Jiffy
Phrasebook
SPANISH

Langenscheidt
NEW YORK

Phonetic Transcriptions: Walter Glanze Word Books
(The Glanze Intersound System)

Jiffy Phrasebooks are also available for many other languages.

*Jiffy Travel Packs combine the Jiffy Phrasebooks with a
travel-oriented 60-minute cassette. Each can be used independently
of the other.*
(Jiffy Travel Pack Spanish ISBN 0-88729-975-x)

*For detailed information please contact
Langenscheidt Publishers, Inc.
46-35 54th Road, Maspeth, NY 11378
(718) 784-0055*

INFORMATION

GUIDE TO THE USE OF THE PHRASEBOOK

This Spanish phrasebook offers you all the important words and phrases you may need on a visit to Spain. The phonetic transcriptions which follow the Spanish expressions are designed as an aid to correct pronunciation, and the systematic arrangement of the phrasebook will help you to find what you are looking for in the shortest possible time.

Structure of the phrasebook

The phrasebook is divided into 20 chapters. It begins with general words and phrases, followed by sections on transportation, accommodations, food and drink, and many other important aspects of travel abroad. There are chapters on shopping, health, cultural activities, and entertainment; the appendix gives you lists of common signs and abbreviations, weights and measures, and colors. For easy reference, English words and phrases are printed in heavy black type, while the Spanish translations are in blue. Following these are the phonetic transcriptions of the Spanish phrases in normal black type.

Occasionally two or more phrases have been combined and the interchangeable elements given in italics. For example, the sentence "Is it going to *rain (snow)?*" corresponds to the Spanish "¿Va a *llover (nevar)?*" Thus "Is it going to rain?" is translated "¿Va a llover?" and "Is it going to snow?" becomes "¿Va a nevar?"

In the boxes you will find help on certain language difficulties, tips on general etiquette, and information on travel, eating out, using the telephone, etc., which will help you get by in everyday situations you may encounter while traveling abroad.

An asterisk at the beginning of a sentence indicates that this is something someone else might say to you.

Spanish pronunciation

On pp. 8–11 you will find a detailed guide to Spanish pronuncia
Most of the symbols used in the phonetic system are taken from
Latin alphabet, so you should have no difficulty getting accustome
the transcriptions.

Spanish grammar

If you would like to get to know some important aspects of Spa
grammar, the brief survey on pp. 195–203 will give you a b
grounding. Apart from offering you an insight into the structure o
Spanish language and helping you to understand the expressions i
phrasebook, this grammatical survey will also enable you to
simple sentences of your own.

Traveler's Dictionary and Index

The glossary at the end of the book is 53 pages long and is for q
reference to words and phrases. The translations are followe
phonetic transcriptions and page references, so that this glossary s
as an index as well.

Carry this phrasebook with you all the time to make the most of
stay.

CONTENTS

SPANISH PRONUNCIATION

The sounds of a foreign language have to be learned by hearing and imitating a native or near-native speaker of that language. No amount of written information will teach you the true pronunciation of a foreign word or phrase. Many transcription systems have been devised toward this purpose; but all of them use either unfamiliar combinations of letters or odd-looking new characters—combinations or characters that have to be learned in addition to learning the foreign language.

The pronunciation system that was developed for the Langenscheidt Jiffy Phrasebooks* is entirely different: The symbols you find here are the ones you are likely to be familiar with from your use of high-school, college, or desk dictionaries of the English language. (That is, the symbols are the same ordinary letters of the alphabet with the same markings, such as [ē] for the vowel sound in *he*.)

This new pronunciation system is meant to be an approximation, serving practical needs, as encountered by the traveler. But, then, even those complicated systems remain an approximation. The true sounds, as we have said, must be learned by listening.

The basic symbols you see in the table are the same that you will find in other Langenscheidt Jiffy Phrasebooks for speakers of English. Therefore, when using these Phrasebooks in traveling from country to country, you don't have to shift from one set of symbols to another.

For Spanish, words of more than one syllable are shown with an accent mark, and occasionally with two equal accent marks: *general* [heneräl′], *norteamericano* [nōr′te·ämerēkä′nō].

To avoid ambiguity, two neighboring vowel symbols (and occasionally two consonant symbols) are separated by a raised dot [·]. This separation is meant to be a convenience to the eye and usually does not mean a break in pronunciation: *ahora* [ä·ō′rä], *sangría* [säng·grē′ä].

The transcription is that of individual words, even in a sentence. The rhythm of a sentence or phrase has to be learned by ear.

The pronunciation of this Jiffy Phrasebook reflects the Spanish of the Americas, rather than classical or Castillian Spanish. (See also the remarks on regional Spanish beneath the table.)

---

* The Glanze Intersound System

Symbol	Approximate Sound	Examples
	Vowels	
[ä]	The a of father or watch; the o of doll or box.	*casa* [kä′sä]
[e]	The e of met (but tending towards the a of fate).	*meses* [me′ses]
[ē]	The e of he.	*camino* [kämē′nō] *ir* [ēr]
[ī]	The i of time.	*hay* [ī] *mosáico* [mōsī′kō]
[ō]	The o of nose (but without the "upglide").	*como* [kō′mō] *norte* [nōr′te]
[oi]	The oi of voice.	*estoy* [estoi′]
[o͞o]	The u of rule.	*agudo* [ägo͞o′dō]
[ou]	The ou of house.	*causa* [kou′sa]
	Consonants	
[b]	A Spanish sound that has to be learned by listening. Until you have learned this sound, use the b of bed. See also [v].	*hablar* [äblär′]
[d]	The d of door.	*rendir* [rendēr′]
[f]	The f of fat.	*efecto* [efek′tō]
[g]	The g of go.	*gato* [gä′tō]

Symbol	Approximate Sound	Examples
[*h*]	A sound that has to be learned by listening. (This "guttural" sound resembles the ch in Scottish *loch* and German *Bach* and, more remotely, the *r* in French *Paris*.) Until you have learned this sound, use the *h* of *hot*.	*Juan* [hōō·än'] *gente* [hen'te]
[k]	The c of can.	*cubo* [kōō'bō]
[l]	The l in love. (Not the l in old.) (See also the combination [ly] below.)	*lado* [lä'dō]
[m]	The m of more.	*mesa* [me'sä]
[n]	The n of nest. (See also the combination [ny] next page.)	*andar* [ändär']
[ng]	The ng of sing.	*banco* [bäng'kō]
[p]	The p of pen.	*poco* [pō'kō]
[r]	The r of run, but stronger "trilled" in many words, especially all words with rr.	*rico* [rē'kō] *grande* [grän'de] *perro* [pe'rrō]
[s]	The s of sun. (See also [z].)	*servir* [servēr']
[t]	The t of tea.	*tiempo* [tyem'pō]
[tsh]	The ch of much.	*muchacha* [mōōtshä'tshä]
[v]	A Spanish sound that is usually identical to the [b] above. But this pronunciation varies greatly, and for the sake of simplicity, the letter *v* is represented by the symbol [v].	*vida* [vē'dä] *huevo* [ōō·e'vō]

Symbol	Approximate Sound	Examples
[y]	The y of year. (See also the combinations [ly] and [ny] below.)	*yo* [yō] *hielo* [ye′lō]
[z]	The z of zeal. (Note: Spanish s is pronounced [z] before the "voiced" consonants b, d, g, l, m, n, and r.)	*mismo* [mēz′mō] *desde* [dez′de]

Note also these combinations:

[ly] as in *caballo* [käbä′lyō], *julio* [hōō′lyō]
[ny] as in *año* [ä′nyō], *junio* [hōō′nyō]
[o͞o·e] as in *bueno* [bo͞o·e′nō]
[o͞o·ä] as in *cuanto* [ko͞o·än′tō]
[o͞o′ē] as in *muy* [mo͞o′ē]
[o͞o·ō] as in *cuota* [ko͞o·ō′tä]
[e·ē] as in *rey* [re′ē]
[e·o͞o] as in *neumático* [ne·o͞omä′tēkō]
[ä·ē] as in *caída* [kä·ē′dä]
(Each of these combinations should be pronounced as almost one "gliding" sound.)

Among other aspects of Spanish that may be learned through listening and practice are:

- The great regional differences in pronunciation (and vocabulary) not only between the "Castillian" Spanish of Spain and the Spanish of the Americas, but also generally among the speech habits of the twenty countries where Spanish is spoken.

- The typical pronunciation of many letters: the *b* and *v*, the final *d*, the *c* and *z*, the *r*, *rr*, *l*, *y*, and *h*, and other letters and their combinations.

The Spanish Alphabet

A a	B b	C c	Ch ch	D d	E e	F f	G g	H h	I i	J j
ä	be	se	tshe	de	e	e′fe	*he*	ä′tshe	ē	hō′tä

K k	L l	Ll ll	M m	N n	Ñ ñ	O o	P p	Q q	R r	S s
kä	e′le	e′lye	e′me	e′ne	e′nye	ō	pe	ko͞o	e′re	e′se

T t	U u	V v	W w	X x	Y y	Z z				
te	o͞o	be	dō′blebe	e′kēs	ēgrē·egä	se′tä				

GENERAL WORDS AND PHRASES

Greetings

Good morning!	**Good afternoon!**	**Good evening!**
¡Buenos días!	¡Buenas tardes!	¡Buenas noches!
bōō·e′nōs dē′äs	bōō·e′näs tär′des	bōō·e′näs nō′tshes

> "Buenos días" *is used in the morning until lunchtime, and* "buenas tardes" *from lunchtime until dark.*

*Welcome! (Pleased to see you!)
¡Bienvenido! (Encantado/Encantada de verlo/*Sp* verle) (*fam* verte)
byenbenē′dō (enkäntä′dō/enkäntä′dä de ver′lō/ver′le) (ver′te)

Hi!
¡Hola!
ō′lä

*Did you have a good trip?
¿Tuvo/*Sp* a tenido/un buen viaje?
tōō′vō/ä tenē′dō/ōōm bōō·em′ byä′*he*

I'm delighted to see you!
Me alegro mucho de verlo/*Sp* verle.
me äle′grō mōō′tshō de ver′lō/ver′le

How are you?
¿Cómo está usted?
kō′mō estä′ ōōste′

How're you doing?
¿Qué tal?
ke täl

How's it going?
¿Cómo le va?
kō′mō le vä

Thanks, just fine.
Muy bien, gracias.
mōō′ē byen, grä′syäs

And you?
¿Y usted?
ē ōōste′

How's the family?
¿Cómo está la familia?
kō′mō estä′ lä fämē′lyä

My ... is sick.
Mi ... está enfermo/enferma.
mē ... estä′ emfer′mō/em-fer′mä

Did you sleep well?
¿Descansó?/*Sp* ¿Ha dormido bien?
deskänsō′/ä dōrmē′dō byen

We're feeling fine.
Nos encontramos bien.
nōs enkōnträ′mōs byen

Thanks for your cordial welcome.
Gracias por la cordial acogida.
grä′syäs pōr lä kōrdyäl′ äkōhē′dä

Forms of Address

Mr. *(name)*	Señor	senyōr′
Mrs. *(name)*	Señora	senyō′rä
Madam/Sir	señora/señor	senyō′rä/senyōr′
Miss	señorita	senyōrē′tä
Ladies and	¡Señoras y	senyō′räs ē
Gentlemen!	Señores!/¡Damas y	senyō′res/dä′mäs ē
	caballeros!	käbälye′rōs
your wife	su esposa (su mujer)	soo espō′sä (soo moo_her′)
your husband	su esposo (su marido)	soo espō′sō (soo märē′do)
Doctor *(when address-*	doctor/doctora	dōktōr′, dōktō′rä
ing him or her)		
Professor	profesor/profesora	prōfesōr′, prōfe-sō′rä

Don *and* Doña + *first name is a form of affectionate respect used for older men and women.*

Letters

The "double" last name in Spanish speaking countries consists of both the father's and the mother's paternal surnames: Fernando Rivera García.

Dear Mr. López	Distinguido	dēstēngē′dō
	Sr. López	senyōr′ lō′pes
Dear Mrs. López	Distinguida	dēstēngē′dä
	Sra. López	senyō′rä lō′pes
Dear Miss López	Distinguida	dēstēngē′dä
	Srta. López	senyōrē′tä lō′pes
Dear Sirs, Gentlemen	Muy Sres. míos	moo′ē senyō′res mē′ōs
Dear Mr. Cook *(to a*	Estimado Sr. Cook	estēmä′dō se-nyōr′
respected friend)		
Dear Mrs. Cook	Estimada Sra. Cook	estēmä′dä senyō′rä
Dear Peter	Querido Pedro	kerē′dō pe′drō
Yours sincerely,	Con un saludo	kōn oon säloo′dō
Cordially yours,	cordial	kōrdyäl′

Introductions

My name is ...
Me llamo ...
me lyä′mō ...

Let me introduce	Le presento a	le presen′tō ä
my son	mi hijo	mē ē′hō
my daughter	mi hija	mē ē′hä
my friend *(male)*	mi amigo	mē ämē′gō
my friend *(female)* ..	mi amiga	mē ämē′gä
my friends	mis amigos	mēs ämē′gōs
my boyfriend	mi novio	mē nō′vyō
my girlfriend	mi novia	mē nō′vyä
my fiancé	mi prometido /	mē prōmetē′dō,
	mi novio	mē nō′vyō
my fiancée	mi prometida /	mē prōmetē′dä
	mi novia	mē nō′vyä

> Novio/novia *mean both boyfriend/girlfriend and fiancé/fiancée. At a wedding, the bride and groom are* "los novios."

Glad to meet you (How do you do?)
¡Encantado! / ¡Encantada!
enkäntä′dō/enkäntä′dä

Haven't we seen each other before?
¿No nos conocemos ya de vista?
nō nōs kōnōse′mōs yä de vēs′tä

Do you live here?
¿Vive usted aquí?
vē′ve ōōste′ äkē′

Are you *Mr. (Mrs., Miss)* Smith?
¿Es usted *el señor (la señora, la señorita)* Smith?
es ōōste′ el senyōr′ (lä senyō′rä, lä senyōrē′tä) Smith

What is your name, please?
¿Cómo se llama usted, por favor?
kō′mō se lyä′mä ōōste′, pōr fävōr′

Where are you from?
¿De dónde es usted?
de dōn′de es ōōste′

We've been here for a week.
Llevamos aquí una semana.
lyevä′mōs äkē′ ōō′nä semä′nä

Do you like it here?
¿Le gusta aquí?
le gōōs′tä äkē′

Are you here alone?
¿Está usted aquí solo/sola?
estä′ ōōste′ äkē′ sō′lō/sō′lä

Where do you work?
¿Dónde trabaja usted?
dōn'de träbä'*h*ä ōōste'

What do you do for a living?
¿Cuál es su profesión?
kōō·äl' es sōō prōfesyōn'

What are you studying? (What's your major?)
¿Qué estudia usted?
ke estōō'dyä ōōste'

Got some time?
¿Tiene tiempo?
tye'ne tyem'pō

Shall we go to the . . .?
¿Vamos al (a la) . . .?
vä'mōs äl (ä lä) . . .

What time shall we meet?
¿A qué horas / *Sp* a qué hora /
nos encontramos?
ä ke ō'räs / ä ke ō'rä /
nōs enkōnträ'mōs

May I pick you up?
¿Quiere que lo / *Sp* le / (la) recoja?
kye're ke lō / le / (lä) rekō'*h*ä

Please leave me alone!
¡Por favor, déjeme en paz!
pōr fävōr', de'*h*eme em päs

Get lost! (Buzz off!)
¡Váyase ya!
vä'yäse yä

A Visit

Is *Mr. (Mrs., Miss)* . . . at home?
¿Está en casa *el señor (la señora, la señorita)* . . .?
estä' en kä'sä el senyōr' (lä senyō'rä, lä senyōrē'tä) . . .

Could I speak to *Mr. (Mrs., Miss)* . . .?
¿Podría hablar con *el señor (la señora, la señorita)* . . .?
pōdrē'ä äblär' kōn el senyōr' (lä senyō'rä, lä senyōrē'tä) . . .

Does *Mr. (Mrs., Miss)* . . . live here?
¿Vive aquí *el señor (la señora, la señorita)* . . .?
vē've äkē' el senyōr' (lä senyō'rä, lä senyōrē'tä) . . .

I'm looking for . . .
Busco . . .
bōōs'kō . . .

When will *he (she)* be home?
¿A qué hora estará en casa?
ä ke ō'rä estärä' en kä'sä

I'll drop by again later.
Volveré más tarde.
vōlvere' mäs tär'de

When *can I (shall we)* come?
¿A qué hora *puedo (debemos)* venir?
ä ke ō'rä pōō·e'dō (debe'mōs) venēr'

I'd (We'd) love to come.
Voy (Vamos) encantado(s).
voi (vä′mōs) enkäntä′dō(s)

*Come in!
¡Adelante! / ¡Pase!
ädelän′te / pä′se

*Please have a seat.
Siéntese, por favor.
syen′tese, pōr fävōr′

*Just a minute, please.
Un momento, por favor.
ōōn mōmen′tō, pōr fävōr′

Thanks so much for the invitation.
Muchísimas gracias por la invitación.
mōōtshē′sēmäs grä′syäs pōr lä ēmbētäsyōn′

Am I bothering you?
¿Lo / *Sp* le / molesto?
lō / le / mōles′tō

Please don't go to a lot of trouble.
No se moleste, por favor.
nō se mōles′te, pōr fävōr′

*What'll you have?
¿Desea tomar algo?
dese′ä tōmär′ äl′gō

What may I offer you?
¿Puedo ofrecerle algo?
pōō•e′dō ōfreser′le äl′gō

***Mr. (Mrs.)* Smith sends you *his (her)* regards (love).**
Muchos saludos de parte *del señor (de la señora)* Smith.
mōō′tshōs sälōō′dōs de pär′te del senyōr′ (de lä senyō′rä) Smith

I'm afraid I've got to go now.
Lo siento, ahora tengo que marcharme.
lō syen′tō, ä·ō′rä ten′gō ke märtshär′me

Thanks so much for *a lovely evening (coming)*.
Muchas gracias por *esta agradable velada (su visita)*.
mōō′tshäs grä′syäs pōr es′tä ägrädä′ble velä′dä (sōō vēsē′tä)

Please give *Mr. (Mrs.)* . . . my best regards.
Salude por favor *al señor (a la señora)* . . . de mi parte.
sälōō′de pōr fävōr′ äl senyōr′ (ä lä senyō′rä) . . . de mē pär′te

I'll tell him (her) you said hello.
Le daré un saludo de su parte con mucho gusto.
le däre′ ōōn sälōō′dō de sōō pär′te kōn mōō′tshō gōōs′tō

I hope we'll meet again soon.
Espero que volveremos a vernos pronto.
espe′rō ke vōlvere′mōs ä ver′nōs prōn′tō

Farewells

Good-bye!	**See you soon!**	**Good night!**
¡Adiós!	¡Hasta luego!	¡Buenas noches!
ädyōs′	äs′tä lōo·e′gō	bōo·e′näs nōtshes

See you tomorrow!	**All the best!**	**Have a good trip!**
¡Hasta mañana!	¡Que le / te *(fam)* / vaya	¡Buen viaje!
äs′tä mänyä′nä	bien!	bōo·em′ byä′*he*
	ke le / te / vä′yä byen	

I'd like to say good-bye!	**I'm afraid we have to go.**
Quisiera despedirme.	Lo siento, ahora tenemos que irnos.
kēsye′rä despedēr′me	lō syen′tō, ä·ō′rä tene′mōs ke ēr′nōs

Thanks so much for coming.	**Come again soon!**
Muchas gracias por venir.	Vuelva / vuelve *(fam)* / pronto.
mōo′tshäs grä′syäs pōr venēr′	vōo·el′vä / vōo·el′ve / prōn′tō

When can we get together again?	**I'll give you a call tomorrow.**
¿Cuándo nos veremos?	Lo / *Sp* le / te *fam* / llamo mañana.
kōo·än′dō nōs vere′mōs	lō / le / te / lyä′mō mänyä′nä

Can I give you a lift home?	**It's pretty late.**
¿Quiere que lo / *Sp* le / te *fam* / lleve a su / tu *fam* /	Ya es tarde.
casa?	yä es tär′de
kye′re ke lō / le / te / lye′ve ä sōo / tōo / kä′sä	

Give ... my best!	**Thanks very much.**	**I had a lovely time.**
¡Saludos a ...!	¡Muchísimas gracias!	Ha sido muy agradable.
sälōo′dōs ä ...	mōotshē′sēmäs	ä sē′dō mōo′ē ägrä-
	grä′syäs	dä′ble

I enjoyed myself very much.	**Till next time.**
Me ha gustado mucho.	Hasta la próxima.
me ä gōostä′dō mōo′tshō	äs′tä lä prō′ksēmä

I'll *take you to (give you a lift to)* the ...
Le / te *(fam)* / *acompaño (llevo* / *Mex* doy un aventón) a ...
le / te / äkōmpä′nyō (lye′vō / doi ōon äventōn′) ä ...

---

*In Spanish-speaking countries, "Adiós" (good-bye) is also used as a
greeting in passing when you have no time to stop and chat.*

General Questions

When?	Why?	What?	What kind of ...?
¿Cuándo?	¿Por qué?	¿Qué?	¿Qué clase de ...?
kōō·än'dō	pōr ke	ke	ke klä'se de ...

Which?	To whom?	With whom?	Whose?
¿Cuál?	¿A quién?	¿Con quién?	¿De quién?
kōō·äl'	ä kyen	kōn kyen	de kyen

Who?	How?	How long?
¿Quién?	¿Cómo?	¿Cuánto tiempo?
kyen	kō'mō	kōō·än'tō tyem'pō

How *much (many)*?	Where?	Where from?
¿*Cuánto?* (¿*Cuántos?*)	¿Dónde?	¿De dónde?
kōō·än'tō (kōō·än'tōs)	dōn'de	de dōn'de

Where to?	What for?	Can I ...?
¿Adónde?	¿Para qué?	¿Puedo ...?
ädōn'de	pä'rä ke	pōō·e'dō ...

Is ... allowed here?	Do you need ...?
¿Se puede ... aquí?	¿Necesita / necesitas *(fam)* ...?
se pōō·e'de ... äke'	nesesē'tä / nesesē'täs ...

Have you got ...?	When can I get ...?
¿Tiene/tienes *(fam)* ...?	¿Cuándo puedo tener ...?
tye'ne/tye'nes ...	kōō·än'dō pōō·e'dō tener' ...

What time do you *open (close)*?	What would you like? (What can I do for you? May I help you?)
¿A qué hora *abren (cierran)*?	¿Qué desea? (¿En qué puedo servirle?)
ä ke ō'rä ä'bren (sye'rrän)	ke dese'ä (en ke pōō·e'dō servēr'le)

What's *this/that*?	What happened?	What does that mean?
¿Qué es *esto/eso*?	¿Qué pasó?	¿Qué significa eso?
ke es es'tō/e'sō	ke päsō'	ke sēgnēfē'kä e'sō

How much does that cost?	What are you looking for?
¿Cuánto cuesta? (¿Cuánto vale?)	¿Qué busca usted?
kōō·än'tō kōō·es'tä (kōō·än'tō vä'le)	ke bōōs'kä ōōste'

Whose is that?	*Whom do you wish to see?
¿De quién es?	¿A quién quiere ver?
de kyen es	ä kyen kye're ver

Who's there?

¿Quién es?
kyen es

Who can (Can anyone) ...?

¿Quién puede ...?
kyen poo·e'de ...

What's your name?

¿Cómo se llama/te llamas *(fam)*?
kō'mō se lyä'mä / te lyä'mäs

How do you say ... in Spanish?

¿Cómo se dice ... en español?
kō'mō se dē'se ... en espänyōl'

How do I get to ...?

¿Por favor, cómo se va a ...?
pōr fävōr, kō'mō se vä ä ...

How does that work?

¿Cómo funciona eso?
kō'mō foonsyō'nä e'sō

How long does it take?

¿Cuánto tiempo tarda?
koo·än'tō tyem'pō tär'dä

How much do I get?

¿Cuánto recibo?
koo·än'tō resē'bō

How much is it?

¿Cuánto vale?
koo·än'tō vä'le

Where can I find ... (is ... located)?

¿Dónde se encuentra ...?
dōn'de se enkoo·en'trä ...

Where *is (are)* ...?

¿Dónde *está (están)* ...?
dōn'de estä' (estän') ...

Where's the nearest ...?

¿Dónde está el/la ... más cercana?
dōn'de estä' el / lä ... mäs serkä'nä

Where can I ...?

¿Dónde puedo ...?
dōn'de poo·e'dō ...

Where can I get (find) ...?

¿Dónde puedo conseguir ...?
dōn'de poo·e'dō konsegēr' ...

Where is (are) there ...?

¿Dónde hay ...?
dōn'de ī ...

Where do you live?

¿Dónde vive/vives *(fam)*?
dōn'de vē've / vē'ves

Where are we?

¿Dónde estamos?
dōn'de estä'mōs

Where do you come from?

¿De dónde viene/vienes *(fam)*?
de dōn'de vye'ne / vye'nes

Where are you going?

¿Adónde va/vas *(fam)*?
ädōn'de vä / väs

Where does *this road (street)* lead?

¿Adónde conduce *este camino (esta calle)*?
ädōn'de kōndoo'se es'te kämē'nō (es'tä kä'lye)

Wishes, Requests

> *As in any language, the liberal use of polite expressions – such as por favor, gracias, con permiso, perdón, etc., – not only reflects well on you, the speaker, but helps in getting things done, solving problems, making friends and, in general, having a more enjoyable trip.*

Would you please *bring (give, show)* me ...?
¿Por favor, *tráigame (déme, enséñeme)* ...?
pōr fàvōr', trī'gäme (de'me, ense'nyme) ...

Would you please tell me ...?
¿Por favor, podría/podrías *(fam)* / decirme ...?
pōr fàvōr', pōdrē'ä / pōdrē'äs / desēr'me ...

Beg your pardon?
¿Perdón? (¿Cómo?/*Mex* ¿Mande?)
perdōn' (kō'mō / män'de)

What can I do for you? **May I help you?** *I'd like (We'd like)* ...
¿En qué puedo servirle? ¿Puedo ayudarle? *Quisiera (Quisiéramos)* ...
en ke po͞o·e'dō servēr'le? po͞o·e'dō äyo͞odär'le kēsye'rä(kēsyer'ämōs)...

I need ... **I'd rather have ...**
Necesito ... Prefiero ...
nesesē'tō ... prefye'rō ...

Could I *have (get)* ...? **Please help me!**
¿Podría *tener (conseguir)* ...? ¡Ayúdeme!/¡Ayúdame! *(fam)*/, por favor.
pōdrē'ä tener' (kōnsegēr') ... äyo͞o'deme / äyo͞o'däme / pōr fàvōr'

Certainly! (Sure!) **Allow me? (Excuse me?)**
¡Cómo no! ¿Permiso?
kō'mō nō permē'sō

Get well soon! **All the best!**
¡Que se mejore / te mejores *(fam)*! ¡Que le / te *(fam)* / vaya bien!
ke se mehō're / te mehō'res ke le / te / vä'yä byen

Have a good time! **I wish you ...**
¡Diviértase! / ¡Diviértete! *(fam)* Le / te *(fam)* / deseo ...
dēvyer'täse / dēvyer'tete ʼ le / te / dese'ō ...

Thanks

Thanks (Thank you) very much!
¡Gracias!, ¡Muchísimas gracias!
grä′syäs, mōōtshē′sēmäs grä′syäs

Thanks a lot!
¡Muchas gracias!
mōō′tshäs grä′syäs

Thank you too!
¡Gracias a usted/a ti *(fam)*!
grä′syäs ä ōōste′/ä tē/

No, thanks.
No, gracias.
nō, grä′syäs

I'm very grateful to you.
Le/te *(fam)*/estoy muy agradecido.
le/te/estoi′ mōō′ē ägrädesē′dō

You're welcome.
De nada.
de nä′dä

Thanks very much for *your help (all your trouble)*!
Muchas gracias por *su/tu (fam)/ayuda (sus/tus (fam)/gestiones)*.
mōō′tshäs grä′syäs pōr sōō/tōō/äyōō′dä (sōōs/tōōs/*h*estyō′nes)

I (We) thank you so much for …
Le/te *(fam)/agradezco (agradecemos)* mucho por …
le/te/ägrädes′kō (ägrädese′mōs) mōō′tshō pōr …

Thanks a million!	**Don't mention it.**	**Glad to do it.**
¡Mil gracias!	No hay de qué.	Con mucho gusto.
mēl grä′syäs	nō ī de ke	kōn mōō′tshō gōōs′tō

Yes and No

Yes.	**Certainly.**	**Of course.**	**Good! (Fine!)**
Sí.	Desde luego.	Por supuesto.	¡Muy bien!
sē	des′de lōō·e′gō	pōr sōōpōō·es′tō	mōō′ē byen

I'd be glad to.	**Right!**	**Terrific!**	**With pleasure!**
Con mucho gusto.	¡Eso es!	¡Estupendo!	Con mucho gusto.
kōn mōō′tshō gōōs′tō	e′sō es	estōōpen′dō	kōn mōō′tshō gōōs′tō

No.	**Never.**	**Nothing.**	**Out of the question!**
No.	Nunca.	Nada.	¡Ni hablar!
nō	nōōng′kä	nä′dä	nē äblär′

Certainly not! (No way!)	**I'd rather not!**
¡De ninguna manera!	Más bien no quiero hacerlo.
de nēngōō′nä mäne′rä	mäs byen nō kye′rō äser′lō

I *don't want to (can't)*.	**Perhaps (Maybe).**	**Probably.**
No *quiero (puedo)*.	Quizá(s).	Probablemente.
nō kye′rō (pōō·e′dō)	kēsä(s)′	prōbäblemen′te

Pardon

Excuse me!
¡Discúlpeme!/¡Discúlpame! *(fam)*
dēskōōl'peme/dēskōōl'päme

I beg your pardon!
¡Perdón!
perdōn'

Please excuse me!
¡Discúlpeme/discúlpame *(fam)*/, por favor!
dēskōōl'peme/dēskōōl'päme/, pōr fävōr'

I'm very sorry.
Lo siento mucho.
lō syen'tō mōō'tshō

I'm extremely sorry.
Lo siento muchísimo.
lō syen'tō mōōtshē'sēmō

I must apologize to you.
Tengo que pedirle/pedirte *(fam)*/
perdón.
'ten'gō ke pedēr'le/pedēr'te/perdōn'

Please don't be angry.
Por favor, no se enfade/no te enfades *(fam)*/Mex no se enoje/no te
enojes *(fam)*.
pōr fävōr', nō se enfä'de/no te enfä'des/nō se enō'he/nō te enō'hes

Regrets

What a pity! (Too bad!)
¡Qué lástima! ¡Qué pena!
ke läs'tēmä, ke pe'nä

To my (great) regret ...
Con (gran) pesar mío ...
kōn (grän) pesär' mē'ō ...

What a shame that ...
Es una lástima que ...
es ōō'nä läs'tēmä ke ...

I'm afraid that isn't possible.
Lo siento, pero no es posible.
lō syen'tō, pe'rō nō es posē'ble

Congratulations and Condolences

> The "día del santo" *(patron saint's day)* is an important day and is
> widely celebrated.

Congratulations!
¡Felicitaciones!
felēsētäsyō'nes

I congratulate you ...
Quiero felicitarle/te *(fam)* ...
kyē'rō felēsētär'le/te/ ...

on your birthday .... por su/tu *(fam)*/
cumpleaños .... pōr sōō/tōō/
kōōmple·ä'nyōs

on your marriage .... por su/tu *(fam)*/boda . pōr sōō/tōō/bō'dä

All the best! (Best wishes!)
¡Muchas felicidades!
mōo'tshäs felēsēdä'des

Happy birthday!
¡Feliz cumpleaños!
felēs' kōomple·ä'nyōs

Merry Christmas!
¡Feliz Navidad!
felēs' nävēdäd'

Happy New Year!
¡Próspero Año Nuevo!
prōs'perō ä'nyō nōo·e'vō

---

*The Christmas season itself extends from about Dec. 16 to Jan. 6,
"día de los reyes magos". In most families children receive presents
both on Christmas and on Epiphany, (from the reyes magos, 3
kings).*

I (We) wish you ...
Le/te *(fam)/deseo (deseamos)* ...
le/te/dese'ō (dese·ä'mōs) ...

Good luck!
¡Mucha suerte!
mōo'tshä sōo·er'te

Success!
¡Mucho éxito!
mōo'tshō e'ksētō

All the best!
¡Qué le/te *(fam)/vaya bien!
ke le/te/vä'yä byen

My sincerest condolences.
¡Le/te *(fam)/acompaño en el
sentimiento!/¡Mi sentido pésame!
le/te/äkōmpä'nyō en el sentē-
myen'tō/mē sentē'dō pe'säme

Our warmest sympathy.
¡Le/te *(fam)/acompañamos en el
sentimiento!
le/te/äkōmpänyä'mōs en el sen-
tēmyen'tō

Complaints

I'd like to register a complaint.
Quisiera hacer una reclamación/
un reclamo.
kēsye'rä äser' ōo'nä reklämäsyōn'/ōon reklä'mō

**I'd like to speak to the *manager
(owner).***
Quisiera hablar con el *director or
gerente (dueño).*
kēsye'rä äblär' kōn el dērektōr'
(heren'te) (dōo·e'nyo)

I'm afraid I'll have to make a complaint about ...
Tengo que hacer una reclamación/un reclamo/por ...
ten'gō ke äser' ōo'nä reklämäsyōn'/ōon reklä'mō/pōr ...

... is (are) missing.
Falta (faltan) ...
fäl'tä (fäl'tän) ...

... doesn't work.
... no funciona.
... nō fōonsyō'nä

... is not in order.
... no está *or* no va bien.
... nō estä' (nō vä byen)

Communication

Do you speak English?
¿Habla/hablas *(fam)*/inglés?
äb´lä/äb´läs/ēngles´

German?
¿Alemán?
älemän´

French?
¿Francés?
fränses´

Can you understand me?
¿Me entiende/entiendes *(fam)*?
me entyen´de/entyen´des

I understand.
Entiendo.
entyen´dō

I can't understand a thing.
No entiendo nada.
nō entyen´dō nä´dä

Would you please speak a little slower?
Por favor, hable/habla *(fam)*/más despacio.
pōr fävōr, äb´le/äb´lä/mäs despä´syō

How do you say ... in Spanish?
¿Cómo se dice ... en español?
kō´mō se dē´se ... en espänyōl´

How do you say that in Spanish?
¿Cómo se dice eso en español?
kō´mō se dē´se e´sō en espänyōl´

What does that mean?
¿Qué significa eso?
ke sēgnēfē´kä e´sō

I beg your pardon?
¿Perdón? ¿Cómo?/*Mex* ¿Mande?
perdōn´ kō´mō/män´de

How do you pronounce this word?
¿Cómo se pronuncia esta palabra?
kō´mō se prōnoon´syä es´tä pälä´brä

Would you please translate this for me?
¿Podría/podrías *(fam)*/traducírmelo?
pōdrē´ä/pōdrē´äs/trädoosēr´melō

Would you please write that down for me?
¿Podría/podrías *(fam)*/escribírmelo?
pōdrē´ä/pōdrē´äs/eskrēbēr´melō

Would you spell that, please?
¿Podría/podrías *(fam)*/deletrearlo, por favor?
pōdrē´ä/pōdrē´äs/deletre·är´lō, pōr favōr´

Weather

How's the weather going to be?
¿Qué tiempo hará?
ke tyem′pō ärä′

What's the weather report?
¿Qué anuncia el parte meteorológico?
ke änōōn′syä el pär′te mete·ōrō-
lō′hēkō

The barometer's *rising (falling)*.
El barómetro está *subiendo (bajando)*.
el bärō′metrō estä′ sōōbyen′dō (bähän′dō)

We're going to have …
Va a hacer …
vä ä äser′ …

good weather …….	buen tiempo ……….	bōō·en tyem′pō
bad weather ……..	mal tiempo …………	mal tyem′pō
changeable weather ..	tiempo variable …….	tyem′pō värē·ä′ble

It's going to stay nice.
El tiempo sigue bueno.
el tyem′pō sē′ge bōō·e′nō

Is it going to *rain (snow)*?
¿Va a *llover (nevar)*?
vä ä lyōver′ (nevär′)

How are the road conditions between here and …?
¿Qué tal está la carretera entre … y …?
ke täl estä′ lä kärrete′rä en′tre … ē …

It's very slippery.
Está resbaladizo/
resbaloso.
estä′ resbälädē′sō/
resbälō′sō

– very hot.
Hace mucho calor.
ä′se mōō′tshō kälōr′

– foggy (misty).
Hay niebla (neblina).
ī nye′blä (neblē′nä)

– very muggy.
Hace bochorno.
ä′se bōtshōr′nō

– very windy.
Hace viento/aire.
ä′se vyen′tō/ī′re

– stormy.
El viento es muy fuerte.
el vyen′tō es mōō′ē fōō·er′te

What's the temperature?
¿A cuántos grados estamos?
ä kōō·än′tōs grä′dōs estä′mōs

It's … *above (below)* zero.
Tenemos … grados *sobre (bajo)* cero.
tene′mōs … grä′dōs sō′bre (bä′hō)
se′rō

It's *cold (hot)*.
Hace frío.(Hace calor.)
ä′se frē′ō (ä′se kälōr′)

I'm *cold (hot)*.
Tengo frío.(Tengo calor.)
ten′gō frē′ō (ten′gō kälōr′)

Is the weather going to stay nice?
¿Sigue el buen tiempo?
sē′ge el bōō·en tyem′pō

The weather's going to change.
El tiempo va a cambiar.
el tyem'pō vä ä kämbyär'

It'll be nice again.
Ya vuelve a hacer buen tiempo.
yä vōō·el've ä äser' bōō·en tyem'pō

The wind has dropped.
El viento ha amainado.
el vyen'tō ä ämīnä'dō

The wind has changed.
El viento ha cambiado (de rumbo).
el vyen'tō ä kämbyä'dō (de rōōm'bō)

We're going to have a thunderstorm.
Va a haber tormenta.
vä ä äber' tōrmen'tä

There's going to be a storm.
Habrá tempestad.
äbrä' tempestäd'

Is the fog going to lift?
¿Se disipará la niebla?
se dēsēpärä' lä nye'blä

It's stopped raining.
Ha dejado de llover.
ä dehä'dō de lyōver'

The sun is shining.
Hace sol.
ä'se sōl

The sun is burning hot.
El sol quema.
el sōl ke'mä

The sky is clear.
El cielo está despejado.
el sye'lō estä' despehä'dō

In Spanish-speaking countries, temperatures are measured in degrees Centigrade. To convert
Fahrenheit to Centigrade: $°F - 32 \times 55 = °C$
Centigrade to Fahrenheit: $°C + 17.8 \times 1.8 = °F$

---

air	aire *m*	ī're
atmospheric pressure	presión *f* atmosférica . .	presyōn' ätmōs-fe'rēkä
barometer	barómetro *m*	bärō'metrō
blizzard	ventisca *f*	ventēs'kä
climate	clima *m*	klē'mä
cloud	nube *f*	nōō'be
cloudburst	chaparrón *m*	tshäpärrōn'
cloud cover, cloudy skies, cloudy	nuboso, nublado	nōōbō'sō, nōōblä'dō
dew	rocío *m*	rōsē'ō
dusk	crepúsculo *m*	krepōōs'kōōlō
earthquake	terremoto *m*, temblor *m*	terremō'tō, temblōr'

fog	niebla *f*	nye′blä
frost	helada *f*	elä′dä
heat	calor *m*	kälōr′
high pressure (system)	anticiclón *m*	äntēsēklōn′
hurricane	ciclón *m*, huracán *m*	sēklōn′, ōōrräkän′
ice	hielo *m*	ye′lō
icy road	carretera *f* helada	kärrete′rä elä′dä
it's freezing	está helando	estä′ elän′dō
it's hailing	cae granizo	kä′e gräne′sō
it's raining	está lloviendo	estä′ lyōvyen′dō
it's snowing	está nevando	estä′ nevän′dō
it's thawing	deshiela	desye′lä
it's windy	hace viento	ä′se vyen′tō
lightning	relámpago *m*	reläm′pägō
low pressure (system)	de baja presión	de bä′hä presyōn′
mist	neblina *f*	neblē′nä
moon	luna *f*	lōō′nä
***north (east)* wind**	viento *m* del *norte (este)*	vyen′tō del nōr′te (es′te)
precipitation	precipitaciones *fpl*	presēpētäsyō′nes
road conditions	estado *m* de las carreteras	estä′dō de läs kärrete′räs
shower	chubasco *m*	tshōōbäs′kō
snow	nieve *f*	nye′ve
snow flurries	copos *mpl* de nieve	kō′pōs de nye′ve
***south (west)* wind**	viento *m* del *sur (oeste)*	vyen′tō del sōōr (ō·es′te)
star	estrella *f*	estre′lyä
storm	tormenta *f*	tōrmen′tä
sun	sol *m*	sōl
sunrise	salida *f* del sol	sälē′dä del sōl
sunset	puesta *f* del sol	pōō·es′tä del sōl
temperature	temperatura *f*	temperätōō′rä
thaw	deshielo *m*	desye′lō
thunder	trueno *m*	trōō·e′nō
thunderstorm	tempestad *f*	tempestäd′
weather	tiempo *m*	tyem′pō
weather prediction	pronóstico *m*	prōnōs′tēkō
weather report	parte *m* meteorológico	pär′te mete·ōrō-lō′hēkō
wind	viento *m*	vyen′tō

Numbers

Cardinal Numbers

0	.....	cero.....	se′rō				
1	.....	un, uno .	ōon, ōo′nō	**6**	.....	seis	se′ēs
2	.....	dos	dōs	**7**	.....	siete	sye′te
3	.....	tres	tres	**8**	.....	ocho	ō′tshō
4	.....	cuatro ...	kōo·ä′trō	**9**	.....	nueve ...	nōo·e′ve
5	.....	cinco....	sēng′kō	**10**	.....	diez	dyes

11	.. once..................	ōn′se
12	.. doce.................	dō′se
13	.. trece.................	tre′se
14	.. catorce	kätōr′se
15	.. quince	kēn′se
16	.. dieciséis	dyesēse′ēs
17	.. diecisiete	dyesēsye′te
18	.. dieciocho	dyesē·ō′tshō
19	.. diecinueve	dyesēnōo·e′ve
20	.. veinte	ve′ēnte
21	.. veintiuno, -a	ve′ēntē·ōo′nō, -ä
22	.. veintidós	ve′ēntēdōs′
23	.. veintitrés	ve′ēntētres′
30	.. treinta	tre′ēntä
40	.. cuarenta	kōo·ären′tä
50	.. cincuenta	sēngkōo·en′tä
60	.. sesenta	sesen′tä
70	.. setenta	seten′tä
80	.. ochenta	ōtshen′tä
90	.. noventa	nōven′tä
100	.. cien, ciento	syen, syen′tō
200	.. doscientos, -as	dōsyen′tōs, -äs
1,000	.. mil	mēl
1,000,000	.. un millón	ōon mēlyōn′
1,000,000,000	.. mil millones	mēl mēlyō′nes

When writing numbers, the use of commas and periods in Spanish is the opposite of their use in English. For example:

8,700 *people* = 8.700 *personas*   35.7% = 35,7%
4,500 *pesetas* = 4.500 *pesetas* $ 10.50 = 10,50 $

Ordinal Numbers

> The ordinal numbers between 1 and 10 are commonly used, those
> between 11 and 20 are seldom used and from 21 on are occasionally
> used in writing (never in speech), being replaced by the cardinal
> numbers.
>
> Ordinals are abbreviated by a period and an upraised "°":
> *primero* = 1.°; *segundo* = 2.°; *tercero* = 3.° etc.

1st	......	primero	prēme'rō
2nd	......	segundo	segōōn'dō
3rd	......	tercero	terse'rō
4th	......	cuarto	kōō·är'tō
5th	......	quinto	kēn'tō
6th	......	sexto	seks'tō
7th	......	séptimo	sep'tēmō
8th	......	octavo	ōktä'vō
9th	......	noveno/nono	nōve'nō/nō'nō
10th	......	décimo	de'sēmō
11th	......	undécimo	ōōnde'sēmō
12th	......	duodécimo	dōō·ōde'sēmō
13th	......	décimo tercero	de'sēmō terse'rō
14th	......	décimo cuarto	de'sēmō kōō·är'tō
20th	......	vigésimo	vēhe'sēmō
21st	......	vigésimo primero	vēhe'sēmō prēme'rō
22nd	......	vigésimo segundo	vēhe'sēmō segōōn'dō
30th	......	trigésimo	trēhe'sēmō
40th	....	cuadragésimo	kōō·ädrähe'sēmō
50th	......	quincuagésimo	kēnkōō·ähe'sēmō
60th	......	sexagésimo	seksähe'sēmō
70th	......	septuagésimo	septōō·ähe'sēmō
80th	......	octogésimo	ōktōhe'sēmō
90th	......	nonagésimo	nōnähe'sēmō
100th	......	centésimo	sente'sēmō
1,000th	......	milésimo	mēle'sēmō

> The 100 year anniversary of an event is the centenario; the 1,000 year
> anniversary is the milenario.

Time

What time is it?
¿Qué hora es?
ke ō'rä es

Have you got the exact time?
¿Tiene/tienes *(fam)*/la hora exacta?
tye'ne/tye'nes/lä ō'rä eksäk'tä

It's one o'clock.
Es la una.
es lä ōō'nä

It's about two o'clock.
Son las dos aproximadamente.
sōn läs dōs äprōksēmädämen'te

It's exactly three o'clock.
Son las tres en punto.
sōn läs tres em pōōn'tō

It's quarter past five.
Son las cinco y cuarto.
sōn läs sēng'kō ē kōō·är'tō

It's half past six.
Son las seis y media.
sōn läs se'ēs ē me'dyä

It's quarter to nine.
Son las nueve menos cuarto.
sōn läs nōō·e've me'nōs kōō·är'tō

It's five (minutes) past four.
Son las cuatro y cinco.
sōn läs kōō·ä'trō ē sēng'kō

It's ten (minutes) to eight.
Son las ocho menos diez.
sōn läs ō'tshō me'nōs dyes

The time of day is expressed by the cardinal numbers preceded by la *or* las: *It's one o'clock* = Es la una.
It's two o'clock = Son las dos. *etc.*

When?
¿Cuándo?
kōō·än'dō

At ten o'clock (10:00).
A las diez.
ä läs dyes

At eleven sharp.
A las once en punto.
ä läs ōn'se em pōōn'tō

At *four (eight-fifteen)* p.m.
A las *cuatro de la tarde (ocho y cuarto de la noche).*
ä läs kōō·ä'trō de lä tär'de (ō'tshō ē kōō·är'tō de lä nō'tshe)

From eight to nine a.m.
De las ocho a las nueve
de la mañana.
de läs ō'tshō ä läs nōō·e've
de lä mänyä'nä

Between ten and twelve a.m.
Entre las diez y las once
de la mañana.
en'tre läs dyes ē läs ōn'se
de lä mänyä'nä

The 24 hour clock is used in written Spanish in general. In spoken Spanish, however, you can use the 12 hour clock, adding de la mañana, de la tarde, *or* de la noche *to the time if there is any doubt.*

In half an hour.
Dentro de media hora.
den'trō de me'dyä ō'rä

In two hours.
Dentro de dos horas.
den'trō de dōs ō'räs

Not before seven.
No antes de las siete.
nō än'tes de läs sye'te

Shortly after eight.
Poco después de las ocho.
pō'kō despoo·es' de läs ō'tshō

It's (too) late.
Es (demasiado) tarde.
es (demäsyä'dō) tär'de

It's still too early.
Es aún temprano.
es ä·o͞on' temprä'nō

Is this clock right?
¿Va bien este reloj?
vä byen es'te relō*h*'

It's too *fast (slow)*.
Va *adelantado (retrasado)*.
vä ädeläntä'dō (reträsä'dō)

Times of the Day

During the day.	**In the morning.**	**In the afternoon.**
De día.	Por la mañana.	Por la tarde.
de dē'ä	pōr lä mänyä'nä	pōr lä tär'de

At noon.	**Yesterday.**	**Today.**	**Tomorrow.**
A mediodía.	Ayer.	Hoy.	Mañana.
ä medyōdē'ä	äyer'	oi	mänyä'nä

In the evening.	**At night.**	**Tonight.**
Por la tarde *or* noche.	Por la noche.	Esta noche.
pōr lä tär'de (nō'tshe)	pōr lä nō'tshe	es'tä nō'tshe

At midnight.	**Daily (every day).**	**Hourly (every hour).**
A medianoche.	Todos los días.	Cada hora.
ä medyänō'tshe	tō'dōs lōs dē'äs	kä'dä ō'rä

The day before yesterday.
Anteayer.
änte·äyer'

The day after tomorrow.
Pasado mañana.
päsä'dō mänyä'nä

A week from now.
De hoy en ocho días.
de ōi en ō'tshō dē'äs

A week from Wednesday.
Del miércoles en ocho días.
del myer'kōles en ō'tshō dē'äs

Two weeks from now.
De hoy en quince días.
de ōi en kēn'se dē'äs

This *morning (afternoon, evening)*.
Esta *mañana (tarde)*.
es'tä mänyä'nä (tär'de)

This noon.	**A month ago.**	**For the last ten days.**
Hoy al mediodía.	Hace un mes.	Desde hace diez días.
oi äl medyōdē′ä	ä′se ōon mes	des′de ä′se dyes dē′äs

During this time (meanwhile).	**Within a week.**
Mientras tanto.	Dentro de una semana.
myen′träs tän′tō	den′trō de ōo′nä semä′nä

This coming week.	*Last (next)* **year.**
La semana que viene.	El año *pasado (que viene).*
lä semä′nä ke vye′ne	el ä′nyō päsä′dō (ke vye′ne)

Every year (annually).	**Every week (weekly).**
Todos los años.	Cada semana.
tōdōs lōs ä′nyōs	kä′dä semä′nä

From time to time.	**Now and then.**	**At the moment.**
De vez en cuando.	A veces.	De momento.
de ves en kōo·än′dō	ä veses	de mōmen′tō

a little while ago	hace poco	ä′se pō′kō
any time now	de un momento a otro .	de ōon mōmen′tō ä ō′trō
earlier	antes	än′tes
later	más tarde	mäs tär′de
now	ahora	ä·ō′rä
on time	a la hora, a tiempo	ä lä ō′rä, ä tyem′pō
previously (before) ...	antes	än′tes
recently	recientemente	resyentemen′te
since	desde	des′de
sometimes	a veces	ä ve′ses
soon	pronto	prōn′tō
temporarily (for the time being)	por el momento	pōr el mōmen′tō
until	hasta	äs′tä
second	segundo *m*	segōon′dō
minute	minuto *m*	mēnōo′tō
hour	hora *f*	ō′rä
day	día *m*	dē′ä
week	semana *f*	semä′nä
month	mes *m*	mes
year	año *m*	ä′nyō
half year	medio año *m*	me′dyō ä′nyō
quarter, three months	trimestre *m*	trēmes′tre

Days of the Week

Monday	lunes *m*	lōō'nes
Tuesday	martes *m*	mär'tes
Wednesday	miércoles *m*	myer'kōles
Thursday	jueves *m*	hōō·e'ves
Friday	viernes *m*	vyer'nes
Saturday	sábado *m*	sä'bädō
Sunday	domingo *m*	dōmēn'gō

Months of the Year

January	enero *m*	ene'rō
February	febrero *m*	febre'rō
March	marzo *m*	mär'sō
April	abril *m*	äbrēl'
May	mayo *m*	mä'yō
June	junio *m*	hōō'nyō
July	julio *m*	hōō'lyō
August	agosto *m*	ägōs'tō
September	se(p)tiembre *m*	se(p)tyem'bre
October	octubre *m*	ōktōō'bre
November	noviembre *m*	novyem'bre
December	diciembre *m*	dēsyem'bre

Seasons

Spring	primavera *f*	prēmäve'rä
Summer	verano *m*	verä'nō
Autumn	otoño *m*	ōtō'nyō
Winter	invierno *m*	ēmbyer'nō

Holidays

New Year's Eve	Año Viejo	ä'nyō vye'hō
New Year's Day	Año Nuevo	ä'nyō nōō·e'vō
Good Friday	Viernes Santo	vyer'nes sän'tō
Easter	Pascua	päs'kōō·ä
Christmas Eve	Nochebuena	nōtshebōō·e'nä
Christmas	Navidad	nävēdäd'

The Date

What's the date today?	**It's the second of July.**
¿A cuántos estamos?	Hoy es el dos de julio.
ä kōō·än'tōs estä'mōs	ōi es el dōs de hōō'lyō

On the twenty ninth of August, 19 ...
El veintinueve de agosto de mil novecientos ...
el ve·ēntēnōō·e've de ägōs'tō de mēl nōvesyen'tōs ...

On the fifteenth *of this (next)* **month**
El quince *de este (del próximo) mes.*
el kēn'se de es'te (del prō'ksēmō) mes

Until the twenty fourth of April.
Hasta el veinticuatro de abril.
äs'tä el ve'ēntēkōō·ä'trō de äbrēl'

On June first *of this (last)* **year.**
El primero de junio *de este año (del año pasado).*
el prēme'rō de hōō'nyō de es'te ä'nyō (del ä'nyō päsä'dō)

We leave on the nineteenth of September.
Salimos el diecinueve de se(p)tiembre.
sälē'mōs el dyesēnōō·e've de se(p)tyem'bre

We arrived on the twelfth of January.
Llegamos el doce de enero.
lyegä'mōs el dō'se de ene'rō

The letter was mailed on the ninth of October.
La carta fue expedida el nueve de octubre.
lä kär'tä fōō·e' ekspedē'dä el nōō·e've de ōktōō'bre

Thank you for your letter of February 2nd.
Le agradecemos su carta del dos de febrero.
le ägrädese'mōs sōō kär'tä del dōs de febre'rō

Age

How old are you?	**I'm twenty years old.**
¿Cuántos años tiene/tienes *(fam)*?	Tengo veinte años.
kōō·än'tōs ä'nyōs tye'ne/tye'nes/	ten'gō ve'ēnte ä'nyōs
I'm over 18.	**Children under 14.**
Soy mayor de edad.	Niños menores de 14 años.
sōi mäyōr' de edäd'	nē'nyōs menō'res de kätōr'se ä'nyōs

I was born on the ...	**He's *younger (older)*.**	**– under age.**
Nací el ...	El es *más joven (mayor)*.	menor de edad.
näsē′ el ...	el es mäs hō′ven (mäyōr′)	menōr′ de edäd′
– grown up.	**At the age of ...**	**At my age.**
adulto.	A la edad de ...	A mi edad.
ädool′tō	ä lä edäd′ de ...	ä mē edäd′

Family

aunt	tía *f*	tē′ä
boy	niño *m*, muchacho *m* ..	nē′nyō, mootshä′tshō
brother	hermano *m*	ermä′nō
brother-in-law	cuñado *m*	koonyä′dō
cousin *(female)*	prima *f*	prē′mä
cousin *(male)*	primo *m*	prē′mō
daughter	hija *f*	ē′hä
family	familia *f*	fämē′lyä
father	padre *m*/*Mex* papá *m* ..	pä′dre/päpä′
father-in-law	suegro *m*	soo·e′grō
girl	niña *f*, muchacha *f*	nē′nyä, mootshä′tshä
grandchild	nieto *m*	nye′tō
granddaughter	nieta *f*	nye′tä
grandfather	abuelo *m*	äboo·e′lō
grandmother	abuela *f*	äboo·e′lä
grandparents	abuelos *mpl*	äboo·e′lōs
grandson	nieto *m*	nye′tō
husband	esposo *m*, marido *m* ...	espō′sō, märē′dō
mother	madre *f*/*Mex* mamá *f* .	mä′dre/mämä′
mother-in-law	suegra *f*	soo·e′grä
nephew	sobrino *m*	sōbrē′nō
niece	sobrina *f*	sōbrē′nä
parents	padres *mpl*	pä′dres
sister	hermana *f*	ermä′nä
sister-in-law	cuñada *f*	koonyä′dä
son	hijo *m*	ē′hō
uncle	tío *m*	tē′ō
wife	esposa *f*, mujer *f*	espō′sä, mooher′

Occupations

apprentice	aprendiz *m*	äprendēs′
artist	artista *m + f*	ärtēs′tä
auto mechanic	mecánico *m* de carros/	mekä′nēkō de
	Sp de coches	kä′rrōs/de kō′tshes
baker	panadero *m*	pänäde′rō
bank teller	cajero *m*	kä*he*′rō
bookkeeper	tenedor *m* de libros	tenedōr′ de lē′brōs
bookseller	librero *m*	lēbre′rō
bricklayer	albañil *m*	älbänyēl′
butcher	carnicero *m*	kärnēse′rō
cabinetmaker	ebanista *m*	ebänēs′tä
carpenter	carpintero *m*	kärpēnte′rō
chef	jefe *m* de cocina	*he*′fe de kōsē′nä
civil servant	funcionario *m*	fōōnsyōnär′yō
clergyman	clérigo *m*	kle′rēgō
confectioner	pastelero *m*	pästele′rō
cook	cocinero *m*	kōsēne′rō
dentist	dentista *m + f*	dentēs′tä
doctor	médico *m + f*	me′dēkō
dressmaker	costurera *f*	kōstōōre′rä
driver	conductor *m*,	kōndōōktōr′,
	chófer *m*	tshō′fer
driving instructor	profesor *m*	prōfesōr′
	de auto-escuela	de outōeskōō·e′lä
electrician	electricista *m*	elektrēsēs′tä
engineer *(scientific)*	ingeniero *m*	ēn*h*enye′rō
engineer *(railroad)*	maquinista *m*	mäkēnēs′tä
farmer	agricultor *m*	ägrēkōōltōr′
fisherman	pescador *m*	peskädōr′
forest ranger	guarda *m* forestal	gōō·är′dä fōrestäl′
gardener	jardinero *m*	*h*ärdēne′rō
glazier	vidriero *m*	vēdrē·e′rō
hairdresser	peluquero *m*	pelōōke′rō
interpreter	intérprete *m + f*	ēnter′prete
(translator)		
journalist	periodista *m + f*	peryōdēs′tä
judge	juez *m + f*	*h*ōō·es′
kindergarten teacher	maestra *f* de párvulos,	mä·es′trä de
		pär′vōōlōs,

	maestra *f* de preescolar	mä·es'trä de pre·es-kōlär'
lawyer	abogado *m* + *f*	äbōgä'dō
librarian	bibliotecario *m*	bēblē-ōtekär'yō
locksmith	cerrajero *m*	serrä*h*e'rō
mailman	cartero *m*	kärte'rō
metalworker	metalúrgico *m*	metälōor'*h*ēkō
midwife	comadrona *f*, partera *f*	kōmädrō'nä, pärte'rä
miner	minero *m*	mēne'rō
musician	músico *m* + *f*	mōō'sēkō
notary	notario *m*	nōtär'yō
nurse *(female)*	enfermera *f*	emferme'rä
nurse *(male)*	enfermero *m*	emferme'rō
optician	óptico *m*	ōp'tēkō
painter	pintor *m*	pēntōr'
pastry chef	pastelero *m*	pästele'rō
pharmacist	farmacéutico *m*	färmäse'·ōotēkō
plumber	plomero *m*/*Sp.* fontanero *m*	plōme'rō/fōntäne'-rō
postal clerk	empleado *m* de correos	emple·ä'dō de kōrre'ōs
pupil	alumno *m*	älōōm'nō
railroad man	ferroviario *m*	ferrōvyär'yō
retailer	comerciante *m*	kōmersyän'te
retiree	pensionista *m* + *f*	pensyōnēs'tä
salesperson	dependiente *m*	dependyen'te
scholar	erudito *m*	erōōdē'tō
scientist	científico *m*	syentē'fēkō
sculptor	escultor *m*	eskōoltōr'
secretary	secretaria *f*	sekretär'yä
shoemaker	zapatero *m*	säpäte'rō
storekeeper	tendero *m*	tende'rō
student	estudiante *m* + *f*	estōōdyän'te
tailor	sastre *m*	säs'tre
teacher	profesor *m*, maestro *m*	prōfesōr', mä·es'trō
technician	técnico *m*	tek'nēkō
trainee	aprendiz *m*	äprendēs'
translator	traductor *m*	trädōōktōr'
truck driver	chófer *m*, camionero *m*	tshō'fer, kämyōne'rō

veterinarian	veterinario m	veterēnär'yō
waiter	camarero m/Mex mesero m	kämäre'rō/mese'rō
waitress	camarera f/Mex mesera f	kämäre'rä/mese'rä
watchmaker	relojero m	relōhe'rō
wholesaler	mayorista m + f	mäyōrēs'tä
worker	obrero m	ōbre'rō
writer	escritor m	eskrētōr'

> To form the feminine form of the occupations given above, change the -o ending to -a (for example: *el peluquero, la peluquera*) or, for endings other than -o, simply add an -a (for example: *el aprendiz, la aprendiza*). In cases where the same noun is used for men and women, only the article is changed from *el* to *la* (for example: *el médico, la médico*). These are designated by m + f.

Education

Where are you studying? (What college or university do you attend?)
¿Dónde estudia/estudias *(fam)*?
dōn'de estōo'dyä/estōo'dyäs

I'm at ... college (university).
Estudio en ...
estōo'dyō en ...

I'm studying (majoring in) ...
Estudio ...
estōo'dyō ...

I got to (am attending) the ... school.
Voy a la escuela ...
vōi ä lä eskōo·e'lä ...

class	clase f	klä'se
major	asignatura f principal	äsēgnätōo'rä prēnsēpäl'
school	escuela f	eskōo·e'lä
– boarding school	internado m	ēnternä'dō
– business school	escuela f de comercio	eskōo·e'lä de kōmer'syō
– grammar school	escuela f primaria, colegio m	eskōo·e'lä prēmär'yä, kōle'hyō
– high school	instituto m de bachillerato	ēnstētōo'tō de bätshēlyerä'tō

– vocational school	escuela f de formación profesional	eskōō·e'lä de fōrmäsyōn' prōfesyōnäl'
subject	asignatura f	äsēgnätōō'rä
– American studies	estudios mpl americanos	estōō'dyōs ämerēkä'nōs
– archaeology	arqueología f	ärke·ōlōhē'ä
– architecture	arquitectura f	ärkētektōō'rä
– art history	historia f de arte	ēstōr'yä de är'te
– biology	biología f	bē·ōlōhē'ä
– business administration	economía f de empresas	ekōnōmē'ä de empre'säs
– chemistry	química f	kē'mēkä
– dentistry	odontología f	ōdōntōlōhē'ä
– economics	ciencias fpl económicas	syen'syäs ekōnō'mēkäs
– education	pedagogía f	pedägōhē'ä
– English	filología f inglesa	fēlōlōhē'ä ēngle'sä
– geology	geología f	he·ōlōhē'ä
– German	filología f germánica	fēlōlōhē'ä hermä'nēkä
– history	historia f	ēstōr'yä
– journalism	periodismo m	peryōdēz'mō
– law	derecho m	dere'tshō
– mathematics	matemáticas fpl	mätemä'tēkäs
– mechanical engineering	construcción f	kōnstrōōksyōn'
	mecánica	mekä'nēkä
– medicine	medicina f	medēsē'nä
– musicology	música f	mōō'sēkä
– painting	pintura f	pēntōō'rä
– pharmacy	farmacia f	färmä'syä
– physics	física f	fē'sēkä
– political science	ciencias fpl políticas	syen'syäs pōlē'tēkäs
– psychology	psicología f	sēkōlōhē'ä
– Romance languages	filología f románica	fēlōlōhē'ä rōmä'nēkä
– Slavic languages	eslavística f	eslävēs'tēkä
– sociology	sociología f	sōsyōlōhē'ä
– veterinary medicine	veterinaria f	veterēnär'yä
– zoology	zoología f	sō·ōlōhē'ä
technical college	escuela f superior técnica	eskōō·e'lä sōōperyōr' tek'nēkä
university	universidad f	ōōnēversēdäd'

ON THE ROAD AGAIN

Asking the Way

Where *is (are)* ...?
¿Dónde *está (están)* ...?
dōn'de estä' (estän') ...

How do I get to ...?
¿Cómo se va a ...?
kō'mō se vä ä ...

How many kilometers is it to the next town?
¿A cuántos kilómetros está la ciudad más cerca?
ä kōō·än'tōs kēlō'metrōs estä' lä syōōdäd' mäs ser'kä

> 8 kilometers = 5 miles

Is this the road to ...?
¿Es ésta la carretera a ...?
es es'tä lä kärrete'rä ä ...

Is this the right way to ...?
¿Voy bien a ...?
vōi byen ä ...

Would you please show me that on the map?
Por favor, enséñemelo en el mapa.
pōr fävōr', ense'nyemelo en el mä'pä

Do I have to go ...?
¿Tengo que ir ...?
ten'gō ke ēr ...

Right.	**Left.**	**Straight ahead.**	**Turn around.**
A la derecha.	A la izquierda.	Todo derecho.	Dar la vuelta.
ä lä dere'tshä	ä lä ēskyer'dä	tō'dō dere'tshō	där lä vōō·el'tä
Here.	**There.**	**This way.**	**As far as ...**
Aquí.	Allá.	Por allí.	Hasta ...
äkē'	älyä'	pōr älyē'	äs'tä ...

How long?
¿Cuánto tiempo?
kōō·än'tō tyem'pō

Where (to)?
¿A dónde?
ä dōn'de

How far is it to ...?
¿A qué distancia está ...?
ä ke dēstän'syä estä' ...

Vehicles

camping trailer	caravana *f/Mex* trayler *m*	kärävä'nä/trīler
camper vehicle	cámper *m*	käm'per
car	automóvil *m*	outōmō'vēl
– **delivery truck, van** .	furgoneta *f*, camioneta *f* ...	fōōrgōne'tä, kä-myōne'tä
– **passenger car**	carro *m/Sp* coche *m* ...	kä'rrō/kō'tshe
– **ranch station wagon**	camioneta *f/Mex* combi *f*	kämyōne'tä/kōm'bē
– **truck**	camión *m*	kämyōn'

bicycle	bicicleta *f*	bēsēkle′tä
horse cart	carro *m*/*Mex* carreta *f*	kä′rrō/kärre′tä
moped, motorbike	ciclomotor *m*	sēklōmōtōr′
motorcycle	motocicleta *f*, moto *f*	mōtōsēkle′tä, mō′tō
motor home	casa rodante *f*,	kä′sä rōdän′te,
	coche-vivienda *m*	kō′tshe-vēvyen′dä
motor scooter	escúter *m*	eskōō′ter
trailer	remolque *m*	remōl′ke
vehicle	vehículo *m*	ve·ē′kōōlō

Renting a Car

Where can I rent a car?
¿Dónde puedo alquilar/*Mex* rentar/un carro/*Sp* un coche?
dōn′de pōō·e′dō älkēlär′/rentär′/ōōn kä′rrō/ōōn kō′tshe

I'd like to rent a car.
Quisiera alquilar/*Mex* rentar/un carro/*Sp* un coche.
kēsye′rä älkēlär′/rentär′/ōōn kä′rrō/ōōn kō′tshe

... with chauffeur.
... con chófer.
... kōn tshō′fer

... for 2 (6) people.
... para *dos (seis)* personas.
... pä′rä dōs (se′ēs) persō′näs

... for *one day (one week, two weeks)*.
... por *un día (una semana (8 días), dos semanas (15 días))*.
... pōr ōōn dē′ä (ōō′nä semä′nä (ō′tshō dē′äs), dōs semä′näs (kēn′se dē′äs))

How much will it cost?
¿Cuánto cuesta?
kōō·än′tō kōō·es′tä

... including full coverage insurance?
... con seguro incluido?
... kōn segōō′rō ēnklōō·ē′dō

Will I have to pay for the gasoline myself?
¿Tengo que pagar yo la gasolina?
ten′gō ke pägär′ yō lä gäsōlē′nä

How much will I have to deposit?
¿Cuánto debo depositar?
kōō·än′tō de′bō depōsētär′

When (Where) can I pick up the car?
¿Cuándo (Dónde) puedo recoger el carro/*Sp* el coche?
kōō·än′dō (dōn′de) pōō·e′dō rekōher′ el kä′rrō/el kō′tshe

Will somebody be there when I bring the car back?
¿Habrá alguien cuando devuelva el carro/*Sp* el coche?
äbrä′ äl′gyen kōō·än′dō devōō·el′vä el kä′rrō/el kō′tshe

On a Drive

I'm *going (driving)* to ...	Are you going to ...?
Voy *(en carro)* a ...	¿Va/vas *(fam)*/a ...?
vōi (en kä'rrō) ä ...	vä/väs/ä ...

To go by *car (motorcycle, bicycle).*		Fast.	Slow.
Ir en *carro*/*Sp coche*/*(motocicleta, bicicleta).*		Rápido.	Despacio.
ēr en kä'rrō/kō'tshe (mōtōsēkle'tä, bēsēkle'tä)		rä'pēdō	despä'syō

access road	acceso m	äkse'sō
bike lane	pista *f* de bicicletas	pēs'tä de bēsēkle'täs
bridge	puente *m*	pōō·en'te
curve	curva *f*	kōōr'vä
detour	desviación *f*	desvē·äsyōn'
direction sign	indicador *m* de camino	ēndēkädōr' de kämē'nō
driver's license	carnet *m* de conducir/ *Mex* licencia *f* de manejar	kärnet' de kōndōō- sēr'/lēsen'syä de mänehär'
driveway	calzada *f*	kälsä'dä
exit	salida *f*	sälē'dä
falling rocks	desprendimiento *m* de piedras/*Mex* zona *f* de derrumbes	desprendēmyen'tō de pye'dräs/sō'nä de derrōōm'bes
highway	autopista *f*	outōpēs'tä
intersection	cruce *m*/*Mex* crucero *m*	krōō'se/krōōse'rō
lane	carril *m*	kärrēl'
limited parking zone	zona *f* de estaciona- miento limitado	sō'nä de estäsyōnä- myen'tō lēmētä'dō
maximum speed	velocidad *f* máxima	velōsēdäd' mä'ksē- mä
no parking	estacionamiento *m* prohibido	estäsyōnämyen'tō prō·ēbē'dō
no passing	prohibido adelantar/ *Mex* no rebase	prō·ēbē'dō ädelän- tär'/nō rebä'se
no stopping	prohibido detenerse	prō·ēbē'dō dete- ner'se
parking disc	disco *m* de estaciona- miento	dēs'kō de estäsyō- nämyen'tō
parking lot	aparcamiento *m*	äpärkämyen'tō
parking meter	parquímetro *m*	pärkē'metrō

path (footpath)	camino *m* (senda *f*) ...	kämē'nō (sen'dä)
railroad crossing ...	paso *m* a nivel/*Mex*	pä'sō ä nēvel'/
	cruce *m* de F.C.	krōō'se de e'fe se
registration	papeles *mpl* del	päpe'les del kä'rrō/
	carro/*Sp* coche	kō'tshe
right of way	preferencia *f* de paso .	preferens'yä de pä'sō
road	carretera *f*, camino *m* .	kärrete'rä, kämē'nō
– country road	camino *m* vecinal	kämē'no vesēnäl'
– cross road	travesía *f*	trävesē'ä
– main road (street)	carretera *f* (calle *f*)	kärrete'rä (kä'lye)
	principal	prēnsēpäl'
road sign	señal *f* de circulación .	senyäl' de
		sērkōōläsyōn'
road under construc-	obras *fpl*/*Mex* hombres	ō'bräs/ōm'bres trä-
tion	*mpl* trabajando	bä*h*än'dō
route	ruta *f*	rōō'tä
side wind	viento *m* de costado ..	vyen'tō de kōstä'dō
slippery road	piso *m* resbaloso/*Sp*	pē'sō resbälō'sō/
	resbaladizo	resbälädē'sō
speed limit	límite *m* de velocidad .	lē'mēte de velōsēdäd'
steep downgrade ...	bajada *f* (peligrosa) ...	bä*h*ä'dä (pelēgrō'sä)
steep upgrade	cuesta *f*, subida *f*	kōō'es'tä, sōōbē'dä
toll	peaje *m*/*Mex* cuota *f* .	pe·ä'*h*e/kōō·ō'tä
traffic.............	circulación *f*, tráfico *m*	sērkōōläsyōn',
		trä'fēkō
traffic circle	glorieta *f*	glōrye'tä
traffic light	semáforo *m*, disco *m* .	semä'fōrō, dēs'ko
trip (journey)	viaje *m*	vyä'*h*e
– brake	frenar	frenär'
– drive	conducir, manejar	kōndōōsēr, mäne*h*är'
– get in lane (merge)	tomar fila	tōmär' fē'lä
– get out (of car) ...	bajar (del carro/*Sp* co-	bä'*h*är (del kä'rrō/
	che)	kō'tshe)
– park	estacionar/*Sp* aparcar	estäsyōnär'/äpärkär'
– stop	parar	pärär'
– turn (the car)	dar la vuelta, virar ...	där lä vōō·el'tä, vērär'
– turn (into a road) .	entrar en	enträr' en
– turn off (a road) ..	doblar/*Sp* torcer	dōblär'/tōrser'
winding road	camino *m* sinuoso	kämē'nō sēnōō·ō'sō
zebra crossing	paso *m* de peatones, pa-	pä'sō de pe·ätō'nes,
	so *m* cebra	pä'sō se'brä

Garage, Parking Lot

Where can I leave my car (for safekeeping)?
¿Dónde hay un estacionamiento/*Sp* aparcamiento/(vigilado) por aquí?
dōn'de ī ōōn estäsyōnämyen'tō/äpärkämyen'tō/(vēhēlä'dō) pōr äkē'

Is there a garage near here?
¿Hay un garaje cerca de aquí?
ī ōōn gärä'*h*e ser'kä de äkē'

Have you still got *a vacant garage (parking space)*?
¿Tiene todavía *un garaje (un sitio)* libre?
tye'ne tōdävē'ä ōōn gärä'*h*e (ōōn sē'tyō) lē'bre

Where can I leave the car?
¿Dónde puedo dejar el carro/*Sp* el coche?
dōn'de pōō·e'dō de*h*är' el kä'rrō/el kō'tshe

Can I leave it here?
¿Puedo dejarlo aquí?
pōō·e'dō de*h*är'lō äkē'

Can I park here?
¿Puedo aparcar/estacionar/aquí?
pōō·e'dō äpärkär'/estäsyōnär'/äkē'

Is this parking lot guarded?
¿Está vigilado el parqueadero/*Sp* vigilado el aparcamiento?
estä' vēhēlä'dō el pärke·äde'rō/vēhēlä'dō el äpärkämyen'tō

Is there a space free?
¿Queda todavía un sitio libre?
ke'dä tōdävē'ä ōōn sē'tyō lē'bre

How long can I park here?
¿Cuánto tiempo puedo aparcar/estacionar/aquí?
kōō·än'tō tyem'pō pōō·e'dō äpärkär'/estäsyōnär'/äkē'

How much does it cost to park here *overnight (until …)*?
¿Cuál es el precio del estacionamiento *por una noche (hasta …)*?
kōō·äl' es el pre'syō del estäsyōnämyen'tō pōr ōō'nä nō'tshe (äs'tä …)

Is the garage open all night?
¿Está abierto toda la noche?
estä' äbyer'tō tō'dä lä nō'tshe

When do you close?
¿A qué hora cierran?
ä ke ō'rä sye'rrän

I'll be leaving *this evening (tomorrow morning at eight)*.
Me voy *esta noche (mañana a las ocho)*.
me vōi es'tä nō'tshe (mänyä'nä ä läs ō'tshō)

I'd like to take my car out of the garage.
Quisiera sacar mi carro/*Sp* mi coche/del garaje.
kēsye'rä säkär' mē kä'rrō/mē kō'tshe/del gärä'*h*e

Gas Station, Car Repair

Where's the nearest gas station?
¿Dónde está la bomba de gasolina (*or* estación de servicio) más próxima?
dōn'de estä' lä bōm'bä de gäsōlē'nä (estä-syōn' de servē'syō) mäs prō'ksēmä

How far is it?
¿A qué distancia está?
ä ke dēstän'syä estä'

Fifteen liters of *regular (high test)* please.
Quince litros de gasolina *normal (extra)*, por favor.
kēn'se lē'trōs de gäsōlē'nä nōrmäl' (eks'trä), pōr fävōr'

> *1 gallon = 3.8 liters*

I'd like 20 liters of diesel, please.
Quisiera veinte litros de gasóleo/*Mex* diesel/ por favor.
kēsye'rä ve'ēnte lē'trōs de gäsō'le·ō/ dyesel'/pōr fävōr'

Fill it up, please.
Lleno, por favor.
lye'nō, pōr fävōr'

I need water (coolant).
Necesito agua para el radiador.
nesesē'tō ä'gōō·ä pä'rä el rädyädōr'

A road map, please.
Un mapa de carreteras, por favor.
ōon mä'pä de kärrete'räs, pōr fävōr'

Would you please fill up the radiator?
Póngame agua en el radiador, por favor.
pōn'gäme ä'gōō·ä en el rädyädōr', pōr fävōr'

Would you please check the brake fluid?
Revise el líquido de frenos, por favor.
revē'se el lē'kēdō de fre'nōs, pōr fävōr'

brake fluid	líquido *m* de frenos	lē'kēdō de fre'nōs
car repair service	taller *m* mecánico	tälyer' mekä'nēkō
coolant	agua *f* para el radiador	ä'gōō·ä pä'rä el rä-dyädōr'
gasoline	gasolina *f*	gäsōlē'nä
gasoline can	bidón *m* de gasolina	bēdōn'de gäsōlē'nä
gas station	gasolinera *f*, estación *f* de servicio	gäsōlēne'rä, estä-syōn' de servē'syō
oil	aceite *m*	äse'ēte
spark plug	bujía *f*	bōōhē'ä
water	agua *f*	ä'gōō·ä
– distilled water	agua *f* destilada	ä'gōō·ä destēlä'dä

Oil

Please check the oil.
Por favor, revise el nivel de aceite.
pōr fàvōr', revē'se el nēvel'
de äse'ēte

Please change the oil.
Cambie el aceite, por favor.
käm'bye el äse'ēte, pōr favōr'

Please fill up the oil tank.
Ponga el aceite que falta, por favor.
pōn'gä el äse'ēte ke fäl'tä, pōr fàvōr'

... liters of oil, please.
... litros de aceite, por favor.
... lē'trōs de äse'ēte, pōr fàvōr'

---

1 liter = approx. 2 pints

---

gear oil	aceite *m* lubricante	äse'ēte lōōbrēkän'te
lubrication	lubricación *f*	lōōbrēkäsyōn'
motor oil	aceite *m* para el motor .	äse'ēte pä'rä el mō-tōr'
oil	aceite *m*	äse'ēte
– special/standard . . .	especial/normal	espesyäl'/nōrmäl'
oil can	aceitera *f*	äse·ē'te'rä
oil change	cambio *m* de aceite	käm'byō de äse'ēte
oil level	nivel *m* de aceite	nēvel' de äse'ēte

Tires

Can you *repair (retread)* this tire?
¿Se puede *arreglar (recauchutar)* este neumático/*Mex* esta llanta?
se pōō·e'de ärreglär' (rekoutshōōtär') es'te ne·ōōmä'tēkō/es'tä
lyän'tä

Can this inner tube be patched?
¿Se puede poner un parche a esta cámara/*Mex* tubo/de aire?
se pōō·e'de pōner' ōōn pär'tshe ä es'tä kä'märä/tōō'bō/de ī're

Please change this tire.
Por favor, cámbieme el
neumático/*Mex* la llanta.
pōr fàvōr', käm'byeme el ne·ōō-
mä'tēkō/lä lyän'tä

A new inner tube, please.
Una nueva cámara/*Mex* tubo/
de aire, por favor.
ōō'nä nōō·e'vä kä'märä/tōō'bō/
de ī're, pōr fàvōr'

One of my tires had a blow-out.
He tenido un reventón (*or* pinchazo).
e tenē'dō ōōn reventōn' (pēntshä'sō)

Would you please check the tire pressure?
Revise la presión de los neumáticos/*Mex* las llantas/por favor.
revē'se lä presyōn' de lōs ne·ōōmä'tēkōs/läs lyän'täs/pōr fävōr'

The front tires are 22.7 and the rear ones are 28.4.
Los de delante necesitan 22.7 y los de atrás 28.4.
lōs de delän'te nesesē'tän ve'ēntēdōs' pōōn'tō sye'te ē lōs de äträs'
ve'ēntē·ō'tshō pōōn'tō kōō·ä'trō

blow-out	pinchazo *m*, reventón *m*	pēntshä'sō, reventōn'
inner tube	cámara *f*/*Mex* tubo *m*/	kä'märä/tōō'bō/
	de aire	de ī're
jack	gato *m*	gä'tō
puncture	pinchazo *m*	pēntshä'sō
tires *(in general)* .	neumáticos *mpl*/*Mex*	ne·ōōmä'tēkōs/
	llantas *fpl*	lyän'täs
tire	neumático *m*/*Mex*	ne·ōōmä'tēkō/
	llanta *f*	lyän'tä
tire change	cambio *m* de neu-	käm'byō de ne·ōō-
	mático/*Mex* de llanta . .	mä'tēkō/de lyän'tä
tire pressure	presión *f* de los neu-	presyōn' de lōs ne·ōō-
	máticos/*Mex* las llantas	mä'tēkōs/läs lyän'täs
valve	válvula *f*	väl'vōōlä
wheel	rueda *f*	rōō·e'dä
– back wheel	rueda *f* trasera	rōō·e'dä träse'rä
– front wheel	rueda *f* delantera	rōō·e'dä delänte'rä
– reserve wheel . .	rueda *f* de repuesto/	rōō·e'dä de repōō·es'tō/
	Sp de recambio	de rekäm'byō
– wheels	ruedas *fpl*	rōō·e'däs

Car Wash

Please wash *the windshield (the windows)*.
Por favor, limpie *el parabrisas (los cristales)*.
pōr fävōr', lēm'pye el päräbrē'säs (lōs krēstä'les)

I'd like my car washed, please.
Por favor, láveme el carro/*Sp* el coche.
pōr fävōr', lä'veme el kä'rrō/el kō'tshe

Please clean out the inside, too.
Por favor, limpie el carro/*Sp* el coche/también por dentro.
pōr fävōr', lēm'pye el kä'rrō/el kō'tshe/tämbyen' pōr den'trō

Breakdown, Accident

I've (We've) had a breakdown.
Tengo (Tenemos) una falla mecánica/Sp una avería.
ten'gō (tene'mōs) ōō'nä fä'lyä mekä'nēkä/ōō'nä ävere'ä

I've had an accident.
He tenido un accidente.
e tenē'do ōōn äksēden'te

Would you please call the police?
¿Por favor, avise a la policía.
pōr fävōr', ävē'se ä lä pōlēsē'ä

Call an ambulance quickly!
¡Llame en seguida una ambulancia!
lyä'me en segē'dä ōō'nä ämbōōlän'syä

Please help me!
¡Ayúdeme, por favor!
äyōō'deme, pōr fävōr'

Could you ...?
¿Podría ...?
pōdrē'ä ...

– give me a lift?
– llevarme en carro/*Sp* coche/
  Mex darme un aventón?
– lyevär'me en kä'rrō/kō'tshe/
  där'me ōōn äventōn'

May I use your phone?
¿Puedo telefonear?
pōō·e'dō telefōne·är'

Could you lend me ...?
¿Podría prestarme ...?
pōdrē'ä prestär'me ...

Get a doctor!
¡Llame a un médico!
lyä'me ä ōōn me'dēkō

I need bandages.
Necesito vendajes/*Mex* vendas.
nesesē'tō vendä'*hes*/ven'däs

– look after the injured?
– cuidar de los heridos?
– kōō·ēdär' de lōs erē'dōs

– tow my car?
– remolcar el carro/*Sp* el coche?
– remōlkär' el kä'rrō/el kō'tshe

– get me *a mechanic (a tow truck)*?
– enviarme *un mecánico (una grúa/Sp un coche grúa)?*
– embyär'me ōōn mekä'nēkō (ōō'nä grōō'ä/ōōn kō'tshe grōō'ä)

Where is there *a service station (repair shop)*?
¿Dónde hay *una gasolinera (un taller mecánico)*?
dōn'de ī ōō'nä gäsōlēne'rä (ōōn tälyer' mekä'nēkō)

Would you please give me your name and address?
Déme su nombre y dirección, por favor.
de'me sōō nōm'bre ē dēreksyōn', pōr fävōr'

It's your fault.
Usted tiene la culpa.
ōōste' tye'ne lä kōōl'pä

I had the right of way.
Yo tenía preferencia.
yō tenē'ä preferen'syä

Nobody's hurt.
Nadie está herido.
nä'dye estä' erē'dō

Where is your car insured?
¿En qué compañía tiene asegurado su carro/Sp coche?
en ke kōmpänyē'ä tye'ne äsegōōrä'dō sōō kä'rrō/kō'tshe

You've damaged ...
Ha dañado/Sp estropeado ...
ä dänyä'dō/estrōpe·ä'dō ...

... is (badly) injured.
... está (gravemente) herido.
... estä' (grävemen'te) erē'dō

Will you be my witness?
¿Puede servirme de testigo?
pōō·e'de servēr'me de testē'gō

ambulance	ambulancia f	ämbōōlän'syä
bandages	vendajes mpl/Mex	vendä'hes/
	vendas fpl	ven'däs
body and fender damage	daños mpl en la carrocería	dä'nyōs en lä kärrōserē'ä
breakdown	avería f/Mex falla f	äverē'ä/fä'lyä
	mecánica	mekä'nēkä
collision	choque m	tshō'ke
damage	daños mpl	dä'nyōs
danger!	¡peligro!	pelē'grō
dealership garage	taller m concesionario .	tälyer' kōnsesyōnär'yō
emergency ward .	sala f de emergencias ..	sä'lä de emerhen'syäs
fire department ..	bomberos mpl	bōmbe'rōs
first aid station ..	puesto m de socorro/	pōō·es'tō de sōkō'rrō/
	Mex primeros auxilios.	prēme'rōs ouksē'lyōs
head-on collision .	choque m de frente	tshō'ke de fren'te
help	ayuda f	äyōō'dä
hospital	hospital m	ōspētäl'
injury	herida f	erē'dä
insurance	seguro m	segōō'rō
mechanic	mecánico m	mekä'nēkō
police	policía f	pōlesē'ä
rear-end collision	accidente m en cadena .	äksēden'te en käde'nä
service station ...	gasolinera f, estación f	gäsōlēne'rä, estäsyōn'
	de servicio	de servē'syō
towing service ...	servicio m de remolque	servē'syō de remōl'ke
tow line	cable m de remolque ..	kä'ble de remōl'ke
tow truck	grúa f/Sp coche m grúa	grōō'ä/kō'tshe grōō'ä

Repair Workshop

Where's the nearest *garage (... garage)*?
¿Dónde está el *taller mecánico (taller concesionario de ...)* más cercano?
dōn'de estä' el tälyer' mekä'nēkō (tälyer' kōnsesyōnär'yō de ...) mäs serkä'nō

... isn't working right.
... no funciona bien.
... nō fōōnsyō'nä byen

... is out of order (isn't working).
... está estropeado/dañado.
... estä' estrōpe·ä'dō/dänyä'dō

Can you fix it?
¿Puede arreglarlo?
pōō·e'de arreglär'lō

Where can I have this fixed?
¿Dónde se puede arreglarlo?
dōn'de se pōō·e'de ärreglär'lō

Would you please check the ...?
¿Podría revisar el/la ...?
pōdrē'ä revēsär' el (lä) ...

Would you please give me ...?
¿Podría darme ...?
pōdrē'ä där'me ...

Would you please fix this?
¿Podría arreglar eso?
pōōdrē'ä ärreglär e'sō

Have you got manufacturer's spare parts for ...?
¿Tiene piezas de repuesto originales de ...?
tye'ne pye'säs de repōō·es'tō ōrēhēnä'les de ...

How soon can you get the spare parts?
¿Cuándo recibirá las piezas de repuesto?
kōō·än'dō resēbērä' läs pye'säs de repōō·es'tō

I need a new ...
Necesito un nuevo ...
nesese'tō ōōn nōō·e'vō ...

Can I still drive it?
¿Puedo seguir circulando con esto?
pōō·e'dō segēr' sērkōōlän'dō kōn es'tō

Just do the essentials, please.
Haga sólo lo más necesario, por favor.
ä'gä sō'lō lō mäs nesesär'yō, pōr fàvōr'

When will it be ready?
¿Cuándo estará listo?
kōō·än'dō estärä' lēs'tō

How much *does (will)* it *cost*?
¿Cuánto *cuesta (va a costar)*?
kōō·än'tō kōō·es'tä (vä ä kōstär')

Car Parts, Repairs

accelerator	acelerador *m*	äselerädōr'
air filter	filtro *m* de aire	fēl'trō de ī're
automatic trans- mission	dispositivo *m* auto- mático	dēspōsētē'vō outō- mä'tēkō
axle	eje *m*	e'*he*
backfire	petardeo *m*	petärde'ō
ball bearings	cojinete *m* de bolas/*Mex* baleros *mpl*	kō*h*ēne'te de bō'läs/ bäle'rōs
battery	batería *f*/*Mex a* acumulador *m*	bäterē'ä/ äkōōmōōlädōr'
blinker	intermitente *m*/*Mex* direccionales	ēntermēten'te/ dēreksyōnä'les
body	carrocería *f*	kärrōserē'ä
bolt	tornillo *m*	tōrnē'lyō
– nut	tuerca *f*	tōō·er'kä
brake drum	tambor *m* de freno	tämbōr' de fre'nō
brake fluid	líquido *m* de frenos	lē'kēdō de fre'nōs
brake lights	luces *fpl* de freno	lōō'ses de fre'nō
brake lining	guarnición *f* de freno/*Mex* balata *f*	gōō·ärnēsyōn' de fre'nō/bälä'tä
brake pedal	pedal *m* de freno	pedäl' de fre'nō
brakes	frenos *mpl*	fre'nōs
– disc brake	freno *m* de disco	fre'nō de dēs'kō
– foot brake	freno *m* de pedal	fre'nō de pedäl'
– hand brake	freno *m* de mano	fre'nō de mä'nō
bulb	bombilla *f*	bōmbē'lyä
– change the bulb	cambiar la bombilla	kämbyär' lä bōmbē'lyä
bumper	parachoques *m*, defensa *f*	pärätshō'kes/ defen'sä

The battery *has run down (needs charging)*.
La batería *está descargada (debe cargarse)*.
lä bäterē'ä estä' deskärgä'dä (de'be kärgär'se)

The brakes aren't working right. They're *slack (too tight)*.
Los frenos no funcionan bien.   Están *flojos (demasiado tensos)*.
lōs fre'nōs nō fōōnsyō'nän byen   estän' flō'*h*ōs (demäsyä'dō ten'sōs)

The brake drums are getting too hot.
Los tambores de freno se calientan demasiado.
lōs tämbō'res de fre'nō se kälyen'tän demäsyä'dō

cable	cable *m*	kä′ble
camshaft	árbol *m* de levas	är′bōl de le′väs
carburetor	carburador *m*	kärbōōrädōr′
carburetor jet . . .	esprea *f*	espre′ä
car door	puerta *f* del carro/*Sp*	pōō·er′tä del kä′rrō/
	del coche	del kō′tshe
car keys	llaves *fpl* del carro/*Sp*	lyä′ves del kä′rrō/
	del coche	del kō′tshe
chains	cadenas *fpl*	käde′näs
– **snow chains** . . .	cadenas *fpl* antidesli-	käde′näs äntēdezlē-
	zantes	sän′tes
chassis	chasís *m*/*Sp* chasis *m* . .	tshäsēs′/tshä′sēs
clutch	cloche *m*/*Sp* embrague *m*	klō′tshe/embrä′ge
compression	compresión *f*	kōmpresyōn′
condenser	condensador *m*	kōndensädōr′
connecting rod . . .	biela *f*	bye′lä
– **connecting rod**	cojinete *m* de biela/*Mex*	kōhēne′te de bye′lä/
bearing	metales *mpl* de bielas . .	metä′les de bye′läs
contact	contacto *m*	kōntäk′tō
crankshaft	cigüeñal *m*	sēgōō·enyäl′
cylinder	cilindro *m*	sēlēn′drō
– **cylinder head** . .	culata *f*/*Mex* cabeza *f*/	kōōlä′tä/käbe′sä/
	del cilindro	del sēlēn′drō
– **cylinder head**	junta *f* de la culata/*Mex*	hōōn′tä de lä kōōlä′tä/
gasket	empaque *m* de cabeza .	empä′ke de käbe′sä
diesel nozzle	tobera *f*	tōbe′rä
differential	diferencial *m*	dēferensyäl′
dip stick	varilla *f* del nivel de	värē′lyä del nēvel′
	aceite	de äse′ēte
distributor	distribuidor *m*	dēstrēbōō·ēdōr′
door lock	cerradura *f*, chapa *f* . .	serrädōō′rä/tshä′pä
drive shaft	árbol *m* del cardán . . .	är′bōl del kärdän′
dynamo	dínamo *m* + *f*/*Sp* *f*	dē′nämō
exhaust	escape *m*	eskä′pe

The dynamo isn't charging.   **There's oil leaking out of the gear-box.**
La dínamo no da corriente.   Gotea aceite de la caja de cambios.
lä dē′nämō nō dä kōrryen′te   gōte′ä äse′ēte de lä kä′*h*ä de käm′byōs

It won't stay in … gear.
La … marcha no agarra/el cambio no entra.
lä … mär′tshä nō ägä′rrä/el käm′byō no en′trä

fan	ventilador *m*	ventēlädōr'
fan belt	correa *f* de ventilador/ *Mex* banda *f* de ventilador	kōrre'ä de ventēlädōr'/bän'dä de ventēlädōr'
fender	guardabarros *m*	gōo·ärdäbä'rrōs
fire extinguisher	extintor *m*, extinguidor *m*	ekstēntōr', ekstēngēdōr'
fuel injector	bomba *f* de inyección	bōm'bä de ēnyeksyōn'
fuel lines	conducto *m* de gasolina	kōndōok'tō de gäsōlē'nä
fuel pump	bomba *f* de gasolina	bōm'bä de gäsōlē'nä
fuse	fusible *m*	fōosē'ble
gas	gasolina *f*	gäsōlē'nä
gasket	junta *f*, empaque *m*	hōon'tä, empä'ke
gear	marcha *f*/*Mex* engrane *m*	mär'tshä/engrä'ne
– neutral	punto *m* muerto	pōon'tō mōo·er'tō
– reverse	marcha *f* atrás	mär'tshä äträs'
– to put in gear	meter la marcha	meter' lä mär'tshä
gear box	caja *f* de cambios	kä'hä de käm'byōs
gear lever, gear shift	palanca *f* de cambios	pälän'kä de käm'byōs
handle	manecilla *f*, manija *f*	mänesē'lyä, mänē'hä
headlight	faro *m*/*Mex* focos *mpl*	fä'rō/fō'kōs
– dipped headlights	luz *f* de cruce	lōos de krōo'se
– full beam	luz *f* de carretera	lōos de kärrete'rä
– parking lights	luz *f* de población	lōos de pōbläsyōn'
– rear lights	luz *f* trasera	lōos träse'rä
heating system	calefacción *f*	kälefäksyōn'
hood	capó *m*, capota *f*	käpō', käpō'tä
horn	bocina *f*, claxon *m*, pito *m*	bōsē'nä, klä'ksōn, pē'tō
hub	cubo *m*	kōo'bō
hub cap	tapacubos *m*, copa *f*	täpäkōo'bōs, kō'pä

The heating doesn't work.
La calefacción no funciona.
lä kälefäksyōn' nō fōonsyō'nä

The radiator has sprung a leak.
Se escapa agua del radiador.
se eskä'pä ä'gōo·ä del rädyädōr'

The clutch *slips (won't disengage)*.
El cloche/*Sp* el embrague/*patina (no se suelta)*.
el klō'tshe/el embrä'ge/pätē'nä (nō se sōo·el'tä)

ignition	encendido *m*	ensendē′dō
– ignition cable ...	cable *m* (del encendido)	kä′ble (del ensen-dē′dō)
– ignition key	llave *f* de contacto	lyä′ve de kōntäk′tō
– ignition lock	interruptor *m* (del encendido)	ēnterrōōptōr′ (del ensendē′dō)
insulation	aislamiento *m* :......	īzlämyen′tō
interrupter	ruptor *m*	rōōptōr′
lamp	lámpara *f*	läm′pärä
license plate	matrícula *f*, placa *f*	mätrē′kōōlä, plä′kä
lighting system	alumbrado *m*, luces *fpl*	älōōmbrä′dō, lōō′ses
lubricant	lubricante *m*	lōōbrēkän′te
mileage indicator ..	cuentakilómetros *m* ...	kōō•entäkēlō′metrōs
motor	motor *m*	mōtōr′
– diesel motor	motor *m* diesel	mōtōr′ dyesel′
– rear motor	motor *m* trasero	mōtōr′ träse′rō
– two-stroke motor	motor *m* de dos tiempos	mōtōr′ de dōs tyem′pōs
nationality plate ..	placa *f* de nacionalidad	plä′kä de näsyōnä-lēdäd′
oil filter	filtro *m* de aceite	fēl′trō de äse′ēte
oil pump	bomba *f* de aceite	bōm′bä de äse′ēte
paint job	pintura *f*/*Sp* barniz *m* .	pēntōō′rä/bärnēs′
pedal	pedal *m*	pedäl′
piston	émbolo *m*, pistón *m* ...	em′bōlō, pēstōn′
– piston ring	segmento *m* de émbolo (de pistón)	segmen′tō de em′-bōlō (de pēstōn′)
pipe	tubo *m*	tōō′bō
power brake	servofreno *m*	servōfre′nō
power steering	servodirección *f*	servōdēreksyōn′
radiator	radiador *m*	rädyädōr′
– radiator grill	rejilla *f* del radiador ...	re*h*ē′lyä del rädyädōr′

The motor lacks power.	– is overheating.
El motor no tira/no tiene fuerza.	– se calienta.
el mōtōr′ nō tē′rä/ nō tye′ne fōō•er′sä	– se kälyen′tä

– knocks.	– suddenly stalls.	– misses.
– golpea, pica/*Mex* suena.	– se cala/se apaga.	– da sacudidas
– gōlpe′ä, pē′kä/sōō•e′nä	– se kä′lä/se äpä′gä	– dä säkōōdē′däs

rear view mirror	espejo *m* retrovisor	espe'hō retrōvēsōr'
repair	reparación *f*	repäräsyōn'
reserve fuel can	tarro *m* de reserva/*Sp*	tä'rrō de reser'vä/
	bidón *m* de reserva	bēdōn' de reser'vä
roof	capota *f*	käpō'tä
screw	tornillo *m*	tōrnē'lyō
seat belt	cinturón *m* de seguridad	sēntōōrōn' de
		segōōrēdäd'
shock absorber	amortiguador *m*	ämōrtēgōō·ädōr'
short circuit	cortocircuito *m*	kōrtōsērkōō·ē'tō
sliding sun roof	techo *m* corredizo	te'tshō kōrredē'sō
solder	soldar	sōldär'
speedometer	taquímetro *m*	täkē'metrō
spoke	rayo *m* (de rueda)	rä'yō (de rōō·e'dä)
seat	asiento *m*	äsyen'tō
– back seat	asiento *m* trasero ....:	äsyen'tō träse'rō
– driver's seat	asiento *m* del conductor	äsyen'tō del
		kōndōōktōr'
– front seat	asiento *m* delantero ...	äsyen'tō delänte'rō
– front passenger seat	asiento *m* delantero del	äsyen'tō delänte'rō
	pasajero	del päsähe'rō
spare part	pieza *f* de recambio, de	pye'sä de rekäm'-
	repuesto	byō, de repōō·e'stō
spare wheel	rueda *f* de recambio, de	rōō·e'dä de rekäm'-
	repuesto	byō, de repōō·e'stō
spark	chispa *f*	tshēs'pä
spark plug	bujía *f*	bōōhē'ä
spring	ballesta *f*	bälyes'tä
starter	arranque *m*/*Mex*	ärrän'ke, mär'tshä
	marcha *f*	

The windshield wiper *smears (is broken off)*.

El limpiaparabrisas *ensucia el vidrio*/*Sp el cristal (está roto)*.

el lēmpyäpäräbrē'säs ensōō'syä el vē'drē·ō/el krēstäl' (estä' rō'tō)

This screw needs *tightening (loosening)*.

Hay que *apretar (aflojar)* este tornillo.

ī ke äpretär' (äflōhär') es'te tōrnē'lyō

The fuse has blown.

Los fusibles están fundidos.

lōs fōōsē'bles estän' fōōndē'dōs

steering	dirección *f*	dēreksyōn′
– steering wheel	volante *m*	vōlän′te
switch	interruptor *m*	ēnterrōōptōr′
thermostat	termostato *m/Mex* toma *f* de agua	termōstä′tō/tō′mä de ä′gōō·ä
(screw) thread	rosca *f*	rōs′kä
top	capota *f*	käpō′tä
transmission	transmisión *f*	tränsmēsyōn′
trunk	portamaletas *m*, maletero *m/Mex* cajuela *f*	pōrtämäle′täs, mälete′rō/kähōō·e′lä
turn signal flasher	intermitente *m/Mex* destallador *m*	ēntermēten′te/destälyädōr′
valve	válvula *f*	väl′vōōlä
warning triangle	triángulo *m* de peligro	trē·än′gōōlō de pelē′grō
washer	arandela *f*	ärande′lä
wheel	rueda *f*	rōō·e′dä
windshield	parabrisas *m*	päräbrē′säs
windshield washer	lavaparabrisas *m*	läväpäräbrē′säs
windshield wiper	limpiaparabrisas *m*	lēmpyäpäräbrē′säs

Would you please straighten out my bumper?
Por favor, enderece el parachoques, la defensa.
pōr fàvōr′, endere′se el pärätshō′kes, lä defen′sä

Would you please *check (clean)* the carburetor?
Por favor, *revise (limpie)* el carburador.
pōr fàvōr′, revē′se (lēm′pye) el kärbōōrädōr′

Would you please change the spark plugs?
Por favor, cámbieme las bujías.
pōr fàvōr′, käm′byeme läs bōōhē′äs

Tools

Can you loan me ...?
¿Puede/puedes *(fam)*/prestarme ...?
pōō·e'de/pōō·e'des/prestär'me ...

I need ...
Necesito ...
nesesē'tō ...

air pump	bomba *f* de aire	bōm'bä de ī're
bolt	tornillo *m*	tōrnē'lyō
– **nut**	tuerca *f*	tōō·er'kä
cable	cable *m*	kä'ble
chisel	cincel *m*	sēnsel'
cloth	paño *m*	pä'nyō
drill	taladro *m*	tälä'drō
file	lima *f*	lē'mä
funnel	embudo *m*	embōō'dō
hammer	martillo *m*	märtē'lyō
inspection light	lámpara *f* piloto *or* de prueba	läm'pärä pēlō'tō (de prōō·e'bä)
jack	gato *m*	gä'tō
nail	clavo *m*	klä'vō
pincers	tenazas *fpl*	tenä'säs
pliers	alicates *mpl*, pinzas *fpl*	älēkä'tes, pēn'säs
rag	trapo *m*	trä'pō
sandpaper	papel *m* de lija	päpel' de lē'hä
screw	tornillo *m*	tōrnē'lyō
screwdriver	destornillador *m*/*Mex* desarmador *m*	destōrnēlyädōr'/ desärmädōr'
socket wrench	llave *f* de dado	lyä've de dä'dō
string	cordel *m*, cuerda *f*	kōrdel', kōō·er'dä
tools	herramientas *fpl*	errämyen'täs
– **tool box (kit)**	caja *f* de herramientas	kä'hä de errämyen'täs
wire	alambre *m*	äläm'bre
– **a piece of wire**	un trozo de alambre	ōōn trō'sō de äläm'bre
wrench	llave *f* inglesa	lyä've ēngle'sä

TRAFFIC SIGNS

1 DANGER Peligro · 2 YIELD RIGHT OF WAY Ceda el paso ·
3 INTERSECTION Cruce · 4 DO NOT ENTER Acceso prohibido · 5
NO VEHICLES ALLOWED Circulación prohibida a todos los
vehículos · 6 ONE WAY STREET Calle de dirección única · 7 SPEED
LIMIT Velocidad máxima · 8 NO PASSING Prohibido adelantar ·
9 PRIORITY ROAD Cruce con prioridad · 10 END OF PRIORITY
ROAD Fin de prioridad · 11 STOP Alto, Pare · 12 NO STOPPING
Prohibida la parada · 13 NO PARKING Estacionamiento prohibido ·
14 EXPRESSWAY/FREEWAY Autopista · 15 RAILROAD CROSS-
ING NO GATES Paso a nivel sin barreras · 16 CUSTOMS Aduana

Road signs are color and shape-coded. Triangular signs with a red
rim are *warning signs*; round blue signs are *regulatory signs*; round
signs with a red rim are *prohibit movement signs*; rectangular
yellow signs with a black rim are *destination signs*; rectangular
blue signs with white letters are *destination signs* on highways.

ON THE BUS

Where do the buses to … stop?
¿Dónde paran los buses/*Mex* camiones/para …?
dōn'de pä'rän lōs bōō'ses/kämyō'nes/pärä …

Is that far?
¿Está lejos?
estä' le'*h*ōs

When does *a (the first, the last)* bus leave for …?
¿A qué hora sale un *(el primer, el último)* autobús/*Mex* camión/para …?
ä ke ō'rä sä'le ōōn (el prēmer', el ōōl'tēmō) outōbōōs'/kämyōn'/
pä'rä …

Which bus goes to …?
¿Qué bus/*Mex* camión/va a …?
ke bōōs/kämyōn'/vä ä …

Where does the bus go?
¿A dónde va el bus/*Mex* camión?
ä dōn'de vä el bōōs/kämyōn'

***Is there a bus (Does this bus go)* to …?**
¿Hay un autobús *(Va este autobús)* a …?
ī ōōn outōbōōs' (vä es'te outōbōōs') ä …

When do we get to …?
¿Cuándo llegamos a …?
kōō·än'dō lyegä'mōs ä …

Do I have to change buses for …?
¿Tengo que cambiar para …?
ten'gō ke kämbyär' pä'rä …

Where do I have to change?
¿Dónde tengo que cambiar?
dōn'de ten'gō ke kämbyär'

One (two) round-trip ticket(s), please.
Un *(dos)* boleto(s)/*Sp* billete(s)/de ida y
vuelta para …
ōōn (dōs) bōle'tō(s)/bēlye'te(s)/de ē'dä
ē vōō·el'tä pä'rä …

bus	bus *m*, autobús *m*/*Mex* camión *m*	bōōs, outōbōōs'/ kämyōn'
bus terminal	estación *f* de autobuses	estäsyōn' de outōbōō'ses
direction	dirección *f*	dēreksyōn'
driver	conductor *m*, chófer *m*	kōndōōktōr', tshō'fer
last stop	terminal *f or m*	termēnäl'
luggage	equipaje *m*	ekēpä'*h*e
route	línea *f*	lē'ne·ä
stop	parada *f*	pärä'dä
ticket	boleto *m*/*Sp* billete *m* ..	bōle'tō/bēlye'te
ticket checker ...	cobrador *m*	kōbrädōr'
transfer	correspondencia *f*	kōrrespōnden'syä

BY TRAIN

At the Station

Where is the *station (main station)*?
¿Dónde está *la estación (central)*
de ferrocarril?
dōn'de estä' lä estäsyōn' (senträl')
de ferrōkärrēl'

Where *is (are)* ...?
¿Dónde *está (están)* ...?
dōn'de estä' (estän') ...

the information office	información *f*	ēnfōrmäsyōn'
the money exchange	oficina *f* de cambio	ōfēsē'nä de käm'byō
the rest room	lavabos *mpl*/servicios *mpl*/*Mex* baños *mpl*	lävä'bōs/servē'syōs/ bä'nyōs
the ticket window	despacho *m* de billetes, taquilla *f*	despä'tshō de bē- lye'tes, täkē'lyä
a time table	horario *m*	ōrär'yō
the waiting room	sala *f* de espera	sä'lä de espe'rä

Time Table

arrival/departure	llegada *f*/salida *f*	lyegä'dä/sälē'dä
connection	combinación *f*/*Sp* enlace *m*	kōmbēnäsyōn'/ enlä'se
couchette sleeper	coche-literas *m*/*Mex* cama *f* alta, baja	kō'tshe-lēte'räs/ kä'mä äl'tä, bä'hä
dining bar	coche-restaurante *m*	kō'tshe restourän'te
express train	expreso *m*	ekspre'sō
fast train	tren *m* rápido	tren rä'pēdō
long distance express	expreso *m* de largo recorrido	ekspre'sō de lär'gō rekōrrē'dō
motorail service	autotrén *m*	outōtren'
platform	andén *m*	änden'
railroad car	coche *m*	kō'tshe
sleeper/sleeping car	coche-cama *m*/*Mex* camarín *m*, alcoba *f*	kō'tshe-kä'mä/ kämärēn', älkō'bä

A couchette car provides overnight travelers with a simple bench or a berth to stretch out on during the night. A sleeping car contains little bedrooms complete with private washing facilities.

supplemental fare .	suplemento *m*	sōōplemen'tō
system time table ..	guía *f* de ferrocarriles .	gē'ä de ferrōkärrē'les
through car	coche *m* directo	kō'tshe dērek'tō
track	vía *f*	vē'ä

Information

When is there a *fast (express)* train to ...?
¿Cuándo sale un tren *rápido (expreso)* para ...?
kōō·än'dō sä'le ōōn tren rä'pēdō (ekspre'sō) pä'rä ...

Where is the train to ...?
¿Dónde está el tren para ...?
dōn'de estä' el tren pä'rä ...

Is this the train to ...?
¿Es éste el tren para ...?
es es'te el tren pä'rä ...

Does this train stop in ...?
¿Para este tren en ...?
pä'rä es'te tren en ...

Is the train from ... late?
¿Tiene retraso el tren de ...?
tye'ne reträ'sō el tren de ...

Can we make a connection to ...?
¿Tenemos conección para ...?
tene'mōs kōneksyōn' pä'rä ...

When does it get to ...?
¿Cuándo llega a ...?
kōō·än'dō lye'gä ä ...

Do we have to change trains?
¿Tenemos que hacer transbordo?
tene'mōs ke äser' tränsbōr'dō

Where?
¿Dónde?
dōn'de

Is there a dining car (are there sleepers) on the train?
¿Hay *un coche-restaurante (coche-camas/Mex camarines, alcobas)* en el tren?
ī ōōn kō'tshe-restourän'te (kō'tshe-kä'mäs/kämärē'nes, älkō'bäs) en el tren

Can I interrupt the trip in ...?
¿Puedo interrumpir el viaje en ...?
pōō·e'dō ēnterrōōmpēr' el vyä'*he* en ...

What platform does the train from ... come in on?
¿En qué andén entra el tren de ...?
en ke änden' en'trä el tren de ...

What platform does the train for ... leave from?
¿De qué andén sale el tren para ...?
de ke änden' sä'le el tren pä'rä ...

Tickets

One ticket (two full fares and two reduced fares) to ..., please.
*Un boleto/Sp billete/(dos boletos/Sp billetes/a precio normal y dos a precio
reducido) a ..., por favor.*
ōon bōle'tō/bēlye'te/(dōs bōle'tōs/bēlye'tes/ä pre'syō normäl ē dōs ä
pre'syō redōōsē'dō) ä ... pōr fävōr'

– round trip.	– one way.	– first class.	– second class.
– de ida y vuelta.	– de ida solo.	– de primera clase.	– de segunda clase.
– de ē'dä ē vōō·el'tä	– de ē'dä sō'lō	– de prēme'rä klä'se	– de segōōn'dä klä'se

I'd like to reserve a seat on the twelve o'clock train to ...
¿Quisiera reservar un asiento para el tren de las doce a ...
kēsye'rä reservär' ōon äsyen'tō pä'rä el tren de läs dō'se ä ...

How long is the ticket valid?
¿Cuánto tiempo es válido este boleto/*Sp* billete?
kōō·än'tō tyem'pō es vä'lēdō es'te bōle'tō/bēlye'te

I'd like to interrupt the trip in ...
Quiero interrumpir el viaje en ...
kye'rō ēnterrōōmpēr' el vyä'*he* en ...

How much is the fare to ...?
¿Cuánto cuesta el boleto/*Sp* billete/a ...?
kōō·än'tō kōō·es'tä el bōle'tō/bēlye'te/ä ...

I'd like to reserve ...
Quisiera reservar ...
kēsye'rä reservär' ...

fare	precio *m* del boleto/*Sp* billete *m*	pre'syō del bōle'tō/ bēlye'te
group fare ticket	boleto *m* colectivo	bōle'to kōlektē'vō
half fare	boleto *m* de media tarifa	bōle'tō de me'dyä tärē'fä
reduced fare	boleto *m* a precio reducido	bōle'tō ä pre'syō redōōsē'dō
seat reservation	reserva *f* de asiento	reser'vä de äsyen'tō
sleeper reservation	boleto *m*/*Sp* billete *m*/ de coche-cama/*Mex* de camarín, de alcoba	bōle'tō/bēlye'te/de kō'-tshe-kä'mä/de kämä-rēn', de älkō'bä
supplemental fare ticket	suplemento *m*	sōōplemen'tō
ticket	boleto *m*/*Sp* billete *m*	bōle'tō/bēlye'te

Baggage

I'd like to ...	– send this luggage on to ...
Quisiera ...	– facturar este equipaje para ...
kēsye'rä ...	– fäktōōrär' es'te ekēpä'he pä'rä ...

– leave this luggage here.	– *insure (claim)* my luggage.
– dejar aquí este equipaje.	– *asegurar (recoger)* mi equipaje.
– de*h*är' äkē' es'te ekēpä'*h*e	– äsegōōrär' (rekō*h*er') mē ekēpä'*h*e

Here's my claim check.
Aquí tiene el talón/recibo/resguardo.
äkē' tye'ne el tälōn'/resē'bō/rezgōō·är'dō

There are two suitcases and a traveling bag.
Son dos maletas y un bolso/una bolsa/de viaje.
sōn dōs mäle'täs ē ōōn bōl'sō/ōō'nä bōl'sä/de vyä'*h*e

Will my baggage be on the same train?	**When does it get to ...?**
¿Sale el equipaje en el mismo tren?	¿Cuándo llegará a ...?
sä'le el ekēpä'*h*e en el mēz'mō tren	kōō·än'dō lyegärä' ä ...

These aren't mine.	**One suitcase is missing.**
No son míos.	Falta una maleta.
nō sōn mē'ōs	fäl'tä ōō'nä mäle'tä

baggage	equipaje *m*	ekēpä'*h*e
baggage check area	depósito *m*/*Mex* "guarda equipaje"	depō'sētō/gōō·är'dä ekēpä'*h*e
baggage claim area	entrega *f* de equipaje/*Mex* andenes *mpl* de equipaje	entre'gä de ekēpä'*h*e/ände'nes de ekēpä'*h*e
baggage room	despacho *m* de equipaje	despä'tshō de ekēpä'*h*e
claim check	talón *m*/recibo *m*/resguardo *m*	tälōn'/resē'bō/rezgōō·är'dō
hand luggage	bultos *mpl* de mano	bōōl'tōs de mä'nō
luggage	equipaje *m*	ekēpä'*h*e
luggage locker	consigna *f* automática	kōnsēg'nä outōmä'tēkä
suitcase	maleta *f*	mäle'tä
traveling bag	bolso *m*/bolsa *f*/de viaje	bōl'sō/bōl'sä/de vyä'*h*e

Porter

porter . . . . mozo *m* . . . . mō'sō

Please bring *this luggage (suitcase)* . . .
Por favor, *estos bultos (esta maleta)* . . .
pōr fävōr' es'tōs bōōl'tōs (es'tä mäle'tä)

– to the . . . train.	– to Platform 2
– al tren de . . .	– al andén 2.
– äl tren de . . .	– äl änden' dōs . . .

– to the baggage check area.	– to the exit.
– a la consigna/*Mex* guarda equipaje.	– a la salida.
– ä lä kōnsēg'nä/gōō·är'dä ekēpä'*he*	– ä lä sälē'dä

– to a taxi.	– to the . . . bus.
– al taxi.	– al autobús/*Mex* al camión/para . . .
– äl tä'ksē	– äl outōbōōs'/äl kämyōn'/pä'rä . . .

On the Platform

Is this the train *to (from)* . . . ?	**Where is . . . ?**
¿Es éste el tren *para (procedente de)* . . . ?	¿Dónde está . . . ?
es es'te el tren pä'rä (prōseden'te de) . . .	dōn'de estä' . . .

– first class?	– the through car to . . . ?
– la primera clase?	– el coche directo para . . . ?
– lä prēme'rä klä'se	– el kō'tshe dērek'tō pä'rä

– the couchette car?	– the sleeping car?
– el coche literas/*Mex* las camas?	– el coche-cama/*Mex* los camarines, las alcobas?
– el kō'tshe lēte'räs/läs kä'mäs	– el kō'tshe-kä'mä/lōs kämärē'nes, läs älkō'bäs

– the dining car?	– the luggage car?
– el coche-restaurante?	– el furgón?
– el kō'tshe-restourän'te	– el fōōrgōn'

– car number . . . ?	
– el coche número . . . ?	
– el kō'tshe nōō'merō . . .	

There.	**Up front.**	**In the middle.**
Allí.	En la cabeza.	En el centro.
älyē′	en lä käbe′sä	en el sen′trō

At the rear.	**What time does the train arrive?**
En la cola.	¿A qué hora llega el tren?
en lä kō′lä	ä ke ō′rä lye′gä el tren

INSPECCION	INFORMACION	SALIDA
Station Master	**Information**	**Exit**

PASO A LOS ANDENES	REFRESCOS
To trains	**Refreshments**

ENTREGA DE EQUIPAJES	VIA
Luggage Checking	**Platform (Track)**

PUESTO DE SOCORRO *Mex* PRIMEROS AUXILIOS	AGUA POTABLE
First Aid	**Drinking Water**

SERVICIOS *Am* BAÑOS	CABALLEROS	SEÑORAS
Rest Rooms	**Men**	**Ladies**

SALA DE ESPERA
Waiting Room

On the Train

Is this seat taken?
¿Está libre este asiento?
estä′ lē′bre es′te äsyen′tō

That's my seat.
Este es mi asiento.
es′te es mē äsyen′tō

Mind if I *open (close)* the window?
¿Puedo *abrir (cerrar)* la ventanilla?
pō͞o·e′dō äbrēr′ (serrär′) lä ventänē′lyä

Allow me (to get past you)?
¿Me permite?
me permē′te

Could you please help me?
¿Puede ayudarme, por favor?
pōō·e'de äyōōdär'me, pōr fävōr'

Would you mind changing places?
¿Le importaría cambiar el asiento conmigo?
le ēmpōrtärē'ä kämbyär' el äsyen'tō kōnmē'gō

I don't like riding backwards.
No me gusta viajar de espaldas.
nō me gōōs'tä vyähär' de espäl'däs

***Tickets, please.**
Boletos/*Sp* billetes/por favor.
bōle'tōs/bēlye'tes/pōr fävōr'

I'd like to *pay the excess fare (pay the supplement, pay now)*.
Quisiera *pagar la diferencia (el suplemento, ahora)*.
kēsye'rä pägär' lä dēferen'syä (el sōōplemen'tō, ä·ō'rä)

How many stations before …?
¿Cuántas estaciones hasta …?
kōō·än'täs estäsyō'nes äs'tä …

Where are we now?
¿Dónde estamos ahora?
dōn'de estä'mōs ä·ō'rä

Will we get to … on time?
¿Llegaremos sin retraso a …?
lyegäre'mōs sēn reträ'sō ä …

How long do we stop here?
¿Cuánto tiempo paramos aquí?
kōō·än'tō tyem'pō pärä'mōs äkē'

***All change, please!**
¡Cambio de tren!
käm'byō de tren

***Passengers for … change at …**
Pasajeros con destino a … cambian en …
päsähe'rōs kōn destē'nō ä … käm'byän en …

***Passengers for … get on in the *front (rear)* of the train.**
Pasajeros con destino a … suben por las portezuelas/puertas/*delanteras (de atrás)*.
päsähe'rōs kōn destē'nō ä … sōō'ben pōr läs pōrtesōō·e'läs/pōō·er'täs/delänte'räs (de äträs')

NO FUMADORES	FUMADORES	ALARMA
No smoking	Smoking	Emergency Brake

COCHE-RESTAURANTE	COCHE-CAMA *Mex* CAMARINES
Dining Car	Sleeping Car

LAVABO	LIBRE	OCUPADO
Rest Room	Vacant	Occupied

*all aboard!	¡Señores pasajeros, al tren!	senyō'res päsä*he*'rōs, äl tren
arrival	llegada *f*	lyegä'dä
arrive	llegar	lyegär'
baggage	equipaje *m*	ekēpä'*he*
barrier	barrera *f*	bärre'rä
car	coche *m*, vagón *m*	kō'tshe, vägōn'
car door	portezuela *f*, puerta *f*	pōrtesoo·e'lä, poo·er'tä
change trains	hacer transbordo	äser' tränsbōr'dō
compartment	departamento *m*, compartim(i)ento *m*	depärtämen'tō, kōmpärtēm(y)en'tō
conductor	conductor *m*	kōndooktōr'
connection	enlace *m*, corresponden-cia *f*	enlä'se, kōrrespōn-den'syä
depart	salir	sälēr'
departure	salida *f*	sälē'dä
entrance	entrada *f*	enträ'dä
exit	salida *f*	sälē'dä
fare	precio *m* del boleto	pre'syō del bōle'tō
– discount	tarifa *f* reducida	tärē'fä redoose'dä
get *in (aboard)*	subir (a)	soobēr' (ä)
get off	bajar (de)	bä*h*är' (de)
heating	calefacción *f*	kälefäksyōn'
– cold	frío	frē'ō
– hot	caliente	kälyen'te
locomotive	locomotora *f*	lōkōmōtō'rä
luggage rack	rejilla *f*	re*h*ē'lyä
passenger	pasajero *m*	päsä*he*'rō
platform	andén *m*	änden'
railroad	ferrocarril *m*	ferrōkärrēl'
route	línea *f*	lē'ne·ä
station	estación *f*	estäsyōn'
station master	jefe *m* de estación	*he*'fe de estäsyōn'
stop	parada *f*	pärä'dä
system time table	guía *f* de ferrocarriles	gē'ä de ferrōkä-rrē'les
ticket	boleto *m*/*Sp* billete *m*	bōle'tō/bēlye'te
train	tren *m*	tren
window seat	asiento *m* de ventanilla	äsyen'tō de ventä-nē'lyä

BY PLANE

Information and Reservations

Is there a (direct) flight to …?
¿Hay un vuelo (directo) para …?
ī ōon vōo·e'lō (dērek'tō) pä'rä

Is there a connection to …?
¿Hay conexión para …?
ī kōneksyōn' pä'rä …

When is there a plane *today (tomorrow)* to …?
¿A qué hora sale *hoy (mañana)* un avión para …?
ä ke ō'rä sä'le oi (mänyä'nä) ōon ävyōn' pä'rä …

When is the next plane to …?
¿Cuándo sale el próximo avión para …?
kōo·än'dō sä'le el prō'ksēmō ävyōn' pä'rä …

Does the plane make a stopover in …?
¿Hace escala en …?
ä'se eskä'lä en …

When do we get to …?
¿Cuándo llegaremos a …?
kōo·än'dō lyegäre'mōs ä …

Are there still seats available?
¿Hay todavía plazas libres?
ī tōdävē'ä plä'säs lē'bres

How much is a (round-trip) flight to …?
¿Cuánto cuesta un pasaje (de ida y vuelta) para …?
kōo·än'tō kōo·es'tä ōon päsä'*he* (de ē'dä ē vōo·el'tä) pä'rä …

What's the luggage allowance?
¿Cuántos kilos de equipaje se pueden llevar?
kōo·än'tōs kē'lōs de ekēpä'*he* se pōo·e'den lyevär'

How much does excess baggage cost?
¿Cuánto cuesta el exceso de equipaje?
kōo·än'tō kōo·es'tä el ekse'sō de ekēpä'*he*

How much is the airport service charge?
¿Cuánto cuesta la tasa del aeropuerto?
kōo·än'tō kōo·es'tä lä tä'sä del ä·erōpōo·er'tō

How do I get to the airport?
¿Cómo se va al aeropuerto?
kō'mō se vä äl ä·erōpōo·er'tō

When is check-in time?
¿A qué hora tengo que estar allí?
ä ke ō'rä ten'gō ke estär' älyē'

I'd like to reserve a seat on the Friday flight to …

Quisiera hacer una reserva para el vuelo del viernes a …
kēsye′rä äser′ ōō′nä reser′vä pä′rä el vōō·e′lō del vyer′nes ä …

I'd like to reserve a round-trip ticket to … on the 2nd of July.

Quisiera reservar, para el dos de julio, un boleto/*Sp* billete/de ida y
vuelta a …
kēsye′rä reservär′, pä′rä el dōs de *hōō*′lyō, ōon bōle′tō/bēlye′tē/de
ē′dä ē vōō·el′tä ä …

– First Class.	– Economy Class.
– primera clase.	– clase turista.
– prēme′rä klä′se	– klä′se tōōrēs′tä

How long is the ticket valid?

¿Por cuánto tiempo es válido el pasaje?
pōr kōō·än′tō tyem′pō es vä′lēdō el päsä′*he*

I have to *cancel (change)* my reservation.

Tengo que *anular/cancelar (cambiar)* mi vuelo.
ten′gō ke änōōlär′/känselär′ (käm′byär′) mē vōō·e′lō

What is the cancellation fee?

¿Cuánto cuesta la cancelación/*Sp* anulación/del pasaje?
kōō·än′tō kōō·es′tä lä känseläsyōn′/änōōläsyōn′/del päsä′*he*

At the Airport

Can I take this along as hand luggage?

¿Puedo llevar esto como equipaje de
mano?
pōō·e′dō lyevär′ es′tō kō′mō ekēpä′*he*
de mä′nō

How much does it cost?

¿Cuánto cuesta?
kōō·än′tō kōō·es′tä

Where is *the waiting room (Exit B, Gate B)*?

¿Dónde está *la sala de espera (salida B, puerta B)*?
dōn′de estä′ lä sä′lä de espe′rä (sälē′dä be, pōō·er′tä be)

Where's the duty-free shop?

¿Dónde se venden mercancías libres de impuestos de aduana?
dōn′de se ven′den merkänsē′äs lē′bres de ēmpōō·es′tōs de ädōō·ä′nä

Is the plane to … late?

¿Tiene retraso el avión a …?
tye′ne reträ′sō el ävyōn′ ä …

Has the plane from … landed already?

¿Ha aterrizado ya el avión de …?
ä äterrēsä′dō yä el ävyōn′ de …

On the Plane

*Kindly refrain from smoking.
No fumen, por favor.
nō foo'men, pōr fävōr'

*Please fasten your seat belts.
Abróchense los cinturones
de seguridad, por favor.
äbrō'tshense lōs sēntoorō'nes de
segoorēdäd, pōr fävōr'

How high are we flying?
¿A qué altura volamos?
ä ke ältoo'rä vōlä'mōs

Where are we now?
¿Dónde estamos ahora?
dōn'de estä'mōs ä·ō'rä

What *mountains are those (river is that)*?
¿Qué *montaña es ésta (río es éste)*?
ke mōntä'nyä es es'tä (rē'ō es es'te)

I feel sick.
Me siento mal.
me syen'tō mäl

Have you got an air-sickness remedy?
¿Tiene un medicamento contra el mareo?
tye'ne oon medēkämen'tō kōn'trä el märe'ō

Can I have …?
¿Me puede dar …?
me poo·e'de där …

When do we land?
¿Cuándo aterrizamos?
koo·än'dō äterrēsä'mōs

How's the weather in …?
¿Qué tiempo hace en …?
ke tyem'pō ä'se en …

aircraft	avión *m*	ävyōn'
air jet *(over seat)*	tobera *f* de aire fresco .	tōbe'rä de ī're fres'kō
airline	compañía *f* aérea	kōmpänyē'ä ä·e're·ä
airport	aeropuerto *m*	ä·erōpoo·er'tō
air sickness	mareo *m*	märe'ō
approach	vuelo *m* de aproxima-	voo·e'lō de äprōksēmä-
	ción	syōn'
arrival	llegada *f*	lyegä'dä
charter plane	avión *m* chárter	ävyōn' tshär'ter
climb	ganar altura, subir	gänär' ältoo'rä, soobēr'
crew	tripulación *f*	trēpooläsyōn'
destination	destino *m*	destē'nō
duty-free goods ..	mercancías *fpl* libres de	merkänsē'äs lē'bres de
	impuestos de aduana ..	empoo·es'tōs de
		ädoo·ä'nä
emergency chute .	rampa *f* de emergencia	räm'pä de emerhen'syä
emergency exit ..	salida *f* de emergencia .	sälē'dä de emerhen'syä
emergency landing	aterrizaje *m* forzoso ...	äterēsä'he fōrsō'sō
engine	motor *m*, propulsor *m* .	mōtōr', prōpoolsōr'

excess baggage	exceso *m* de equipaje ..	ekse′sō de ekēpä′*h*e
exit	salida *f*	sälē′dä
flight	vuelo *m*	voo·e′lō
flight attendant	azafata *f*/aeromoza *f*,	äsäfä′tä/ä·erō-
	cabinera *f*	mō′sä, käbēne′rä
fly	volar	vōlär′
flying time	duración *f* de vuelo ...	dōōräsyōn′ de
		voo·e′lō
fog	niebla *f*	nye′blä
gate	puerta *f*	poo·er′tä
hand luggage	equipaje *m* de mano ...	ekēpä′*h*e de mä′nō
helicopter	helicóptero *m*	elēkōp′terō
information	información *f*	ēnfōrmäsyōn′
information counter .	mostrador *m* de infor-	mōsträdōr′ de ēn-
	mación	fōrmäsyōn′
jet plane	jet *m*/*Sp* avión *m* a reac-	*h*et/ävyōn′ ä re·äk-
	ción	syōn′
land	aterrizar	äterrēsär′
landing	aterrizaje *m*	äterrēsä′*h*e
landing gear	tren *m* de aterrizaje ...	tren de äterrēsä′*h*e
life jacket	chaleco *m* salvavidas ..	tshäle′kō sälvä-
		vē′däs
pilot	piloto *m*	pēlō′tō
plane	avión *m*	ävyōn′
reservation	reserva *f*	reser′vä
return flight	vuelo *m* de regreso	voo·e′lō de regre′sō
scheduled flight	avión *m* de línea	ävyōn′ de lē′ne·ä
seat belt	cinturón *m* de seguridad	sēntoorōn′ de
		segoorēdäd′
– fasten seat belts ...	abróchense los cinturo-	äbrō′tshense lōs
	nes de seguridad	sēntoorō′nes de
		segoorēdäd′
stopover	escala *f*	eskä′lä
system time table ...	horario *m* de vuelos ...	ōrär′yō de
		voo·e′lōs
take off	despegue *m*/descolaje *m*	despe′ge deskōlä′*h*e
thunderstorm	tormenta *f*	tormen′tä
ticket	billete *m*, pasaje *m*	bēlye′te, päsä′*h*e
waiting room	sala *f* de espera	sä′lä de espe′rä
weather	tiempo *m*	tyem′pō
wing	ala *f*	ä′lä

BY SHIP

Information, Tickets

When does *a ship (the ferry)* leave for …?
¿Cuándo sale un barco (el transbordador, el ferry) para …?
kōō·än'dō sä'le ōon bär'kō (el tränsbōrdädōr', el fe'rē) pä'rä …

Where?
¿Dónde?
dōn'de

How often does the car ferry go to …?
¿Cuántas veces sale un transbordador para …?
kōō·än'täs ve'ses sä'le ōon tränsbōrdädōr' pä'rä …

How long does the crossing from … to … take?
¿Cuánto tiempo dura la travesía de … a …?
kōō·än'tō tyem'pō dōō'rä lä trävesē'ä de … ä …

How far is the railroad station from the harbor?
¿A qué distancia del puerto queda la estación?
ä ke dēstän'syä del pōō·er'tō ke'dä lä estäsyōn'

What are the ports of call?
¿En qué puertos hacemos escala?
en ke pōō·er'tōs äse'mōs eskä'lä

Where can we get tickets?
¿Dónde se sacan los pasajes?
dōn'de se sä'kän lōs päsä'hes

When do we *dock (land)* at …?
¿Cuándo atracamos (desembarcamos) en …?
kōō·än'dō äträkä'mōs (desembärkä'mōs) en …

Can I get a connection to …?
¿Hay conexión *or* empalme para …?
ī kōneksyōn' (empäl'me) pä'rä …

Can we go ashore at …?
¿Es posible desembarcar en …?
es pōsē'ble desembärkär' en …

For how long?
¿Por cuánto tiempo?
pōr kōō·än'tō tyem'pō

Will there be any land excursions?
¿Se organizan excursiones a tierra?
se ōrgänē'sän ekskōōrsyō'nes ä tye'rrä

When do we have to be back on board?
¿Cuándo tenemos que estar a bordo?
kōō·än'dō tene'mōs ke estär' ä bōr'dō

I'd like ...
Quisiera ...
kēsye'rä ...

– to book passage to ...
– un pasaje para ...
– ōon päsä'*h*e pä'rä ...

– two tickets on the ... to ... tomorrow.
– para mañana dos pasajes en el ... para ...
– pä'rä mänyä'nä dōs päsä'*h*es en el ... pä'rä ...

– a round-trip ticket from ... to ...
– un pasaje de ... a ..., ida y vuelta.
– ōon päsä'*h*e de ... ä ..., ē'dä ē vōō·el'tä

– a ticket for a car.
– un billete de transporte para un carro/*Sp* un coche.
– ōon bēlye'te de tränspōr'te pä'rä ōon kä'rrō/ōon kō'tshe

– a single cabin.
– un camarote/*Mex* una cabina/individual.
– ōon kämärō'te/ōo'nä käbē'nä/ēndēvēdōo·äl'

– an *outside (inside)* cabin.
– un camarote/*Mex* una cabina/*exterior (interior)*.
– ōon kämärō'te/ōo'nä käbē'nä/eksteryōr' (ēnteryōr')

– a double cabin.
– un camarote/*Mex* una cabina/doble.
– ōon kämärō'te/ōo'nä käbē'nä/dō'ble

– First Class
– Primera clase
– prēme'rä klä'se

– Tourist class
– Clase turista
– klä'se tōorēs'tä

In the Harbor

Where is the "..." docked?
¿Dónde está atracado el "..."?
dōn'de estä' äträkä'dō el ...

Where does the "..." dock?
¿Dónde atraca el "..."?
dōn'de äträ'kä el ...

Does this ship sail to ...?
¿Va este barco a ...?
vä es'te bär'kō ä ...

When does it sail?
¿Cuándo zarpa? ¿Cuándo sale?
kōo·än'dō sär'pä, kōo'ändō sä'le

Where is the *shipping company's office (harbor police station, customs office)*?
¿Dónde está *la oficina de la compañía naviera (de la policía del puerto, de la administración de aduanas)*?
dōn'de estä' lä ōfēsē'nä de lä kōmpänyē'ä nävye'rä (de lä pōlēsē'ä del pōo·er'tō, de lä ädmēnēsträsyōn' de ädōo·ä'näs)

On Board

I'm looking for cabin n⁰ ...	Where's my baggage?
Busco el camarote/*Mex* la cabina/	¿Dónde está mi equipaje?
número ...	dōn'de estä' mē ekēpä'*he*
bōōs'kō el kämärō'te/lä käbē'nä/	
nōō'merō ...	

Have you got ... on board?	Please, where is ...?
¿Tienen ... a bordo?	¿Por favor, dónde está ...?
tye'nen ... ä bōr'dō	pōr fävōr', dōn'de estä' ...

the bar	el bar	el bär
the barber shop, beauty parlor	la peluquería	lä pelōōkerē'ä
the dining room	el comedor	el kōmedōr'
the lounge	el salón	el sälōn'
the purser's office	la oficina del contador	lä ōfēsē'nä del kōntädōr'
the radio room	la cabina de radio	lä käbē'nä de rä'dyō
the reading room	la sala de lectura	lä sä'lä de lektōō
the ship's photographer	el fotógrafo (de a bordo)	el fōtō'gräfō (de bōr'dō)
the sick bay	el hospital	el ōspētäl'
the swimming pool	la piscina	lä pēsē'nä
the tour guide's office	la dirección del crucero	lä dēreksyōn' de krōōse'rō

I'd like to speak to the ...
Quisiera hablar con el ...
kēsye'rä äblär' kōn el ...

– captain	capitán *m*	käpētän'
– chief steward	jefe *m* de camareros	*he*'fe de kämäre
– deck officer	oficial *m* de guardia	ōfēsyäl' de gōō·är'dyä
– luggage master	oficial *m* encargado de equipajes	ōfēsyäl' enkärgä de ekēpä'*hes*
– purser	contador *m*	kōntädōr'
– ship's doctor	médico *m* de a bordo	me'dēkō de ä bō
– tour guide	guía *m*	gē'ä

Steward, please bring me ...
Camarero/*Mex* mesero/tráigame ..., por favor.
kämäre'rō/mese'rō/trī'gäme ..., pōr fävōr'

Please call the ship's doctor.
Llame al médico, por favor.
lyä'me äl me'dēkō, pōr fävōr'

What is the voltage here?
¿Qué voltaje hay aquí?
ke vōltä'*he* ī äkē'

Have you got anything for seasickness?
¿Tiene un medicamento contra el mareo?
tye'ne ōon medēkämen'tō kōn'trä el märe'ō

air conditioning .	aire *m* acondicionado ..	ī're äkōndēsyōnä'dō
anchor	ancla *f*	äng'klä
bank	orilla *f*	ōrē'lyä
barge	barcaza *f*/*Mex* chalana *f*	bärkä'sä/tshälä'nä
bay	bahía *f*	bä·ē'ä
blanket	manta *f*/cobija *f*	män'tä/kōbē'*h*ä
board (to)	ir a bordo	ēr ä bōr'dō
– on board	a bordo	ä bōr'dō
boat	barco *m*, lancha *f*	bär'kō, län'tshä
– fishing trawler .	barco *m* pesquero	bär'kō peske'rō
– launch	lancha *f*	län'tshä
– lifeboat	bote *m* salvavidas	bō'te sälvävē'däs
– motorboat	lancha *f* motora/vola-	län'tshä mōtō'rä/vōlä-
	dora *f*/*Mex* motonauta *f*	dō'rä/mōtōnou'tä
– sailboat	barco *m* de vela, velero *m*	bär'kō de ve'lä, vele'rō
bow	proa *f*	prō'ä
breeze	brisa *f*	brē'sä
bridge	puente *m* de mando ...	pōo·en'te de män'dō
buoy	boya *m*	bō'yä
cabin	camarote *m*/*Mex* cabina *f*	kämärō'te/käbē'nä
cable	cable *m*	kä'ble
call *(at port)*	hacer escala	äser' eskä'lä
canal	canal *m*	känäl'
captain	capitán *m*	käpētän'
captain's table ..	mesa *f* del capitán	me'sä del käpētän'
coast	costa *f*	kōs'tä
course	rumbo *m*	rōom'bō
crew	tripulación *f*	trēpōoläsyōn'
crossing	travesía *f*	trävesē'ä
cruise	crucero *m*	krōose'rō

deck	cubierta *f*	ko͞obyer′tä
– boat deck	cubierta *f* de botes	ko͞obyer′tä de bō′tes
– foredeck	cubierta *f* de proa	ko͞obyer′tä de prō′ä
– main deck	cubierta *f* principal	ko͞obyer′tä prēnsēpäl′
– poop deck	cubierta *f* de popa	ko͞obyer′tä de pō′pä
– promenade deck	cubierta *f* de paseo	ko͞obyer′tä de päse′ō
– steerage	entrepuente *m*	entrepo͞o·en′te
– sun deck	cubierta *f* del sol	ko͞obyer′tä del sōl
– upper deck	cubierta *f* superior	ko͞obyer′tä so͞operyōr′
deck chair	silla *f* de cubierta, tumbona *f*, hamaca *f*	sē′lyä de ko͞obyer′tä, to͞ombō′nä, ämä′kä
disembark	desembarcar	desembärkär′
dock *(noun)*	muelle *m*, embarcadero *m*	mo͞o·e′lye, embärkäde′rō
dock *(verb)*	atracar	äträkär′
excursion	excursión *f*	eksko͞orsyōn′
excursion program	programa *m* de la excursión	prōgrä′mä de lä eksko͞orsyōn′
farewell dinner . .	comida *f* de despedida .	kōmē′dä de despedē′dä
ferry	transbordador *m*, ferry *m*	tränsbōrdädōr′, fe′rrē
– car ferry	transbordador *m*, ferry *m*	tränsbōrdädōr′, fe′rrē
– train ferry	transbordador *m* de trenes	tränsbōrdädōr′ de tre′nes
first officer	segundo comandante *m*	sego͞on′dō kōmändän′te
gangway	plancha *f*	plän′tshä
harbor	puerto *m*	po͞o·er′tō
harbor police	policía *f* del puerto	pōlēsē′ä del po͞o·er′tō
helm	timón *m*	tēmōn′
helmsman	timonel *m*	tēmōnel′
island	isla *f*	ēz′lä
jetty	malecón *m*, muelle *m* . .	mälekōn′, mo͞o·e′lye
knot	nudo *m*	no͞o′dō
lake	lago *m*	lä′gō
land *(noun)*	tierra *f*	tye′rrä
land *(verb)*	tomar tierra	tōmär′ tye′rrä
landing stage	embarcadero *m*	embärkäde′rō
life belt	salvavidas *m*	sälvävē′däs
life jacket	chaleco *m* salvavidas . .	tshäle′kō sälvävē′däs

lighthouse	faro *m*	fä′rō
mast	mástil *m*	mäs′tēl
mole	malecón *m*, muelle *m*	mälekōn′, mōō·e′lye
ocean	océano *m*	ōse′änō
passenger	pasajero *m*	päsä*he*′rō
pier	embarcadero *m*	embärkäde′rō
playroom	cuarto *m* de niños	kōō·är′tō de nē′nyōs
port *(land)*	puerto *m*	pōō·er′tō
port *(side)*	babor *m*	bäbōr′
port fees	tasa *f* portuaria	tä′sä pōrtōō·är′yä
quay	muelle *m*	mōō·e′lye
railing	baranda *f*	bärän′dä
river	río *m*	rē′ō
rope	cuerda *m*, cabo *m*	kōō·er′dä, kä′bō
rough seas	marejada *f*	märe*hä*′dä
rudder	timón *m*	tēmōn′
sail	navegar	nävegär′
sailor	marinero *m*	märēne′rō
sea	mar *m*	mär
– on the high seas	en alta mar	en äl′tä mär
seasickness	mareo *m*	märe′ō
ship	barco *m*, buque *m*	bär′kō, bōō′ke
– freighter	carguero *m*	kärge′rō
– passenger ship	barco *m* de pasajeros	bär′kō de päsä*he*′rōs
– warship	buque *m* de guerra	bōō′ke de ge′rrä
ship's doctor	médico *m* de a bordo	me′dēkō de ä bōr′dō
shipboard party	fiesta *f* de a bordo	fyes′tä de ä bōr′dō
shipping agency	agencia *f* marítima	ä*h*en′syä märē′tēmä
shipping company	compañía *f* naviera	kōmpänyē′ä nävye′rä
shore (on)	en tierra	en tye′rrä
starboard	estribor *m*	estrēbōr′
steamer	vapor *m*	väpōr′
stern	popa *f*	pō′pä
steward	camarero *m*/*Mex* mesero *m*	kämäre′rō/mese′rō
strait	estrecho *m*	estre′tshō
tourist class	clase *f* turista	klä′se tōōrēs′tä
tug	remolcador *m*	remōlkädōr′
voyage	viaje *m* (por mar)	vyä′*he* (pōr mär)
wave	ola *f*	ō′lä
yacht	yate *m*	yä′te

AT THE BORDER

Passport Control

When do we get to the border?
¿Cuándo llegamos a la frontera?
kōō·än'dō lyegä'mōs ä lä frōnte'rä

*Your passport, please.
Su pasaporte, por favor.
sōō päsäpōr'te, pōr fävōr'

*Your papers, please.
La documentación, por favor.
lä dōkōōmentäsyōn', pōr fävōr'

Here they are.
Tenga usted.
ten'gä ōōste'

I'll be staying _a week (two weeks, until the . . .)._
Me quedaré _una semana (dos semanas, hasta el . . .)._
me kedäre' ōō'nä semä'nä (dōs semä'näs, äs'tä el . . .)

I'm here _on business (on vacation)._
Hago un viaje de negocios (Estoy de vacaciones).
ä'gō ōōn vyä'he de negō'syōs (estoi' de väkäsyō'nes)

I am visiting (We are visiting) . . .
Visito . . . (Visitamos . . .)
vēsē'tō . . . (vēsētä'mōs . . .)

Do I have to fill in this form?
¿Tengo que (re)llenar el formulario?
ten'gō ke (re)lyenär' el fōrmōōlär'yō

I haven't got a vaccination certificate.
No tengo un certificado de vacunación.
nō ten'gō ōōn sertēfēkä'dō de väkōōnäsyōn'

What should I do?
¿Qué debo hacer?
ke de'bō äser'

I _have (haven't)_ had a _smallpox (cholera)_ vaccination.
(No) estoy vacunado contra _la viruela (el cólera)._
(nō) estoi' väkōōnä'dō kōn'trä lä vērōō·e'lä (el kō'lerä)

I'm traveling with the . . . group.
Pertenezco al grupo del . . .
pertenes'kō äl grōō'pō del . . .

The children are entered in my passport.
Los niños figuran en mi pasaporte.
lōs nē'nyōs fēgōō'rän en mē päsäpōr'te

Can I get my visa here?
¿Puedo conseguir la visa/_Sp_ el visado/aquí?
pōō·e'dō kōnsegēr' lä vē'sä/el vēsä'dō/äkē'

May I please phone my consulate?
¿Puedo telefonear al consulado?
pōō·e'dō telefōne·är' äl kōnsōōlä'dō

border	frontera *f*	frōnte'rä
date of birth	fecha *f* de nacimiento	fe'tshä de näsē-myen'tō
departure	salida *f*	sälē'dä
driver's license	carnet *m* de conducir	kärnet' de kōndōōsēr'
entry	entrada *f*	enträ'dä
entry visa	visa *f*/*Sp* visado *m*/de entrada	vē'sä/vēsä'dō/de enträ'dä
exit visa	visa *f*/*Sp* visado *m*/de salida	vē'sä/vēsä'dō/de sälē'dä
identity card	documento *m*/*Sp* carnet *m*/de identidad	dōkōōmen'tō/kärnet'/de ēdentēdäd'
insurance certificate	tarjeta *f* de seguro	tär*h*e'tä de segōō'rō
international vaccination certificate	certificado *m* internacional de vacunación	sertēfēkä'dō ēnternäsyōnäl' de väkōōnäsyōn'
maiden name	nombre *m* de soltera	nōm'bre de sōlte'rä
marital status	estado *m* civil	estä'dō sēvēl'
– **single**	soltero (-a)	sōlte'rō (-ä)
– **married**	casado (-a)	käsä'dō (-ä)
– **widowed**	viudo (-a)	vyōō'dō (-ä)
– **divorced**	divorciado (-a)	dēvōrsyä'dō (-ä)
name	nombre *m*	nōm'bre
– **first name**	nombre *m* de pila	nōm'bre de pē'lä
– **middle name**	nombre *m* segundo	nōm'bre segōōn'dō
– **last name**	apellido *m*	äpelyē'dō
nationality	nacionalidad *f*	näsyōnälēdäd'
nationality plate	placa *f* de nacionalidad	plä'kä de näsyōnälēdäd'
number	número *m*	nōō'merō
occupation	profesión *f*	prōfesyōn'
passport	pasaporte *m*	päsäpōr'te
passport control	control *m* de pasaportes	kōntrōl' de päsäpōr'tes
place of birth	lugar *m* de nacimiento	lōōgär' de näsēmyen'tō
place of residence	lugar *m* de residencia	lōōgär' de resēden'syä
renew	renovar	renōvär'
signature	firma *f*	fēr'mä
valid	válido	vä'lēdō

Customs Control

*Do you have anything to declare?
¿Tiene algo que declarar?
tye'ne äl'gō ke deklärär'

That's my suitcase.
Esa es mi maleta.
e'sä es mē mäle'tä

I only have articles for my personal use.
Sólo tengo objetos de uso personal.
sō'lō ten'gō ōb*he*'tōs de ōō'sō persōnäl'

That isn't mine.
No es mío.
nō es mē'ō

*Please open.
Abra, por favor.
äb'rä, pōr fävōr'

This is a *present (souvenir)*.
Es un *regalo (recuerdo)*.
es ōōn regä'lō (rekōō·er'dō)

I have ... *cigarettes (a bottle of perfume)*.
Tengo ... *cigarrillos/Mex cigarros/(una botella de perfume)*.
ten'gō ... sēgärrē'lyōs/sēgä'rrōs/(ōō'nä bōte'lyä de perfōō'me)

*What's in here?
¿Qué hay dentro?
ke ī den'trō

That's all.
Es todo.
es tō'dō

*All right!
¡Está bien!
estä' byen

I'd like to declare this.
Quisiera declarar esto.
kēsye'rä deklärär' es'tō

Do I have to pay duty on this?
¿Tengo que pagar derechos de aduana?
ten'gō ke pägär' dere'tshōs de ädōō·ä'nä

How much can I bring in duty free?
¿Qué cantidad está libre de aduanas?
ke käntēdäd' estä' lē'bre de ädōō·ä'näs

What do I have to pay for it?
¿Cuánto tengo que pagar por esto?
kōō·än'tō ten'gō ke pägär' pōr es'tō

border	frontera *f*	frōnte'rä
border crossing . .	paso *m* de la frontera . .	pä'sō de lä frōnte'rä
customs	aduana *f*	ädōō·ä'nä
customs control .	control *m* aduanero . . .	kōntrōl' ädōō·äne'rō
customs declara-	declaración *f* de aduana	dekläräsyōn' de
tion		ädōō·ä'nä
customs office . . .	edificio *m* de aduanas .	edēfē'syō de
		ädōō·ä'näs
customs officer . .	aduanero *m*	ädōō·äne'rō
duty	derechos *mpl* de aduana	dere'tshōs de ädōō·ä'nä
– export duty . . .	derechos *mpl* de salida .	dere'tshōs de sälē'dä
– import duty . . .	derechos *mpl* de entrada	dere'tshōs de enträ'dä

ACCOMMODATIONS

Checking it out

Where is *the ... hotel (pension)*?
¿Dónde está *el hotel (la pensión)* ...?
dōn'de estä' el ōtel (lä pensyōn')

Is (Are) there ... *near here*?
¿Hay ... por aquí?
ī ... pōr äkē'

Can you recommend a good hotel?
¿Puede recomendarme un buen hotel?
pōō·e'de rekōmendär'me ōōn bōō·en' ōtel'

accommodations	alojamiento *m*	älōhämyen'tō
apartments	apartamentos *mpl*	äpärtämen'tōs
a boarding house	una casa de huéspedes .	ōō'nä kä'sä de ōō·es'pedes
bungalows	bungalows *mpl/Mex* bungalos *mpl*, cabañas *fpl*	bōōngä'lōs/ bōōngä'lōs, käbä'nyäs
a camping site	un camping/*Mex* un campamento	ōōn kämpen'/ōōn kämpämen'tō
a hotel	un hotel	ōōn ōtel'
an inn	una posada, un hostal .	ōō'nä pōsä'dä, ōōn ōstäl'
a motel	un motel	ōōn mōtel'
a pension	una pensión	ōō'nä pensyōn'
a room in private homes	una habitación/*Mex* un cuarto/en casa particular	ōō'nä äbētäsyōn'/ ōōn kōō·är'tō/en kä'sä pärtēkōōlär'
a youth hostel	un albergue juvenil	ōōn älber'ge hōōvenēl'

– near the beach	**– *in a quiet place (centrally located)*.**
– cerca de la playa.	– *tranquilo (céntrico)*.
– ser'kä de lä plä'yä	– trängkē'lō (sen'trēkō)

How *are the prices (is the food)* there?
¿Qué tal *son los precios (es la comida)*?
ke täl sōn lōs pre'syōs (es lä kōmē'dä)

In Spain and Mexico, only first class and luxury hotels have complete bathrooms attached to every room. Most economical hotels have a sink in each room (sometimes a shower), but usually all showering, bathing and toilet facilities are located down the hall.

Checking in

I reserved a room here.	... **six weeks ago.**
He reservado aquí una habitación/	... hace seis semanas.
Mex un cuarto.	... ä'se se'ēs semä'näs
e reservä'dō äkē' o͞o'nä äbētäsyōn'/	
o͞on ko͞o·är'tō	

The ... travel agency reserved a room for *me (us)*.
La agencia de viajes ... ha reservado una habitación/*Mex* un
cuarto/*para mí (para nosotros)*.
lä ä*h*en'syä de vyä'*h*es ... ä reservä'dō o͞o'nä äbētäsyōn'/o͞on
ko͞o·är'tō/pä'rä mē (pä'rä nōsō'trōs)

Have you got a single room available?
¿Tiene una habitación individual/*Mex* un cuarto sencillo/libre?
tye'ne o͞o'nä äbētäsyōn' ēndēvēdo͞o·äl'/o͞on ko͞o·är'tō sensē'lyō/lē'bre

I'd like to have ...
Quisiera ...
kēsye'rä ...

– **an apartment** ..	un apartamento	o͞on äpärtämen'tō
– **a double room** .	una habitación/*Mex* un cuarto/doble	o͞o'nä äbētäsyōn'/o͞on ko͞o·är'tō/dō'ble
– **a quiet room** .	una habitación/*Mex* un cuarto/tranquilo (-a) ..	o͞o'nä äbētäsyōn'/o͞on ko͞o·är'tō/ trängkē'lō (-ä)
– **a room**	una habitación/*Mex* un cuarto	o͞o'nä äbētäsyōn'/o͞o'n ko͞o·är'tō
– **for ... persons** .	para ... personas	pä'rä ... persō'näs
– **on the second floor**	en el segundo piso	en el sego͞on'dō pē'sō
– **with balcony** ...	con balcón	kōn bälkōn'
– **with bath**	con baño completo	kōn bä'nyō kōmple'tō
– **with running water**	con agua corriente	kōn ä'go͞o·ä kōrryen'te
– **with shower** ...	con ducha/*Mex* con regadera	kōn do͞o'tshä/kōn regäde'rä
– **with terrace** ...	con terraza	kōn terrä'sä
– **with toilet**	con wáter, con lavabo/ *Mex* con excusado	kōn o͞o·ä'ter, kōn lä- vä'bō/kōn eksko͞osä'dō

... for *one night (two nights, one week, four weeks)*.
... para *una noche (dos días, ocho días, cuatro semanas)*.
... pä'rä o͞o'nä nō'tshe (dōs dē'äs, ō'tshō dē'äs, ko͞o·ä'trō semä'näs)

Can I have a look at the room?
¿Podría ver la habitación/*Mex* el cuarto?
pōdrē'ä ver lä äbētäsyōn'/el ko͞o·är'tō

I like it.	***I'll (We'll) take it.***
Me gusta.	*Me quedo (Nos quedamos) con ella.*
me go͞os'tä	me ke'dō (nōs kedä'mōs) kōn e'lyä

Could you show me another room?
¿Podría mostrarme/*Sp* enseñarme/otra habitación/*Mex* otro cuarto?
pōdrē'ä mōsträr'me/ensenyär'me/ōt'rä äbētäsyōn'/ōt'rō ko͞o·är'tō

Could you put in *an extra bed (a crib)*?
¿Podría poner *una cama adicional (una cuna)*?
pōdrē'ä pōner' o͞o'nä kä'mä ädēsyōnäl' (o͞o'nä ko͞o'nä)

Price

How much is the room *per day (week)*?
¿Cuánto cuesta la habitación/*Mex* el cuarto/*por día (por semana)*?
ko͞o·än'tō ko͞o·es'tä lä äbētäsyōn'/el ko͞o·är'tō/pōr dē'ä (pōr semä'nä)

– with breakfast.	**– with two meals a day.**	**– American plan.**
– con desayuno.	– con media pensión.	– con pensión completa.
– kōn desäyo͞o'nō	– kōn me'dyä pensyōn'	– kōn pensyōn'kōmple'tä

Is *everything (service)* included?
¿*Está todo* incluido? ¿*Va* incluido *el servicio*?
estä' tō'dō ēnklo͞o·ē'dō/vä ēnklo͞o·ē'dō el serve'syō

What's the *single room surcharge (seasonal surcharge)*?
¿Cuánto es el suplemento *por habitación individual*/*Mex por cuarto sencillo*/*(por temporada)*?
ko͞o·än'tō es el so͞oplemen'tō pōr äbētäsyōn' ēndēvēdo͞o·äl'/pōr ko͞o·är'tō sensē'lyo/(pōr tempōrä'dä)

Are there reduced rates for children?
¿Hay una rebaja (*or* un descuento) para niños?
ī o͞o'nä rebä'*h*ä (o͞on desko͞o·en'tō) pä'rä nē'nyōs

How much deposit do I have to pay?	**How much is that altogether?**
¿Cuánto debo pagar a cuenta?	¿Cuánto es en total?
ko͞o·än'tō de'bō pägär' ä ko͞o·en'tä	ko͞o·än'tō es en tōtäl'

Registration, Luggage

I'd like to register (check in).
Quisiera inscribirme.
kēsye'rä enskrēbēr'me

Do you need our passports?
¿Necesitan los pasaportes?
nesesē'tän lōs päsäpōr'tes

When do you want back the registration form?
¿Cuándo debo devolver la ficha?
ko͞o·än'dō de'bō devōlver' lä fē'tshä

What do I have to fill out here?
¿Qué tengo que (re)llenar?
ke ten'gō ke (re)lyenär'

*I just need your signature.
Basta con la firma.
bäs'tä kōn lä fēr'mä

Would you have my luggage picked up?
¿Podrían recoger mi equipaje?
pōdrē'än rekō̄her' mē ekēpä'he

It's still *at the station (airport)*.
Está todavía *en la estación (en el aeropuerto)*.
estä' tōdävē'ä en lä estäsyōn' (en el ä·erōpo͞o·er'tō)

Here's the baggage check.
Aquí el resguardo/*Sp* el talón.
äkē' el rezgo͞o·är'dō/el tälōn'

Where's my luggage?
¿Dónde está mi equipaje?
dōn'de estä' mē ekēpä'he

Is my baggage already up in the room?
¿Está mi equipaje ya en la habitación/*Mex* el cuarto?
estä' mē ekēpä'he yä en lä äbētäsyōn'/el ko͞o·är'tō

Can I leave my luggage here?
¿Puedo dejar aquí mi equipaje?
po͞o·e'dō dehär' äkē' mē ekēpä'he

Would you put these valuables in the safe?
¿Podría guardar estos objetos de valor en la caja?
pōdrē'ä go͞o·ärdär' es'tōs ōbhe'tōs de välōr' en lä kä'hä

Do you have a *garage (parking lot)*?
¿Tiene *garaje (estacionamiento/Sp aparcamiento)*?
tye'ne gärä'he (estäsyōnämyen'tō/äpärkämyen'tō)

Reception, Desk Clerk

Where is room 308?
¿Dónde está la habitación/*Mex* el cuarto/número trescientos ocho?
dōn'de estä' lä äbĕtäsyōn'/el kōo·är'tō/nōo'merō tresyen'tōs ō'tshō

The key, please.
La llave, por favor.
lä lyä've, pōr fävōr'

Number ..., please.
El número ..., por favor.
el nōo'merō ..., pōr fävōr'

Has anyone asked for me?
¿Ha preguntado alguien por mí?
ä pregōontä'dō äl'gyen pōr mē

Is there any mail for me?
¿Hay correo para mí?
ī kōrre'ō pä'rä mē

What time does the mail come?
¿A qué hora llega el correo?
ä ke ō'rä lye'gä el kōrre'ō

Do you have any *stamps (picture postcards)*?
¿Tiene *estampillas/Sp sellos/Mex timbres/(postales)*?
tye'ne estämpē'lyäs/se'lyōs/tēm'bres/(pōstä'les)

What's the postage on *a letter (postcard)* to the United States?
¿Cuánto cuesta *una carta (una postal)* a los Estados Unidos?
kōo·än'tō kōo·es'tä ōo'nä kär'tä (ōo'nä pōstäl') ä lōs estä'dōs ōo-nē'dōs

Where can I *get (rent)* ...?
¿Dónde se puede *conseguir (alquilar/Mex rentar)* ...?
dōn'de se pōo·e'de kōnsegēr' (älkēlär'/rentär') ...

Where do I sign up for the excursion to ...?
¿Dónde puedo inscribirme para la excursión a ...?
dōn'de pōo·e'dō ēnskrēbēr'me pä'rä lä ekskōorsyōn' ä ...

Where can I *make a phone call (change some money)*?
¿Dónde puedo *telefonear (cambiar dinero)*?
dōn'de pōo·e'dō telefōne·är' (kämbyär' dēne'rō)

I'd like to place a long distance call to ...
Quisiera pedir una llamada a larga distancia/*Sp* una conferencia/con ...
kēsye'rä pedēr' ōo'nä lyämä'dä ä lär'gä dēstän'syä/ōo'nä kōnferen'syä/kōn ...

I'm expecting a long distance call from the United States.
Estoy esperando una llamada de los Estados Unidos.
estoi' esperän'dō ōo'nä lyämä'dä de lōs estä'dōs ōonē'dōs

Where can I get an American newspaper?
¿Dónde se venden periódicos norteamericanos?
dōn'de se ven'den perē·ō'dēkōs nōr'te·ämerēkä'nōs

Where is (are) …?
¿Dónde está (están) …?
dōn'de estä' (estän') …

Could you get me …?
¿Puede conseguirme …?
pōō·e'de kōnsegēr'me …

What's the voltage here?
¿Qué voltaje hay aquí?
ke vōltä'*he* ī äkē'

I'll be back in ten minutes (a couple of hours, right away).
Vuelvo en 10 minutos (en dos horas, en seguida).
vōō·el'vō en dyes mēnōō'tōs (en dōs ō'räs, en segē'dä)

We're going down to the beach (into town).
Vamos a la playa (a la ciudad).
vä'mōs ä lä plä'yä (ä lä syōōdäd')

I'll be in the lounge (bar).
Estaré en el salón (en el bar).
estäre' en el sälōn' (en el bär)

I lost my key (left my key in the room).
He perdido la llave (He dejado la llave en la habitación/Mex el cuarto).
e perdē'dō lä lyä've (e de*hä*'dō lä lyä've en lä äbētäsyōn'/el kōō·är'tō)

What time are meals served?
¿A qué hora son las comidas?
ä ke ō'rä sōn läs kōmē'däs

Where's the dining room?
¿Dónde está el comedor?
dōn'de estä' el kōmedōr'

Can we have breakfast in the room?
¿Se puede desayunar en la habitación/Mex el cuarto?
se pōō·e'de desäyōōnär' en lä äbētäsyōn'/el kōō·är'tō

Could we have breakfast at seven tomorrow morning, please?
¿Podríamos desayunar mañana a las siete, por favor?
pōdrē'ämōs desäyōōnär' mänyä'nä ä läs sye'te, pōr fävōr'

I'd like a box lunch tomorrow morning, please.
Quisiera una bolsa de merienda para mañana por la mañana, por favor.
kēsye'rä ōō'nä bōl'sä de meryen'dä pä'rä mänyä'nä pōr lä mänyä'nä, pōr fävōr'

Please wake me at 7:30 tomorrow.
Despiérteme/Sp llámeme/mañana a las siete y media, por favor.
despyer'teme/lyä'meme/mänyä'nä ä läs sye'te ē me'dyä, pōr fävōr'

Maid

Come in!	**Just a moment, please!**	
¡Adelante!	¡Un momento, por favor!	
ädelän'te	ōōn mōmen'tō, pōr fàvōr'	

Could you wait another *five (ten)* minutes?
¿Puede esperar unos *cinco (diez)* minutos?
pōō·e'de esperär' ōō'nōs sēng'kō (dyes) mēnōō'tōs

We'll be going out *in another quarter hour (half hour)*.
Nos vamos dentro de *un cuarto de hora (una media hora)*.
nōs vä'mōs den'trō de ōōn kōō·är'tō de ō'rä (ōō'nä me'dyä ō'rä)

Please *bring me (us)* ...
Por favor, *tráigame (tráiganos)* ...
pōr fàvōr', trī'gäme (trī'gänōs) ...

another blanket	otra cobija, otra frazada/*Sp* otra manta .	ōt'rä kōbē'*h*ä, ōt'rä fräsä'dä/ōt'rä män'tä
another pillow	otra almohada	ōt'rä älmō·ä'dä
another towel	otra toalla	ōt'rä tō·ä'lyä
an ash tray	un cenicero	ōōn senēse'rō
a blanket	una cobija, una frazada/*Sp* una manta ..	ōō'nä kōbē'*h*ä, ōō'nä fräsä'dä/ōō'nä män'tä
breakfast	el desayuno	el desäyōō'nō
a cake of soap	una pastilla de jabón	ōō'nä pästē'lyä de *h*äbōn'
a couple of clothes hangers	algunas perchas/ algunos ganchos	älgōō'näs per'tshäs/ älgōō'nōs gän'tshōs

How does this thing work?	**Is our room ready?**
¿Cómo funciona esto?	¿Está ya arreglada (-o) nuestra (-o) habitación/*Mex* cuarto?
kō'mō fōōnsyō'nä es'tō	estä' yä ärreglä'dä (-ō) nōō·es'trä (-ō) äbētäsyōn'/kōō·är'tō

Would you have these things laundered for me?
¿Puede mandar a lavar esta ropa?
pōō·e'de mändär' ä lävär' es'tä rō'pä

Thanks very much!	**This is for you.**
¡Muchas gracias!	Es para usted.
mōō'tshäs grä'syäs	es pä'rä ōōste'

Complaints

I'd like to speak to the manager, please.
Quisiera hablar con el gerente (director del hotel), por favor.
kēsyeʹrä äblärʹ kōn el *h*erenʹte (dērektōrʹ del ōtelʹ), pōr fävōrʹ

There's no ...	**There are no ...**	**... doesn't work.**
Falta ...	Faltan ...	... no funciona.
fälʹtä ...	fälʹtän ...	... nō fo͞onsyōʹnä

There's no light in my room.
En mi habitación/*Mex* cuarto/
no hay luz.
en mē äbētäsyōnʹ/ko͞oʹärʹtō/nō ī
lo͞os

The bulb has burned out.
Esta bombilla/*Mex* este foco/
está fundida (-o).
esʹtä bōmbēʹlyä/esʹte fōʹkō/
estä foͦondēʹdä (-ō)

The socket is broken.
El enchufe/*Mex* el soquet, el dado/
está estropeado/roto.
el ent*sh*o͞oʹfe/el sōketʹ, el däʹdō/
estäʹ estrōpe·äʹdō/rōʹtō

The fuse has blown.
El fusible se ha fundido.
el fo͞osēʹble se ä foͦondēʹdō

The bell (heating) doesn't work.
El timbre (La calefacción) no funciona.
el tēmʹbre (lä kälefäksyōnʹ) nō fo͞onsyōʹnä

The key doesn't fit.
La llave no entra en la cerradura.
lä lyäʹve nō enʹträ en lä serrädo͞oʹrä

The rain comes in.
Aquí entra la lluvia.
äkēʹ enʹträ lä lyo͞oʹvyä

This window *won't shut properly (won't open).*
La ventana *no cierra bien (no abre).*
lä ventäʹnä nō syeʹrrä byen (nō äbʹre)

There's no (hot) water.
No hay agua (caliente).
nō ī äʹgoͦo·ä (kälyenʹte)

The faucet drips.
El grifo gotea.
el grēʹfō gōteʹä

The toilet won't flush.
El sifón no funciona.
el sēfōnʹ nō fo͞onsyōʹnä

There's a leak in this pipe.
La tubería tiene fugas/escape.
lä to͞oberēʹä tyeʹne fo͞o·gäs/eskäʹpe

The drain is stopped up.
El desagüe está tapado/*Sp* atascado.
el desäʹgoͦo·e estäʹ täpäʹdō/ätäskäʹdō

Checking out

I'll be leaving tomorrow.
Me marcho mañana.
me mär′tshō mänyä′nä

We're continuing on tomorrow.
Seguiremos el viaje mañana.
segēre′mōs el vyä′he mänyä′nä

Would you please make up my bill?
Prepáreme la cuenta, por favor.
prepä′reme lä kōō·en′tä, pōr fävōr′

Could I please have *my (our)* bill?
¿Me puede dar *mi (nuestra)* cuenta?
me pōō·e′de där mē (nōō·es′trä) kōō·en′tä

Please wake me early tomorrow morning.
Despiérteme/*Sp* llámeme/mañana temprano.
despyer′teme/lyä′meme/mänyä′nä temprä′nō

Please order a taxi for me tomorrow morning at 8.
Pídame un taxi para mañana a las ocho.
pē′däme ōōn tä′ksē pä′rä mänyä′nä ä läs ō′tshō

Would you have my luggage taken *to the station (airport)*?
¿Puede mandarme el equipaje *a la estación (al aeropuerto)*?
pōō·e′de mändär′me el ekēpä′he ä lä estäsyōn′ (äl ä·erōpōō·er′tō)

When does *the bus (train)* leave?
¿Cuándo sale *el autobús/Mex el camión/(el tren)* para ...?
kōō·än′dō sä′le el outōbōōs′/el kämyōn′/(el tren) pä′rä ...

Please forward my mail.
Remita mi correo a esta dirección, por favor.
remē′tä mē kōrre′ō ä es′tä dēreksyōn′, pōr fävōr′

Thanks for everything!
¡Gracias por todo!
grä′syäs pōr tō′dō

We had a very good time here.
Hemos tenido una estancia (estadía) muy agradable.
e′mōs tenē′dō ōō′nä estän′syä (estädē′ä) mōō′ē ägrädä′ble

accommodations ..	alojamiento *m*	älōhämyen'tō
adapter plug	enchufe *m* intermedio .	entshōō'fe ēnter-me'dyō
air conditioning ...	aire *m* acondicionado ..	ī're äkōndēsyōnä'dō
alternating current	corriente *f* alterna	kōrryen'te älter'nä
American plan	pensión *f* completa	pensyōn' kōmple'tä
apartment	apartamento *m*	äpärtämen'tō
apartment building	casa *f* de pisos	kä'sä de pē'sōs
armchair	butaca *f*, sillón *m*	bōōtä'kä, sē'lyōn
arrival	llegada *f*	lyegä'dä
ash tray	cenicero *m*	senēse'rō
balcony	balcón *m*	bälkōn'
basement	sótano *m*	sō'tänō
bathroom	cuarto *m* de baño	kōō·är'tō de bä'nyō
bed	cama *f*	kä'mä
– bedspread	colcha *f*, cubrecama *m*,	kōl'tshä, kōōbre-
	sobrecama *m*	kä'mä, sōbrekä'mä
– blanket	cobija *f*, frazada *f*/*Sp*	kōbē'hä, fräsä'dä/
	manta *f*	män'tä
– crib	cuna *f*	kōō'nä
– mattress	colchón *m*	kōltshōn'
– pillow	almohada *f*	älmō·ä'dä
bed and two meals .	media pensión *f*	me'dyä pensyōn'
bed linen	ropa *f* de cama	rō'pä de kä'mä
– cover	sábana *f*	sä'bänä
– pillowcase	funda *f*	fōōn'dä
– sheets	sábanas *fpl*	sä'bänäs
bed rug	alfombrilla *f*,	älfōmbrē'lyä,
	pie *m* de cama	pye de kä'mä
bedside table	mesita *f* de noche	mesē'tä de nō'tshe
bell	timbre *m*	tēm'bre
bill	cuenta *f*	kōō·en'tä
breakfast	desayuno *m*	desäyōō'nō
– eat breakfast	desayunar	desäyōōnär'
breakfast room	sala *f* de desayuno	sä'lä de desäyōō'nō
bucket	cubo *m*, balde *m*	kōō'bō, bäl'de
carpet	moqueta *f*/*Mex* tapete *m*	mōke'tä/täpe'te
category	categoría *f*	kätegōrē'ä
ceiling	techo *m*	te'tshō
cellar	sótano *m*	sō'tänō
central heating	calefacción *f* central ...	kälefäksyōn' senträl'

chair	silla *f*	sē'lyä
check in *(verb)*	inscribirse	ēnskrēbēr'se
check-in *(noun)*	inscripción	ēnskrēpsyōn'
chimney	chimenea *f*	tshēmene'ä
closet	armario *f*	ärmär'yō
clothes hanger	percha *f*, gancho *m*	per'tshä, gän'tshō
complaint	reclamación *f*,	reklämäsyōn',
	reclamo *m*	reklä'mō
concierge	conserje *m*	kōnser'*he*
corridor	pasillo *m*, corredor *m*	päsē'lyō, kōrredōr'
curtain	cortina *f*	kōrtē'nä
day bed	sofá-cama *m*	sōfä'-kä'mä
deck chair	silla *f* de cubierta, hama-	sē'lyä de kōōbyer'tä,
	ca *f*, tumbona *f*	ämä'kä, tōōmbō'nä
departure	salida *f*	sälē'dä
deposit	pago *m* a cuenta	pä'gō ä kōō·en'tä
dining room	comedor *m*	kōmedōr'
dinner	cena *f*	se'nä
door	puerta *f*	pōō·er'tä
door handle	picaporte *m*	pēkäpōr'te
drawer	cajón *m*, gaveta *f*	kähōn', gäve'tä
elevator	ascensor *m*/*Mex* eleva-	äsensōr'/elevädōr'
	dor *m*	
entrance	entrada *f*	enträ'dä
exit	salida *f*	sälē'dä
extension cord	cordón *m*, cable *m* de	kōrdōn', kä'ble de
	empalme/*Mex* cable *m*	empäl'me/kä'ble de
	de extensión	ekstensyōn'
extra week	semana *f* suplementaria	semä'nä sōōplemen-
		tär'yä
fan	ventilador *m*	ventēlädōr'
faucet	grifo *m*	grē'fō
fireplace	chimenea *f*	tshēmene'ä
floor	piso *m*	pē'sō
front desk	recepción *f*	resepsyōn'
front door	puerta *f* de entrada	pōō·er'tä de
		enträ'dä
fuse	fusible *m*	fōōsē'ble
garden umbrella	sombrilla *f*, parasol *m*	sōmbrē'lyä, päräsōl'
grill room	parrilla *f*	pärrē'lyä
guest house	casa *f* de huéspedes	kä'sä de ōō·es'pedes

hall	hall *m*, vestíbulo *m*	äl, vestē'bōōlō
head clerk	jefe *m* de recepción	*he*'fe de resepsyōn'
heating	calefacción *f*	kälefäksyōn'
hotel	hotel *m*	ōtel'
– beach hotel	hotel *m* de playa	ōtel' de plä'yä
hotel restaurant	restaurante *m* del hotel	restourän'te del ōtel'
house	casa *f*	kä'sä
house key	llave *f* de la casa	lyä've de lä kä'sä
inquiry	informe *m*	ēnfōr'me
key	llave *f*	lyä've
kitchen	cocina *f*	kōsē'nä
kitchenette	rincón-cocina *m*, cocineta *f*	rēnkōn'-kōsē'nä, kōsēne'tä
lamp	lámpara *f*	läm'pärä
laundry	lavandería *f*	lävänderē'ä
– do laundry	lavar	lävär'
– dry	secar	sekär'
– iron	planchar	pläntshär'
light bulb	bombillo *m*/*Sp* bombilla *f*/*Mex* foco *m*	bōmbē'lyō/bōmbē'lyä/fō'kō
lights	luces *fpl*	lōō'ses
lobby	vestíbulo *m*	vestē'bōōlō
lock	cerrar con llave	serrär' kōn lyä've
– lock up	encerrar	enserrär'
– unlock	abrir con llave	äbrēr' kōn lyä've
lunch	almuerzo *m*, comida *f*	älmōō·er'sō, kōmē'dä
maid	camarera *f*/*Mex* recamarera *f*	kämäre'rä/rekämäre'rä
mirror	espejo *m*	espe'*h*ō
move	mudarse	mōōdär'se
move in	instalarse	ēnstälär'se
move out	abandonar	äbändōnär'
night's lodging	alojamiento *m* para una noche	älō*h*ämyen'tō pä'rä ōō'nä nō'tshe
pail	balde *m*/*Sp* cubo *m*/*Mex* a cubeta *f*	bäl'de/kōō'bō/kōōbe'tä
patio	patio *m*	pä'tyō
pension	pensión *f*	pensyōn'
plug	clavija *f* de enchufe	klävē'*h*ä de entshōō'fe
pot	olla *f*, puchero *m*	ō'lyä, pōōtshe'rō

price	precio m	pre'syō
private beach	playa f privada	plä'yä prēvä'dä
radiator	radiador m	rädyädōr'
reading lamp	lámpara f para leer	läm'pärä pä'rä le·er'
reception desk	recepción f	resepsyōn'
refrigerator	frigorífico m/Mex refrigerador m	frēgōrē'fēkō/refrē-herädōr'
registration	inscripción f	ēnskrēpsyōn'
rent (noun)	alquiler m/arriendo m	älkēler'/ärryen'dō
rent (verb)	alquilar, rentar	älkēlär', rentär'
rest room	baños mpl/Sp servicios mpl	bä'nyōs/serve'syōs
– ladies' room	Señoras	senyō'räs
– men's room	Caballeros	käbälye'rōs
room	cuarto m	kōō·är'tō
– bedroom	dormitorio m, alcoba f/Mex recámara f	dōrmētōr'yō, äl-kō'bä/rekä'märä
– living room	salón m, sala f de estar	sälōn', sä'lä de estär'
– nursery	cuarto m de niños	kōō·är'tō de nē'nyōs
season	temporada f	tempōrä'dä
service	servicio m	serve'syō
shower	ducha f/Mex regadera f	dōō'tshä/regäde'rä
sink	lavabo m, lavatorio m	lävä'bō, lävätōr'yō
socket	enchufe m/Mex soquet m, dado m	entshōō'fe/sōket', dä'dō
staircase	escalera f	eskäle'rä
stairwell	hueco m de escalera	ōō·e·kō de eskäle'rä
stove	estufa f/Sp cocina f	estōō'fä/kōsē'nä
swimming pool	piscina f/Mex alberca f	pēsē'nä/älber'kä
switch (light)	interruptor m	ēnterrōōptōr'
table	mesa f	me'sä
tablecloth	mantel m	mäntel'
telephone	teléfono m	tele'fōnō
terrace	terraza f	terrä'sä
toilet paper	papel m higiénico or sanitario	päpel' ēhē·e'nēkō (sänētär'yō)

tour guide	guía *m*	gē'ä
travel agency	agencia *f* de viajes	ähen'syä de vyä'*h*es
vacate the room ...	dejar libre la habitación/	dehär' lē'bre lä
	Mex vencer el cuarto ..	äbētäsyōn'/venser' el
		kōō·är'tō
ventilation	ventilación *f*	ventēläsyōn'
voltage	voltaje *m*	vōltä'*h*e
wall	pared *f*, tabique *m*	päred', täbē'ke
water	agua *f*	ä'gōō·ä
– cold water	agua *f* fría	ä'gōō·ä frē'ä
– hot water	agua *f* caliente	ä'gōō·ä kälyen'te
water glass	vaso *m* para agua	vä'sō pä'rä ä'gōō·ä
window	ventana *f*	ventä'nä
windowpane	vidrio *m*/*Sp* cristal *m* ..	vē'drē·o/krēstäl'

Camping, Youth Hostels

Is there a *camping site (youth hostel)* near here?
¿Hay un *camping/Mex campamento/(albergue juvenil)* cerca de aquí?
ī ōōn kämpēn′/kämpämen′tō/(älber′ge hōōvenēl′) ser′kä de äkē′

Can we camp here?
¿Podemos acampar aquí?
pōde′mōs äkämpär′ äkē′

Is the site guarded at night?
¿Está vigilado durante la noche?
estä′ vēhēlä′dō dōōrän′te lä nō′tshe

Do you have room for another tent?
¿Hay sitio para montar otra carpa/*Sp* tienda, *Mex a* casita/de campaña?
ī sē′tyō pä′rä mōntär′ ōt′rä kär′pä/tyen′dä, käsē′tä/de kämpä′nyä

How much does it cost to stay overnight?
¿Cuánto cuesta una noche?
kōō·än′tō kōō·es′tä ōō′nä nō′tshe

How much is it for *the car (trailer)*?
¿Cuál es el precio por *el carro/Sp el coche/(el remolque)*?
kōō·äl′ es el pre′syō pōr el kä′rrō/el kōtshe/(el remōl′ke)

I'll be staying ... *days (weeks)*.
Me quedo ... *días (semanas)*.
me ke′dō ... dē′äs (semä′näs)

Can we ... here?
¿Podemos ... aquí?
pōde′mōs ... äkē′

Is there a grocery store near here?
¿Hay por aquí una tienda de comestibles/*Mex* tienda de abarrotes?
ī pōr äkē′ ōō′nä tyen′dä de kōmestē′bles/tyen′dä de äbärrō′tes

Can I *rent bottles gas (exchange gas bottles)* here?
¿Se *alquilan (cambian)* aquí *botellas/cilindros/de gas*?
se älkē′län (käm′byän) äkē′ bōte′lyäs/sēlēn′drōs/de gäs

Where are the *rest rooms (wash rooms)*?
¿Dónde están *los baños/Sp los servicios (los lavabos)*?
dōn′de estän lōs bä′nyōs/lōs serve′syōs (lōs lävä′bōs)

Are there any electrical connections here?
¿Hay enchufes/*Mex* soquetes, dados/aquí?
ī entshōō′fes/sōke′tes, dä′dōs/äkē′

Can we drink the water?
¿Se puede tomar el agua?
se pōō·e'de tōmär' el ä'gōō·ä

Can I rent ...?	**Where can I ...?**
¿Puedo rentar/*Sp* alquilar ...?	¿Dónde se puede ...?
pōō·e'dō rentär'/älkēlär' ...	dōn'de se pōō·e'de ...

advance reservation .	reserva *f* de plaza	reser'vä de plä'sä
camp bed	cama *f* de campaña ...	kä'mä de käm- pä'nyä
camping	camping *m*/*Mex* cam- pismo *m*	kämpēn'/käm- pēz'mō
camping ID	tarjeta *f* de camping ...	tärhe'tä de käm- pēn'
camp out	acampar	äkämpär'
camp site	camping *m*/*Mex* campa- mento *m*	kämpēn'/kämpä- men'tō
canteen	cantimplora *f*	käntēmplō'rä
check-in	inscripción *f*	ēnskrēpsyōn'
check-out	aviso *m* de salida	ävē'sō de sälē'dä
cook	cocinar	kōsēnär'
cooking utensils	batería *f* de cocina	bäterē'ä de kōsē'nä
day room	sala *f* de estar	sä'lä de estär'
dishes	vajilla *f*	vähē'lyä
dormitory	dormitorio *m*	dōrmētōr'yō
drinking water	agua *f* potable	ä'gōō·ä pōtä'ble
get	conseguir	kōnsegēr'
go swimming	ir a nadar, ir a bañarse	ēr ä nädär', ēr ä bänyär'se
hostel parents	encargados *mpl* del albergue	enkärgä'dōs del älber'ge
– hostel mother	encargada *f* del albergue	enkärgä'dä del älber'ge
– hostel father	encargado *m* del alber- gue..........	enkärgä'dō del älber'ge
iron	planchar	pläntshär'
membership card	tarjeta *f*/*Sp* carnet *m* / de miembro	tärhe'tä/kärnet'/de myem'brō
park	parque *m*	pär'ke
playground	parque *m* infantil	pär'ke ēnfäntēl'
recreation room	salón *m* de recreo	sälōn' de rekre'ō

rent	rentar/*Sp* alquilar	rentär'/älkēlär'
rental fee	tarifa *f* de alquiler	tärē'fä de älkēler'
sleeping bag	saco *m*/*Mex* bolsa *f*/de dormir	sä'kō/bōl'sä/de dōrmēr'
take a bath	bañarse	bänyär'se
tent	carpa *f*/*Sp* tienda *f*, *Mex* casita *f*/de campaña ...	kär'pä/tyen'dä, kä-sē'tä/de kämpä'nyä
trailer	caravana *f*/*Mex* remolque *m*, trayler *m*	kärävä'nä/remōl'ke, trīler'
wash	lavar	lävär'
youth group	grupo *m* juvenil	grōō'pō hōōvenēl'
youth hostel	albergue *m* juvenil	älber'ge hōōvenēl'
youth hostel card	carnet *m* de alberguista/ *Mex* tarjeta *f* para albergues	kärnet' de älber-gēs'tä/tärhe'tä pä'rä älber'ges

Youth Hostels

Although youth hostels are primarily for those under 26 in possession of a youth hostel card, there are also rates for those over 26, families and groups. In Spain there are 122 youth hostels which offer various lodging and eating arrangements from 375 to 950 pesetas a day (1985 rates). Information: Instituto de la Juventud, Calle José Ortega y Gasset 71, 28006 Madrid. For information on youth hosteling in Mexico: Asociación Mexicana de Albergues de la Juventud, Calle Madero 6, México 1, Distrito Federal.

EATING AND DRINKING

Ordering

Is there a *good (economical) restaurant (with regional specialities)*?
¿Hay por aquí *un buen restaurante (un restaurante económico, un restaurante con especialidades de la región)*?
ī pōr äkē' ōon boo·en' restourän'te (ōon restourän'te ekōnō'mēkō, ōon restourän'te kōn espesyälēdä'des de lä rehyōn')

Would you please reserve a table for four at eight p.m.?
¿Nos reserva una mesa para cuatro personas para las ocho de la noche, por favor?
nōs reser'vä ōo'nä me'sä pä'rä koo·ät'rō persō'näs pä'rä läs ō'tshō de lä nō'tshe, pōr fävōr'

Is *this table (seat)* taken?
¿Está libre *esta mesa (este asiento)*?
estä' lē'bre es'tä me'sä (es'te äsyen'tō)

Waiter!	**Waitress!**	**We'd like a drink.**
¡Camarero!/*Mex* ¡Mesero!	¡Señorita!	Quisiéramos tomar algo.
kämäre'rō/mese'rō	senyōrē'tä	kēsye'rämōs tōmär' äl'gō

Is this your table?	**I'd like a meal.**
¿Sirve usted en esta mesa?	Quisiera comer algo.
sēr've ōoste' en es'tä me'sä	kēsye'rä kōmer' äl'gō

Could I see *the menu (wine list)* please?
¿Me trae *la carta/Am el menú/(la lista de vinos)*, por favor?
me trä'e lä kär'tä/el menōo'/(lä lēs'tä de vē'nōs), pōr fävōr'

What can we have right away?	**Do you have …?**
¿Qué plato nos puede servir en seguida?	¿Hay …?
ke plä'tō nōs poo·e'de servēr' en segē'dä	ī …

Do you have *vegetarian (diet)* food, too?
¿Tienen también platos *vegetarianos (de régimen)*?
tye'nen tämbyen' plä'tōs vehetäryä'nōs (de re'hēmen)

Please bring us *one portion (two portions)* of …
Por favor, *una ración (dos raciones)* de …
pōr fävōr', ōo'nä räsyōn' (dōs räsyō'nes) de …

A cup (glass, bottle) of …, please.
Por favor, *una taza (un vaso, una botella)* de …
pōr fävōr', ōo'nä tä'sä (ōom bä'sō, ōo'nä bōte'lyä) de …

Table Service

ash tray	cenicero *m*	senēse′rō
bottle	botella *f*/*Mex* a frasco *m*	bōte′lyä/fräs′kō
bowl	tazón *m*	täsōn′
bread basket	cestilla *f*/canasta *f*/del pan	sestē′lyä/känäs′tä/del pän
carafe	garrafa *f*	gärrä′fä
cup	taza *f*	tä′sä
– saucer	platillo *m*	plätē′lyō
cutlery	cubiertos *mpl*	kōōbyer′tōs
decanter	jarra *f*	*h*ä′rrä
egg cup	huevera *f*	ōō·eve′rä
fork	tenedor *m*	tenedōr′
glass	vaso *m*	vä′sō
– water glass	vaso *m* para agua	vä′sō pä′rä ä′gōō·ä
– wine glass	vaso *m* para vino	vä′sō pä′rä vē′nō
knife	cuchillo *m*	kōōtshē′lyō
napkin	servilleta *f*	servēlye′tä
pepper mill	molinillo *m* de pimienta	mōlēnē′lyō de pēmyen′tä
pepper shaker	pimentero *m*	pēmente′rō
pitcher	jarra *f*	*h*ä′rrä
– cream pitcher	jarra *f* para leche	*h*ä′rrä pä′rä le′tshe
place setting	cubierto *m*	kōōbyer′tō
plate	plato *m*	plä′tō
– bread plate	platillo *m*	plätē′lyō
– soup plate	plato *m* sopero	plä′tō sōpe′rō
pot	olla *f*	ō′lyä
– coffee pot	cafetera *f*	käfete′rä
– tea pot	tetera *f*	tete′rä
salt shaker	salero *m*	säle′rō
serving dish	fuente *m*	fōō·en′te
spoon	cuchara *f*	kōōtshä′rä
– soup spoon	cuchara *f* sopera	kōōtshä′rä sōpe′rä
– teaspoon	cucharita *f*	kōōtshärē′tä
sugar bowl	azucarera *f*/*Sp* azucarero *m*	äsōōkäre′rä/äsōōkäre′rō
tablecloth	mantel *m*	mäntel′
toothpick	palillo *m*	pälē′lyō
tray	charola *f*/*Sp* bandeja *f*	tshärō′lä/bände′*h*ä

Breakfast

bread	pan *m*	pän
– whole wheat bread	pan *m* de trigo integral . .	pän de trē´gō ēntegräl´
breakfast	desayuno *m*	desäyōō´nō
– eat breakfast . .	desayunar	desäyōōnär´
butter	mantequilla *f*	mäntekē´lyä
cereal	cereales *mpl*	sere·ä´les
coffee	café *m*	käfe´
– black (espresso)	solo *m*/*Mex* expreso	sō´lō/espre´sō
– decaffeinated . .	descafeinado	deskäfe·ēnä´dō
– and milk	con leche	kōn le´tshe
cold cuts	fiambres *mpl*/*Mex* carnes *fpl* frías	fyäm´bres/kär´nes frē´äs
croissant	croissant *m*	krō·äsänt´
egg	huevo *m*/*Mex* blanquillo *m*	ōō·e´vō/blängkē´lyō
– soft-boiled	pasado por agua/*Mex* tibio	päsä´dō pōr ä´gōō·ä/tē´byō
– ham and eggs . .	huevos *mpl* con jamón . .	ōō·e´vōs kōn hämōn´
– fried eggs	fritos/*Mex* estrellados . . .	frē´tōs/estrelyä´dōs
– scrambled eggs	revueltos	revōō·el´tōs
fruit juice	jugo *m*/*Sp* zumo *m*	hōō´gō/sōō´mō
– grapefruit juice	jugo *m*/*Sp* zumo *m*/de pomelo/*Mex* de toronja ·	hōō´gō/sōō´mō/de pōme´lō/de tōrōn´hä
– orange juice . . .	jugo *m*/*Sp* zumo *m*/de naranja	hōō´gō/sōō´mō/de närän´hä
honey	miel *f*	myel
hot chocolate	chocolate *m*	tshōkōlä´te
jam	mermelada *f*	mermelä´dä
milk	leche *f*	le´tshe
– condensed milk	leche *f* evaporada	le´tshe eväpōrä´dä
roll	panecillo *m*/*Mex* bolillo *m*	pänesē´lyō/bōlē´lyō
sausage	salchicha *f*	sältshē´tshä
sugar	azúcar *m*	äsōō´kär
tea	té *m*	te
– camomile tea . .	té *m* de manzanilla	te de mänsänē´lyä
– mint tea	té *m* de menta/*Mex* de hierba buena	te de men´tä/de yer´bä bōō·e´nä
toast	pan *m* tostado	pän tōstä´dō

> *Breakfast in Latin America and Spain is not as large as in the U.S. It usually consists of coffee, tea or hot chocolate, some sort of bread or pastry, and perhaps butter and jam.*

Lunch and Dinner

I'd (We'd) like to have ...
Quisiera (Quisiéramos) ...
kēsye′rä (kēsye′rämōs) ...

Would you bring us ...?
¿Nos trae ...?
nōs trä′e ...

Please pass ...
Páseme/Pásame *(fam)/* ..., por favor.
pä′seme/pä′säme/ ..., pōr fàvōr′

What's the name of this dish?
¿Cómo se llama este plato?
kō′mō se lyä′mä es′te plä′tō

*Would you like seconds on anything?
¿Desean algo más?
dese′än äl′gō mäs

Yes, please.
Sí, por favor.
sē, pōr fävōr′

Yes, indeed.
Con mucho gusto.
kōn mōō′tshō gōōs′tō

Just a little.
Un poquito, nada más.
ōōn pōkē′tō, nä′dä mäs

Thanks, that's enough.
Gracias, nada más.
grä′syäs, nä′dä mäs

No, thanks.
No, gracias.
nō grä′syäs

I've had enough.
Estoy bien.
estoi′ byen

Nothing more, thanks.
Nada más, gracias.
nä′dä mäs, grä′syäs

*Did you like it?
¿Le/te *(fam)/*ha gustado?
le/te/ä gōōstä′dō

Delicious!
¡Muy rico!
mōō′ē rē′kō

Cheers!
¡Salud!
sälōōd′

This dish (The wine) is delicious!
Este plato (El vino) es excelente.
es′te plä′tō (el vē′nō) es ĕkselen′te

I'm not allowed to have any alcohol.
No debo beber alcohol.
nō de′bō beber′ älkō·ōl′

> *To wish others at the table an enjoyable meal, say "¡Que aproveche!" or "¡Buen provecho!", which, freely translated, means "make the most of it!"*

Cooking

baked	asado, horneado	äsä'dō, ōrne·ä'dō
barbecue	barbacoa *f*	bärbäkō'ä
boiled	cocido	kōsē'dō
breaded	empanado	empänä'dō
cold	frío	frē'ō
fat	grasa *f*	grä'sä
fresh	fresco	fres'kō
fried	frito	frē'tō
grilled	asado a la parrilla	äsä'dō ä lä pärrē'lyä
hard	duro	dōō'rō
hot	caliente	kälyen'te
hot *(spicy)*	picante	pēkän'te
juicy	jugoso	*hōō*gō'sō
lean	magro/*Mex a* macizo	mäg'rō/mäsē'sō
medium *(done)*	medio cocido/*Sp* medio asado	me'dyō kōsē'dō/ me'dyō äsä'dō
pickled	escabechado	eskäbetshä'dō
rare	casi crudo/*Sp a* la inglesa	kä'sē krōō'dō/ä lä ēngle'sä
raw	crudo	krōō'dō
roasted	asado, horneado	äsä'dō, ōrne·ä'dō
salted	salado	sälä'dō
seasoned	condimentado	kōndēmentä'dō
smoked	ahumado	ä·ōōmä'dō
soft	blando	blän'dō
steamed	cocido al vapor	kōsē'dō äl väpōr'
stewed	estofado, guisado	estōfä'dō, gēsä'dō
stuffed	relleno	relye'nō
tender	tierno	tyer'nō
tough	duro	dōō'rō
well done	bien hecho, bien asado, bien cocido	byen e'tshō, byen äsä'dō, byen kōsē'dō

Ingredients

bacon	tocino *m*	tōsē'nō
butter	mantequilla *f*	mäntekē'lyä
capers	alcaparras *fpl*	älkäpä'rräs

caraway	semillas *fpl* de Alcaravea	semē'lyäs de älkä-räve'ä
chives	cebollino *m*	sebōlyē'nō
cinnamon	canela *f*	käne'lä
cloves	clavos *mpl* de especia	klä'vōs de espe'syä
cumin seeds	cominos *mpl*	kōmē'nōs
dill	eneldo *m*	enel'dō
garlic	ajo *m*	ä'hō
ginger	jengibre *m*	*h*en*h*ē'bre
herbs	hierbas *fpl*	yer'bäs
honey	miel *f*	myel
horseradish	rábano *m* picante	rä'bänō pēkän'te
jelly *(fruit)*	jalea *f*, gelatina *f*	*h*äle'ä, *h*elätē'nä
ketchup	salsa *f* de tomate	säl'sä de tōmä'te
lard	manteca *f* (de cerdo)	mänte'kä (de ser'dō)
lemon	limón *m*/*Mex* lima *f*	lēmōn'/lē'mä
lime	lima *f*/*Mex* limón *m*	lē'mä/lēmōn'
margarine	margarina *f*	märgärē'nä
mayonnaise	mayonesa *f*	mäyōne'sä
mushrooms	champiñones *mpl*, hongos *mpl*, setas *fpl*	tshämpēnyō'nes, ōn'gōs, se'täs
mustard	mostaza *f*	mōstä'sä
nutmeg powder	nuez *f* moscada	nōō·es' mōskä'dä
oil	aceite *m*	äse'ēte
olives	aceitunas *fpl*	äse·ētōō'näs
onion	cebolla *f*	sebō'lyä
paprika (cayenne pepper)	pimentón *m*	pēmentōn'
parsley	perejil *m*	pere*h*ēl'
pepper *(spice)*	pimienta *f* (negra)	pēmyen'tä (ne'grä)
pickles	pepinillos *mpl*	pepēnē'lyōs
raisins	pasas *fpl*	pä'säs
rosemary	romero *m*	rōme'rō
salt	sal *f*	säl
sauce	salsa *f*	säl'sä
– gravy	salsa *f* de asado	säl'sä de äsä'dō
seasoning *(spice)*	especias *fpl*	espe'syäs
thyme	tomillo *m*	tōmē'lyō
vanilla	vainilla *f*	vīnē'lyä
vinegar	vinagre *m*	vēnä'gre

THE MENU

Appetizers

aceitunas *fpl*	äse·ētoō'näs	olives
alcachofas *fpl*	älkätshō'fäs	artichokes
almejas *fpl*	älme'häs	clams
anchoas *fpl*	äntshō'äs	anchovies
boquerones *mpl*	bōkerō'nes	type of anchovy
– fritos	frē'tōs	fried
calamares *mpl*	kälämä'res	squid
– a la romana	ä lä rōmä'nä	breaded and fried
– en su tinta	en soō tēn'tä	in their own ink
cangrejos *mpl*	kängre'hōs	snails
ceviche *m*	sevē'tshe	raw fish, marinated
croquetas *fpl*	krōke'täs	croquettes
empanadas	empänä'däs	stuffed savory pastries
fiambres *mpl*/*Mex*	fyäm'bres/kär'nes	cold cuts
carnes *fpl* frías	frē'äs	
gambas *fpl*/*Mex*	gäm'bäs/kämärō'nes	shrimp
camarones *mpl*		
– al ajillo	äl ähē'lyō	in garlic
jamón	hämōn'	ham
mejillones *mpl*	mehēlyō'nes	mussels
– en salsa vinagreta	en säl'sä vēnägre'tä	in vinaigrette sauce
ostras *fpl*/*Mex*	ōs'träs/	
ostiones *fpl*	ōstyō'nes	oysters
salchichón *m*	sältshētshōn'	salami
sardinas *fpl*	särdē'näs	sardines
– en escabeche	– en eskäbe'tshe	pickled

Salads

ensalada *f*	ensälä'dä	salad
– de lechuga	– de letshoō'gä	lettuce salad
– de lechuga y tomate	– de letshoō'gä ē tōmä'te	lettuce and tomato salad
– mixta	mē'kstä	mixed salad
ensaladilla *f* rusa	ensälädē'lyä roō'sä	vegetable salad in mayonnaise dressing

Soups

caldo *m*	käl'dō	broth, bouillon
– de gallina	de gälyē'nä	chicken broth
consomé *m*	kōnsōme'	clear soup
crema *f*	kre'mä	cream soup
potaje *m*	potä'he	stew
pote *m* gallego *(Sp)*	pō'te gälye'gō	stew with beans, meat, potatoes, greens
puré *m*	pōore'	purée
sopa *f*	sō'pä	soup
– de ajo	de ä'hō	garlic soup
– de fideos	de fēde'ōs	noodle soup
– de lentejas	de lente'häs	lentil soup
– de pescado	de peskä'dō	fish soup
– de tomate	de tōmä'te	tomato soup
– de verduras	de verdōo'räs	vegetable soup
juliana	hōolyä'nä	vegetable soup

Rice

arroz *m*	ärrōs'	rice
– a la marinera	ä lä märēne'rä	rice with fish
– a la cubana	ä lä kōobä'nä	rice with egg and banana
– blanco	bläng'kō	plain white rice

Eggs

huevos *mpl/Mex a* blanquillos *mpl*	ōo·e'vōs/blänkē'lyōs	eggs
– a la andaluza	ä lä ändälōo'sä	with ham and eggplant
– al plato	äl plä'tō	sunny side up
– rancheros *(Mex)*	räntshe'rōs	in chile sauce
– rellenos	relye'nōs	stuffed eggs, deviled eggs
omelet *m (Mex)*	ōmelet'	omelette
tortilla *f* francesa *(Sp)*	tōrtē'lyä fränse'sä	omelette
– paisana *(Sp)*	pīsä'nä	Spanish tortilla with beans, ham and tomatoes

Some Typical Spanish Dishes

bacalao a la vizcaína	bäkälä′ō ä lä vēskä·ē′nä	cod with tomato-onion sauce
callos a la madrileña	kä′lyōs ä lä mädrēle′nyä	tripe with sausage and spices
cochinillo	kōtshēnē′lyō	roasted baby pig
cocido madrileño . . .	kōsē′dō mädrēle′nyō	stewed chick peas, cabbage, sausages, bacon
fabada asturiana	fäbä′dä ästōōryä′nä .	stew of beans, ham, bacon
gazpacho	gäspä′tshō	cold tomato soup with garnish of cucumbers peppers and onions
paella valenciana	pä·e′lyä välensyä′nä .	saffron rice with seafood, chicken and vegetables
pisto manchego	pēs′tō mäntshe′gō . . .	fried vegetables, usually eggplant, pepper, onion, in spicy tomato sauce
sopa de ajo	sō′pä de ä′hō	garlic soup topped with an egg
tapas	tä′päs	Spanish appetizers
tortilla española	tōrtē′lyä espänyō′lä .	round, cake-shaped potato omelette

Fish and Shellfish

abulón m (Mex)	äbōōlōn′	abalone
almeja f	älme′hä	clam
anguila f	ängē′lä	eel
arenque m	ären′ke	herring
atún m	ätōōn′	tuna
bacalao m	bäkälä′ō	(dried) cod
besugo m	besōō′gō	sea bream
bogavante m	bōgävän′te	lobster
bonito m	bōnē′tō	striped tuna
caballa f	käbä′lyä	mackerel
cabrilla f (Mex)	käbrē′lyä	rock fish
camarón m (Mex) . .	kämärōn′	shrimp

cangrejo *m*	kängre'*h*ō	large crab
carpa *f*	kär'pä	carp
esturión *m*	estōōryōn'	sturgeon
gambas *fpl* (*Sp*)	gäm'bäs	shrimp
huachinango *m* (*Mex*)	ōō·ätshēnän'gō	red snapper
langosta *f*	läng·gōs'tä	spiny lobster
langostinos *mpl*	läng·gōstē'nōs	crayfish
lenguado *m*	leng·gōō·ä'dō	sole
lucio *m*	lōō'syō	pike
mariscos *mpl*	märēs'kōs	shellfish
mejillones *mpl*	me*h*ēlyō'nes	mussels
merluza *f*	merlōō'sä	hake
mero *m*	me'rō	grouper
pargo *m* (*Mex*)	pär'gō	sea bass or snapper
perca *f*	per'kä	perch
pescado *m*	peskä'dō	fish
pulpo *m*	pōōl'pō	octopus
rodaballo *m*	rōdäbä'lyō	turbot
roballo (*Mex*)	rōbä'lyō	snook
salmón *m*	sälmōn'	salmon
salmonete *m*	sälmōne'te	red mullet
sierra *f* (*Mex*)	sye'rrä	Spanish mackerel
trucha *f*	trōō'tshä	trout

Poultry

codornices *fpl*	kōdōrnē'ses	quails
capón *m*	käpōn'	capon
faisán *m*	fīsän'	pheasant
gallina *f*	gälyē'nä	hen, fowl
ganso *m*	gän'sō	goose
guajolote *m* (*Mex*)	gōō·ä*h*ōlō'te	turkey
menudillos *mpl*	menōōdē'lyōs	giblets
pata *f* (*Sp*)	pä'tä	thigh, drumstick
pato *m*	pä'tō	duck
pierna *f* (*Mex*)	pyer'nä	thigh, drumstick
pavo *m* (*Sp*)	pä'vō	turkey
pechuga *f*	petshōō'gä	breast
perdigón *m*	perdēgōn'	young partridge
perdiz *f*	perdēs'	partridge
pichón *m*	pētshōn'	young pigeon
pollo *m*	pō'lyō	chicken

Meat

albóndigas *fpl*	älbōn'dēgäs	meatballs
horneado/*Sp* asado	ōrne·ä'dō/äsä'dō	roasted
bistec *m*	bēstek'	steak
buey *m*	bōō·e'ē	ox
carne *f*	kär'ne	meat
– molida/*Sp* picada	mōlē'dä/pēkä'dä	ground meat
callos *mpl*	kä'lyōs	tripe
carnero *m*	kärne'rō	mutton
cerdo *m*/puerco *m*	ser'dō/pōō·er'kō	pork
cochinillo *m*, lechón *m*	kōtshēnē'lyō, letshōn'	baby pig
conejo *m*	kōne'hō	rabbit
cordero *m*	kōrde'rō	lamb
– lechal	letshäl'	baby lamb
costillas *fpl*	kōstē'lyäs	ribs
chuleta *f*	tshōōle'tä	chop
escalope *m*	eskälō'pe	scallops
filete *m*	fēle'te	fillet
hígado *m*	ē'gädō	liver
jabalí *m*	*h*äbälē'	wild boar
jamón *m*	*h*ämōn'	ham
lacón *m*	läkōn'	shoulder of pork
liebre *f*	lye'bre	hare
lomo *m*	lō'mō	loin
pierna *f* de ternera, pernil *m*	pyer'nä de terne'rä, pernēl'	veal leg shank
riñones *mpl*	rēnyō'nes	kidneys
rosbif *m*	rōsbēf'	roast beef
salchicha *f*	sältshē'tshä	sausage
solomillo *m*	sōlōmē'lyō	sirloin
ternera *f*/*Mex* ternero *m*	terne'rä/terne'rō	veal

Some Typical Mexican Dishes

antojitos	äntō*h*ē'tōs	Mexican hors d'oeuvres
burritos	bōōrrē'tōs	filled flour tortillas
chicharrones	tshētshärrō'nes	pig cracklings

chile	tshē′le	generic name of various types of peppers (mild to hot) used extensively in Mexican cuisine
chile relleno	tshē′le relye′nō	mild *Poblano* chiles stuffed with cheese and deep fried
enchiladas	entshēlä′däs	rolled, stuffed tortillas in hot sauce
– suizas	sōo·ē′säs	with sour cream and cheese
frijoles refritos	frē*h*ō′les refrē′tōs	beans refried in lard
gorditas	gōrdē′täs	round stuffed tortilla dough, fried
guacamole	gōo·äkämō′le	spicy avocado dip
mole	mō′le	sauce of chocolate, chile, spices, nuts and herbs
taco	tä′kō	folded, fried tortilla with filling
tamales	tämä′les	steamed, filled corn dough in banana leaf or corn husk
tostada	tōstä′dä	crisp corn tortillas stacked with beans, meat, cheese, etc.
tortilla	tōrtē′lyä	thin pancake-shaped staple of Mexican diet, made of unleavened corn meal or flour
quesadillas	kesädē′lyäs	cheese and chile fried in tortilla dough

Vegetables

acelgas *fpl*	äsel′gäs	Swiss chard
aguacate *m*	ägōo·äkä′te	avocado
alcachofa *f*	älkätshō′fä	artichoke
alubias *fpl (Sp)*	älōo′byäs	white beans
apio *m*	ä′pyō	celery

batatas *fpl*/ camotes *mpl*	bätä'täs/kämō'tes	sweet potatoes
berenjena *f*	beren*h*e'nä	eggplant
berza *f* lombarda	ber'sä lōmbär'dä	red cabbage
brécol *m*, brócoli *m*	bre'kōl, brō'kōlē	broccoli
cacahuates *mpl* (*Mex*)	käkä·ōō·ä'tes	peanuts
cacahuetes *mpl* (*Sp*)	käkä·ōō·e'tes	peanuts
calabacines *mpl*	käläbäsē'nes	zucchini
calabaza *f*	käläbä'sä	pumpkin
coles *fpl* de Bruselas	kō'les de brōose'läs	Brussel sprouts
coliflor *f*	kōlēflōr'	cauliflower
champiñones *mpl*	tshämpēnyō'nes	mushrooms
chícharos *mpl* (*Mex*)	tshē'tshärōs	peas
ejotes *mpl* (*Mex*)	e*h*ō'tes	green beans
elotes *mpl* (*Mex*)	elō'tes	green corn
escarola *f*	eskärō'lä	endive
espárragos *mpl*	espä'rrägōs	asparagus
espinacas *fpl*	espēnä'käs	spinach
frijoles *mpl*	frē*h*ō'les	beans
garbanzos *mpl*	gärbän'sōs	chick peas
guisantes *mpl* (*Sp*)	gēsän'tes	peas
jitomate *m* (*Mex*)	*h*ētōmä'te	red tomato
judías *fpl* verdes (*Sp*)	*h*ōōdē'äs ver'des	green beans
lechuga *f*	letshōō'gä	lettuce
lentejas *fpl*	lente'*h*äs	lentils
maíz *m*	mīs	corn
nabo *m*	nä'bō	turnip
papas *fpl*	pä'päs	potatoes
patatas *fpl* (*Sp*)	pätä'täs	potatoes
remolachas *fpl* (*Sp*)	remōlä'tshäs	beets
repollo *m*	repō'lyō	cabbage (white)
tomate *m* (*Sp*)	tōmä'te	red tomato
tomate *m* (*Mex*)	tōmä'te	green tomato
zanahorias *fpl*	sänä·ōr'yäs	carrots

Cheese

queso *m*	ke'sō	cheese
– ahumado	ä·ōōmä'dō	smoked cheese
– blanco	bläng'kō	white cheese
– de cabra	de kä'brä	goat cheese

– fundido	fōōndē'dō	melted cheese
– rallado	rälyä'dō	grated cheese
– suizo	sōō·ē'sō	Swiss cheese
requesón *m*	rekesōn'	(type of) cottage cheese

Bread

barra *f* de pan	bä'rrä de pän	loaf of bread, baguette
bocadillo *m (Sp)*	bōkädē'lyō	sandwich on French bread
bolillo *m (Mex)*	bōlē'lyō	French roll
bollos *mpl*	bō'lyōs	sweet rolls, Danish
pan *m*	pän	bread
– dulce *(Mex)*	dōōl'se	sweet bread
– tostado	tōstä'dō	toast
panecillo *m (Sp)*	pänesē'lyō	roll
torta *f (Mex)*	tōr'tä	sandwich on French roll
tostada *f (Sp)*	tōstä'dä	sliced white bread, buttered and grilled

Fruit

albaricoque *m (Sp)*	älbärēkō'ke	apricot
almendra *f*	älmen'drä	almond
avellana *f*	ävelyä'nä	hazelnut
cereza *f*	sere'sä	cherry
ciruela *f*	sērōō·e'lä	plum
– pasa	pä'sä	prune
coco *m*	kō'kō	coconut
chabacano *m (Mex)*	tshäbäkä'nō	apricot
damasco *m*	dämäs'kō	apricot
dátiles *mpl*	dä'tēles	dates
durazno *m*	dōōräz'nō	peach
fresa *f*	fre'sä	strawberry
granada *f*	gränä'dä	pomegranate
guayaba *f*	gōō·äyä'bä	guava
higo *m*	ē'gō	fig
mandarina *f*	mändärē'nä	tangerine
manzana *f*	mänsä'nä	apple

melocotón m (Sp)	melōkōtōn'	**peach**
melón m	melōn'	**melon**
membrillo m	membrē'lyō	**quince**
naranja f	närän'hä	**orange**
nuez f	nōo·es'	**nut**
pera f	pe'rä	**pear**
piña f	pē'nyä	**pineapple**
plátano m	plä'tänō	**banana**
pomelo m	pōme'lō	**grapefruit**
toronja f (Mex)	tōrōn'hä	**grapefruit**
sandía f	sändē'ä	**watermelon**
uva f	ōo'vä	**grape**

Baby Food

baby bottle	biberón m	bēberōn'
baby cereal	papilla f	päpē'lyä
baby food	alimentos mpl infantiles	älēmen'tōs ēnfäntē'les
baby formula	leches fpl infantiles	le'tshes ēnfäntē'les

Desserts

arroz m con leche	ärrōs' kōn le'tshe ..	**rice pudding**
budín m	bōodēn'	**pudding**
buñuelos mpl (Mex) ..	bōonyōo·e'lōs	**fried dough with sugar and honey**
buñuelos mpl (Sp) de viento	bōonyōo·e'lōs de vyen'tō	**(type of) cream puff**
bizcocho m (Sp)	bēskō'tshō	**pound cake**
churros mpl	tshōo'rrōs	**crunchy, deep fried dough**
compota f	kōmpō'tä	**compote**
coctel m de frutas (Mex)	kōktel' de frōo'täs .	**fruit cocktail**
crema f batida (Mex) ..	kre'mä bätē'dä	**whipped cream**
flan m (de caramelo) ..	flän (de käräme'lō) ..	**caramel custard**
galletas fpl	gälye'täs	**plain cookies, biscuits**
helado m	elä'dō	**ice cream**
– de chocolate	de tshōkōlä'te	**chocolate ice cream**
– de fresa	de fre'sä	**strawberry ice cream**
– de vainilla	de vīnē'lyä	**vanilla ice cream**

macedonia f de frutas (Sp)	mäsedō'nyä de froo'täs	**fruit cocktail**
nata f (Sp)	nä'tä	**whipped cream**
natillas fpl	nätē'lyäs	**egg custard**
paleta f (Mex)	päle'tä	**flavored ice on a stick**
pastas fpl (Sp)	päs'täs	**cookies**
rosquilla f (Sp)	rōskē'lyä	**(type of) donut**
tarta f/torta f	tär'tä/tōr'tä	**cake**

BEVERAGES

Wine

champán m	tshämpän'	**champagne**
jerez m	heres'	**sherry**
– fino	fē'nō	**pale, dry**
– amontillado	ämōntēlyä'dō	**full-bodied**
– oloroso	ōlōrō'sō	**sweet**
sangría f	säng·grē'ä	**wine punch with fruit**
vino m	vē'nō	**wine**
– añejo	änye'hō	**vintage**
– blanco	bläng'kō	**white**
– de la casa	de lä kä'sä	**house wine**
– dulce	dool'se	**sweet**
– nuevo	noo·e'vō	**new**
– rosado	rōsä'dō	**rosé**
– seco	se'kō	**dry**
– tinto	tēn'tō	**red**

Beer

caña f (Sp)	kä'nyä	**glass of beer**
cerveza f	serve'sä	**beer**
– de barril	de bärrēl'	**draft beer**
– de botella	de bōte'lyä	**bottled beer**
– negra	ne'grä	**dark beer**
– clara/Sp rubia	klä'rä, roo'byä	**light beer**

Liquor

aguardiente *m*	ägōō·ärdyen'te	clear liquor
anis *m*	änēs'	anisette liqueur
aperitivo *m*	äperētē'vō	apéritif
coñac *m*	kōnyäk'	cognac, brandy
ginebra *f*	*h*ēne'brä	gin
Kahlúa *f (Mex)*	kälōō'ä	coffee liqueur
mezcal *m (Mex)*	mes'käl	mescal
pulque *m (Mex)*	pōōl'ke	fermented sap of maguey cactus
sidra *f*	sē'drä	cider
tequila *f*	tekē'lä	tequila
vodka *f*	vōd'kä	vodka
whisk(e)y *m*	ōō·ēs'kē	whisk(e)y

Other

agua *f*	ä'gōō·ä	water
– dulce	dōōl'se	fresh water
– mineral	mēneräl'	mineral water
– potable	pōtä'ble	drink water
– purificada	pōōrēfēkä'dä	bottled water
atole *m (Mex)*	ätō'le	drinking of ground corn, sugar and water
batidos *mpl (Sp)*	bätē'dōs	shakes
granizado *m*	gränēsä'dō	iced beverage
– de café	de käfe'	iced coffee
– de limón	de lēmōn'	lemon juice and ice
horchata *f (Mex)*	ōrtshä'tä	ground melon seeds and water
horchata *f (Sp)*	ōrtshä'tä	almond milk
jugo *m (Mex)*	hōō'gō	juice
licuado *m (Mex)*	lēkōō·ä'dō	shake
limonada *f*	lēmōnä'dä	lemonade
naranjada *f*	näränhä'dä	orangeade
refresco *m*	refres'kō	drink, soft drink
tónica *f*	tō'nēkä	tonic water
zumo *m (Sp)*	sōō'mō	juice

Complaints, Paying the Check

We need another *portion (set of silverware, glass).*
Falta otra *porción/Sp ración (un cubierto, un vaso).*
fàl'tä ō'trä pōrsyōn'/räsyōn' (ōōn kōōbyer'tō, ōōm bä'sō)

This isn't what I ordered.
Esto no es lo que pedía.
es'tō nō es lō ke pedē'ä

I wanted ...
Quería ...
kerē'ä ...

This is ...
Está ...
estä' ...

too fatty	demasiado grasiento ..	demäsyä'dō grä-syen'tō
too hard	demasiado duro	demäsyä'dō dōō'rō
too hot *(temperature)*	demasiado caliente	demäsyä'dō kälyen'te
too spicy	demasiado picante	demäsyä'dō pē-kän'te
too cold	demasiado frío	demäsyä'dō frē'ō
too salty	demasiado salado	demäsyä'dō sälä'dō
too sour	demasiado agrio	demäsyä'dō ä'grē·ō
too tough	demasiado duro	demäsyä'dō dōō'rō

The check, please!
¡La cuenta, por favor!
lä kōō·en'tä, pōr fävōr'

All together, please.
Todo junto, por favor.
tō'dō *h*ōōn'tō, pōr fävōr'

Separate checks, please.
Cuentas separadas, por favor.
kōō·en'täs sepärä'däs, pōr fävōr'

I don't think this is correct.
Me parece que aquí hay un error.
me päre'se ke äkē' ī ōōn errōr'

We didn't have that.
Esto no nos lo han servido.
es'tō nō nōs lō än servē'dō

Thanks very much.
Muchas gracias.
mōō'tshäs grä'syäs

Keep the change.
Para usted.
pä'rä ōōste'

DOWNTOWN

On the Street

Where is ...?
¿Dónde está ...?
dōn′de estä′

the bus stop	la parada de autobuses/ *Mex* de camiones	lä pärä′dä de outōbōō′ses/de kämyō′nes
the Catholic Church	la iglesia católica	lä ēgle′syä kätō′lēkä
city hall	el ayuntamiento/la alcaldía	el äyōōntämyen′tō/ lä älkäldē′ä
the harbor	el puerto	el pōō·er′tō
the ... Hotel	el hotel	el ōtel′
the museum	el museo	el mōōse′ō
the police station	la comisaría	lä kōmēsärē′ä
the post office	el correo	el kōrre′ō
the Protestant Church	la iglesia protestante	lä ēgle′syä prōte-stän′te
... Square	la plaza	lä plä′sä
... Street	la calle	lä kä′lye
the station	la estación	lä estäsyōn′
the synagogue	la sinagoga	lä sēnägō′gä
a taxi stand	la parada/*Mex* el sitio/ de taxis	lä pärä′dä/el sē′tyō/de tä′ksēs

Is it far from here?
¿Está lejos?
estä′ le′*h*ōs

How far is it to the ...?
A qué distancia está ...?
ä ke dēstän′syä estä′ ...

How many minutes on foot?
¿Cuántos minutos andando?
kōō·än′tōs mēnōō′tōs ändän′dō

A good distance. (Not far.)
Bastante. (No muy lejos.)
bästän′te (nō mōō′ē le′*h*ōs)

Which direction is ...?
¿En qué dirección se encuentra ...?
en ke dēreksyōn′ se enkōō·en′trä ...

What street is ... on?
¿En qué calle está ...?
en ke kä′lye estä′ ...

There.	**Straight ahead.**	**To the right.**	**To the left.**
Allí.	Todo derecho/*Sp* seguido.	A la derecha.	A la izquierda.
älyē′	tō′dō dere′tshō/segē′dō	ä lä dere′tshä	ä lä ēskyer′dä

Bus, Taxi

Can I get there by bus?
¿Va el autobús/*Mex* el camión/a …?
vä el outōbōōs′/el kämyōn′/ä …

Which bus goes to (the) …?
¿Qué autobús/*Mex* camión/va a …?
ke outōbōōs′/kämyōn′/vä ä …

How many stops is it from here?
¿Cuántas paradas hay desde aquí?
kōō·än′täs pärä′däs ī dez′de äke′

Do I have to change?
¿Tengo que cambiar de auto-bús/*Mex* camión?
ten′gō ke kämbyär′ de outō-bōōs′/kämyōn′

Where do I have to *get out (change)*?
¿Dónde tengo que *bajar (cambiar)*?
dōn′de ten′gō ke bäh̠är′ (kämbyär′)

Would you please tell me when we get there?
¿Podría avisarme cuando lleguemos?
pōdrē′ä ävēsär′me kōō·än′dō lyege′mōs

A *one-way (transfer)* ticket to …
Un boleto/*Sp* billete/de ida sólo *(de correspondencia)* para …
ōōn bōle′tō/bēlye′te/de ē′dä sō′lō (de kōrrespōnden′syä) pä′rä …

Where can I get a taxi?
¿Dónde puedo conseguir un taxi?
dōn′de pōō·e′dō kōnseger′ ōōn tä′ksē

Take me to …
Lléveme a …
lye′veme ä …

To the station, please.
A la estación, por favor.
ä lä estäsyōn′, pōr fävōr′

How much is the fare to …?
Cuánto cuesta hasta …?
kōō·än′tō kōō·es′tä äs′tä …

Could you show us some of the sights?
¿Podría enseñarnos algunos monumentos importantes?
pōdrē′ä ensenyär′nōs älgōō′nōs mōnōōmen′tōs ēmpōrtän′tes

Please *wait (stop)* here for a minute.
Espere (Pare) aquí un momento, por favor.
espe′re (pä′re) äke′ ōōn mōmen′tō, pōr fävōr′

Sightseeing and Excursions

Two tickets for the ... tomorrow, please.
Para mañana, dos plazas para ..., por favor.
pä′rä mänyä′nä, dōs plä′säs pä′rä ..., pōr fävōr′

Is lunch included?
¿Está incluido el almuerzo en el precio?
estä′ ēnklōō·ē′dō el älmōō·er′sō en el pre′syō

When (Where) do we meet?
¿A que hora (Dónde) nos encontramos?
ä ke ō′rä (dōn′de) nōs enkōnträ′mōs

We'll be meeting ...
Nos encontramos ...
nōs enkōnträ′mōs ...

When do we get going?
¿A qué hora salimos?
ä ke ō′rä sälē′mōs

Will we be seeing the ... too?
¿Visitamos también ...?
vēsētä′mōs tämbyen′ ...

Will we have some free time?
¿Disponemos de algún tiempo libre?
dēspōne′mōs de älgōōn′ tyem′pō lē′bre

How much?
¿Cuánto?
kōō·än′tō

Will we be able to do some shopping?
¿Podemos ir de compras?
pōde′mōs ēr de kōm′präs

When do we get back?
¿Cuándo volveremos?
kōō·än′dō vōlvere′mōs

How long will we stay in ...?
¿Cuánto tiempo nos quedamos en ...?
kōō·än′tō tyem′pō nōs kedä′mōs en ...

Will we be going to ... too?
¿Iremos también a ...?
ēre′mōs tämbyen′ ä ...

What's worth seeing in ...?
¿Qué cosas de interés turístico hay en ...?
ke kō′säs de ēnteres′ tōōrēs′tēkō ī en ...

When does ... *open (close)*?
¿A qué hora *abren (cierran)* ...?
ä ke ō′rä äb′ren (sye′rrän) ...

How much does *the admission (guided tour)* cost?
¿Cuánto cuesta *la entrada (el guía)*?
kōō·än′tō kōō·es′tä lä enträ′dä (el gē′ä)

Is there an English speaking guide?
¿Hay un guía que hable inglés?
ī ōōn gē′ä ke äb′le ēngles′

I'd like to see the ...	**Can we take a look at ... today?**
Me gustaría ver ...	¿Se puede visitar ... hoy?
me go͞ostärē'ä ver ...	se po͞o·e'de vēsētär' ... oi

the castle	el castillo	el kästē'lyō
the cathedral	la catedral	lä kätedräl'
the church	la iglesia	lä ēgle'syä
the fortress	la fortaleza	lä fōrtäle'sä
the exhibition	la exposición	lä ekspōsēsyōn'
the gallery	la galería	lä gälerē'ä
the monument	el monumento	el mōno͞omen'tō
the museum	el museo	el mo͞ose'ō
the palace	el palacio	el pälä'syō
the zoo	el jardín zoológico	el härdēn' sō·ōlō'hēkō

When does the tour start?	**Can we take pictures?**
¿A qué hora comienza la visita guiada?	¿Se puede sacar fotos?
ä ke ō'rä kōmyen'sä lä vēsē'tä gē·ä'dä	se po͞o·e'de säkär' fō'tōs

What is that *building (monument)*?
¿Qué *edificio (monumento)* es ése?
ke edēfē'syō (mōno͞omen'tō) es e'se

Who *painted this picture (sculpted this statue)*?
¿De quién es *este cuadro (esta estatua)*?
de kyen es es'te ko͞o·ä'drō (es'tä estä'to͞o·ä)

What period does this ... date from?
¿De qué siglo es ...?
de ke sē'glō es ...

When was ... built?	**Who built ...?**
¿Cuándo fue construido ...?	¿Quién construyó ...?
ko͞o·än'dō fo͞o·e' kōnstro͞o·ē'dō ...	kyen kōnstro͞oyō' ...

Where can I find ...?	**Is this ...?**
¿Dónde se encuentra ...?	¿Es éste ...?
dōn'de se enko͞o·en·trä ...	es es'te ...

*This is where ... *lived (was born, died)*.
Aquí vivió ... (nació ..., murió ...)
äkē' vēvyō' ... (näsyō' ..., mo͞oryō' ...)

Vocabulary

airport	aeropuerto *m*	ä·erōpōō·er'tō
alley	callejón *m*	kälyehōn'
amusement park	parque *m* de atracciones	pär'ke de äträk-syō'nes
area	región *f*	rehyōn'
avenue	avenida *f*, paseo *m*	ävené'dä, päse'ō
boat trip	excursión *f* en lancha	eksko͞orsyōn' en län'tshä
botanical gardens	jardín *m* botánico	härdēn' bōtä'nēkō
bridge	puente *m*	pōō·en'te
building	edificio *m*	edēfē'syō
bus	autobús *m*/*Mex* camión *m*	outōbo͞os'/kämyōn'
capital	capital *f*	käpētäl'
castle	castillo *m*	kästē'lyō
cathedral	catedral *f*	kätedräl'
cave	cueva *f*	ko͞o·e'vä
cemetery	cementerio *m*	sementer'yō
church	iglesia *f*	ēgle'syä
churchyard	campo *m* santo	käm'pō sän'tō
city	ciudad *f*	syo͞odäd'
city hall	alcaldía *f*/*Sp* ayuntamiento *m*	älkäldē'ä/äyo͞ontämyen'tō
consulate	consulado *m*	kōnso͞olä'dō
corner	esquina *f*	eskē'nä
countryside	campo *m*	käm'pō
courthouse	tribunal *m*, juzgado *m*	trēbo͞onäl', ho͞ozgä'dō
covered market	mercado *m* cubierto	merkä'dō ko͞obyer'tō
dead-end street	callejón *m* sin salida	kälyehōn' sēn sälē'dä
district of town	barrio *m*	bärr'yō
ditch	zanja *f*	sän'hä
downtown	centro *m* ciudad, centro *m* urbano	sen'trō syo͞odäd, sen'trō o͞orbä'nō
embassy	embajada *f*	embähä'dä
excavations	excavaciones *fpl*	ekskäväsyō'nes

excursion	excursión *f*	ekskōōrsyōn′
exhibition	exposición *f*	ekspōsēsyōn′
factory	fábrica *f*	fä′brēkä
farmhouse	granja *f*/*Mex* cortijo *m*	grän′hä/ kōrtē′hō
fire dept	bomberos *mpl*	bōmbe′rōs
first-aid	puesto *m* de socorros/ *Mex* "primeros auxilios"	pōō·es′tō de sō-kō′rrōs/prēme′rōs ouksē′lyōs
fountain	fuente *f*	fōō·en′te
gallery	galería *f*	gälerē′ä
garden	jardín *m*	*h*ärdēn′
gate	puerta *f*	pōō·er′tä
government office	oficina *f* pública	ōfēsē′nä pōō′blēkä
guide	guía *m*	gē′ä
harbor	puerto *m*	pōō·er′tō
high-rise	edificio *m*, torre *f*	edēfē′syō, tō′rre
hill	colina *f*, cerro *m*	kōlē′nä, se′rrō
hospital	hospital *m*	ōspētäl′
house	casa *f*	kä′sä
house number	número *m* (de la casa)	nōō′mero
landscape	paisaje *m*	pīsä′*h*e
lane	camino *m*, sendero *m*	kämē′nō, sende′rō
library	biblioteca *f*	bēblē·ōte′kä
lost and found office	oficina *f* de objetos perdidos	ōfēsē′nä de ōb-*h*e′tōs perdē′dōs
market	mercado *m*	merkä′dō
main street	calle *f* principal	kä′lye prēnsēpäl′
memorial	monumento *m*	mōnōōmen′tō
ministry	ministerio *m*	mēnēster′yō
moat	foso *m*	fō′sō
monument	monumento *m*	mōnōōmen′tō
mountain	montaña *f*	mōntä′nyä
mountain range	montañas *fpl*, sierra *f*, cordillera *f*	mōntä′nyäs, sye′-rrä, kōrdēlye′rä
museum	museo *m*	mōōse′ō
national park	parque *m* nacional	pär′ke näsyōnäl′
observatory	observatorio *m*	ōbservätōr′yō
old town	parte *f* antigua	pär′te äntē′gōō·ä
open market	mercado *m*	merkä′dō
palace	palacio *m*	pälä′syō

park	parque *m*	pär'ke
part of town	barrio *m*	bärr'yō
path	senda *f*	sen'dä
pavillion	pabellón *m*	päbelyōn'
pedestrian	peatón *m*	pe·ätōn'
– pedestrian crossing	paso *m* de peatones	pä'sō de pe·ätō'nes
police	policía *f*	pōlēsē'ä
police station	comisaría *f*/estación *f* de policía	kōmēsärē'ä/estä-syōn' de pōlēsē'ä
policeman	policía *m*	pōlēsē'ä
port	puerto *m*	poo·er'tō
post office	correos *mpl*	kōrre'ōs
power station	central *f* eléctrica/*Mex* planta *f* eléctrica	senträl' elek'trēkä/plän'tä elek'trēkä
public garden	jardín *m* público	*h*ärdēn' poo'blēkō
public rest room	baños *mpl*/*Sp* servicios *mpl*	bä'nyōs/servē'syōs
river	río *m*	rē'ō
road	camino *m*	kämē'nō
road sign	señal *f* de tráfico	senyäl' de trä'fēkō
ruin	ruina *f*	roo·ē'nä
school	escuela *f*	eskoo·e'lä
sidewalk	acera *f*/*Mex* banqueta *f*	äse'rä/bängke'tä
shop	tienda *f*	tyen'dä
shopping mall	centro *m* comercial	sen'trō kōmersyäl'
side road	calle *f* lateral	kä'lye läteräl'
sightseeing	turismo *m*	toorēz'mō
square	plaza *f*	plä'sä
stadium	estadio *m*	estä'dyō
station	estación *f*	estäsyōn'
stop	parada *f*	pärä'dä
store	tienda *f*	tyen'dä
street	calle *f*	kä'lye
suburbs	afueras *fpl*	äfoo·e'räs
subway	métro *m*	me'trō
surroundings	alrededores *mpl*	älrededō'res
synagogue	sinagoga *f*	sēnägō'gä
taxi	taxi *m*	tä'ksē
taxi stand	parada *f*/*Mex* sitio *m*/de taxis	pärä'dä/sē'tyō/de tä'ksēs
temple	templo *m*	tem'plō

theater	teatro *m*	te·ä′trō
tomb	sepulcro *m*	sepōōl′krō
tower	torre *f*	tō′rre
town	ciudad *f*	syōōdäd′
traffic	tráfico *m*, circulación *f*	trä′fēkō, sērkōōläsyōn′
traffic light	semáforo *m*, disco *m* . .	semä′fōrō, dēs′kō
travel agency	agencia *f* de viajes	ähen′syä de vyä′hes
university	universidad *f*	ōōnēversēdäd′
valley	valle *m*	vä′lye
village	pueblo *m*, aldea *f*	pōō·e′blō, älde′ä
wall *(city)*	muralla *f*	mōōrä′lyä
waterfall	cascada *f*, salto *m* de agua, caída *f* de agua . .	käskä′dä, säl′tō de ä′gōō·ä, kä·ē′dä de ä′gōō·ä
zebra crossing	paso *m* cebra	pä′sō se′brä
zoo	jardín *m* zoológico	*h*ärdēn′ sō·ōlō′*h*ēkō

Religion, Churches

Where is the Catholic church?
¿Dónde está la iglesia católica?
dōn′de estä′ lä ēgle′syä kätō′lēkä

What time *are services (is high mass)*?
¿A qué hora es *el oficio (la misa mayor)*?
ä ke ō′rä es el ōfē′syō (lä mē′sä mäyōr′)

Is there *a wedding (christening)* today?
¿Se celebra hoy *una boda (un bautizo)*?
se sele′brä oi ōō′nä bō′dä (ōōn boutē′sō)

Who's preaching the sermon?
¿Quién predica?
kyen predē′kä

Are there church concerts?
¿Hay conciertos de música sacra?
ī kōnsyer′tōs de mōō′sēkä sä′krä

Have you been to church today?
¿Ha/Has *(fam)*/ido ya a la iglesia?
ä/äs/ē′dō yä ä lä ēgle′syä

Please call *a clergyman (priest)*!
¡Por favor, llame a *un clérigo (un cura)*!
pōr fävōr′, lyä′me ä ōōn kle′rēgō (ōōn kōō′rä)

I am a	Soy	soi
Buddhist	budista *m*	bōōdēs'tä
Christian	cristiano *m*	krēstyä'nō
Jew	judío *m*	hōōdē'ō
Catholic	católico *m*	kätō'lēkō
Moslem	musulmán *m*	mōōsōōlmän'
Protestant	protestante *m*	prōtestän'te

I don't belong to any religious denomination.
No tengo confesión religiosa.
no ten'gō kōnfesyōn' relē*h*yō'sä

abbey	abadía *f*	äbädē'ä
altar	altar *m*	ältär'
arch	arco *m*	är'kō
baptism	bautismo *m*	boutēz'mō
Baroque	barroco *m*	bärrō'kō
bell	campana *f*	kämpä'nä
candlestick	candelabro *m*	kändelä'brō
cathedral	catedral *f*	kätedräl'
Catholic	católico *m*	kätō'lēkō
cemetery	cementerio *m*	sementer'yō
chapel	capilla *f*	käpē'lyä
choir	coro *m*	kō'rō
Christ	Cristo *m*	krēs'tō
christening	bautizo *m*	boutē'sō
Christian	cristiano *m*	krēstyä'nō
Christianity	cristianismo *m*	krēstyänēz'mō
church	iglesia *f*	ēgle'syä
church concert	concierto *m* de música	kōnsyer'tō de
	sacra	mōō'sēkä sä'krä
churchyard	campo *m* santo	käm'pō sän'tō
circumcision	circuncisión *f*	sērkōōnsēsyōn'
clergyman	clérigo *m*	kle'rēgō
communion	comunión *f*	kōmōōnyōn'
confess	confesarse	kōnfesär'se
confession	confesión *f*	kōnfesyōn'
convent	convento *m*	kōnven'tō
creed	credo *m*	kre'dō
cross	cruz *f*	krōōs
crucifix	crucifijo *m*	krōōsēfē'hō
crypt	cripta *f*	krēp'tä

cupola	cúpula *f*	kōō'pōōlä
denomination	confesión *f* religiosa	könfesyōn' relēhyō'sä
dome	cúpula *f*, bóveda *f*	kōō'pōōlä, bō'vedä
font	pila *f* bautismal	pē'lä boutēzmäl'
fresco	fresco *m*	fres'kō
God	Dios	dyōs
Gospel	evangelio *m*	evän*he*'lyō
Gothic	gótico	gō'tēkō
grave	sepultura *f*	sepōōltōō'rä
High Mass	misa *f* mayor	mē'sa mäyōr'
Islam	Islam	ēzläm'
Jewish	judío	*h*ōōdē'ō
Judaism	judaísmo *m*	*h*ōōdä·ēz'mō
mass	misa *f*	mē'sä
meditation	meditación *f*	medētäsyōn'
monastery	monasterio *m*	mōnäster'yō
mosaic	mosaico *m*	mōsī'kō
Moslem	musulmán *m*	mōōsōōlmän'
mosque	mezquita *f*	meskē'tä
nave	nave *f*	nä've
organ	órgano *m*	ōr'gänō
pastor	pastor *m*	pästōr'
pillar	columna *f*	kōlōōm'nä
portal	portal *m*	pōrtäl'
priest	cura *m*, padre *m*	kōō'rä, pä'dre
procession	procesión *f*	prōsesyōn'
Protestant	protestante *m*	prōtestän'te
pulpit	púlpito *m*	pōōl'pētō
rabbi	rabino *m*	räbē'nō
religion	religión *f*	relē*h*yōn'
religious	religioso	relē*h*yō'sō
Romanesque	románico	rōmä'nēkō
rosary	rosario *m*	rōsär'yō
sacristan	sacristán *m*	säkrēstän'
sacristy	sacristía *f*	säkrēstē'ä
sarcophagus	sarcófago *m*	särkō'fägō
sermon	sermón *m*, plática *f*	sermōn', plä'tēkä
service (*Protestant*)	oficio *m* religioso	ōfē'syō relē*h*yō'sō
sexton	sacristán *m*	säkrēstän'
Stations of the Cross	estaciones *fpl* de la vía	estäsyō'nes de lä vē'ä
	Crucis	krōō'sēs

statue	estatua *f*	estä′tōō·ä
synagogue	sinagoga *f*	sēnägō′gä
tomb	tumba *f*	tōōm′bä
tower	torre *f*	tō′rre
vestibule	vestíbulo *m*	vestē′bōōlō

LET'S GO SHOPPING

General Words and Phrases

Where can I *get (buy)* **...?**
¿Dónde se puede *conseguir (comprar)* ...?
dōn′de se pōō·e′de kōnsegēr′ (kōmprär′) ...

Is there a ... shop here?
¿Hay por aquí una tienda de ...?
ī pōr äkē′ ōō′nä tyen′dä de ...

Please give me ...
Déme ..., por favor.
deme ..., pōr fävōr′

Have you got ...?
¿Tienen ...?
tye′nen ...

***I'd (We'd)* like ...**
Quisiera (Quisiéramos) ...
kēsye′rä (kēsye′rämōs) ...

Please show me ...
Muéstreme/*Sp* enséñeme/..., por favor.
mōō·es′treme/ense′nyeme/..., pōr fävōr′

I need ...
Necesito ...
nesesē′tō ...

a bag	una bolsa de	ōō′nä bōl′sä de
a bottle	una botella de	ōō′nä bōte′lyä de
a box	una caja de	ōō′nä kä′*h*ä de
a few	unos	ōō′nōs
a can	una lata de/*Mex* un bote de	ōō′nä lä′tä de/ōōm bo′te de
a pound	una libra de	ōō′nä lē′brä de
a *pack (packet)*	un paquete de	ōōm päke′te de
a pair	un par de	ōōm pär de
a piece	un trozo de	ōōn trō′sō de
a quart	*(approx)* un litro de	ōōn lē′trō de
a quarter pound	*(approx)* cien gramos de	syen grä′mōs de
a roll	un rollo de	ōōn rō′lyō de
a tube	un tubo de	ōōn tōō′bō de
two pounds	*(approx)* un kilo de	ōōn kē′lō de
a yard	*(approx)* un metro de	ōōn me′trō de

That's plenty.
Eso basta.
e′sō bäs′tä

A little more.
Algo más.
äl′gō mäs

Even more.
Todavía más.
tōdävē′ä mäs

Can you order it for me?
¿Puede encargarlo?
pōō·e′de enkärgär′lō

When will you get it in?
¿Cuándo lo tendrá?
kōō·än′dō lō tendrä′

Can I exchange it?
¿Puedo cambiarlo?
pōō·e′dō kämbyär′lō

I don't like *the shape (color)*.
No me gusta *la forma (el color)*.
nō me gōōs′tä lä fōr′mä (el kōlōr′)

This is ...
Esto es ...
es′tō es ...

too big	demasiado grande	demäsyä′dō grän′de
too dark	demasiado oscuro	demäsyä′dō ōskōō′rō
too expensive ...	demasiado caro	demäsyä′dō kä′rō
too light (pale) ..	demasiado claro	demäsyä′dō klä′rō
too narrow	demasiado estrecho ...	demäsyä′dō estre′tshō
too small	demasiado pequeño ...	demäsyä′dō peke′nyō
too wide	demasiado ancho	demäsyä′dō än′tshō
too much	demasiado	demäsyä′dō
not enough	muy poco	mōō′ē pō′kō

Have you got something *a little nicer (less expensive)*?
¿Tiene algo *mejor (no tan caro)*?
tye′ne äl′gō mehōr′ (nō tän kä′rō)

I'll take it.
Me lo llevo.
me lō lye′vō

I like that.
Me gusta.
me gōōs′tä

How much is that?
¿Cuánto vale?
kōō·än′tō vä′le

Thanks, that'll be all.
Gracias, es todo.
grä′syäs, es tō′dō

Can you send my things to the ... Hotel please?
¿Podría mandarme las cosas al hotel ..., por favor?
pōdrē′ä mändär′me läs kō′säs äl ōtel′ ... pōr fävōr′

Do you take *credit cards (traveler's checks)*?
¿Aceptan *tarjetas de crédito (cheques de viaje)*?
äsep′tän tär*h*e′täs de kre′dētō (tshe′kes de vyä′*h*e)

Stores

antique shop	tienda *f* de antigüedades	tyen´dä de äntēgōō·edä´des
art gallery	galería *f* de arte	gälerē´ä de är´te
bakery	panadería *f*	pänäderē´ä
barber shop	peluquería *f*	pelōōkerē´ä
beauty parlor	salón *m* de belleza	sälōn´ de belye´sä
bookshop	librería *f*	lēbrerē´ä
butcher shop	carnicería *f*	kärnēserē´ä
candy store	confitería *f*	kōnfēterē´ä
china shop	artículos *mpl* de porcelana	ärtē´kōōlōs de pōrselä´nä
cosmetic salon	instituto *m* de belleza	ēnstētōō´tō de belye´sä
dairy	lechería *f*	letsherē´ä
department store	grandes almacenes *mpl*	grän´des älmäse´nes
dressmaker's shop	modista *f*	mōdēs´tä
drugstore (*cosmetics & sundries*)	droguería *f*	drōgerē´ä
drugstore (prescription pharmacy)	farmacia *f*	färmä´syä
dry cleaner's	tintorería *f*	tēntōrerē´ä
electrical appliance shop	(tienda *f* de) electrodomésticos *mpl*	(tyen´dä de) elektrōdōmes´tēkōs
fashion boutique	boutique *f*	bō·ōōtē´ke
fish market	pescadería *f*	peskäderē´ä
flower shop	florería *f*/*Sp* floristería *f*	flōrerē´ä/flōrēsterē´ä
fruit market	frutería *f*	frōōterē´ä
furrier	peletero *m*	pelete´rō
furniture store	tienda *f* de muebles	tyen´dä de mōō·e´bles
grocery store	tienda *f* de alimentación/*Mex* de abarrotes	tyen´dä de älēmentä-syōn´/de äbärrō´tes
hardware store	ferretería *f*	ferreterē´ä
hat shop	sombrerería *f*	sōmbrerē´ä
jewelry store	joyería *f*	hōyerē´ä
laundromat	lavandería *f* automática	lävänderē´ä outōmä´tēkä

laundry	lavandería f	lävänderē'ä
leather goods store	artículos mpl de piel, marroquinería f	ärtē'kŏolŏs de pyel, märrōkēnerē'ä
lingerie shop	lencería f, corsetería f	lenserē'ä, kōrseterē'ä
liquor store	tienda f de bebidas alcohólicas/Mex licorerías	tyen'dä de bebē'däs älkō·ō'lēkäs/lēkōrerē'äs
music store	tienda f de música	tyen'dä de mōō'sēkä
newsdealer	vendedor m de periódicos	vendedōr' de perē·ō'dēkōs
optician	óptico m	ōp'tēkō
perfume shop	perfumería f	perfōomerē'ä
photo shop	tienda f de artículos fotográficos	tyen'dä de ärtē'kōolŏs fōtōgrä'fēkōs
photographer's studio	fotógrafo m	fōtō'gräfō
real estate agency	inmobiliaria f	ēnmōbēlyär'yä
record store	tienda f de discos/Mex discoteca f	tyen'dä de dēs'kōs/dēskōte'kä
second-hand bookshop	librería f de viejo/Sp de ocasión	lēbrerē'ä de vye'hō/de ōkäsyōn'
self-service	autoservicio m	outōservē'syō
shoemaker	zapatero m	säpäte'rō
shoe store	zapatería f	säpäterē'ä
souvenir shop	recuerdos mpl	rekōo·er'dōs
sporting goods store	tienda f de artículos de deporte	tyen'dä de ärtē'kōolŏs de depōr'te
stationery store	papelería f	päpelerē'ä
supermarket	supermercado m	sōopermerkä'dō
tabacco store	tabaquería f/Sp estanco m	täbäkerē'ä/estäng'kō
tailor	sastre m	säs'tre
textile store	tienda f de tejidos	tyen'dä de tehē'dōs
toy store	juguetería f	hōogeterē'ä
travel agency	agencia f de viajes	ähen'syä de vyä'hes
vegetable market	verdulería f	verdōolerē'ä
watchmaker's shop	relojería f	relōhere'ä
wine shop	bodega f	bōde'gä

Flowers

bouquet	ramo *m* de flores	rä′mō de flō′res
carnation	clavel *m*	klävel′
flower pot	tiesto *m*, maceta *f*	tyes′tō, mäse′tä
flowers	flores *fpl*	flō′res
gladioli	gladiolos *mpl*	glädyō′lōs
lilacs	lilas *fpl*	lē′läs
orchids	orquídeas *fpl*	ōrkē′de·äs
roses	rosas *fpl*	rō′säs
tulips	tulipanes *mpl*	tŏŏlēpä′nes
vase	florero *m*	flōre′rō
violets	violetas *fpl*	vyōle′täs

Bookshop

autobiography	autobiografía *f*	outōbē·ōgräfē′ä
biography	biografía *f*	bē·ōgräfē′ä
book	libro *m*	lē′brō
brochure	folleto *m*	fōlye′tō
catalogue	catálogo *m*	kätä′lōgō
children's book	libro *m* para niños	lē′brō pä′rä nē′nyōs
city map	plano *m* de la ciudad	plä′nō de lä syŏŏdäd′
detective novel	novela *f* policíaca	nōve′lä pōlēsē′äkä
dictionary	diccionario *m*	dēksyōnär′yō
guide book	guía *f*	gē′ä
map	mapa *m*	mä′pä
novel	novela *f*	nōve′lä
paperback	libro *m* de bolsillo	lē′brō de bōlsē′lyō
phrase book	libro *m* de frases	lē′brō de frä′ses
record	disco *m*	dēs′kō
reference book	libro *m* de consulta	lē′brō de kōnsŏŏl′tä
road map	mapa *m* de carreteras	mä′pä de kärrete′räs
story book	libro *m* de cuentos	lē′brō de kŏŏ·en′tōs
street map	plano *m* de la ciudad	plä′nō de lä syŏŏdäd′
text book	manual *m*	mänŏŏ·äl′
thriller	novela *f* de suspense, de misterio	nōve′lä de sŏŏspen′se, de mēster′yō
translation	traducción *f*	trädŏŏksyōn′
volume	tomo *m*, volumen *m*	tō′mō, vōlŏŏ′men

Photo Shop

Would you please develop this film?
¿Puede revelarme este rollo/*Sp* este carrete/por favor?
pōō·e'de revelär'me es'te rō'lyō/es'te kärre'te/pōr fävōr'

One print (enlargement) of each negative, please.
Una copia (una ampliación) de cada negativo, por favor.
ōō'nä kō'pyä (ōō'nä ämplē·äsyōn') de kä'dä negätē'vō, pōr fävōr'

– **three by four inches.**
– siete por diez centímetros.
– sye'te pōr dyes sentē'metrōs

– **three and a half by three and a half inches.**
– nueve por nueve centímetros.
– nōō·e've pōr nōō·e've sentē'metrōs

I'd like ...
Quisiera ...
kēsye'rä ...

– **a cartridge film.**
– un rollo/*Sp* un carrete.
– ōōn rō'lyō/ōōn kärre'te

– **a super eight color film.**
– una película súper de ocho milímetros, en color.
– ōō'nä pelē'kōōlä sōō'per de ō'tshō mēlē'metrōs, en kōlōr'

– **a sixteen millimeter color film.**
– una película de dieciséis milímetros, en color.
– ōō'nä pelē'kōōlä de dyesēse'ēs mēlē'metrōs en kōlōr'

– **a black and white eight millimeter film.**
– una película de ocho milímetros, en blanco y negro.
– ōō'nä pelē'kōōlä de ō'tshō mēlē'metrōs, en bläng'kō ē ne'grō

– **a thirty-five millimeter film.**
– una película de treinta y cinco milímetros.
– ōō'nä pelē'kōōlä de tre'ēntä e sēng'kō mēlē'metrōs

– **a film for color slides.**
– una película para transparencias/*Sp* diapositivas/en color.
– ōō'nä pelē'kōōlä pä'rä tränspären'syäs/dyäpōsētē'väs/en kōlōr'

– **a *twenty (thirty-six)* exposure film.**
– Un rollo/*Sp* un carrete/*de veinte (de treinta y seis)* fotografías.
– ōōn rō'lyō/ōōn kärre'te/de ve'ēnte (de tre'ēntä ē se'ēs) fōtōgräfē'äs

Would you please put the film in the camera for me?
Por favor, me puede poner el rollo/*Sp* el carrete?
pōr fävōr' me pōō·e'de pōner' el rō'lyō/el kärre'te

camera	máquina *f* fotográfica .	mä′kēnä fōtō-grä′fēkä
color film	película *f* en color	pelē′kōōlä en kōlōr′
daylight color film . .	película *f* en color para luz diurna	pelē′kōōlä en kōlōr′ pä′rä lōōs dyōōr′nä
develop	revelar, desarrollar . . .	revelär′, desärrōlyär′
diaphragm	diafragma *m*	dyäfräg′mä
8-mm film	película *f* de ocho mili-metros	pelē′kōōlä de ō′tshō mēlē′metrōs
enlargement	ampliación *f*	ämplē·äsyōn′
exposure	exposición *f*	ekspōsēsyōn′
exposure meter	fotómetro *m*	fōtō′metrō
film	1) rollo *m/Sp* carrete *m*	rō′lyō/kärre′te
	2) *for movies:* película *f*	pelē′kōōlä
film *(verb)*	filmar	fēlmär′
flash bulb	bombilla *f*, foco *m* de flash	bōmbē′lyä, fō′kō de fläsh
flash cube	cubo *m* de flash	kōō′bō de fläsh
lens	objetivo *m*	ōbhetē′vō
movie camera	tomavistas *m*, cámara *f*, filmadora *f*	tōmävēs′täs, kä′-märä, fēlmädō′rä
negative	negativo *m*	negätē′vō
paper	papel *m*	päpel′
– glossy	brillante	brēlyän′te
– matte	mate	mä′te
photo	fotografía *f*	fōtōgräfē′ä
photograph *(verb)* . .	fotografiar	fōtōgräfē·är′
picture	foto *f*	fō′tō
print	copia *f*	kō′pyä
– color print	copia *f* en color	kō′pyä en kōlōr′
reversal film	película *f* reversible . . .	pelē′kōōlä reversē′-ble
roll film	carrete *m*, rollo *m*	kärre′te, rō′lyō
shutter	obturador *m*	ōbtōōrädōr′
shutter (release)	disparador *m*	dēspärädōr′
slide	transparencia *f/Sp* dia-positiva *f*	tränspären′syä/dyä-pōsētē′vä
take pictures	sacar fotos/*Mex* retra-tar	säkär′ fō′tōs/reträ-tär′
view finder	visor *m*	vēsōr′
yellow filter	filtro *m* amarillo	fēl′trō ämärē′lyō

Jeweler

amber	ámbar *m*	äm'bär
bracelet	pulsera *f*	po͞olse'rä
brooch	broche *m*, prendedor *m*	brō'tshe, prendedōr'
costume jewelry	bisutería *f*, fantasia *f*	bēso͞oterē'ä, fàntäse'ä
cufflinks	gemelos *mpl*/*Mex* man-	heme'lōs/män-
	cuernas *fpl*	ko͞o·er'näs
diamond	diamante *m*	dyämän'te
earclips	zarcillos *mpl*, aretes *mpl*	särsē'lyōs, äre'tes
earrings	pendientes *mpl*	pendyen'tes
emerald	esmeralda *f*	ezmeräl'dä
gold	oro *m*	ō'rō
gold plated	dorado	dōrä'dō
jewelry	joyas *fpl*	hō'yäs
necklace	collar *m*	kōlyär'
pearls	perlas *fpl*	per'läs
ring	sortija *f*, anillo *m*	sōrtē'hä, änē'lyō
ruby	rubí *m*	ro͞obē'
sapphire	zafiro *m*	säfē'rō
silver	plata *f*	plä'tä
silver plated	plateado	pläte·ä'dō
wedding ring	anillo *m* de boda	änē'lyō de bō'dä

Clothing

May I try it on?	I take size ...	This is ...
¿Me lo puedo probar?	Necesito la talla ...	Esto es ...
me lō po͞o·e'dō prōbär'	nesesē'tō lä tä'lyä ...	es'tō es ...

too long	demasiado largo	demäsyä'dō lär'gō
too short	demasiado corto	demäsyä'dō kōr'tō
too tight	demasiado estrecho	demäsyä'dō estre'-tshō
too wide	demasiado ancho	demäsyä'dō än'tshō

Can it be altered?	... *fits just fine (doesn't fit).*
¿Pueden arreglarmelo (a mi medida)?	... *me queda bien (no me queda).*
po͞o·e'den ärreglär'melō (ä mē me-dē'dä)	... me ke'dä byen (nō me ke'dä)

apron	delantal *m*	deläntäl′
baby clothes	ropa *f* infantil	rō′pä enfäntēl′
bathing cap	gorro *m* de baño	gō′rrō de bä′nyō
bathing trunks	bañador *m (Sp)*	bänyädōr′
bathrobe	bata *f/Sp* albornoz *m*	bä′tä/älbōrnōs′
belt	cinturón *m*	sēntōōrōn′
bikini	bikini *m*	bēkē′nē
blouse	blusa *f*	blōō′sä
blue jeans	pantalón *m* vaquero, tejanos *mpl*, jeans *mpl*	päntälōn′ väke′rō, tehä′nōs, hens
bra, brassiére	sostén *m*, sujetador *m*	sōsten′, sōōhetädōr′
cap	gorra *f*, gorro *m*	gō′rrä, gō′rrō
coat	sobretodo *m/*abrigo *m*	sōbretō′dō/äbrē′gō
corset	corpiño *m*	kōrpē′nyō
dress	vestido *m*	vestē′dō
dressing gown	bata *f*	bä′tä
fur coat	abrigo *m* de piel	äbrē′gō de pyel
fur jacket	chaquetón *m* de piel	tshäketōn′ de pyel
garter belt	portaligas *m*, liguero *m*	pōrtälē′gäs, lēge′rō
girdle	faja *f*	fä′hä
gloves	guantes *mpl*	gōō·än′tes
handkerchief	pañuelo *m*	pänyōō·e′lō
hat	sombrero *m*	sōmbre′rō
– straw hat	sombrero *m* de paja	sōmbre′rō de pä′hä
jacket *(lady's)*	chaqueta *f*	tshäke′tä
jacket *(man's)*	saco *m/Sp* americana *f*, chaqueta *f*	sä′kō/ämerēkä′nä, tshäke′tä
knee socks	medias *fpl* cortas	me′dyäs kōr′täs
leather coat	abrigo *m* de cuero	äbrē′gō de kōō·e′rō
leather jacket	chaquetón *m* de cuero	tshäketōn′ de kōō·e′rō
lingerie	ropa *f* interior	rō′pä ēnteryōr′
maternity clothes	ropa *f* pre-mamá	rō′pä pre-mämä′
night shirt	camisa *f* de dormir	kämē′sä de dōrmēr′
nightgown	camisón *m*	kämēsōn′
outfit	conjunto *m*	kōnhōōn′tō
pajamas	pijama *m*	pēhä′mä
panties	bragas *fpl/Mex* pantaletas *fpl*	brä′gäs/päntäle′täs

pants	pantalón m	päntälōn'
pants suit	traje m de pantalón	trä'he de päntälōn'
panty hose	panty m/Mex pantimedias fpl	pän'tē/päntē-me'dyäs
parka	anorac m	änōräk'
petticoat	enaguas fpl	enä'gōō·äs
raincoat	impermeable m	ēmperme·ä'ble
scarf	bufanda f	bōōfän'dä
shirt	camisa f	kämē'sä
– drip-dry	"no se plancha"	nō se plän'tshä
– short-sleeved	de manga corta	de män'gä kōr'tä
shorts	pantalón m corto	päntälōn' kōr'tō
skirt	falda f	fäl'dä
slacks	pantalones mpl	päntälō'nes
slip	combinación f/Mex medio fondo m	kōmbēnäsyōn'/me'dyō fōn'dō
socks	medias fpl/Sp calcetines mpl	me'dyäs/kälsetē'nes
sport shirt	camisa f deportiva	kämē'sä depōrtē'vä
sportswear	trajes mpl de deportes	trä'hes de depōr'tes
stockings	medias fpl	me'dyäs
stole	estola f	estō'lä
suède coat	abrigo m de ante	äbrē'gō de än'te
suède jacket	chaqueta f de ante	tshäke'tä de än'te
suit (lady's)	traje m de chaqueta, traje m sastre	trä'he de tshäke'tä, trä'he säs'tre
suit (man's)	traje m	trä'he
summer dress	vestido m de verano	vestē'dō de verä'nō
suspenders	tirantes mpl	tērän'tes
sweater	jersey m, suéter	her'sē, sōō·e'ter
swimsuit	traje m de baño	trä'he de bä'nyō
tie	corbata f	kōrbä'tä
track suit	chandal m/sudadera f	tshändäl'/sōōdäde'rä
trench coat	gabardina f	gäbärdē'nä
two-piece	de dos piezas	de dōs pye'säs
underpants (men's)	calzoncillos mpl	kälsōnsē'lyōs
undershirt	camiseta f	kämēse'tä
underwear	ropa f interior	rō'pä ēnteryōr'
vest	chaleco m	tshäle'kō
windbreaker	cazadora f	käsädō'rä

Dry Goods

accessories	accesorios *mpl*	äksesōr'yōs
belt	cinturón *m*, correa *f*, cinto *m*	sēntōōrōn', kōrrē'ä, sēn'tō
buckle	hebilla *f*	ebē'lyä
button	botón *m*	bōtōn'
basting thread	hilo *m* para hilvanar	ē'lō pä'rä ēlvänär'
darning thread	hilo *m* para zurcir	ē'lō pä'rä sōōrsēr'
dry goods store	mercería *f*	merserē'ä
elastic	cinta *f* de goma, caucho *m*	sēn'tä de gō'mä, kou'tshō
garters	ligas *fpl*	lē'gäs
hooks and eyes	corchetes *mpl*, ganchos *mpl* de macho y hembra	kōrtshe'tes, gän'tshōs de mä'tshō ē em'brä
lining	forro *m*	fō'rrō
needle	aguja *f*	ägōō'hä
– sewing needle	aguja *f* de coser	ägōō'hä de kōser'
pin	alfiler *m*	älfēler'
ribbon	cinta *f*	sēn'tä
safety pin	imperdible *m/Mex* seguro *m*	ēmperdē'ble/ segōō'rō
scissors	tijeras *fpl*	tēhe'räs
silk thread	hilo *m* de seda	ē'lō de se'dä
snap	botón *m* de presión	bōtōn' de presyōn'
suspenders	tirantes *mpl*	tērän'tes
synthetic thread	hilo *m* sintético	ē'lō sēnte'tēkō
tape	cinta *f*	sēn'tä
tape measure	cinta *f* métrica	sēn'tä me'trēkä
thimble	dedal *m*	dedäl'
thread	hilo *m*	ē'lō
wool	lana *f*	lä'nä
zipper	cierre *m/Sp* cremallera *f*	sye'rre/kremälye'rä

Fabrics

cloth	paño *m*, tela *f*	pä'nyō, te'lä
corduroy	pana *f*	pä'nä
cotton	algodón *m*	älgōdōn'

fabric	tela *f*	te'lä
– **checked**	a cuadros	ä koo·ä'drōs
– **printed**	estampado	estämpä'dō
– **solid color**	de un solo color	de oon sō'lō kōlōr'
– **striped**	a rayas, rayado	ä rä'yäs, räyä'dō
flannel	franela *f*	fräne'lä
jersey	jersey *m*	*h*er'sē
lace	encaje *m*	enkä'*h*e
linen	lino *m*	lē'nō
material	tejido *m*, tela *f*	te*h*ē'dō, te'lä
nylon	nilón *m*	nēlōn'
silk	seda *f*	se'dä
– **artificial**	seda *f* artificial	se'dä ärtēfēsyäl'
synthetic fibre	fibra *f* sintética	fē'brä sēnte'tēkä
velvet	terciopelo *m*	tersyōpe'lō
wool	lana *f*	lä'nä
– **pure wool**	lana *f* pura	lä'nä poo'rä
– **pure virgen wool**	pura lana *f* virgen	poo'rä lä'nä vēr'*h*en
worsted	estambre *m*	estäm'bre

Cleaning, Alterations, Repairs

I'd like to have *this dress (suit)* cleaned.
Quiero que me limpien *este vestido (este traje)*.
kye'rō ke me lēm'pyen es'te vestē'dō (es'te trä'*h*e)

I'd like to have these things laundered.
Quisiera mandar a lavar esta ropa.
kēsye'rä mändär' ä lävär' es'tä rō'pä

Would you please *press this (take out this stain)*?
¿Podría *plancharme esto (quitarme esta mancha)*?
pōdrē'ä pläntshär'me es'tō (kētär'me es'tä män'tshä)

Could you *darn this (sew on this button)*?
¿Puede *zurcirme esto (coserme este botón)*?
poo·e'de soorsēr'me es'tō (kōser'me es'te bōtōn')

Could you *lengthen (shorten)* this?
¿Podría *alargarme (acortarme)* esto?
pōdrē'ä älärgär'me (äkōrtär'me) es'tō

Optician

Can you fix these glasses?
¿Puede arreglarme estos lentes, anteojos/*Sp* estas gafas?
po͞o·e'de ärreglär'me es'tōs len'tes, änte·ō'hōs/es'täs gä'fäs

Can you replace these lenses?	**I'm *near-sighted (far-sighted).***
¿Puede reponer los lentes?	Soy *miope (présbita).*
po͞o·e'de repōner' lōs len'tes	soi mē·ō'pe (pres'bētä)

binoculars	prismáticos *mpl*	prēsmä'tēkōs
compass	brújula *f*	bro͞o'ho͞olä
contact lenses	lentes *fpl* de contacto,	len'tes de kōn-
	lentillas *fpl*	täk'tō, lentē'lyäs
frame	montura *f*	mōnto͞o'rä
glasses	lentes *fpl*, anteojos *mpl*/	len'tes, änte·ō'hōs/
	Sp gafas *fpl*	gä'fäs
sunglasses	lentes *fpl*, anteojos *mpl*/	len'tes, änte·ō'hōs/
	Sp gafas *fpl*/de sol	gä'fäs/de sōl

Stationery

ball point pen	bolígrafo *m*/*Mex* pluma *f*	bōlē'gräfō/plo͞o'mä
crayons	lápices *mpl* de color	lä'pēses de kōlōr'
envelope	sobre *m*	sō'bre
eraser	goma *f*, borrador *m*	gō'mä, bōrrädōr'
fountain pen	pluma *f*	plo͞o'mä
glue	pegamento *m*	pegämen'tō
ink	tinta *f*	tēn'tä
pad	bloc *m*	blōk
– scratch pad	bloc *m* de notas	blōk de nō'täs
– sketch pad	bloc *m* de dibujos	blōk de dēbo͞o'hōs
paper	papel *m*	päpel'
– typewriter paper .	papel *m* para la máquina	päpel' pä'rä lä
	de escribir	mä'kēnä de
		eskrēbēr'
– wrapping paper ..	papel *m* de envolver/*Sp* de	päpel' de embōl-
	embalar	ver'/ de embälär'
– writing paper	papel *m* de carta	päpel' de kär'tä
pencil	lápiz *m*	lä'pēs
photocopies	fotocopias *fpl*	fōtōkō'pyäs

Shoes

I take size …	**I'd like a pair of …**
Calzo el número …	Quisiera un par de …
käl′sō el nōō′merō …	kēsye′rä ōon pär de …

beach sandals	sandalias *fpl* para la playa	sändä′lyäs pä′rä lä plä′yä
bedroom slippers	zapatillas *fpl*, pantuflas *fpl*	säpätē′lyäs, päntōōf′läs
boots	botas *fpl*	bō′täs
ladies' shoes	zapatos *mpl* de señora	säpä′tōs de senyō′rä
loafers	zapatos *mpl* sin cordones, mocasín *m*	säpä′tōs sēn kōr-dō′nes, mōkäsēn′
rubber boots	botas *fpl* de goma	bō′täs de gō′mä
sandals	sandalias *fpl*	sändä′lyäs
tennis shoes, gym shoes	zapatos *mpl* de tenis/*Sp* playeras *fpl*	säpä′tōs de te′nēs/pläye′räs
walking shoes	botas *fpl* para caminar	bō′täs pä′rä kämēnär′

They're too *tight* (*wide*).
Me están *estrechos* (*anchos*).
me estän′ estre′tshōs (än′tshōs)

They pinch here.
Me aprietan aquí.
me äprē·e′tän äkē′

Could you fix these shoes for me?
¿Puede arreglarme estos zapatos?
pōō·e′de ärreglär′me es′tōs säpä′tōs

crepe sole	suela *f* de crepe	sōō·e′lä de kre′pe
heel	tacón *m*	täkōn′
– flat	bajo	bä′hō
– high	alto	äl′tō
in-sole	plantilla *f*	pläntē′lyä
leather	cuero *m*	kōō·e′rō
leather sole	suela *f* de cuero	sōō·e′lä de kōō·e′rō
rubber sole	suela *f* de goma	sōō·e′lä de gō′mä
shoe horn	calzador *m*	kälsädōr′
shoe laces	cordones *mpl*	kōrdō′nes
shoe polish	betún *m*	betōon′
sole *(noun)*	suela *f*	sōō·e′lä
sole *(verb)*	poner suela	pōner′ sōō·e′lä
suède	ante *m*	än′te

Cigar Store

A pack of ... *cigarettes (tobacco)*, please.
Un paquete/*Mex* una cajetilla/de *cigarrillos*/*Mex cigarros*/*(tabaco)*, por favor.
ōōm päke′te/ōō′nä kä*h*etē′lyä/de sēgärrē′lyōs/sēgä′rrōs/(täbä′kō), pōr fävōr′

Do you have American cigarettes?
¿Tiene cigarrillos/*Mex* cigarros/norteamericanos?
tye′ne sēgärrē′lyōs/sēgä′rrōs/nōr′te·ämerēkä′nōs

A dozen cigars, please.
Doce puros, por favor.
dō′se pōō′rōs, pōr fävōr′

Would you please refill my lighter?
¿Puede llenarme el encendedor?
pōō·e′de lyenär′me el ensendedōr′

Could I please have a light?
¿Tiene fuego?
tye′ne fōō·e′gō

A box of matches, please.
Una caja de fósforos/*Sp* cerillas, *Mex* cerillos/por favor.
ōō′nä kä′*h*ä de fōs′fōrōs/serē′lyäs, serē′lyōs/pōr fävōr′

cigar	puro *m*	pōō′rō
cigarette	cigarrillo *m*/*Mex* cigarro *m*	sēgärrē′lyō/sēgä′rrō
– filtered	con filtro	kōn fēl′trō
– unfiltered	sin filtro	sēn fēl′trō
cigarillo	purito *m*	pōōrē′tō
lighter	encendedor *m*	ensendedōr′
lighter fluid	gasolina *f* para el encendedor	gäsōlē′nä pä′rä el ensendedōr′
matches	fósforos *mpl*/*Sp* cerillas *fpl*, *Mex* cerillos *mpl*	fōs′fōrōs/serē′lyäs, serē′lyōs
pipe	pipa *f*	pē′pä
tobacco	tabaco *m*	täbä′kō

Toiletries

after shave	loción *f* para después del afeitado	lōsyōn′ pä′rä despōō·es′ del äfe·ētä′dō
bath salts	sales *fpl* de baño	sä′les de bä′nyō

bobby pins	horquillas *fpl*, clips *mpl*	ōrkē′lyäs, klēps
body lotion	loción *f* corporal	lōsyōn′ kōrpōräl′
brush	cepillo *m*	sepē′lyō
comb	peine *m*	pe′ēne
compact	polvera *f*	pōlve′rä
cream	crema *f*	kre′mä
curler	rulero *m*/*Sp* rulo *m* ..	ro͞ole′rō/ro͞o′lō
deodorant	desodorante *m*	desōdōrän′te
dye	tinte *m*	tēn′te
eye liner	trazado *m* de párpado .	träsä′dō de pär′pädō
eye shadow	sombra *f* de ojos	sōm′brä de ō′hōs
eyebrow pencil	lápiz *m* de cejas	lä′pēs de se′häs
face cream	crema *f* para el cutis ..	kre′mä pä′rä el ko͞o′tēs
hair spray	spray *m*, laca *f*	spre′ē, lä′kä
hairbrush	cepillo *m* del pelo	sepē′lyō del pe′lō
hairpins	horquillas *fpl*, clips *mpl*	ōrkē′lyäs, klēps
lipstick	lápiz *m* de labios/*Mex* colorete *m*	lä′pēs de lä′byōs/ kōlōre′te
make up	maquillaje *m*	mäkēlyä′he
mascara	pestañina *f*/*Sp* rimel *m*	pestänyē′nä/rē′mel
mirror	espejo *m*	espe′hō
mouthwash	agua *f* dentífrica	ä′go͞o·ä dentē′frēkä
nail file	lima *f* de uñas	lē′mä de o͞o′nyäs
nail polish	esmalte *m*	ezmäl′te
nail polish remover	quitaesmalte *m*	kētä·ezmäl′te
nail scissors	tijeras *fpl* de uñas	tēhe′räs de o͞o′nyäs
perfume	perfume *m*	perfo͞o′me
powder	polvos *mpl*	pōl′vōs
prophylactics	preservativos *mpl*	preservätē′vōs
razor (safety)	rasuradora *f*/*Sp* maquinilla *f* de afeitar	räso͞orädō′rä/mä- kēnē′lyä de äfe·ētär′
– electric shaver ...	máquina *f* de afeitar eléctrica	mä′kēnä de äfe·ētär′ elek′trēkä
– straight razor ...	navaja *f*	nävä′hä
razor blades	hojas *fpl* de afeitar, cuchillas *fpl*	ō′häs de äfe·ētär′, ko͞otshē′lyäs
sanitary napkins ...	compresas *fpl*	kōmpre′säs
scissors	tijeras *fpl*	tēhe′räs
shampoo	champú *m*	tshämpo͞o′
shaving brush	brocha *f* de afeitar	brō′tshä de äfe·ētär′

shaving cream	crema *f* de afeitar	kre'mä de äfe·ētär'
shaving foam	espuma *f* de afeitar	espo͞o'mä de äfe·ētär'
shaving soap	jabón *m* de afeitar	häbōn' de äfe·ētär'
soap	jabón *m*	häbōn'
sponge	esponja *f*	espōn'hä
sun tan cream	crema *f* solar/*Mex* bronceadora *f*	kre'mä sōlär'/brōn-se·ädō'rä
– sun tan lotion	loción *f* solar/*Mex* loción *f* para broncearse	lōsyōn' sōlär'/lōsyōn' pä'rä brōnse·är'se
– sun tan oil	aceite *m* solar/*Mex* bronceador *m*	äse'ēte sōlär'/brōn-se·ädōr'
talcum powder	talco *m*	täl'kō
tampon	tampón *m*	tämpōn'
tissues	pañuelos *mpl* de papel	pänyo͞o·e'lōs de päpel'
toilet articles, toiletries	artículos *mpl* de tocador	ärtē'ko͞olōs de tōkädōr'
toilet kit	neceser *m*	neseser'
toilet paper	papel *m* higiénico, papel *m* sanitario	päpel' ēhē·e'nēkō, päpel' sänētär'yō
toothbrush	cepillo *m* de dientes	sepē'lyō de dyen'tes
toothpaste	pasta *f* de dientes	päs'tä de dyen'tes
towel	toalla *f*	tō·ä'lyä
– bath towel	toalla *f* de baño	tō·ä'lyä de bä'nyō
tweezers	pinzas *fpl*	pēn'säs
wash cloth	manopla *f* de baño	mänō'plä de bä'nyō

Watchmaker

Can you fix this *watch (clock)*?
¿Puede arreglarme el *reloj*?
po͞o·e'de ärreglär'me el relō(h)'

How much will the repair cost?
¿Cuánto costará la reparación?
ko͞o·än'tō kōstärä' lä repäräsyōn'

It's running *fast (slow)*.
Va *adelantado (atrasado)*.
vä ädeläntä'dō (äträsä'dō)

alarm clock	despertador *m*	despertädōr'
crystal	vidrio *m*/*Sp* cristal *m*	vē'drē·ō/krēstäl'
clock	reloj *m*	relō(h)'
face	esfera *f*	esfe'rä
hands	agujas *fpl*, manecillas *fpl*	agōō'häs, mäne-sē'lyäs
pocket watch	reloj *m* de bolsillo	relō(h)' de bōlsē'lyō
spring	resorte *m*, muelle *m*	resōr'te, mōō·e'lye
stop watch	cronómetro *m*	krōnō'metrō
watch	reloj *m*	relō(h)'
watch band	pulsera *f* de reloj	pōōlse'rä de relō(h)'
wrist watch	reloj *m* de pulsera/*Mex* de pulso	relō(h)' de pōōlse'rä/ de pōōl'sō

Sundries

ash tray	cenicero *m*	senēse'rō
bag	saco *m*, bolsa *f*	sä'kō, bōl'sä
ball	pelota *f*	pelō'tä
basket	cesta *f*, cesto *m*, canasta *f*	ses'tä, ses'tō, känäs'tä
battery	pila *f*, batería *f*	pē'lä, bäterē'ä
beach bag	bolsa *f* para la playa	bōl'sä pä'rä lä plä'yä
bottle opener	destapador *m*/*Sp* abridor *m*	destäpädōr'/äbrēdōr'
briefcase	maletín *m*/*Sp* cartera *f*.	mäletēn'/kärte'rä
camp stove	brasero *m*	bräse'rō
can opener	abrelatas *m*	äbrelä'täs
candle	vela *f*	ve'lä
– beeswax	cera *f* de abejas	se'rä de äbe'häs
candlestick	candelero *m*	kändele'rō
candy	caramelos *mpl*	käräme'lōs
canned goods	conservas *fpl*, enlatados *mpl*	kōnser'väs, enlä-tä'dōs
cassette	cassette *m or f*	käse'te
ceramics	cerámica *f*	serä'mēkä
china	porcelana *f*	pōrselä'nä
computer	ordenador *m*	ōrdenädōr'
corkscrew	sacacorchos *m*, descorchador *m*	säkäkōr'tshōs, deskōrtshädōr'

detergent	detergente *m*	deterhen'te
doll	muñeca *f*	mōōnye'kä
figurine	figura *f*	fēgōō'rä
flashlight	linterna *f*/*Mex* foco *m*, luz *f*	lēnter'nä/fō'kō, lōōs
hammock	hamaca *f*	ämä'kä
handbag	bolso *m*, cartera *f*/*Mex* bolsa *f*	bōl'sō, kärte'rä/bōl'sä
handicrafts	labores *mpl* de mano	läbō'res de mä'nō
kerchief	pañuelo *m* de cabeza	pänyōō·e'lō de käbe'sä
jackknife	navaja *f*	nävä'hä
leash	cuerda *f*	kōō·er'dä
paper napkins	servilletas *fpl* de papel	servēlye'täs de päpel'
phonograph record	disco *m*	dēs'kō
picture	cuadro *m*	kōō·ä'drō
plastic bag	bolsa *f* de plástico	bōl'sä de pläs'tēkō
playing cards	cartas *fpl*, naipes *mpl*	kär'täs, nī'pes
pocket knife	navaja *f*	nävä'hä
recording tape	cinta *f* magnetofónica	sēn'tä mägnetō-fō'nēkä
rucksack	mochila *f*	mōtshē'lä
Scotch tape	cinta *f* adhesiva/*Sp* cinta *f* celo	sēn'tä ädesē'vä/sēn'tä se'lō
sled	trineo *m*	trēne'ō
spot remover	quitamanchas *m*	kētämän'tshäs
string	cuerda *f*, cordel *m*	kōō·er'dä, kōrdel'
stuffed animal	animal *m* de trapo	änēmäl' de trä'pō
suitcase	maleta *f*	mäle'tä
tape recorder	magnetófono *m*/*Mex* grabadora *f*	mägnetō'fōnō/grä-bädō'rä
thermometer	termómetro *m*	termō'metrō
thermos bottle	termo *m*	ter'mō
toy	juguete *m*	hōōge'te
umbrella	paraguas *m*	pärä'gōō·äs
vase	florero *m*	flōre'rō
video camera	cámara *f* de video	kä'märä de vē'de·ō
video cassette	cassette *m or f* de vídeo	käse'te de vē'de·ō
wallet	monedero *m*	mōnede'rō
washing line	cuerda *f*, soga *f*, lazo *m*	kōō·er'dä, sō'gä, lä'sō
wood carvings	tallas *fpl* de madera	tä'lyäs de mäde'rä

Post Office   THE POST OFFICE

Where is the post office?
¿Dónde está el correo/*Sp* la oficina de correos?

dōn'de estä' el kōrre'ō/lä ōfēsē'nä de kōrre'ōs

Where is there a mail box?
¿Dónde hay un buzón?

dōn'de ī ōon bōosōn'

How much is airmail for this postcard?
¿Cuánto cuesta esta postal por avión?

kōo·än'tō kōo·es'tä es'tä pōstäl' pōr ävyōn'

– to Canada.
– para Canadá.

– pä'rä känädä'

– to the United States.
– para los Estados Unidos.

– pä'rä lōs estä'dōs ōonē'dōs

What's the postage for this letter?
¿Cuánto cuesta esta carta?

kōo·än'tō kōo·es'tä es'tä kär'tä

this air mail letter .	esta carta por avión ...	es'tä kär'tä pōr ävyōn'
this letter abroad ..	esta carta para el extranjero	es'tä kär'tä pä'rä el eksträn*he*'rō
this local letter	esta carta local	es'tä kär'tä lōkäl'
this local post card	esta postal local	es'tä pōstäl' lōkäl'
this parcel	este paquete	es'te päke'te
this post card	esta (tarjeta) postal	es'tä (tär*he*'tä) pōstäl'
this printed matter .	estos impresos	es'tōs ēmpre'sōs
this registered letter	esta carta certificada, registrada	es'tä kär'tä sertēfē-kä'dä, re*h*ēstra'dä
this small parcel ...	este paquete pequeño ..	es'te päke'te peke'nyō
this special delivery letter ...	esta carta exprés, urgente	es'tä kär'tä ekspres', ōor*h*en'te

Five fifty cents stamps, please.
Cinco timbres *(Mex.)* de ciucuanta céntimos, por favor.

sēng'kō tēm'bres de sinkōōäntä sen'timōs, pōr fävōr'

Three one euro stamps, please.
Tres sellos *(Sp.)* de un euro, por favor.

tres se'lyōs de ōon eōo'rō, pōr fävōr'

When sending letters or postcards to the US from Latin America or Spain be sure to specify por avión (air mail), *otherwise they might be sent by regular mail* (correo ordinario).

Do you have any special issues?
¿Tiene estampillas/*Sp* sellos, *Mex* timbres/especiales?
tye′ne estämpē′lyäs/se′lyōs, tēm′bres/espesyä′les

This set of stamps, please.
Esta serie, por favor.
es′tä ser′ye, pōr fävōr′

Two of each, please.
Dos de cada uno, por favor.
dōs de kä′dä o͞o′nō, pōr fävōr′

Aerograms (thin, prestamped letter sheets) are handy for longer messages, and save the trouble of having to get paper, envelopes and stamps.

I'd like to send this letter by *registered mail (special delivery).*
Quisiera enviar esta carta *registrada/Sp certificada/(exprés o urgente).*
kēsye′rä embyär′ es′tä kär′tä re*h*ēsträ′dä/sertēfēkä′dä/(ekspres′, o͞or*h*en′te)

How long does it take for *a letter (package)* to get to ...?
¿Cuánto tarda *una carta (un paquete)* para ...?
ko͞o·än′tō tär′dä o͞o′nä kär′tä (o͞om päke′te) pä′rä ...

Can I withdraw money from my postal savings account?
¿Puedo sacar dinero con mi libreta postal de ahorros?
po͞o·e′dō säkär′ dēne′rō kōn mē lēbre′tä pōstäl′ de ä·ō′rrōs

Is there any mail here for me?
¿Hay correo para mí?
ī kōrre′ō pä′rä mē

My name is ...
Mi nombre es ...
mē nōm′bre es ...

Where can I *mail (pick up)* a package?
¿Dónde puedo *enviar (recoger)* un paquete?
dōn′de po͞o·e′dō embyär′ (rekō*h*er′) o͞om päke′te

*Sign here, please.
Firme aquí, por favor.
fēr′me äkē′, pōr fävōr′

Do I need a customs declaration?
¿Hay que hacer una declaración de aduana?
ī ke äser′ o͞o′nä dekläräsyōn′ de ädo͞o·ä′nä

This is my new address.
Aquí está mi dirección
(*or* están mis señas).
äkē′ estä′ mē dēreksyōn′
(estän′ mēs se′nyäs)

I'd like to have my mail forwarded to ...
Quisiera que me remitan mi correspondencia a ...
kēsye′rä ke me remē′tän mē kōrrespōnden′syä ä ...

Telegrams

A telegram form, please.
Un impreso de telegrama, por favor.
ōōn ĕmpre′sō de telegrä′mä, pōr fävōr′

I'd like to send ...
Quisiera poner/*Mex* mandar/ ...
kēsye′rä pōnĕr′/mändär′

a telegram	un telegrama	ōōn telegrä′mä
– with prepaid reply .	con respuesta pagada ..	kōn respōō-es′tä pagä′dä
an urgent telegram ..	un telegrama urgente ..	ōōn telegrä′mä ōōrĕn′te

How much do ten words to ... cost?
¿Cuánto cuestan diez palabras para ...?
kōō-än′tō kōō-es′tän dyes pälä′bräs pä′rä ...

When will it arrive at ...?
¿Cuándo llegará a ...?
kōō-än′dō lyegärä′ ä ...

Telephone

It is wise to place long distance calls at the telephone office (central de teléfonos; *in Mexico*, oficina de teléfonos), *as many hotels make sizeable surcharges for use of the phone.*

Where is the nearest phone?
¿Dónde está el teléfono más próximo?
dōn′de estä′ el tele′fōnō mäs prō′ksēmō

May I use your phone?
¿Puedo utilizar su teléfono?
pōō-e′dō ōōtēlēsär′ sōō tele′fōnō

Where can I make a phone call?
¿Dónde puedo telefonear?
dōn′de pōō-e′dō telefōne-är′

What's the area code for ...?
¿Cuál es el prefijo de ...?
kōō-äl′ es el prefe′hō de ...

The phone book, please.
El directorio/*Sp* la guía (de teléfonos)/, por favor.
el dĕrektōr′yō/lä gē′ä (de tele′fōnōs)/pōr fävōr′

Can I direct dial to ...?
¿Puedo llamar directamente a ...?
pōō-e′dō lyämär′ dĕrektämen′te ä ...

You can direct dial from both Spain and Mexico.
to US from Mexico: 95 & area code & tel. number
to US from Spain: 07-1 & area code & tel. number

A long distance call to …, please.
Una llamada a larga distancia/*Sp* una
conferencia/, por favor.

o͞o'nä lyämä'dä ä lär'gä dēstän'syä/
o͞o'nä kōmferen'syä/, pōr fävōr'

How long will that take?
¿Cuánto tiempo tardará?

ko͞o·än'to tyem'pō tärdärä'

Can I have some coins for the pay phone?
¿Tiene monedas (cambio) para el teléfono público?

tye'ne mōne'däs (käm'byō) pä'rä el tele'fōnō po͞o'blēkō

How much does *a local call (call to …)* cost?
¿Cuánto cuesta *una llamada urbana*/*Mex interna*/(*una llamada a …*)?

ko͞o·än'tō ko͞o·es'tä o͞onä lyämä'dä o͞orbä'nä/ēnter'nä/(o͞o'nä
lyämä'dä ä …)

What time does the night rate begin?
¿A partir de qué hora hay tarifa nocturna?

ä pärtēr' de ke ō'rä ī tärē'fä nōkto͞or'nä

*What's your number?
¿Cuál es su número?

ko͞o·äl es so͞o no͞o'merō

*Your call is ready in booth four.
Su llamada/*Sp* su conferencia/es en
la cabina cuatro.

so͞o lyämä'dä/so͞o kōmferen'syä/es en
lä käbē'nä ko͞o·ä'trō

Wrong number!
¡Se ha equivocado de
número!

se ä ekēvōkä'dō de
no͞o'merō

Please connect me with …
Póngame con (comuníqueme con) … por favor.

pōn'gäme kōn (kōmo͞onē'keme kōn) … pōr fävōr'

The line is *busy (out of order)*.
Está *ocupado (interrumpido)*.

estä' ōko͞opä'dō (ēnterro͞ompē'dō)

There's no answer at that number.
El número no contesta.

el no͞o'merō nō kōntes'tä

Hello!
¡Díga(me)!/*Mex* ¡Bueno!

dē'gä(me)/bo͞o·e'nō

May I speak to *Mr. (Mrs., Miss)* …?
¿Puedo hablar con *el señor (la señora, la señorita)* …?

po͞o·e'dō äblär' kōn el senyōr' (lä senyō'rä, lä senyōrē'tä) …

Speaking!
¡Soy yo!

soi yō

This is … speaking.
Aquí …

äkē' …

Who is this?
¿Quién habla?

kyen äb'lä

Please hold the line.
¡Por favor, no cuelgue!

pōr fävōr', nō ko͞o·el'ge

Would you please cancel that call.
Por favor, cancelen/*Sp* anulen/la llamada.

pōr fävōr', känse'len/äno͞o'len/lä lyämä'dä

Code Alphabet

A	Antonio	[äntō'nyō]	M	México	[me'hēkō]
B	Bogotá	[bōgōtä']	N	Nicaragua	[nēkärä'gōō·ä]
C	Carmen	[kär'men]	Ñ	Ñoño	[nyō'nyō]
CH	Chocolate	[tshōkōlä'te]	O	Océano	[ōse'änō]
D	Dora	[dō'rä]	P	Paraguay	[pärägōō·ī']
E	Enrique	[enrē'ke]	Q	Querido	[kerē'dō]
F	Francisco	[fränsēs'kō]	R	Ramón	[rämōn']
G	Gibraltar	[hēbrältär']	S	Sábado	[sä'bädō]
H	Historia	[ēstōr'yä]	T	Tomás	[tōmäs']
I	Inés	[ēnes']	U	Ulises	[ōōlē'ses]
J	José	[hōse']	V	Venezuela	[venesōō·e'lä]
K	Kilo	[kē'lō]	W	Washington	[ōō·äshēngtōn']
L	Lorenzo	[lōren'sō]	X	Xiquena	[hēke'nä]
Ll	Llobregat	[lyōbregät']	Y	Yegua	[ye'gōō·ä]
			Z	Zaragoza	[särägō'sä]

address	dirección f/señas fpl	dēreksyōn'/se'nyäs
addressee	destinatario m	destēnätär'yō
air mail	correo m aéreo	kōrre'ō ä·er'e·ō
area code	prefijo m/Mex clave f	prefē'hō/klä've
c.o.d.	envío m contra reembolso	embē'ō kōn'trä re·embōl'sō
counter	ventanilla f	ventänē'lyä
customs declaration	declaración f de aduana	dekläräsyōn' de ädōō·ä'nä
destination	destino m	destē'nō
dial (noun)	disco m	dēs'kō
dial (verb)	marcar	märkär'
direct dialing	llamada f directa	lyämä'dä dērek'tä
general delivery	lista f de correos	lēs'tä de kōrre'ōs
insured mail	correo m asegurado	kōrre'ō äsegōōrä'dō
letter	carta f	kär'tä
local call	llamada f urbana/Mex interna	lyämä'dä ōōrbä'nä/ēnter'nä
long distance call	conferencia f/Mex llamada f de larga distancia	kōmferen'syä/lyämä'dä de lär'gä dēstän'syä
mail box	buzón m	bōōsōn'

operator	telefonista m & f/Mex operador m & f	telefōnēs'tä/ōperä-dōr'
package	paquete m	päke'te
parcel	paquete m	päke'te
post card	postal f or tarjeta f postal	pōstäl', tärhe'tä pōstäl'
postage	porte m, franqueo m	pōr'te, frängke'ō
postal clerk	empleado m de correos .	emple·ä'dō de kōrre'ōs
postal savings book	libreta f postal de aho-rros	lēbre'tä pōstäl' de ä·ō'rrōs
postman	cartero m	kärte'rō
printed matter .	impresos mpl	ēmpre'sōs
receipt	recibo m/Sp resguardo m	resē'bō/rezgo͞o·är'dō
register	certificar, registrar	sertēfēkär', rehēsträr'
registered letter	carta f certificada, registrada	kär'tä sertēfēkä'dä, rehēsträ'dä
registered parcel with declared value	paquete m registrado/Sp certificado/con declara-ción de valor	päke'te rehēsträ'dō/sertēfēkä'dō/kōn dekläräsyōn' de välōr'
return postage .	porte m de vuelta	pōr'te de vo͞o·el'tä
sender	remitente m	remēten'te
small parcel	paquete m pequeño	päke'te peke'nyō
special delivery .	exprés, urgente, entrega f inmediata	ekspres', o͞orhen'te, entre'gä ēnmedyä'tä
special delivery letter	carta f exprés, carta f de entrega inmediata/Sp urgente	kär'tä ekspres', kär'tä de entre'gä ēnmedyä'tä/o͞orhen'te
special issue stamp	estampilla f/Sp sello m, Mex timbre m/conmemo-rativo	estämpē'lyä/se'lyō, tēm'bre/kōnmemō-rätē'vō
stamp	estampilla f/Sp sello m, Mex timbre m	estämpē'lyä/se'lyō, tēm'bre
stamp (verb) . . .	franquear	frängke·är'
stamp machine .	distribuidor m automá-tico de estampillas/Sp sellos, Mex timbres	dēstrēbo͞o·ēdōr' outō-mä'tēkō de estämpē'-lyäs/se'lyōs, tēm'bres
telegram	telegrama m	telegrä'mä
telephone	teléfono m	tele'fōnō
unstamped	sin franquear	sēn frängke·är'
value declaration	declaración f de valor . . .	dekläräsyōn' de välōr'

BANK, CURRENCY EXCHANGE

Where can I change some money?
¿Dónde se puede cambiar dinero?
dōn'de se pōō·e'de kämbyär' dēne'rō

Where is the bank?
¿Dónde está el banco?
dōn'de estä' el bäng'kō

I need a hundred dollars in ...
Quisiera cambiar cien dólares en ...
kēsye'rä kämbyär' syen dō'läres en ...

How much will I get for ...?
¿Cuánto me dan por ...?
kōō·än'tō me dän pōr ...

What's the rate of exchange?
¿Cómo es el cambio?
kō'mō es el käm'byō

Can you change ... into *pesos (euros)* for me?
¿Puede cambiar ... en *pesos (euros)*?
pōō·e'de kämbyär' ... en pe'sōs (eōō'rōs)

Could I have some change, please?
¿Tiene dinero suelto (cambio), por favor?
tye'ne dēne'rō sōō·el'tō (käm'byō), pōr
fävōr'

Can you change this?
¿Puede cambiar esto?
pōō·e'de kämbyär' es'tō

I'd like to cash this *check (traveler's check)*.
Quisiera cobrar este *cheque (cheque de viaje)*.
kēsye'rä kōbrär' es'te tshe'ke (tshe'ke de vyä'*he*)

Has some money arrived for me?
¿Ha llegado dinero para mí?
ä lyegä'do dēne'rō pä'rä mē

amount	importe *m*	ēmpōr'te
bank	banco *m*	bäng'kō
bank account	cuenta *f* bancaria	kōō·en'tä bäng-kär'yä
bank charges	derechos *mpl* del banco	dere'tshōs del bäng'kō
bank draft	cheque *m* del banco	tshe'ke del bäng'kō
bank note	billete *m* de banco	bēlye'te de bäng'kō
bank transfer	giro *m* bancario	*h*ē'rō bängkär'yō
bill	billete *m*	bēlye'te
branch manager	gerente *m or* director *m* de la sucursal	heren'te (dērektōr') de lä sōōkōōrsäl'

cash *(verb)*	cobrar	kōbrär′
change	cambio *m*	käm′byō
check	cheque *m*, talón *m*	tshe′ke, tälōn′
coin	moneda *f*	mōne′dä
credit	crédito *m*	kre′dētō
– **take out a loan**	tomar crédito	tōmär′ kre′dētō
credit card	tarjeta *f* de crédito	tär*h*e′tä de kre′dētō
currency	moneda *f*	mōne′dä
deposit	ingresar, consignar	ēngresär′, kōnsēg-när′
foreign currency	divisas *fpl*	dēvē′säs
form	formulario *m*	fōrmōōlär′yō
in cash	al contado	äl kōntä′dō
money	dinero *m*	dēne′rō
– **Canadian dollars**	dólares *mpl* canadienses	dō′läres känä-dyen′ses
– **English pounds**	libras *fpl* inglesas	lē′bräs ēngle′säs
– **American dollars**	dólares *mpl* americanos	dō′läres ämerē-kä′nōs
euros	euros	eōō′rōs
money exchange	cambio *m* de moneda	käm′byō de mōne′dä
mortgage	hipoteca *f*	ēpōte′kä
on credit	al fiado, al crédito	äl fyä′dō, äl kre′dētō
pay out	pagar	pägär′
payment	pago *m*	pä′gō
rate of exchange	tipo *m* de cambio	tē′pō de käm′byō
receipt	recibo *m*	resē′bō
savings bank	caja *f* de ahorros	kä′hä de ä·ō′rrōs
savings book	libreta *f* de ahorros	lēbre′tä de ä·ō′rrōs
security	fianza *f*	fyän′sä
share of stock	acción *f*	äksyōn′
signature	firma *f*	fēr′mä
stock	acciones *fpl*	äksyō′nes
telegraphic	telegráfico	telegrä′fēkō
teller's window	caja *f*	kä′hä
transfer	giro *m*	*h*ē′rō
traveler's check	cheque *m* de viaje	tshe′ke de vyä′*h*e
withdraw	retirar	retērär′

POLICE STATION

STOP

POLICE

Reporting

I'd like to report ...
Quisiera denunciar ...
kēsye′rä denōonsyär′ ...

an accident	un accidente	ōon äksēden′te
a blackmail attempt	una extorsión, un chantaje	ōo′nä ekstōrsyōn′, ōon tshäntä′he
a hold-up	un atraco	ōon äträ′kō
a kidnapping	un secuestro	ōon sekōo·es′trō
a loss	una pérdida	ōo′nä per′dēdä
a murder	un asesinato	ōon äsesēnä′tō
a theft	un robo	ōon rō′bō

My ... has been stolen.   **I lost my ...**
Me han robado ...   He perdido mi ...
me än rōbä′dō ...   e perdē′dō mē ...

bag	el saco, la bolsa	el sä′kō, lä bōl′sä
billfold	la cartera	lä kärte′rä
bracelet	la pulsera	lä pōolse′rä
briefcase	la cartera de documentos	lä kärte′rä de dōkōomen′tōs
camera	la máquina fotográfica	lä mä′kēnä fōtōgrä′fēkä
car keys	las llaves del carro/*Sp* del coche	läs lyä′ves del kä′rrō/del kō′tshe
handbag	el bolso/*Mex* la bolsa	el bōl′sō/lä bōl′sä
jewelry	las joyas	läs hō′yäs
key	la llave	lä lyä′ve
money	el dinero	el dēne′rō
necklace	el collar	el kōlyär′
purse	el bolso/*Mex* la bolsa	el bōl′sō/lä bōl′sä
ring	el anillo, la sortija	el änē′lyō, lä sōrtē′hä
suitcase	la maleta	lä mäle′tä
umbrella	el paraguas	el pärä′gōo·äs
wallet	el monedero	el mōnede′rō
watch	el reloj	el relō(h)′
– wrist watch	el reloj de pulsera/*Mex* de pulso	el relō(h)′ de pōolse′rä/de pōol′sō

I have nothing to do with *it (this business).*
Yo no tengo nada que ver con *eso (ese asunto).*
yō nō ten'gō nä'dä ke ver kōn e'sō (e'se äsōōn'tō)

I'm innocent.
Yo soy inocente.
yō soi ēnō̄sen'te

I didn't do it.
Yo no lo he hecho.
yō nō lō e e'tshō

How long do I have to stay here?
¿Cuánto tiempo debo quedarme aquí?
kōō·än'tō tyem'pō de'bō kedär'me äkē'

This man is *bothering (following)* **me.**
Este hombre me está *molestando (persiguiendo).*
es'te ōm'bre me estä' mōlestän'dō (persēgyen'dō)

arrest	detener	detener'
attorney	abogado *m*	äbōgä'dō
confiscate	confiscar	kōnfēskär'
court	tribunal *m*	trēbōōnäl'
crime	delito *m*	delē'tō
criminal	delincuente *m*	delēnkōō·en'te
custody	detención *f*	detensyōn'
– protective custody	custodia *f* preventiva	kōōstō'dyä preventē'vä
drugs	drogas *fpl*	drō'gäs
hold-up	atraco *m*	äträ'kō
judge	juez *m*	hōō·es'
lawyer	abogado *m*	äbōgä'dō
narcotics	narcóticas *fpl*	närkō'tēkäs
pickpocket	ratero *m*	räte'rō
police	policía *f*	pōlēsē'ä
police car	carro *m/Sp* coche *m/de la policía*	kä'rrō/kō'tshe/de lä pōlēsē'ä
police station	estación *f* de policía/*Sp* comisaría *f*	estäsyōn' de pōlēsē'ä/kōmēsärē'ä
prison	cárcel *f*	kär'sel
smuggling	contrabando *m*	kōnträbän'dō
thief	ladrón *m*	lädrōn'
verdict	sentencia *f*	senten'syä

BEAUTY SHOP, BARBER SHOP

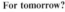

Beauty Shop

May I make an appointment for Saturday?
¿Puede darme hora para el sábado?
pōō·e'de där'me ō'rä pä'rä el sä'bädō

Would you put me down for a permanent wave?
¿Puede hacerme la permanente?
pōō·e'de äser'me lä permänen'te

For tomorrow?
¿Para mañana?
pä'rä mänyä'nä

Will I have to wait?
¿Tengo que esperar?
ten'gō ke esperär'

Will it take long?
¿Tardará mucho tiempo?
tärdärä' mōō'tshō tyem'pō

Wash and set, please.
Lavar y enrular/*Sp* marcar/, por favor.
lävär' ē enrōōlär'/märkär'/, pōr fävōr'

I'd like a permanent (set), please.
Quisiera una permanente.
kēsye'rä ōō'nä permänen'te

Please set my hair for the evening.
Quisiera un peinado de noche.
kēsye'rä ōōm pe·ēnä'dō de nō'tshe

Please *dye (rinse)* my hair.
Por favor, podría *teñirme el pelo (dar reflejos al pelo)*.
pōr fävōr, pōdrē'ä tenyēr'me el pe'lō (där refle'*h*ōs äl pe'lō)

Please cut my hair a little shorter.
Córteme el pelo un poco, por favor.
kōr'teme el pe'lō ōōm pō'kō, pōr fävōr'

Just trim it, please.
Sólo las puntas.
sō'lō läs pōōn'täs

Please cut it wet.
Corte en mojado, por favor.
kōr'te en mō*h*ä'dō, pōr fävōr'

Please pin it up in a bun.
Hágame el moño, por favor.
ä'gäme el mō'nyō, pōr fävōr'

Please tease it a little on the *top (sides)*.

Por favor, enredar/*Sp* cardar/sólo un poco *arriba (a los lados)*.
pōr fävōr', enredär'/kärdär'/sō'lō ōōm pō'kō ärrē'bä (ä lōs lä'dōs)

It's a little too hot under the drier.

Hace demasiado calor bajo el secador.
ä'se demäsyä'dō kälōr' bä'hō el sekädōr'

No *setting lotion (hair spray)*, please.

No ponga *fijador (laca)*, por favor.
nō pōn'gä fēhädōr' (lä'kä), pōr fävōr'

Could you give me a *manicure (pedicure)*?

¿Puede hacerme la *manicura (pedicura)*?
pōō·e'de äser'me lä mänēkōō'rä (pedēkōō'rä)

Please file my nails *round (to a point)*.

Hágame las uñas *redondas (en punta)*.
ä'gäme läs ōō'nyäs redōn'däs (em pōōn'tä)

Just polish them, please.

Por favor, sólo pulir.
pōr fävōr', sō'lō pōōlēr'

***With (without)* nail polish.**

Con (sin) esmalte.
kōn (sēn) ezmäl'te

Please *tweeze (shave)* my eyebrows.

Por favor, *maquilleme (depileme)* las cejas.
pōr fävōr', mäkē'lyeme (depē'leme) läs se'häs

A *facial mask (face massage)*, please.

Por favor, *una mascarilla (un masaje facial)*.
pōr fävōr', ōō'nä mäskärē'lyä (ōōn mäsä'he fäsyäl')

Would you please put *this hairpiece (wig)* on for me?

Por favor, póngame *este postizo (esta peluca)*?
pōr fävōr', pōn'gäme es'te pōstē'sō (es'tä pelōō'kä)

Yes, thank you, that's just fine.

Sí, gracias, está bien así.
sē, grä'syäs, estä' byen äsē'

Very nice!

¡Muy bien!
mōō'ē byen

Barber Shop

(Shave and) a haircut, please.
Cortar el pelo (y afeitar), por favor.
kōrtär′ el pe′lō (ē äfe·ētär′), pōr fävōr′

Not too short, please.
No demasiado corto, por favor.
nō demäsyä′dō kōr′tō, pōr fävōr′

(Very) short, please.
(Muy) corto, por favor.
(mōō′ē) kōr′tō, pōr fävōr′

– at the back.	**– on top.**	**– in front.**	**– on the sides.**
– por detras.	– arriba.	– por delante.	– a los lados.
– pōr deträs′	– ärrē′bä	– pōr delän′te	– ä lōs lä′dōs

A razor cut, please.
Un corte a navaja, por favor.
ōōn kōr′te ä nävä′*h*ä, pōr fävōr′

With (without) part, please.
Con (sin) raya (carrera, línea),
por favor.
kōn (sēn) rä′yä (kärre′rä, lē′-
ne·ä), pōr fävōr′

Part it on the *left (right)*, please.
Hágame la raya (carrera, línea) a la *izquierda (derecha).*
ä′gäme lä rä′yä (kärre′rä, lē′ne·ä) ä lä ēskyer′dä (dere′tshä)

A shampoo too, please.
Láveme también el pelo, por favor.
lä′veme tämbyen′ el pe′lō, pōr fävōr′

Scalp massage, please.
Un poco de masaje, por favor.
ōōm pō′kō de mäsä′*h*e, pōr
fävōr′

Would you trim my *beard (moustache)*, please.
Arréglame un poco *la barba (el bigote)*, por favor.
ärre′gleme ōōm pō′kō lä bär′bä (el bēgō′te), pōr fävōr′

Just a shave, please.
Sólo afeitar, por favor.
sō′lō äfe·ētär′, pōr fävōr′

Please don't shave against the grain.
No me afeite a contrapelo, por favor.
no me äfe′ēte ä kōnträpe′lō, pōr fävōr′

Some hair tonic (a little brilliantine), please.
Loción (un poco de brillantina), por favor.
lōsyōn′ (ōōm pō′kō de brēlyäntē′nä), pōr fävōr′

Please leave it dry.
No los moje, por favor.
nō lōs mō′*h*e, pōr fävōr′

Yes, thank you, that's just great.
Sí, gracias, está bien así.
sē, grä′syäs, estä′ byen äse′

barber	peluquero *m*	pelōōke′rō
beard	barba *f*	bär′bä
beauty parlor ...	salón *m* de belleza	sälōn′ de belye′sä
brilliantine	brillantina *f*	brēlyäntē′nä
comb *(noun)*	peine *m*	pe′ēne
comb *(verb)*	peinar	pe·ēnär′
curls	rizos *mpl*	rē′sōs
cut	cortar	kōrtär′
dandruff	caspa *f*	käs′pä
dye	teñir	tenyēr′
hair	pelo *m*	pe′lō
– dry hair	seco	se′kō
– greasy hair	grasiento	gräsyen′tō
haircut	corte *m* de pelo	kōr′te de pe′lō
hair-do	peinado *m*	pe·ēnä′dō
hairdresser	peluquero *m*	pelōōke′rō
– men's	peluquero *m* de caba- lleros	de käbälye′rōs
– women's	peluquero *m* de señoras	de senyō′räs
hair drier	secador *m*	sekädōr′
hair loss	caída *f* del pelo	kä·ē′dä del pe′lō
hair style	peinado *m*	pe·ēnä′dō
hairpiece	postizo *m*	pōstē′sō
lock of hair	mechón *m*	metshōn′
manicure	manicura *f*	mänēkōō′rä
moustache	bigote *m*	bēgō′te
part	raya *f,* carrera *f,* línea *f*	rä′yä, kärre′rä, lē′ne·ä
pedicure	pedicura *f*	pedēkōō′rä
permanent wave .	permanente *f*	permänen′te
scalp massage ...	masaje *m* de la cabeza .	mäsä′he de lä käbe′sä
set	enrular/*Sp* marcar	enrōōlär′/märkär′
shave	afeitar	äfe·ētär′
sideburns	patillas *fpl*	pätē′lyäs
tease	cardar, crespar, enredar	kärdär′, krespär′, enredär′
tint	dar color, dar reflejos .	där kōlōr′, där re- fle′hōs
toupé	postizo *m*	pōstē′sō
wash	lavar	lävär′
wig	peluca *f*	pelōō′kä

HEALTH

Pharmacy

Where is the nearest pharmacy?
¿Dónde está la farmacia más cercana?
dōn′de estä′ lä färmä′syä mäs serkä′nä

Which pharmacy has night duty?
¿Qué farmacia está de guardia *or* de turno?
ke färmä′syä est′ä de goo·är′dyä, de toor′nō

I'd like this medicine, please.
Quisiera este medicamento, por favor.
kēsye′rä es′te medēkämen′tō, pōr fävōr′

Please give me something for ...   **I'd like ...**
Por favor, déme algo contra ...   Quisiera ...
pōr fävōr′, de′me äl′gō kōn′trä ...   kēsye′rä ...

Do I need a prescription for this medicine?
¿Se necesita receta (fórmula) para este medicamento?
se nesesē′tä rese′tä (fōr′moolä) pä′rä es′te medēkämen′tō

Can you order this medicine for me?
¿Podría encargarme este medicamento?
pōdrē′ä enkärgär′me es′te medēkämen′tō

Where can I pick it up?   **Can I wait for it?**
¿Dónde puedo recogerlo?   ¿Puedo esperar?
dōn′de poo·e′dō rekōher′lō   poo·e′dō esperär′

for external use	para uso externo ....
for internal use	para uso interno ....
before meals	antes de las comidas ....
after meals	después de las comidas ....
three times a day	tres veces al día ....
as prescribed	según prescripción médica ....
on an empty stomach	en ayunas ....

Medication and Bandages

absorbent cotton	algodón *m* hidrófilo ...	älgōdōn' ēdrō'fēlō
adhesive bandage	tela *f* adhesiva	te'lä ädesē'vä
adhesive tape	esparadrapo *m*	espärädrä'pō
alcohol	alcohol *m*	älkō·ōl'
ampule	ampolla *f*	ämpō'lyä
antidote	antídoto *m*	äntē'dōtō
aspirin	aspirina *f*	äspērē'nä
bandage	vendaje *m*/*Mex* venda *f*	vendä'*he*/ven'dä
bicarbonate of soda ..	bicarbonato *m* sódico ..	bēkärbōnä'tō sō'dēkō
boric acid ointment ..	agua *f* bórica	ä'gōō·ä bō'rēkä
burn ointment	pomada *f* para quema-duras	pōmä'dä pä'rä kemädōō'räs
camomile tea	manzanilla *f*	mänsänē'lyä
castor oil	aceite *m* de ricino	äse'ēte de rēsē'nō
charcoal pills	pastillas *fpl* de carbón .	pästē'lyäs de kärbōn'
contraceptive pills ...	píldoras *fpl* anticoncep-tivas	pēl'dōräs äntēkōn-septē'väs
corn plaster	parche *m* para callos ..	pär'tshe pä'rä kä'lyōs
cough medicine	calmante *m* de la tos ..	kälmän'te de lä tōs
cough syrup	jarabe *m* para tos	*h*ärä'be pä'rä tōs
dextrose	dextrosa *f*	dekstrō'sä
digestive tablets	pastillas *fpl* para el estómago	pästē'lyäs pä'rä el estō'mägō
digestive tonic	gotas *fpl* para el estómago	gō'täs pä'rä el estō'mägō
disinfectant	desinfectante *m*	desēnfektän'te
diuretic	diurético *m*	dyōōre'tēkō
drops	gotas *fpl*	gō'täs
ear drops	gotas *fpl* para los oidos	gō'täs pä'rä lōs ō·ēdōs
elastic bandage	venda *f* elástica	ven'dä eläs'tēkä
elastic stocking	media *f* elástica	me'dyä eläs'tēkä
emetic	emético *m*	eme'tēkō
enema	enema *f*	ene'mä
eye drops	gotas *fpl* para los ojos .	gō'täs pä'rä lōs ō'*h*ōs

eye ointment	pomada *f* para los ojos	pōmä′dä pä′rä lōs ō′hōs
fever cure	antipirético *m*, antitérmico *m*	äntēpēre′tēkō, äntēter′mēkō
first-aid kit	botiquín *m*	bōtēkēn′
gargle	gárgaras *fpl*	gär′gäräs
gauze bandage	gasa *f*	gä′sä
glycerine	glicerina *f*	glēserē′nä
hydrogen peroxide .	agua *f* oxigenada	ä′gōō·ä ōksēhenä′dä
injection	inyección *f*	ēnyeksyōn′
insect repellent	insecticida *m*	ēnsektēsē′dä
iodine	yodo *m*	yō′dō
laxative	laxante *m*	läksän′te
liniment	linimento *m*	lēnēmen′tō
medicine	medicina *f*	medēsē′nä
mouthwash	agua *f* para gargarismo	ä′gōō·ä pä′rä gärgärēz′mō
ointment	pomada *f*	pōmä′dä
pain pills	analgésicos *mpl*	änäl*he*′sēkōs
peppermint	menta *f*	men′tä
pill	pastillas *fpl*, píldoras *fpl*	pästē′lyäs, pēl′dōräs
powder	talco *m*	täl′kō
prophylactics	preservativos *mpl*	preservätē′vōs
quinine	quinina *f*	kēnē′nä
remedy	remedio *m*	reme′dyō
salve	pomada *f*	pōmä′dä
sanitary napkins ...	compresas *fpl*	kōmpre′säs
sleeping pills	somníferos *mpl*	sōmnē′ferōs
suppository	supositorio *m*/*Mex a* calillo *m*	sōōpōsētōr′yō/kälē′lyō
tablet	comprimido *m*	kōmprēmē′dō
talcum powder	talco *m*	täl′kō
thermometer	termómetro *m*	termō′metrō
tincture of iodine ..	tintura *f* de yodo	tēntōō′rä de yō′dō
tonic	tónico *m*	tō′nēkō
tranquilizer	calmante *m*, sedante *m*	kälmän′te, sedän′te
valerian drops	gotas *fpl* de valeriana ..	gō′täs de väleryä′nä
vaseline	vaselina *f*	väselē′nä
vitamin pills	pastillas *fpl* de vitaminas	pästē′lyäs de vētämē′näs
wound salve	ungüento *m*	ōōngōō·en′tō

The doctor is in

Quick, call a doctor!
¡Pronto! Llame a un médico.
prōn'tō lyä'me ä ōōn me'dēkō

Is there a doctor in the house?
¿Hay un médico aquí?
ī ōōn me'dēkō äkē'

Please get a doctor!
¡Por favor, busque un médico!
pōr fävōr', bōōs'ke ōōn me'dēkō

Where is there a doctor?
¿Dónde hay un médico?
dōn'de ī ōōn me'dēkō

Can he come here?
¿Puede venir aquí?
pōō·e'de venēr' äkē'

Where is there a hospital?
¿Dónde hay un hospital?
dōn'de ī ōōn ōspētäl'

When does the doctor have office hours?
¿A qué hora tiene consulta?
ä ke ō'rä tye'ne kōnsōōl'tä

Would you please come to the ...
Por favor, venga a ...
pōr fävōr', ven'gä ä ...

I'm sick.
Estoy enfermo.
estoi' enfer'mō

My husband (my wife, our son, our daughter) is sick.
Mi esposo (mi esposa, nuestro hijo, nuestra hija)
está enfermo (-a).
mē espō'sō (mē espō'sä, nōō·es'trō ē'hō, nōō·es'-
trä ē'hä) estä' enfer'mō (-ä)

doctor	médico *m*	me'dēkō
dermatologist	dermatólogo *m*	dermätō'lōgō
ear, nose and throat specialist	otorrinolaringólogo *m* .	ōtōrrēnōlärēn-gō'lōgō
eye doctor	optometrista *m*	ōptōmetrēs'tä
general practitioner .	médico *m* general	me'dēkō heneräl'
gynecologist	ginecólogo *m*	hēnekō'lōgō
internist *m*	internista *m*	ēnternēs'tä
neurologist	neurólogo *m*	ne·ōōrō'lōgō
orthopedist	ortopedista *m*	ōrtōpedēs'tä
pediatrician	pediatra *m*	pedyä'trä

psychiatrist	psiquiatra *m*	sēkyä'trä
psychologist	psicólogo *m*	sēkō'lōgō
specialist	especialista *m*	espesyälēs'tä
surgeon	cirujano *m*	sērōōhä'nō
urologist	urólogo *m*	ōōrō'lōgō
doctor's office	consultorio *m*	kōnsōōltōr'yō
office hours	horas *fpl* de consulta ..	ō'räs de kōnsōōl'tä
waiting room	sala *f* de espera	sä'lä de espe'rä

I haven't felt well the last few days.
Hace algunos días que no me encuentro bien.
ä'se älgōō'nōs dē'äs ke nō me enkōō·en'trō byen

My *head (throat, stomach)* hurts.
Me duele *la cabeza (la garganta, el estómago).*
me dōō·e'le lä käbe'sä (lä gärgän'tä, el estō'mägō)

It hurts here.
Me duele aquí.
me dōō·e'le äkē'

I've got a *severe (sharp, dull)* pain here.
Tengo aquí dolores *fuertes (agudos, sordos).*
ten'gō äkē' dōlō'res fōō·er'tes (ägōō'dōs, sōr'dōs)

I've got a (high) fever.   **I've caught a cold.**
Tengo (mucha) fiebre.   Estoy resfriado./ *Sp* Estoy constipado.
ten'gō (mōō'tshä) fye'bre   estoi' resfrē·ä'dō/estoi' kōnstēpä'dō

I can't handle *the heat (food)* here.
Me sienta mal *el calor (la comida).*
me syen'tä mäl el kälōr' (lä kōmē'dä)

I must have done something to my stomach.   **I ate ...**
Tengo una indigestión.   Comí ...
ten'gō ōō'nä ēndēhestyōn'   kōmē' ...

I threw up.   **I feel sick.**
Vomité.   Me siento mal.
vomēte'   me syen'tō mäl

I have *no appetite (diarrhea)*.   **I'm constipated.**
No tengo apetito. (Tengo diarrea.)   Tengo estreñimiento.
nō ten'gō äpetē'tō (ten'gō dyärre'ä)   ten'gō estrenyēmyen'tō

My eyes hurt.
Me duelen los ojos.
me doo·e'len lōs ō'hōs

I have an earache.
Me duele el oído.
me doo·e'le el ō·ē'dō

I can't sleep.
No puedo dormir.
nō poo·e'dō dōrmēr'

I feel nauseated.
Me mareo.
me märe'ō

I've got chills.
Tengo escalofríos.
ten'gō eskälōfrē'ōs

I can't move ...
No puedo mover ...
nō poo·e'dō mōver' ...

I'm diabetic.
Soy diabético.
soi dyäbe'tēkō

I'm expecting a baby.
Estoy embarazada.
estoi' embäräsä'dä

I fell.
Me he caído.
me e kī'dō

I sprained my ankle.
Me he torcido el tobillo.
me e tōrsē'dō el tōbē'lyō

... is (are) swollen.
... está(n) hinchado(s).
... estä(n)' ēntshä'dō(s)

Is it serious?
¿Es algo grave?
es äl'gō grä've

I'm feeling a little (much) better.
Ya me siento algo (mucho) mejor.
yä me syen'tō äl'gō (moo'tshō) mehōr'

Could you give me a prescription for ...?
¿Puede recetarme ...?
poo·e'de resetär'me ...

I'd like to be vaccinated against ...
Quiero vacunarme contra ...
kye'rō väkoonär'me kōn'trä ...

The doctor will tell you:

Take your clothes off, please.
Quítese la ropa, por favor.
kē'tese lä rō'pä, pōr fävōr'

Breathe deeply.
Respire profundamente.
respē're prōfoondämen'te

Does this hurt?
¿Le duele aquí?
le doo·e'le äkē'

Open your mouth.
Abra la boca.
ä'brä lä bō'kä

Let me see your tongue.
¡Saque la lengua!
sä′ke lä len′gōō·ä

Cough!
¡Tosa!
tō′sä

What have you been eating?
¿Qué ha comido usted?
ke ä kōmē′dō ōōste′

How long have you been ill?
¿Desde cuándo está enfermo?
dez′de kōō·än′dō estä′ enfer′mō

We'll have to do a *blood test (urinalysis)*.
Es necesario hacer un *análisis de sangre (de orina)*.
es nesesär′yō äser′ ōōn änä′lēsēs de säng′gre (de ōrē′nä)

You're going to need an operation.
Tiene que someterse a una operación.
tye′ne ke sōmeter′se ä ōō′nä ōperäsyōn′

I'll have to refer you to ...
Le remitiré a ...
le remētēre′ ä ...

You must stop *drinking (smoking)*.
Debe abstenerse de *beber (fumar)*.
de′be äbstener′se de beber′ (fōōmär′)

You'll have to stay *in bed (on a strict diet)*.
Debe *quedarse en cama (seguir una dieta rigurosa)*.
de′be kedär′se en kä′mä (segēr′ ōō′nä dye′tä rēgōōrō′sä)

Spend the next few days in bed.
Guarde cama algunos días.
gōō·är′de kä′mä älgōō′nōs dē′äs

Take *two tablets (ten drops)* three times a day.
Tome *dos comprimidos (diez gotas)* tres veces al día.
tō′me dōs kōmprēmē′dōs (dyes gō′täs) tres ve′ses äl dē′ä

It's nothing serious.
No es nada grave.
nō es nä′dä grä′ve

Come back and see me a week from now.
Vuelva a verme dentro de ocho días.
vōō·el′vä ä ver′me den′trō de ō′tshō dē′äs

Parts of the Body and their Functions

abdomen	abdomen *m*	äbdō'men
ankle	tobillo *m*	tōbē'lyō
appendix	apéndice *m*	äpen'dēse
arm	brazo *m*	brä'sō
armpit	sobaco *m*, axila *f*	sōbä'kō, äksē'lä
artery	arteria *f*	ärter'yä
back	espalda *f*	espäl'dä
bile	bilis *f*	bē'lēs
bladder	vejiga *f*	ve*h*ē'gä
blood	sangre *f*	säng'gre
blood pressure	presión *f* de la sangre, tensión *f*	presyōn' de lä säng'gre, tensyōn'
body	cuerpo *m*	koo·er'pō
bone	hueso *m*	oo·e'sō
bowel movement	deposición *f*	depōsēsyōn'
brain	cerebro *m*	sere'brō
breast	pecho *m*, seno *m*	pe'tshō, se'nō
breathing	respiración *f*	respēräsyōn'
buttocks	nalgas *fpl*	näl'gäs
calf	pantorilla *f*	päntōrē'lyä
cheek	mejilla *f*	me*h*ē'lyä
chest	pecho *m*	pe'tshō
chin	barbilla *f*, mentón *m*	bärbē'lyä, mentōn'
circulation	circulación *f*	sērkooläsyōn'
collarbone	clavícula *f*	klävē'koolä
digestion	digestión *f*	dē*h*estyōn'
disc	disco *m* intervertebral	dēs'kō ēnterverte-bräl'
ear	oreja *f*	ōre'*h*ä
eardrum	tímpano *m*	tēm'pänō
elbow	codo *m*	kō'dō
eye	ojo *m*	ō'*h*ō
– eyeball	globo *m* del ojo	glō'bō del ō'*h*ō
– eyelid	párpado *m*	pär'pädō
face	cara *f*, rostro *m*	kä'rä, rōs'trō
finger	dedo *m*	de'dō
– thumb	pulgar *m*	poolgär'
– index finger	dedo *m* índice	de'dō ēn'dēse
– middle finger	dedo *m* del corazón	de'dō del kōräsōn'

– ring finger	dedo *m* anular	de′dō änōōlär′
– pinkie	dedo *m* meñique	de′dō menyē′ke
foot	pie *m*	pye
forehead	frente *f*	fren′te
frontal sinus	seno *m* frontal	se′nō frōntäl′
gall bladder	vesícula *f*	väsē′kōōlä
genital organs	órganos *mpl* genitales	ōr′gänōs henētä′les
gland	glándula *f*	glän′dōōlä
hair	pelo *m*, cabello *m*	pe′lō, käbe′lyō
hand	mano *f*	mä′nō
head	cabeza *f*	käbe′sä
heart	corazón *m*	kōräsōn′
heel	talón *m*	tälōn′
hip	cadera *f*	käde′rä
intestine	intestino *m*	ēntestē′nō
– large intestine	intestino *m* grueso	ēntestē′nō grōō·e′sō
– small intestine	intestino *m* delgado	ēntestē′nō delgä′dō
jaw	maxilar *m*, mandíbula *f*	mäksēlär′, mändē′bōōlä
– upper jaw	maxilar *m*, mandíbula *f* superior	-sōōperyōr′
– lower jaw	maxilar *m*, mandíbula *f* inferior	-ēnferyōr′
joint	articulación *f*	ärtēkōōläsyōn′
kidney	riñón *m*	rēnyōn′
knee	rodilla *f*	rōdē′lyä
kneecap	rótula *f*	rō′tōōlä
larynx	laringe *f*	lärēn′he
leg	pierna *f*	pyer′nä
– thigh	muslo *m*	mōōs′lō
limbs	miembros *mpl*	myemb′rōs
lip	labio *m*	lä′byō
liver	hígado *m*	ē′gädō
lung	pulmón *m*	pōōlmōn′
maxillary sinus	seno *m* maxilar	se′nō mäksēlär′
menstruation	menstruación *f*, período *m*	menstrōō·äsyōn′, perē′ōdō

metabolism	metabolismo *m*	metäbōlēz'mō
mouth	boca *f*	bō'kä
mucous membrane	mucosa *f*	mōōkō'sä
muscle	músculo *m*	mōōs'kōōlō
nail	uña *f*	ōō'nyä
neck	cuello *m*	kōō·e'lyō
– nape of the neck	nuca *f*	nōō'kä
nerve	nervio *m*	ner'vyō
nerves	nervios *mpl*	ner'vyōs
nose	nariz *f*	närēs'
palate	paladar *m*	pälädär'
pancreas	páncreas *m*	pän'kre·äs
pelvis	pelvis *f*	pel'vēs
penis	pene *m*	pe'ne
pregnancy	embarazo *m*	embärä'sō
respiration	respiración *f*	respēräsyōn'
rib	costilla *f*	kōstē'lyä
shin	espinilla *f*	espēnē'lyä
shoulder	hombro *m*	ōm'brō
sinew	tendón *m*	tendōn'
skin	piel *f*, cutis *m*	pyel, kōō'tēs
skull	cráneo *m*	krä'ne·ō
sole	planta *f*	plän'tä
spinal cord	médula *f* espinal	me'dōōlä espēnäl'
spine	espina *f* dorsal	espē'nä dōrsäl'
spleen	bazo *m*	bä'sō
stomach	estómago *m*	estō'mägō
temple	sien *f*	syen
tendon	tendón *m*	tendōn'
thorax	tórax *m*	tōräks'
throat	garganta *f*	gärgän'tä
toe	dedo *m* del pie	de'dō del pye
tongue	lengua *f*	len'gōō·ä
tonsils	amígdalas *fpl*	ämēg'däläs
tooth	diente *m*	dyen'te
urine	orina *f*	ōrē'nä
uterus	útero *m*	ōō'terō
vagina	vagina *f*	vähē'nä
vein	vena *f*	ve'nä
wrist	muñeca *f*	mōōnye'kä

What's wrong?

abscess	absceso *m*	äbse′sō
AIDS	SIDA *m*	sē′dä
airsickness	mareo *m*	märe′ō
allergy	alergia *f*	äler*h*yä
anemia	anemia *f*	äne′myä
appendicitis	apendicitis *f*	äpendēsē′tēs
arthritis	artritis *f*	ärtrē′tēs
asthma	asma *m*	äz′mä
attack	ataque *m*	ätä′ke
bite *(insect)*	mordedura *f/Mex* mordida *f*	mōrdedoo′rä/mōrdē′dä
bleeding	hemorragia *f*	emōrrä′hyä
blood poisoning	intoxicación *f* de la sangre	ēntōksēkäsyōn′ de lä säng′gre
blood pressure	presión *f* de la sangre, tensión *f*	presyōn′ de lä säng′gre, tensyōn′
– high pressure	tensión *f* alta	tensyōn′ äl′tä
– low pressure	tensión *f* baja	tensyōn′ bä′hä
breathing problems	dificultades *fpl* respiratorias	dēfēkooltä′des respērätōr′yäs
bronchitis	bronquitis *f*	brōngkē′tēs
bruise	contusión *f*	kōntoosyōn′
burn	quemadura *f*	kemädoo′rä
cardiac infarction	infarto *m* del miocardio	ēnfär′tō del mē·ōkär′dyō
chicken pox	varicela *f*	värēse′lä
chills	escalofríos *mpl*	eskälōfrē′ōs
cholera	cólera *m*	kō′lerä
circulatory problems	trastornos *mpl* circulatorios	trästor′nōs sērkoolätōr′yōs
cold	resfriado *m*	resfrē·ä′dō
colic	cólico *m*	kō′lēkō
concussion	conmoción *f* cerebral	kōnmōsyōn′ serebräl′
conjunctivitis	conjuntivitis *f*	kōn*h*oontēvē′tēs
constipation	estreñimiento *m*	estrenyēmyen′tō
cough	tos *f*	tōs
cramps	calambres *mpl*	käläm′bres
cut	herida *f*, corte *m*	erē′dä, kōr′te

diabetes	diabetes *f*	dyäbe′tes
diarrhea	diarrea *f*	dyärre′ä
diphtheria	difteria *f*	dēfte′ryä
disease	enfermedad *f*	enfermedäd′
– **contagious disease** .	enfermedad *f* contagiosa	enfermedäd′ kōntä*h*yō′sä
dislocation	dislocación *f*	dēslōkäsyōn′
dizziness	mareo *m*, vértigo *m* ...	märe′ō, ver′tēgō
dysentery	disentería *f*	dēsenterē′ä
fainting	desmayo *m*	desmä′yō
fever	fiebre *f*/*Mex* calentura *f*	fye′bre/kälentoo′rä
flatulence	flatulencia *f*	flätoolen′syä
flu	gripe *f*	grē′pe
food poisoning	intoxicación *f* alimenticia	ēntōksēkäsyōn′ älēmentē′syä
fracture	fractura *f*/*Mex a* quebradura *f*	fräktoo′rä/ kebrädoo′rä
gall stones	cálculos *mpl* biliares ...	käl′koolōs bēlyä′res
German measles	rubéola *f*	roobe′ōlä
hay fever	fiebre *f* del heno	fye′bre del e′nō
heart attack	ataque *m* cardíaco	ätä′ke kärdē′äkō
heart problems	problemas *mpl* cardíacas	prōble′mäs kärdē′äkäs
heartburn	ardor *m* del estómago .	ärdōr′ del estō′mägō
hemorrhage	hemorragia *f*	emōrrä′*h*yä
hemorrhoids	hemorroides *fpl*	emōrroi′des
hoarseness	ronquera *f*	rōnke′rä
hypertension	hipertensión *f*	ēpertensyōn′
indigestion	trastornos *mpl* digestivos	trästōr′nōs dē*h*estē′vōs
inflammation	inflamación *f*	ēnflämäsyōn′
influenza	gripe *f*	grē′pe
injury	herida *f*, lesión *f*	erē′dä, lesyōn′
insomnia	insomnio *m*	ēnsōm′nyō
intestinal catarrh	enteritis *f*	enterē′tēs
jaundice	ictericia *f*	ēkterē′syä
kidney stones	cálculos *mpl* renales ...	käl′koolōs renä′les
liver problems	trastornos *mpl* del hígado	trästōr′nōs del ē′gädō

measles	sarampión *m*	särämpyōn'
middle ear inflammation	otitis *f* media	ōtē'tēs me'dyä
mumps	paperas *fpl*	päpe'räs
nausea	náuseas *fpl*	nou'se·äs
nephritis	nefritis *f*	nefrē'tēs
neuralgia	neuralgia *f*	ne-ōōräl'*h*yä
nosebleed	hemorragia *f* nasal	emōrrä'*h*yä näsäl'
pain	dolor *m*	dōlōr'
paralysis	parálisis *f*	pärä'lēsēs
peptic ulcer	úlcera *f* gástrica	ōōl'serä gäs'trēkä
piles	almorranas *fpl*	älmōrrä'näs
pleurisy	pleuresía *f*	ple·ōōresē'ä
pneumonia	pulmonía *f*	pōōlmōnē'ä
poisoning	envenenamiento *m*, intoxicación *f*	envenenämyen'tō, ēntōksēkäsyōn'
pregnancy	embarazo *m*	embärä'sō
pulled tendon	distorsión *f* de un tendón	dēstōrsyōn' de ōōn tendōn'
rash	erupción *f* cutánea/*Mex* salpullido *m*	erōōpsyōn' kōōtä'ne·ä/sälpōōlye'dō
rheumatism	reumatismo *m*	re·ōōmätēz'mō
scarlet fever	escarlatina *f*	eskärlätē'nä
sciatica	ciática *f*	syä'tēkä
seasickness	mareo *m*	märe'ō
shock	shock *m* nervioso	shōk nervyō'sō
skin disease	enfermedad *f* de la piel	enfermedäd' de lä pyel
skin lesion	lesión *f* de la piel	lesyōn' de lä pyel
smallpox	viruela *f*	vērōō·e'lä
sore throat	dolor *m* de garganta	dōlōr' de gärgän'tä
sprain	torcedura *f*, falseo *m*	tōrsedōō'rä, fälse'ō
sting	picadura *f*	pēkädōō'rä
stitch in the side	puntadas *fpl* en el costado	pōōntä'däs en el kōstä'dō
stomach pain	dolores *mpl* de estómago	dōlō'res de estō'mägō
stroke	apoplejía *f*	äpōple*h*ē'ä
sunburn	quemadura *f* del sol	kemädōō'rä del sōl
sunstroke	insolación *f*	ēnsōläsyōn'
suppuration	supuración *f*	sōōpōōräsyōn'
swelling	hinchazón *f*	ēntshäsōn'

tetanus	tétano *m*	te'tänō
tonsillitis	anginas *fpl*	änhē'näs
tumor	tumor *m*	tōōmōr'
typhoid fever	tifoidea *f*	tēfoide'ä
ulcer	úlcera *f*	ōōl'serä
vomiting	náuseas *fpl*	nou'se·äs
wound	herida *f*	erē'dä

In the Hospital

anesthetic	anestesia *f*	äneste'syä
bed	cama *f* (de ruedas)	kä'mä (de rōō·e'däs)
bed pan	orinal *m*, bacín *m*	ōrēnäl', bäsēn'
blood count	hemograma *m*	emōgrä'mä
blood test	muestra *f* de sangre . . .	mōō·es'trä de säng'gre
blood transfusion . .	transfusión *f* de sangre	tränsfōōsyōn' de säng'gre
diagnosis	diagnóstico *m*	dyägnō'stēkō
discharge	dar de alta	där de äl'tä
doctor	médico *m*	me'dēkō
examination	1) *in lab:* análisis *m*	änä'lēsēs
	2) *of person:* reconoci-miento *m*	rekōnōsēmyen'tō
examine	examinar, reconocer . .	eksämēnär', rekōnōser'
head nurse	enfermera *f* jefe	enferme'rä *he*'fe
hospital	hospital *m*	ōspētäl'
infusion	infusión *f*	ēnfōōsyōn'
injection	inyección *f*	ēnyeksyōn'
intensive care unit	unidad *f* de cuidados in-tensivos	ōōnēdäd' de kōō·ē-dä'dōs ēntensē'vōs
medical director . . .	médico-jefe *m*	me'dēkō-*he*'fe
night nurse	enfermera *f* de noche . .	enferme'rä de nō'tshe
nurse	enfermera *f*	enferme'rä
operate	operar	ōperär'
operation	operación *f*	ōperäsyōn'
patient	paciente *m* & *f*	päsyen'te
surgeon	cirujano *m*	sērōō*ha*'nō

temperature	temperatura *f*	temperätoo'rä
temperature chart	curva *f* de temperatura	koor'vä de tempe-rätoo'rä
visiting hours	horas *fpl* de visita	ō'räs de vēsē'tä
ward	unidad *f*, sección *f*	ōōnēdäd', seksyōn'
x-ray *(verb)*	hacer una radiografía	äser' oo'nä rädyō-gräfē'ä

Nurse, could you give me a *pain killer (sleeping pill)*?

¿Podría darme algo contra *el dolor (para dormir)*?

pōdrē'ä där'me äl'gō kōn'trä el dōlōr' (pä'rä dōrmēr')

When can I get out of bed?

¿Cuándo puedo levantarme?

koo·än'dō poo·e'dō leväntär'me

What's the diagnosis?

¿Cuál es el diagnóstico?

koo·äl' es el dyägnōs'tēkō

At the Dentist's

Where is there a dentist here?

¿Dónde hay un dentista por aquí?

dōn'de ī ōon dentēs'tä pōr äkē'

I'd like to make an appointment.

Quisiera pedir hora (cita).

kēsye'rä pedēr ō'rä (sē'tä)

I've got a toothache.

Tengo dolor de muelas.

ten'gō dōlōr' de moo·e'läs

This tooth hurts.

Me duele este diente.

me doo·e'le es'te dyen'te

– up here (an upper tooth).

– arriba.

– ärrē'bä

– down here (a lower tooth).

– abajo.

– äbä'hō

I've lost a filling.

Se ha caído una calza/*Sp* un empaste.

se ä kä·ē'dō oo'nä käl'sä/oon empäs'te

This tooth is loose.

Este diente se mueve.

es'te dyen'te se moo·e've

Does this tooth have to be pulled?

¿Es necesario sacar este diente?

es nesesär'yō säkär' es'te dyen'te

... broke off.

... está roto.

... estä' rō'tō

Can you do a temporary repair on this tooth?

¿Puede tratarme provisionalmente este diente?

poo·e'de trätär'me prōvēsyōnälmen'te es'te dyen'te

Can you fix these dentures?

¿Puede reparar esta dentadura postiza?

poo·e'de repärär' es'tä dentädoo'rä pōstē'sä

*Please don't *eat anything (smoke)* for two hours.
¿Por favor, no *coma (fume)* hasta dentro de dos horas.
pōr fàvōr', nō kō'mä (foo'me) äs'tä den'trō de dōs ō'räs

When do you want me to come back?
¿Cuándo tengo que volver?
koo·än'dō ten'gō ke vōlver'

anesthesia	anestesia *f*	äneste'syä
braces	aparato *m* dental, frenillo *m*	äpärä'tō dentäl', frenē'lyō
bridge	puente *m* dental	poo·en'te dentäl'
cavities	caries *fpl*	kär'yes
crown	corona *f*	kōrō'nä
dental clinic	clínica *f* dental	klē'nēkä dentäl'
dentist	dentista *m*	dentēs'tä
dentures	dentadura *f* postiza	dentädoo'rä pōstē'sä
extract	sacar, extraer	säkär', eksträ·er'
false tooth	diente *m* de espiga	dyen'te de espē'gä
fill	calzar/*Sp* empastar	kälsär'/empästär'
filling	calza *f*/*Sp* empaste *m*	käl'sä/empäs'te
gums	encías *fpl*	ensē'äs
incisor	diente *m* incisivo	dyen'te ēnsēsē'vō
injection	inyección *f*	ēnyeksyōn'
jaw	mandíbula *f*	mändē'boolä
molar	muela *f*	moo·e'lä
nerve	nervio *m*	ner'vyō
oral surgeon	cirujano *m* oral	sēroo*h*ä'nō ōräl'
orthodontist	ortodoncista *m*	ōrtōdōnsēs'tä
plate	plancha *f*	plän'tshä
root	raíz *f* del diente	rä·ēs' del dyen'te
root canal work	tratamiento *m* de la raíz	trätämyen'tō de lä rä·ēs'
tartar	sarro *m* dental, tártaro *m*	sä'rrō dentäl', tär'tärō
temporary filling	empaste *m* provisional	empäs'te prōvēsyōnäl'
tooth	diente *m*	dyen'te
toothache	dolor *m* de muelas	dōlōr' de moo·e'läs
wisdom tooth	muela *f* del juicio	moo·e'lä del *h*oo·ē'syō

Taking a Cure

bath	baño *m.*	bä'nyō
bath attendant	bañero *m.*	bänye'rō
convalescent home	casa *f* de reposo	kä'sä de repō'sō
cure	cura *f,* tratamiento. *m*	kōō'rä, trätä-myen'tō
cure tax	impuesto *m* de turismo	impōō·es'tō de tōōrĕz'mō
diet	régimen *m,* dieta. *f.*	re'hēmen, dye'tä
gymnastics	gimnasia *f.*	hēmnä'syä
health resort	estación *f* climática	estäsyōn' klēmä'tēkä
hot spring	fuente *f* termal	fōō·en'te termäl'
inhale	inhalar	ēnälär'
massage *(noun)*	masaje *m.*	mäsä'he
massage *(verb)*	dar masaje	där mäsä'he
masseur	masajista *m.*	mäsähēs'tä
masseuse	masajista *f.*	mäsähēs'tä
medicinal spring	aguas *fpl* medicinales	ä'gōō·äs medēsēnä'les
mineral bath	baño *m* de aguas minerales	bä'nyō de ä'gōō·äs mēnerä'les
mineral spring	aguas *fpl* minerales	ä'gōō·äs mēnerä'les
minerals	minerales *mpl*	mēnerä'les
mud	lodo. *m.*	lō'dō
mud bath	baño *m* de lodo	bä'nyō de lō'dō
mud pack	envoltura *f.*	envōltōō'rä
radiation therapy	radioterapia. *f.*	rädyōterä'pyä
rest cure	cura *f* de reposo	kōō'rä de repō'sō
sanatorium	sanatorio *m.*	sänätōr'yō
sauna	sauna *f.*	sou'nä
sea water	agua *f* de mar	ä'gōō·ä de mär
short wave	onda *f* corta	ōn'dä kōr'tä
spa	balneario *m.*	bälne·är'yō
steam bath	baño *m* de vapor, baño *m* turco	bä'nyō de väpōr', bä'nyō tōōr'kō
sunlamp	lámpara *f* solar ultravioleta	läm'pärä sōlär' ōōlträvyōle'tä
ultrasonics	ultrasonido *m*	ōōlträsōnē'dō

CONCERT, THEATER, MOVIES

Box Office

What's on tonight?
¿Qué dan esta noche?
ke dän es'tä nō'tshe

When does *the performance (the concert)* start?
¿A qué hora empieza *la función (el concierto)*?
ä ke ō'rä empye'sä lä fōōnsyōn' (el kōnsyer'tō)

Where can we get tickets?
¿Dónde se venden (se despachan) los boletos/*Sp* las entradas?
dōn'de se ven'den (se despä'tshän) lōs bōle'tōs/läs enträ'däs

Are there any discounts for …?
¿Hay una reducción del precio para …?
ī ōō'nä redōōksyōn' del pre'syō pä'rä …

Are there still tickets available for *this (tomorrow)* evening?
¿Quedan boletos/*Sp* entradas/para *esta noche (mañana)*?
ke'dän bōle'tōs/enträ'däs/pä'rä es'tä nō'tshe (mänyä'nä)

One ticket in the *third (tenth)* row, please.
Un asiento en la *tercera (décima)* fila, por favor.
ōōn äsyen'tō en lä terse'rä (de'sēmä) fē'lä, pōr fä'vōr'

Two seats in the third row, orchestra, please.
Dos asientos en el patio (la luneta), tercera fila, por favor.
dōs äsyen'tōs en el pä'tyō (lä lōōne'tä), terse'rä fē'lä, pōr fävōr'

– in the middle.	– on the side.
– en el centro.	– lateral(es).
– en el sen'trō	– läteräl'(es)

Concert, Theater

accompaniment	.....	acompañamiento *m*	...	äkōmpänyä-myen'tō
act	....	acto *m*	....	äk'tō
actor	....	actor *m*	....	äktōr'
actress	....	actriz *f*	....	äktrēs'

advance ticket sales .	venta *f* anticipada	ven'tä äntēsēpä'dä
alto	alto *m*	äl'tō
applause	aplausos *mpl*	äplou'sōs
aria	aria *f*	är'yä
ballet	ballet *m*	bäle'
balcony	paraíso *m*/*Mex* chilla *f* .	pärä·ē'sō/tshē'lyä
band	conjunto *m*, banda *f* ..	kōnhōōn'tō, bän'dä
baritone	baritono *m*	bärē'tōnō
bass	bajo *m*	bä'hō
box office	taquilla *f*	täkē'lyä
box seats	palcos *mpl*	päl'kōs
chamber music	música *f* de cámara ...	mōō'sēkä de kä'märä
check room	guardarropa *m*	gōō·ärdärrō'pä
chorus	coro *m*	kō'rō
coat check	ficha *f* del guardarropa	fē'tshä del gōō·ärdärrō'pä
comedy	comedia *f*	kōme'dyä
composer	compositor *m*	kōmpōsētōr'
concert	concierto *m*	kōnsyer'tō
concert hall	sala *f* de conciertos	sä'lä de kōnsyer'tōs
conductor	director *m* de orquesta	dērektōr' de ōrkes'tä
contralto	contralto *m*	kōnträl'tō
costumes	trajes *mpl*	trä'hes
costume designer	figurinista *m*	fēgōōrēnēs'tä
curtain	telón *m*	telōn'
curtain time	comienzo *m*	kōmyen'sō
dancer	bailarín *m*	bīlärēn'
director	director *m*	dērektōr'
drama	drama *m*	drä'mä
dress circle	anfiteatro *m*	änfēte·ä'trō
duet	dúo *m*	dōō'ō
final curtain	fin *m*	fēn
grand piano	piano *m* de cola	pē·ä'nō de kō'lä
intermission	descanso *m*, intermedio *m*, entreacto *m*	deskän'sō, ēnterme'dyō, entre·äk'tō
libretto	libreto *m*	lēbre'tō
lobby	foyer *m*	fōyer' (fōye')
music	música *f*	mōō'sēkä
musical	musical *m*	mōōsēkäl'

note	nota *f*	nō´tä
opera	ópera *f*	ō´perä
opera glasses	gemelos *mpl* (de teatro)	*h*eme´lōs (de te·ä´trō)
operetta	opereta *f*	ōpere´tä
orchestra	orquesta *f*	ōrkes´tä
orchestra seats	patio *m* (de butacas), platea *f*/luneta *f*	pä´tyō (de bōōtä´käs), pläte´ä/lōōne´tä
overture	obertura *f*	ōbertōō´rä
part/role	papel *m*	päpel´
– leading role	papel *m* principal	päpel´ prēnsēpäl´
performance	representación *f*	representäsyōn´
pianist	pianista *m*	pē·änes´tä
piano recital	recital *m* (de piano)	resētäl´ (de pē·ä´nō)
piece of music	composición *f*	kōmpōsēsyōn´
play	pieza *f* de teatro	pye´sä de te·ä´trō
producer	productor *m*	prōdōōktōr´
production	puesta *f* en escena	pōō·es´tä en ese´nä
program	programa *m*	prōgrä´mä
scenery/settings	decoración *f*	dekōräsyōn´
set designer	escenógrafo *m*	esenō´gräfō
singer	cantante *m*	käntän´te
singing	canto *m*	kän´tō
soloist	solista *m* & *f*	sōlēs´tä
song	canción *f*	känsyōn´
– folk song	canción *f* popular	känsyōn´ pōpōōlär´
song recital	recital *m* (de canto)	resētäl´ (de kän´tō)
soprano	soprano *m*	sōprä´nō
stage	escena *f*, escenario *m*	ese´nä, esenär´yō
stage director	director *m* de escena	dērektōr´ de ese´nä
symphony concert	concierto *m* sinfónico	kōnsyer´tō sēnfō´nēkō
tenor	tenor *m*	tenōr´
theater	teatro *m*	te·ä´trō
theater schedule	programa *m*	prōgrä´mä
ticket	boleto *m*/*Sp* entrada *f*	bōle´tō/enträ´dä
ticket sales	despacho *m* de localidades	despä´tshō de lōkälēdä´des
tragedy	tragedia *f*	trä*h*e´dyä
violin recital	recital *m* (de violín)	resētäl´ (de vē·ōlēn´)
work	obra *f*	ō´brä

Movies

What's on tonight at the movies?
¿Qué película ponen *or* dan hoy?
ke pelē'kōōlä pō'nen (dän) oi

What time does *the box office open (the film start)*?
¿Cuándo empieza *la venta de boletos/Sp entradas (la película)*?
kōō·än'dō empye'sä lä ven'tä de bōle'tōs/entrā'däs (lä pelē'kōōlä)

How long is the picture?
¿Cuánto dura la sesión?
kōō·än'tō dōō'rä lä sesyōn'

audience	espectadores *mpl*	espektädō'res
auditorium	sala *f*	sä'lä
cartoon	dibujos *mpl* animados/	dēbōō'hōs änē-
	Am a monitos *mpl*	mä'dōs/mōnē'tōs
cinema	cine *m*	sē'ne
color film	película *f* en color	pelē'kōōlä en kōlōr'
documentary	documental *m*	dōkōōmentäl'
drive-in movie	cine *m* al aire libre	sē'ne äl ī're lē'bre
dubbed	doblado	dōblä'dō
dubbing	doblaje *m*	dōblä'he
educational film	documental *m*	dōkōōmentäl'
feature film	largometraje *m*	lärgōmeträ'he
film	película *f*, film(e) *m*	pelē'kōōlä, fēlm(e)
film actor	actor *m* de cine	äktōr' de sē'ne
film festival	festival *m* cinematográ-	festēväl' sēnemätō-
	fico	grä'fēkō
film screening	sesión *f* de cine	sesyōn' de sē'ne
motion picture theater	cine *m*	sē'ne
movie	película *f*	pelē'kōōlä
movies	cine *m*	sē'ne
preview	avance *m*	ävän'se
screen	pantalla *f*	päntä'lyä
screenplay	guión *m*	gē·ōn'
short subject	cortometraje *m*	kōrtōmeträ'he
subtitled	subtitulado	sōōbtētōōlä'dō
thriller	película *f* escalofriante	pelē'kōōlä eskälō- frē·än'te
usher	acomodador *m*	äkōmōdädōr'

PASTIMES

Fun and Games

Where is there ...?
¿Dónde hay ...
dōn'de ī ...

a bar	un bar	ōͻn bär
a discothèque	una discoteca	ōͻ'nä dēskōte'kä
an ice skating rink .	una pista de hielo	ōͻ'nä pēs'tä de ye'lō
a miniature golf course	un minigolf	ōͻn mēnēgōlf'
a night club	un club nocturno	ōͻn klōͻb nōktōͻr'nō
a pool hall	una sala de billar	ōͻ'nä sä'lä de bēlyär'
a riding stable	una cuadra	ōͻ'nä kōͻ·ä'drä
a sailing school	una escuela de vela	ōͻ'nä eskōͻ·e'lä de ve'lä
a tennis court	una pista *or* cancha de tenis	ōͻ'nä pēs'tä (kän'tshä) de te'nēs

I'd like to ...
Quisiera ...
kēsye'rä ...

play badminton	jugar al badminton/*Sp* al volante	hōͻ'gär äl bädmēn- tōn'/äl volän'te
play miniature golf	jugar al minigolf	hōͻ'gär äl mēnēgōlf'
play ping pong	jugar al ping pong	hōͻgär' äl pēnpōn'
watch the fashion show	mirar el desfile de mo- das	mē'rär el desfē'le de mō'däs

Do you have television?
¿Tienen televisión?
tye'nen televēsyōn'

Can I listen to the radio here?
¿Puedo escuchar el radio/*Sp* la radio?
pōͻ·e'dō eskōͻtshär' el rä'dyō/lä rä'dyō

What station is that?
¿Qué emisora es ésta?
ke emēsō'rä es es'tä

What's on today?
¿Qué programa hay hoy?
ke prōgrä'mä ī oi

Do you play *chess (ping pong)*?
¿Juega/juegas *(fam)*/ al ajedrez *(ping pong)*?
hōͻ·e'gä/hōͻ·e'gäs/äl ähedres' (pēnpōn')

amusement	pasatiempo *m*	päsätyem'pō
bowling alley	bolera *f*	bōle'rä
card game	juego *m* de cartas	hōō·e'gō de kär'täs
– cut	cortar	kōrtär'
– deal	dar	där
– shuffle	barajar	bärähär'
– ace	as *m*	äs
– jack	valet *m*	välet'
– queen	dama *f*	dä'mä
– king	rey *m*	re'ē
– clubs	tréboles *mpl*	tre'bōles
– diamonds	diamantes *mpl*	dyämän'tes
– hearts	corazones *mpl*	kōräsō'nes
– spades	picos *mpl*	pē'kōs
– joker	comodín *m*	kōmōdēn'
– trick	baza *f*	bä'sä
– trump	triunfo *m*	trē·ōōn'fō
checkers	damas *fpl*	dä'mäs
chess	ajedrez *m*	ähedres'
chessboard	tablero *m*	täble'rō
chessman	pieza *f*	pye'sä
– square	casilla *f*	käsē'lyä
– bishop	alfil *m*	älfēl'
– castle	torre *f*	tō'rre
– king	rey *m*	re'ē
– knight	caballo *m*	käbä'lyō
– pawn, rook	peón *m*	pe·ōn'
– queen	reina *f*	re'ēnä
chip	ficha *f*	fē'tshä
circus	circo *m*	sēr'kō
club	club *m*	klōōb
country fair	fiesta *f* popular	fyes'tä pōpōōlär'
crossword puzzle	crucigrama *m*	krōōsēgrä'mä
dice	dados *mpl*	dä'dōs
– shoot dice	jugar a los dados	hōōgär' ä lōs dä'dōs
gambling casino	casino *m*	käsē'nō
gambling	juego *m*	hōō·e'gō
– banker	banquero *m*	bängke'rō
– bet	apostar	äpōstär'
– draw	mover, jugar	mōver', hōōgär'
– move	jugada *f*	hōōgä'dä

– **piece**	peón *m*, pieza *f*	pe·ōn', pye'sä
– **play**	jugar	*h*ōōgär'
– **stake**	puesta *f*	pōō·es'tä
magazine	revista *f*	revēs'tä
– **fashion magazine**	revista *f* de modas	revēs'tä de mō'däs
– **glossy**	revista *f* ilustrada	revēs'tä ēlōōsträ'dä
newspaper	periódico *m*	peryō'dēkō
party games	juegos *mpl* de sociedad	*h*ōō·e'gōs de sōsye-däd'
pastime	pasatiempo *m*	päsätyem'pō
ping pong	ping pong *m*	pēnpōn'
radio	radio *m*, *Sp f*	ra'dyō
– **FM**	frecuencia *f* modulada	frekōō·en'syä mōdōōlä'dä
– **long wave**	onda *f* larga	ōn'dä lär'gä
– **medium wave**	onda *f* media	ōn'dä me'dyä
– **short wave**	onda *f* corta	ōn'dä kōr'tä
– **radio play**	radioteatro *m*	rä'dyōte·ä'trō
record	disco *m*	dēs'kō
record player	tocadiscos *m*	tōkädēs'kōs
table tennis	ping pong *m*	pēnpōn'
tape recorder	magnetófono *m*	mägnetō'fōnō
television	televisión *f*	televēsyōn'
– **announcer**	presentador *m*	presentädōr'
– **breakdown**	interferencia *f*	ēnterferen'syä
– **news**	noticias *fpl*	notē'syäs
– **program**	programa *m*	prōgrä'mä
– **program schedule**	programas *mpl* de la semana	prōgrä'mäs de lä semä'nä
– **turn off**	apagar	äpägär'
– **turn on**	poner	pōner'
– **television play**	telefilm *m*	telefēlm'

Getting acquainted

Hope you don't mind if I talk to you.
Perdone que me dirija a usted. (*Fam:* Quisiera hablar contigo si no te importa.)
perdō'ne ke me dērē'*h*ä ä ōōste' (kēsye'rä äblär' kōntē'gō sē nō te ēmpōr'tä)

Mind if I join you?
¿Puedo sentarme a su/tu *(fam)*/lado?
po͞o·e'dō sentär'me ä so͞o/to͞o/lä'dō

May I treat you to a *drink (coffee, tea)*?
¿Lo/*Sp* le/te *(fam)*/invito a tomar *algo (un café, un té)*?
lō/le/te/ēmbē'tō ä tōmär' äl'gō (o͞on käfe', o͞on te)

Are you doing anything this evening?
¿Tiene/tienes *(fam)*/un compromiso para esta noche?
tye'ne/tye'nes/o͞on kōmprōmē'sō pä'rä es'tä nō'tshe

Shall we dance?
¿Bailamos?
bīlä'mōs

Is there *a discothèque (a dance hall)* nearby?
¿Hay por aquí *una discoteca (una sala de baile)*?
ī pōr äkē' o͞o'nä dēskōte'kä (o͞o'nä sä'lä de bī'le)

May I have the next dance?
¿Me reserva/reservas *(fam)*/el próximo baile?
me reser'vä/reser'väs/el prō'ksēmō bī'le

We can chat undisturbed here.
Aquí podemos hablar sin que nadie nos moleste.
äkē' pōde'mōs äblär' sēn ke nä'dye nōs mōles'te

May I invite you to a party?
¿Puedo invitarlo/*Sp* le/te *(fam)*/a una fiesta?
po͞o·e'dō ēmbētär'lō/le/te/ä o͞o'nä fyes'tä

I'll be expecting you at ...
Lo/*Sp* le/te *(fam)*/esperaré a las ...
lō/le/te/esperäre' ä läs ...

You look good in that dress.
Ese vestido le/te *(fam)*/queda muy bien.
e'se vestē'dō le/te/ke'dä mo͞o'ē byen

When can you come visit me?
¿Cuándo me va/vas *(fam)*/a visitar?
ko͞o·än'dō me vä/väs/ä vēsētär'

When can we meet again?
¿Cuándo podemos vernos otra vez?
koo·än'dō pōde'mōs ver'nōs ōt'rä ves

May I give you a lift home?
¿Puedo llevarlo/*Sp* le/te *(fam)*/a casa?
poo·e'dō lyevär'lō/le/te/ä kä'sä

Where do you live?
¿Dónde vive/vives *(fam)*?
dōn'de vē've/vē'ves

Won't you come in for a minute?
¿Quiere/quieres *(fam)*/pasar un momentito?
kye're/kye'res/pä'sär oon mōmentē'tō

May I walk part of the way with you?
¿Puedo acompañarlo/*Sp* le/te *(fam)*/un trecho?
poo·e'dō äkōmpänyär'lō/le/te/oon tre'tshō

Thanks very much for a nice evening.
Gracias por una tarde muy agradable.
grä'syäs pōr oo'nä tär'de moo'e ägrädä'ble

accompany	acompañar	äkōmpänyär'
chat	charlar/*Mex a* platicar .	tshärlär'/plätēkär'
dance *(noun)*	baile *m*	bī'le
dance *(verb)*	bailar	bīlär'
dance hall	sala *f* (salón *m*) de baile	sä'lä (salōn') de bī'le
discothèque	discoteca *f*	dēskōte'kä
enjoy oneself	divertirse	dēvertēr'se
expect somebody	esperar a	esperär' ä
flirt	flirteo *m*	flērte'ō
invite	invitar	ēmbētär'
kiss *(noun)*	beso *m*	be'sō
kiss *(verb)*	besar	besär'
live	vivir	vēvēr'
love *(noun)*	amor *m*	ämōr'
love *(verb)*	amar	ämär'
make love	hacer el amor	äser' el ämōr'
meet	encontrarse	enkōnträr'se
meet again	volver a verse	vōlver' ä ver'se
party	fiesta *f*	fyes'tä
take a walk	pasear, dar una vuelta .	päse·är', där oo'nä voo·el'tä
visit	visitar	vēsētär'

On the Beach

Where can we go swimming here?
¿Dónde podemos bañarnos?
dōn'de pōde'mōs bänyär'nōs

Can we go swimming here?
¿Podemos bañarnos aquí?
pōde'mōs bänyär'nōs äkē'

Two tickets (with cabaña), please.
Dos boletos/*Sp* entradas/(con caseta).
dōs bōle'tōs/enträ'däs/(kōn käse'tä)

Can we swim nude here?
¿Podemos bañarnos desnudos aquí?
pōde'mōs bänyär'nōs desnōō'dōs
äkē'

How far out can we swim?
¿Hasta dónde se puede nadar?
äs'tä dōn'de se pōō·e'de nädär'

How *deep (warm)* is the water?
¿Qué *profundidad (temperatura)* tiene el agua?
ke prōfōōndēdäd' (temperätōō'rä) tye'ne el ä'gōō·ä

Is it dangerous for children?
¿Es peligroso para los niños?
es pelēgrō'sō pä'rä lōs nē'nyōs

No swimming!
¡Prohibido bañarse!
prō·ēbē'dō bänyär'se

Is there an undertow here?
¿Hay aquí corrientes?
ī äkē' kōrryen'tes

Where is the lifeguard?
¿Dónde está el vigilante?
dōn'de estä' el vēhēlän'te

A deck chair (umbrella), please.
Por favor, *una hamaca or silla extensible (una sombrilla).*
pōr fàvōr', ōō'nä ämä'kä, sē'lyä ekstensē'ble (ōō'nä sōmbrē'lyä)

How much does ... cost?
¿Cuánto cuesta ...?
kōō·än'tō kōō·es'tä ...

I'd like to rent *a cabaña (boat).*
Quisiera alquilar/*Mex* rentar/*una caseta (un bote).*
kēsye'rä älkēlär'/rentär'/ōō'nä käse'tä (ōōm bō'te)

Where *is (are)* ...?
¿Dónde *está (están)* ...?
dōn'de estä' (estän') ...

I'd like to go water skiing.
Quisiera practicar el esquí acuático.
kēsye'rä präktēkär' el eskē' akōō·ä'tēkō

Where can I go fishing?
¿Dónde se puede pescar?
dōn'de se pōō·e'de peskär'

Would you be good enough to keep an eye on my gear.
Hágame/házme *(fam)*/el favor de cuidar/*Sp* vigilar/mis cosas.
ä'gäme/äz'me/el fàvōr' de kōō·ēdär'/vēhēlär'/mēs kō'säs

air mattress	colchón *m* de aire	kõltshōn' de ī're
air temperature	temperatura *f* del aire	temperätoo'rä del ī're
bathing cap	gorro *m* de baño	gō'rrō de bä'nyō
bathing suit	traje *m* de baño	trä'*he* de bä'nyō
– trunks	bañador *m (Sp)*	bänyädōr'
bathrobe	bata *f/Sp* albornoz *m*	bä'tä/älbōrnōs'
bay	bahía *f*	bä·ē'ä
boat	barca *f*, lancha *f*	bär'kä, län'tshä
– dinghy	bote *m*	bō'te
– motorboat	lancha *f* motora, vola-dora *f*, *Mex* motonauta *f*	län'tshä mōtō'rä, vōlädō'rä, mōtōnou'tä
– pedal boat	patín *m*	pätēn'
– sailboat	barco *m* de vela	bär'kō de ve'lä
cabaña	caseta *f*	käse'tä
dive	bucear	boose·är'
diving board	trampolín *m*	trämpōlēn'
dune	duna *f*	doo'nä
jellyfish	medusa *f/Mex* malagua *f*	medoo'sä/mälä'goo·ä
locker room	vestuario *m*	vestoo·är'yō
non-swimmer	no-nadador *m*	nō-nädädōr'
saline content	salinidad *f*	sälēnēdäd'
sandy beach	playa *f* de arena	plä'yä de äre'nä
scuba diving	bucear	boose·är'
scuba equipment	escafandra *f*, equipo *m* de bucear	eskäfän'drä, ekē'pō de boose·är'
shells	conchas *fpl*	kōn'tshäs
shower	ducha *f*, regadera *f*	doo'tshä, regäde'rä
swim	nadar, bañarse	nädär', bänyär'se
swimmer	nadador *m*	nädädōr'
take a sunbath	tomar el sol	tōmär' el sōl
water	agua *f*	ä'goo·ä
water temperature	temperatura *f* del agua	temperätoo'rä del ä'goo·ä
wave	ola *f*	ō'lä

Sports

What sport events do they have here?

¿Qué pruebas deportivas se organizan aquí?

ke proo·e'bäs depōrtē'väs se ōrgänē'sän äkē'

Where's *the stadium (soccer field)*?
¿Dónde está *el estadio (el campo de fútbol)*?
dōn'de estä' el estä'dyō (el käm'pō de foot'bōl)

... is playing today against ...   **What sports do you like to play?**
Hoy juega ... contra ...   ¿Qué deportes practica/practicas
oi hoo·e'gä ... kōn'trä ...   *(fam)/*?
    ke depōr'tes präktē'kä/präktē'käs/

I'd love to see *the game (race, fight)*.
Tengo ganas de ver *el partido (la carrera, la pelea)*.
ten'gō gä'näs de ver el pärtē'dō (lä kärre'rä, lä pele'ä)

When (Where) **is the soccer game?**
¿*Cuándo (Dónde)* se juega el partido de fútbol?
koo·än'dō (dōn'de) se hoo·e'gä el pärtē'dō de foot'bōl

Can you get us tickets for it?   **Goal!**
¿Podría/podrías *(fam)/*facilitarnos boletos/*Sp* entradas? ¡Gol!
pōdrē'ä/pōdrē'äs/fäsēlētär'nōs bōle'tōs/enträ'däs   gōl

What's the score?   **The score is three to two for ...**
¿Cómo está el partido?   Está tres a dos a favor de ...
kō'mō estä' el pärtē'dō   estä' tres ä dōs ä fävōr' de ...

Is there an *outdoor (indoor)* **swimming pool here?**
¿Hay aquí una piscina/*Mex* alberca/(cubierta)?
ī äkē' oo'nä pēsē'nä/älber'kä/(koobyer'tä)

I'm ...	**I play ...**	**I'm fond of ...**
Soy ...	Juego ...	Soy aficionado a ...
sōi ...	hoo·e'gō ...	sōi äfēsyōnä'dō ä ...

athlete	atleta *m & f*	ätle'tä
auto racing	motorismo *m*	mōtōrēz'mō
– race	carrera *f*	kärre'rä
– race car driver	corredor *m*	kōrredōr'
– racing car	carro *m*/*Sp* coche *m*/de	kä'rrō/kō'tshe/de
	carreras	kärre'räs
basketball	baloncesto *m*	bälōnses'tō
bicycling	ciclismo *m*	sēklēz'mō
– bicycle	bicicleta *f*	bēsēkle'tä
– bicycle race	carrera *f* ciclista	kärre'rä sēklēs'tä
– bicycle rider	ciclista *m*	sēklēs'tä
– ride a bike	ir en bicicleta	ēr en bēsēkle'tä
bowling	bolos *mpl*	bō'lōs
– bowling alley	bolera *f*	bōle'rä

boxing	boxeo *m*	bōkse'ō
– box	boxear	bōkse·är'
– boxer	boxeador *m*	bōkse·ädōr'
bullfight	corrida *f* (de toros)	kōrrē'dä de tō'rōs
– bull	toro *m*	tō'rō
– bullfighter	torero *m*, matador *m*	tōre'rō, mätädōr'
– bullring	plaza *f* de toros	plä'sä de tō'rōs
competition	competición *f*, concurso *m*	kōmpetēsyōn', kōnkōōr'sō
– championship	campeonato *m*	kämpe·ōnä'tō
– defeat	derrota *f*	derrō'tä
– draw	empate *m*	empä'te
– free style	carrera *f* libre	kärre'rä lē'bre
– game	juego *m*	hōō·e'gō
– goal	gol *m*	gōl
– half time	medio tiempo *m*	me'dyō tyem'pō
– match	partido *m*	pärtē'dō
– play	jugar	hōōgär'
– point	punto *m*	pōōn'tō
– practice	entrenarse	entrenär'se
– result	resultado *m*	resōōltä'dō
– start	salida *f*	sälē'dä
– victory	victoria *f*	vēktō'ryä
– win	ganar	gänär'
fencing	esgrima *f*	esgrē'mä
figure skating	patinaje *m* artístico	pätēnä'he ärtēstē'kō
– skate	patinar	pätēnär'
– skates	patines *mpl*	pätē'nes
– skater	patinador *m*	pätēnädōr'
fishing	pesca *f*	pes'kä
– fishing rod	caña *f*	kä'nyä
– go fishing	pescar (con caña)	peskär' (kōn kä'nyä)
– fishing license	licencia *f* de pescar	lēsen'syä de peskär'
golf	golf *m*	gōlf
gymnastics	gimnasia *f*	hēmnä'syä
– gymnast	gimnasta *m* & *f*	hēmnäs'tä
– gymnastics with apparatus	gimnasia *f* con aparatos	hēmnä'syä kōn äpärä'tōs
– horizontal bar	barra *f* fija	bä'rrä fē'hä
– parallel bars	paralelas *fpl*	päräle'läs
– rings	anillas *fpl*	änē'lyäs

handball	balonmano *m*	bälōnmä′nō
hockey	hockey *m*	*hō′*kē
marksmanship	tiro *m*	tē′rō
– clay pigeon shooting	tiro *m* al plato	tē′rō äl plä′tō
– rifle range	campo *m* de tiro	käm′pō de tē′rō
– shoot	tirar	tērär′
– target	blanco	bläng′kō
mountain climbing .	montañismo *m*, alpinismo *m*	mōntänyēz′mō, älpēnēz′mō
– mountain climber	montañero *m*, alpinista *m*	mōntänye′rō, älpēnēs′tä
ninepins	bolos *mpl*	bō′lōs
player	jugador *m*	*hōō*gädōr′
referee	árbitro *m*	är′bētrō
riding	equitación *f*	ekētäsyōn′
– horse	caballo *m*	käbä′lyō
– horse race	carrera *f* de caballos ...	kärre′rä de käbä′lyōs
– jumping	salto *m*	säl′tō
– ride	montar a caballo	mōn′tär ä käbä′lyō
– rider	jinete *m*	*hē*ne′te
rowing	remo *m*	re′mō
– scull	barca *f* de remos	bär′kä de re′mōs
– oarsman	remero *m*	reme′rō
– coxswain	timonel *m*	tēmonel′
sailing	deporte *m* de vela	depōr′te de ve′lä
– sail (*noun*)	vela *f*	ve′lä
– sail (*verb*)	navegar a la vela	nävegär′ ä lä ve′lä
– sailboat	barco *m* de vela	bär′kō de ve′lä
skiing	esquí *m*	eskē′
– ski (*noun*)	esquí *m*	eskē′
– ski (*verb*)	esquiar	eskē·är′
– ski binding	fijación *f*	fē*h*äsyōn′
– ski jump	trampolín *m* de saltos .	trämpōlēn′ de säl′tōs
– ski lift	telesquí *m*	teleskē′
soccer	fútbol *m*	*fōō*t′bōl
– ball	balón *m*	bälōn′
– corner	saque *m* de esquina ...	sä′ke de eskē′nä
– forward	delantero *m*	delänte′rō
– free kick	golpe *m* franco	gōl′pe fräng′kō
– fullback	defensa *m*	defen′sä

– **kick a goal**	meter un gol	meter' ōon gōl
– **goal**	gol *m*	gōl
– **goalie**	portero *m*	pōrte'rō
– **off-side**	fuera de juego	foō·e'rä de hoō·e'gō
– **penalty kick**	penalty *m*	penäl'tē
– **play soccer**	jugar al fútbol	hoōgär' äl foōt'bōl
– **player**	jugador *m*	hoōgädōr'
– **throw-in**	saque *m* de línea	sä'ke de lē'ne·ä
sports	deportes *m*	depōr'tes
– **athletic club**	club *m* deportivo	kloōb depōrtē'vō
– **sports fan**	aficionado *m*	äfēsyōnä'dō
swimming	natación *f*	nätäsyōn'
– **dive**	salto *m*	säl'tō
– **diving board**	trampolín *m*	trämpōlēn'
– **swimmer**	nadador *m*	nädädōr'
team	equipo *m*	ekē'pō
tennis	tenis *m*	te'nēs
– **singles/doubles**	individual/dobles *mpl*	ēndēvēdoō·äl/dō'bles
– **play tennis**	jugar al tenis	hoōgär' äl te'nēs
– **tennis ball**	pelota *f* de tenis	pelō'tä de te'nēs
– **tennis court**	pista *f*, cancha *f* de tenis	pēs'tä, kän'tshä de te'nēs
– **tennis racket**	raqueta *f* de tenis	räke'tä de te'nēs
– **ping pong**	ping pong *m*	pēnpōn'
toboganing	ir en trineo	ēr en trēne'ō
– **toboggan**	trineo *m*	trēne'ō
track and field	atletismo *m* en pista	ätletēz'mō en pēs'tä
umpire	árbitro *m*	är'bētrō
volleyball	vol(e)ibol *m*/*Sp* balónvolea *m*	vōlēbōl'/bälōn'vōle'ä
wrestling	lucha *f*	loō'tshä
– **wrestle**	luchar	loōtshär'
– **wrestler**	luchador *m*	loōtshädōr'

The most popular sport in Spain and Latin America is fútbol *(* soccer *), which draws enormous crowds every week. American football is virtually unknown.*

Signs	APPENDIX		
A LA DERECHA ..	**to the right**	ä lä dere′tshä
A LA IZQUIERDA .	**to the left**	ä lä ēskyer′dä
¡ATENCION!	**Caution!**	ätensyōn′
CABALLEROS	**Men**	käbälye′rōs
CERRAR LA PUERTA	**Close the door**	serrär′ lä pōō·er′tä
¡CUIDADO! ¡PERRO!	**Beware of the dog** ...	kōō·ēdä′dō, pe′rrō
¡DESPACIO!	**Slow!**	despä′syō
¡EMPUJAR!	**Push!**	empōō*h*är′
ENTRADA LIBRE .	**free entrance**	enträ′dä lē′bre
ESTACIONAMIEN-TO/*Sp* APARCA-MIENTO	**Parking**	estäsyōnämyen′tō/äpärkämyen′tō
FUMADORES	**Smokers**	fōōmädō′res
LLEGADA	**Arrival**	lyegä′dä
¡OBRAS!/*Mex* ¡HOMBRES TRABAJANDO! ..	**Construction**	ō′bräs/ōm′bres träbä-*h*än′dō
PARADA	**Stop**	pärä′dä
¡PELIGRO!	**Danger!**	pelē′grō
PRIVADO	**private**	prēvä′dō
PROHIBIDO BAÑARSE	**No Swimming**	prō·ēbē′dō banyär′se
PROHIBIDO EL PASO	**Road Closed**	prō·ēbē′dō el pä′sō
PROHIBIDO FIJAR AFICHES/*Sp* CARTELES ...	**Post no bills**	prō·ēbē′dō fē*h*är′ äfē′tshes/kärte′les
PROHIBIDA LA ENTRADA ...	**No Entry**	prō·ēbē′dä lä enträ′dä
SALIDA	**Exit**	sälē′dä
SE ALQUILA/*Mex* SE RENTA ..	**For Rent**	se älkē′lä/se ren′tä
SEÑORAS	**Ladies**	senyō′räs
SE PROHIBE FUMAR	**No Smoking**	se prō·ē′be fōōmär′
SE VENDE	**For Sale**	se ven′de
¡JALE!/*Sp* ¡TIRAR!	**Pull**	*h*ä′le/tērär′

Abbreviations

a/c	al cuidado de .... [äl kōo·ēdä'dō de]	care of
apdo	apartado (de correos) .... [äpärtä'dō (de kōrre'ōs)]	Post Office Box
avda	avenida [ävenē'dä]	avenue
C/	calle [kä'lye]	street
Cía	Compañía [kōmpänyē'ä]	company
D. Dª ...	Don, Doña [dōn, dō'nyä].....	terms of respect, forms of address
dcha	derecha [dere'tshä]	right
D. F. ...	Distrito Federal .... [dēstrē'tō federäl']	Mexico City (Federal District)
EE. UU.	Estados Unidos .... [estä'dōs ōonē'dōs]	United States
gral. ...	general [heneräl']	general
izq., izda.	izquierda [ēskyer'dä]	left
Kg.	kilogramo [kēlōgrä'mō]	kilogram
Km.	kilómetro [kēlō'metrō]	kilometer
m.	metro [me'trō]	meter
M.N. ...	Moneda Nacional .... [mōne'dä näsyōnäl']	Mexican peso ("national currency")
Nº	número [nōo'merō]	number
pág.	página [pä'hēnä]	page
Ptas. ...	pesetas [pese'täs]	Spanish pesetas
P.V.P. ..	precio de venta al público ..... [pre'syō de ven'tä äl pōo'blēkō]	sale price to the public (Spain)
RENFE .	Red Nacional de los Ferrocarri-les Españoles .... [red näsyōnäl' de lōs ferrōkä-rrē'les espänyō'les]	Spanish national railroad
S. A. ...	Sociedad Anónima .... [sōsyedäd' änō'nēmä]	Corporation, Incorporated
Sr.	Señor [senyōr']	Mr.
Sra.	Señora [senyō'rä]	Mrs.
Srta. ...	Señorita [senyōrē'tä]	Miss
tel., teléf.	teléfono [tele'fōnō]	telephone
Ud.	usted [ōoste']	you
Vd.	usted [ōoste']	you

Weights and Measures

1 millimeter	un milímetro	ōon mēlē'metrō
1 centimeter	un centímetro	ōon sentē'metrō
1 decimeter	un decímetro	ōon desē'metrō
1 meter	un metro	ōon me'trō
1 kilometer	un kilómetro	ōon kēlō'metrō
1 inch	una pie pulgada	ōo'nä pōolgä'dä
1 foot	un pie	ōom pye
1 yard	una yarda	ōo'nä yär'dä
1 (statute) mile	una milla	ōo'nä mē'lyä
1 nautical mile	una milla marítima or náutica	ōo'nä mē'lyä märē'tēmä, nou'tēkä
1 square foot	un pie cuadrado	ōom pye kōo·ädrä'dō
1 square yard	una yarda cuadrada	ōo'nä yär'dä kōo·ädrä'dä
1 square meter	un metro cuadrado	ōon me'trō kōo·ädrä'dō
1 square mile	una milla cuadrada	ōo'nä mē'lyä kōo·ädrä'dä
1 cubic foot	un pie cúbico	ōom pye kōo'bēkō
1 liter	un litro	ōon lē'trō
1 pint	una pinta	ōo'nä pēn'tä
1 quart	un cuarto de galón	ōon kōo·är'tō de gälōn'
1 gallon	un galón	ōon gälōn'
1 ounce	una onza	ōo'nä ōn'sä
1 pound	una libra	ōo'nä lē'brä
1 hundredweight	*approx.* un quintal	ōon kēntäl'
1 ton	una tonelada	ōo'nä tōnelä'dä
a piece (of ...)	una parte, un trozo de	ōo'nä pär'te, ōon trō'sō de
a pair (of ...)	un par de	ōom pär de
a dozen	una docena	ōo'nä dōsē'nä
a pack(et) of	un paquete de	ōom päke'te de

Colors

beige	beige	be′ē*h*e
black	negro	ne′grō
blonde	rubio	rōō′byō
blue	azul	äsōōl′
– light blue	azul claro	äsōōl′ klä′rō
– navy blue	azul marino	äsōōl′ märē′nō
– turquoise	azul turquesa	äsōōl′ tōōrke′sä
brown	marrón/*Mex* café	märrōn′/käfe′
– chestnut brown	castaño	kästä′nyō
brunette	moreno	mōre′nō
color	color	kōlōr′
– colored	de colores	de kōlō′res
– colorful	de muchos colores	de mōō′tshōs kōlō′res
– solid-color	de un solo color	de ōōn sō′lō kōlōr′
gold	dorado	dōrä′dō
gray	gris	grēs
– ash gray	gris ceniza	grēs senē′sä
– dark gray	gris oscuro	grēs ōskōō′rō
– pale gray	gris claro	grēs klä′rō
green	verde	ver′de
– dark green	verde oscuro	ver′de ōskōō′rō
– light green	verde claro	ver′de klä′rō
lavender/mauve	lila, malva	lē′lä, mäl′vä
orange	naranja	närän′*h*ä
pink	rosa	rō′sä
purple	morado	mōrä′dō
red	rojo, colorado	rō*h*ō, kōlōrä′dō
– bright red	rojo vivo	rō′*h*ō vē′vō
– dark red	rojo oscuro	rō*h*ō ōskōō′rō
silver	plateado	pläte·ä′dō
violet	violeta	vyōle′tä
white	blanco	bläng′kō
yellow	amarillo	ämärē′lyō

IMPORTANT GRAMMAR RULES

I. Stress and Accent

1. A word consisting of more than two syllables and ending in **n, s,** or a vowel is stressed on the second last syllable; e.g. *tomo* [tō'mō] I take, *naciones* [näsyō'nes] nations, *joven* [hō'ven] young.

2. A word consisting of more than two syllables and ending in another consonant or in y is stressed on the last syllable; e.g. *papel* [päpel'] paper, *Madrid* [mädrēd'], *estoy* [estōi'] I am.

3. Exceptions to the above rules are indicated by accent marks over the syllable to be stressed; e.g. *está* [estä'] he, she, it is, *nación* [näsyōn'] nation, *jóvenes pl.* [hō'venes] young people, *fácil* [fä'sēl] easy.

4. **i** (and **y** at the end of a word) and **u** next to another vowel are the unstressed (weak) vowels in diphthongs: *auto* [ou'tō] car, *bien* [byen] well, *buey* [bōō·ei'] ox. When i or u are stressed, an accent mark is placed over them.

5. Words of one syllable do not need accent marks, but some are accented in order to distinguish them from words which sound the same but have a different meaning; e.g. *se* [se] -self, *sé* [se] I know.

6. All question words have an accent, e.g. *¿dónde?* where?, *¿quién?* who?.

II. Orthography

Different Spellings for the Same Sound

k = **c:** *saco* [sä'kō] I take out.
qu before e, i: *saque usted* [sä'ke ōōsted'] take out (polite command form)

g = **g:** *pagar* [pägär'] to pay
gu before e, i: *paguemos* [päge'mōs] let's pay

x = **j:** me *dirijo* [me dērē'hō] I turn towards
g before e, i: *dirigirse* [dērēhēr'se] to turn towards

ĭ, j = **i:** *perdió* [perdyō'] he (she) lost
y between vowels: *creyó* [kreyō'] he (she) believed

In Spain:

θ = **z:** la *voz* [lä vōθ] the voice
c before e, i: las *voces* [läs vō'θes] the voices

III. The Article

1. Spanish nouns are either masculine or feminine.

2. The Definite Article:

masculine (*m*): **el** [el], plural (*pl.*) **los** [lōs]; feminine (*f*): **la** [lä], plural **las** [läs]. – *el año* [el ä'nyō] the year, *los años* [lōs ä'nyōs] the years; *el libro* [el lē'brō] the book, *los libros* [lōs lē'brōs] the books; *la casa* [lä kä'sä] the house, *las casas* [läs kä'säs] the houses; *la voz* [lä vōs] the voice, *las voces* [läs vō'ses] the voices.

3. The neuter article **lo** [lō] precedes adjectives when they are used as nouns, numbers and possessive pronouns; e.g. *lo bueno* [lō bōo·e'nō] the good thing, *lo primero* [lō prēme'rō] the first thing, *lo mío* [lō mē·ō] mine.

4. The Indefinite Article:

un *m* [ōon] a, an, **unos** *pl* [ōo'nōs] some, a few **una** *f* [ōo'nä] a, an, **unas** *pl* [ōo'näs] some, a few; e.g.

un año [ōon ä'nyō] a year, *unos años* [ōo'nōs ä'nyōs] some years; *una voz* [ōonä vōs] a voice, *unas voces* [ōo'näs vō'ses] some voices.

5. Before a feminine noun beginning with a stressed a or ha, el is used instead of la and un instead of una; e.g. *el agua* (*f*) [el ä'gōo·ä] the water, *un hacha f* [ōon ä'tshä] an axe; *pl. las, unas.*

IV. The Noun

Plural

1. Nouns and adjectives ending in a vowel form their plurals by adding **-s**; those ending in a consonant or **-y** add **-es**; e.g. *el próximo año* [el prōg'sēmō ä'nyō] next year, *pl. los próximos años*; *un país fértil* [ōom päēs' fer'tēl] a fertile country, *pl. los países fértiles*; *la ley* [lä lei] the law, *pl. las leyes* [läs le'yes].

2. The addition of **-es** changes the accentuation: *la región* [lä rehyōn] the region, *pl. las regiones* [läs rehyō'nes].

V. The Prepositions de and a

1. The preposition **de** [de] is used to indicate possession; in conjunction with the masculine singular definite article (el) it forms the contracted form **del** [del]. When used with the masculine singular el, the preposition **a** forms **al** [äl]; e.g. *la casa* [lä kä'sä] the house, *de la casa, a la casa*; *el mes* [el mes] the month, *del mes, al mes*; *pl. los meses* [lōs me'ses] the months, *de los meses, a los meses.*

2. As in English, subject and object are distinguished by their place in the sentence (preceding or following the verb). When the direct object is a

person or one of the indefinites (alguien, nadie, alguno(s), ninguno(s)) it is preceded by **a**; e.g. *pierdo el tren* [pyer'dō el tren] I miss the train; but: *llamo al camarero* [lyä'mō al kämäre'rō] I call the waiter.

3. When a number or an indefinite article precedes a direct object referring to a person, the **a** is dropped: *busco una secretaria* [boos'kō oo'nä sekretä'ryä] I'm looking for a secretary.

VI. Adjectives and Adverbs

1. Adjectives agree in number and gender with the noun or pronoun they describe.

2. The plural of adjectives is formed in the same way as the plural of nouns.

3. Adjectives ending in **-o** form the feminine by changing the **-o** to **-a**; e.g. *alto* [äl'tō] high, tall, *f alta*; *pl. altos, altas*.

4. All other adjectives have the same form in the masculine and feminine; e.g. *un año feliz* [oon ä'nyō felēs'] a happy year; *una hora feliz* [oo'nä ō'rä felēs'] a happy hour.

5. Adjectives referring to nationality, whatever their ending, can always have a feminine form with **a**; e.g. *español m* [espänyōl'] Spanish, *f española*; as a noun *el español* the Spaniard (*m*), *la española* the Spaniard (*f*).

6. Certain adjectives drop the **-o** when they precede a masculine singular noun, thus *bueno* [booe'·nō] good becomes **buen** [boo·en'], *malo* [mä'lō] bad becomes **mal** [mäl].

7. The adjective usually follows the noun; demonstrative and indefinite adjectives as well as cardinal numbers precede the noun. Other adjectives may also precede the noun for emotional effect.

8. The adverb is formed by adding **-mente** to the feminine singular form of the adjective: e.g. *lento* [len'tō] slow – *lentamente* [lentämen'te] slowly.

9. Irregular Adverbs: **bien** [byen] well, **mal** [mäl] badly.

10. "**Very**" = muy [moo·ē] before adjectives and adverbs; "**very much**" = mucho [moo'tshō] after the verb.

VII. Comparison

1. The comparison of adjectives is formed by placing **más** [mäs] before the adjective; the superlative is obtained by placing the definite article before the comparative; e.g. *más alto* [mäs äl'tō] higher, *el más alto* the highest.

2. Irregular Comparisons: **mejor** [mehōr'] better, **peor** [pe·ōr'] worse; **mayor** [mäyōr] bigger, older, **menor** [menōr'] smaller, younger.

3. **"Than"** after the comparative = que [ke], before numbers de [de], and when the Spanish sentence has two verbs de lo que [de lō ke]; e.g. *España es más grande que Portugal* [Espä'nyä es mäs grän'de ke Pōrtōōgäl'] Spain is bigger than Portugal; *más de tres veces* [mäs de tres ve'ses] more than three times; *España es mas grande de lo que yo pensaba* [Espä'nyä es mäs grän'de de lō ke yō pensä'bä] Spain is bigger than I thought.

VIII. Pronouns

Personal Pronouns

A. Personal Pronouns used in the Accusative and Dative with the Verb

1. Singular (*sg.*)   Plural (*pl.*)

me	[me]	me, to me	*nos*	[nōs]	us, to us
te	[te]	you, to you	*os*	[ōs]	you, to you
lo	[lō]	him, it	*los*	[lōs]	them, you (*m*)
la	[lä]	her, it, you	*las*	[läs]	them, you (*f*)
le	le]	him, you, to him, to her, to you	*les*	[les]	them, you, to them, to you
se	[se]	yourself, himself, herself, itself, yourselves, themselves			

2. Position: The unstressed personal pronouns precede the verb; e.g. *lo sé* [lō se] I know it. However, they are attached to the end of the direct affirmative command, the infinitive and the gerund; e.g. *sígame usted* [sē'gäme ōōsted'] follow me (but: *no me siga usted* [nō me sē'gä ōōsted'] don't follow me).

3. **se** can be used instead of the passive and to express the impersonal form (the English "one"); e.g. *cigarrillos se venden en estancos* [sēgärrē'lyōs se ven'den en estän'kōs] cigarettes are sold in tobacco stores; *aquí se come bien* [äkē' se kō'me byen] one can eat well here.

4. When both the direct and indirect object pronouns are in the third person singular in one sentence, the indirect precedes the direct and is written "**se**" [se] instead of "le" or "les"; le(s) + lo(s), la(s) = se lo(s), la(s).

B. Stressed Personal Pronouns

1. Subject Pronouns:

Singular	Plural
yo [yō] I	*nosotros f -as* [nōsō'trōs, -äs] we
tú [tōō] you (familiar)	*vosotros f -as* [vōsō'trōs, -äs] you (familiar)

él [el] he	*ellos f -as* [e'lyōs, -äs] they
ella [e'lyä] she	*Ustedes* [ōōste'des] you (*pl.*) (polite)
Usted [ōōsted'] you (polite)	

The subject pronoun is usually omitted; it is used when necessary for clarification or emphasis.

2. Pronouns as objects of a preposition; e.g. *a mí* [ä mē] to me, me; *de ti* [de tē] from you, of you; *para él* [pä'rä el] for him; *con ella* [kōn e'lyä] with her; *por ello* [pōr e'lyō] because of that.

3. Irregular: *conmigo* [kōnmē'gō] with me, *contigo* [cōntē'gō] with you, *consigo* [kōnsē'gō] with him, her, it(self) and yourself (polite form).

4. **usted (Ud.)** [ōōsted'] you (sing. polite), *ustedes* (Uds.) [ōōste'des] you (*pl.* polite); also see Remarks.

5. The object pronouns before the verb are often supplemented by the prepositional pronoun when ambiguity exists (that is, in the polite form of "you"); e.g. *le buscaba* **a usted** [le bōōskä'bä ä ōōsted'] I looked for you; *le buscaba* can stand alone when the meaning is clear from the context.

Possessive Pronouns

1. Preceding the noun:

mi [mē] my	*nuestro, f -a* [nōō·es'trō] our
tu [tōō] your	*vuestro, f -a* [vōō·es'trō] your
su [sōō] his, her, their	

2. Nominative function:

el mío [el mē·ō], *la mía* [lä mē·ä] mine
el tuyo [el tōō'yō], *la tuya* [lä tōō'yä] your
el suyo [el sōōy'ō], *la suya* [lä sōō'yä] his, hers, theirs
el nuestro [el nōō·es'trō], *la nuestra* [lä nōō·es'trä] ours
el vuestro [el vōō·es'trō], *la vuestra* [lä vōō·es'trä] your

3. Plurals are formed in the same way as the plural of nouns.

4. *Estas casas son mías* [es'täs kä'säs sōn mē'äs] these houses are mine. – *un amigo suyo* [ōōn ämē'gō sōō'yō] a friend of his, hers, theirs; *un amigo de usted* [ōōn ämē'gō de ōōsted'] a friend of yours.

5. *su amigo de usted* [sōō ämē'gō de ōōsted'] your friend.

Demonstrative Pronouns

1. Preceding the noun: *este m* [es'te], *esta f* [es'tä], *pl. estos, estas* this, these (near speaker).

esa f [e'sä], *ese m* [e'se], *pl. esos, esas* that, those (near listener); *aquel m* [äkel'], *aquella f* [äke'lyä], *pl. aquellos, -as* that, those (over there).

2. When used as the subject or object of a verb or when standing alone, the demonstrative pronouns have an accent placed on the stressed vowel: e.g. *éstos son míos* [es'tōs sōn mē·'ōs] these are mine.

3. Demonstratives are used with prepositions in the same way as nouns.

Question Words

1. *¿quién? pl. ¿quiénes?* [kyen, kye'nes] who?
   ¿qué? [ke] what? which? (before noun)
   ¿cuál? pl. ¿cuáles? [kōō·äl, kōō·ä'les] which? (before *de* "of" and the verb *ser* "to be").
   ¿cuánto, -a, -os, -as? [kōō·än'tō, -ä, -os, -äs] how much?, how many?

2. Interrogatives are used with prepositions in the same way as nouns, e.g. *¿de quién?* [de kyen] whose?, *¿a quién?* [ä kyen] to whom?, *¿de qué?* [de ke] what about?

Relative Pronouns

que [ke]: most frequent relative pronoun, meaning who, that, which; sometimes with the definite article: *el (la, los, las) que*

el (la) cual, los (las) cuales [el (lä) kōō·äl, lōs (läs) kōō·ä'les]: used mostly after prepositions with more than two syllables to mean, who, which, or whom.

quien(es) [kyen'(es)]: whom, refers only to persons, especially following prepositions of one syllable.

cuyo(s), cuya(s) [kōō'yō(s), kōō'yä(s)]: always in adjective meaning "whose", agrees in number and gender with the noun it modifies.

lo que [lō ke], *lo cual* [lō kōō·äl], what, which; *todo lo que* [tō'dō lō ke] everything that.

Definite Pronouns

= the definite article; e.g. *el que* [el ke], he who.

IX. The Verb

Conjugation of regular verbs

Endings are attached to the stem of the verb except in the future and conditional tenses, when they are added to the infinitive.

Verbs are divided into three conjugations with the endings **-ar, -er** and **-ir.**

Infinitive

First Conjugation: *tomar* [tōmär′] to take (stem: *tom-*)
Second Conjugation: *vender* [vender′] to sell (stem: *vend-*)
Third Conjugation: *vivir* [vēvēr′] to live (stem: *viv-*)
Gerund: *tomando* taking, *vendiendo* selling, *viviendo* living. y instead of i is written between two vowels, e.g. *creer* [kre·er] to believe: *Ger. creyendo* [kreyen′dō] believing.
Participle: *tomado* taken, *vendido* sold, *vivido* lived
With an accent: *creer* to believe: *creído* [kre·ē′dō] believed.

Endings

	1st sing.	2nd sing.	3rd sing.	1st pl.	2nd pl.	3rd pl.
Present Indicative						
I take, etc.						
tom-	o	as	a	amos	áis	an
stem { vend-	o	es	e	emos	éis	en
viv-	o	es	e	imos	ís	en
Present Subjunctive						
(that) I (may) take						
tom-	e	es	e	emos	éis	en
stem { vend- } viv-	a	as	a	amos	áis	an
Imperfect						
I used to take,						
I was taking, etc.						
tom-	aba	abas	aba	ábamos	abais	aban
stem { vend- } viv-	ía	ías	ía	íamos	íais	ían

Preterite
I took, etc.

$$\text{stem} \begin{Bmatrix} \text{tom-} \\ \text{vend-} \\ \text{viv-} \end{Bmatrix}$$

é	aste	ó	amos	asteis	aron
í	iste	ió	imos	isteis	ieron

1. Imperfect Subjunctive (-ra)
(that) I might take, etc.

$$\text{stem} \begin{Bmatrix} \text{tom-} \\ \text{vend-} \\ \text{viv-} \end{Bmatrix}$$

ara	aras	ara	áramos	arais	aran
iera	ieras	iera	iéramos	ierais	ieran

2. Imperfect Subjunctive (-se)

$$\text{stem} \begin{Bmatrix} \text{tom-} \\ \text{vend-} \\ \text{viv-} \end{Bmatrix}$$

ase	ases	ase	ásemos	aseis	asen
iese	ieses	iese	iésemos	ieseis	iesen

Imperative
take, etc.

$$\text{stem} \begin{Bmatrix} \text{tom-} \\ \text{vend-} \\ \text{viv-} \end{Bmatrix}$$

a		ad
e		ed
e		id

Future
I will take, etc.

$$\text{Infin-itive} \begin{Bmatrix} \text{tomar} \\ \text{vender} \\ \text{vivir} \end{Bmatrix}$$

é	ás	á	emos	éis	án

Conditional
I would take, etc.

$$\text{Infin-itive} \begin{Bmatrix} \text{tomar} \\ \text{vender} \\ \text{vivir} \end{Bmatrix}$$

ía	ías	ía	íamos	íais	ían

Remarks

1. The familiar forms of address are **tú** [tōo] you *sing.* and **vosotros** [vōsō′trōs] you *pl.* (only in Spain). The polite forms of address are **usted** [ōoste′] you *sing.* and **ustedes** [ōoste′des] you *pl.*

2. The active compound tenses are formed with the auxiliary verb **haber** + the participle. The participle does not change.

Examples:

1. Present Perfect: *he tomado* [e tōmä′dō] I have taken, *hemos estado* [e′mōs estä′dō] we have been.

2. Pluperfect: *habían vendido* [äbē·'än vendē'do] they had sold, *habíamos venido* [äbē'ämōs venē'dō] we had come.

3. The passive is often expressed by an impersonal reflexive construction **(se)** in the third person singular. It is also expressed, as in English, by the auxiliary verb to be **(ser)** + past participle + by **(por)**; e.g. *fué vendido por mí* [foo·e' vendē'dō pōr mē] it was sold by me.

4. The imperfect is used to describe a past progressive action (what was happening or what used to happen) or a physical or emotional state in an incomplete past time. The preterite records an event or a series of events as a single completed occurrence in the past. The present perfect refers to an event in the past which extends into the present.

5. The affirmative command form of *tú* is the same as the third person of the present indicative, except for *tener, poner, venir, salir, hacer, ser, decir* and *ir*, whose forms are *ten, pon, ven, sal, haz, sé, di, ve*. The affirmative imperative of vosotros is formed by changing the final -r of the infinitive to -d. All other persons form the imperative by taking the corresponding form of the present subjunctive (with the negative commands being preceded by *no*); e.g. *toma* [tō'mä] (2nd pers. sing.) take – but: *no tomes* [nō tō'mes] (2nd pers. sing.) don't take; *tome usted* [tō'me ōosted'] (3rd pers. sing.) take, *tomen ustedes* [tō'men ōoste'des] (3rd pers. pl.) take; *tomemos* [tōme'mos] let us take; also *vamos a tomar*.

6. The subjunctive expresses: 1. doubt on the part of the speaker: *no creo que venga* [nō kre'·ō ke ven'gä] I don't think he'll come. – 2. desire and the expression of will: *deseaba que viniese* or *viniera* [deseä'bä ke vēnye'se *or* vēnye'rä] I wanted him to come; commands (see paragraph 5). – 3. possibility: *es posible que venga* [es pōsē'ble ke ven'gä] he might come. – 4. expressions of emotion: *siento que estés enfermo* [syen'tō ke estes' emfer'mō] I'm sorry you're sick.

7. Progressive Action: Progressive action in the present is expressed by the verb estar ("to be") and the present participle of the verb, which is formed by adding -ando to the stem of the -ar verbs and -iendo to the stem of the -er and -ir verbs: *estoy fumando* [estoi' foomän'dō] I am smoking – *seguir* [segēr'], *continuar* [kōntēnoo·är'] + Gerund = to keep on doing something: *sigo* (or *continúo*) *fumando* I keep on smoking.

ENGLISH – SPANISH DICTIONARY

The translations are followed by phonetic transcriptions and page references, so that this dictionary serves as an index as well.

A

abbey abadía f [äbädē'ä] 124

abdomen abdomen m [äbdō'men] 166

above sobre [sō'bre] 25

abscess absceso m [äbse'sō] 169

absorbent cotton algodón m hidrófilo [älgōdōn' ēdrō'fēlō] 160

accelerator acelerador m [äselerädōr'] 51

access road acceso m [äkse'sō] 42

accessories accesorios m/pl. [äksesōr'yōs] 136

accident accidente m [äksēden'te] 153

accommodations alojamiento m [älōhämyen'tō] 81

accompany acompañar [äkōmpänyär'] 184

ace as m [äs] 181

act acto m [äk'tō] 176

actor actor m [äktōr'] 176

actress actriz f [äktrēs'] 176

adapter plug enchufe m intermedio [entshōō'fe ēnterme'dyō] 90

address dirección f [dēreksyōn'] 48

addressee destinatario m [destēnätär'yō] 149

admission entrada f [enträ'dä] 118

advance reservation reserva f de plaza [reser'vä de plä'sä] 96

advance ticket sales venta f anticipada [ve'ntä äntēsēpä'dä] 176

after después [despōō·es'] 159

after shave loción f para después del afeitado [lōsyōn' pä'rä despōō·es' del äfe·ētä'dō] 140

afternoon tarde f [tär'de] 31; **good ~** buenas tardes [bōō·e'näs tär'des] 12; **in the ~** por la tarde [pōr lä tär'de] 31; **this ~** esta tarde [es'tä tär'de] 31

again otra vez [ō'trä ves] 184

against contra [kōn'trä] 164

age edad f [edäd'] 35; **under ~** menor de edad [menō'r de edäd'] 35

ago: a month ~ hace un mes [ä'se ōōn mes] 32

air aire m [ī're] 26; **~ filter** filtro m de aire [fēl'trō de ī're] 51; **~ pump** bomba f de aire [bōm'bä de ī're] 57; **~ sickness** mareo m [märe'ō] 70; **~ temperature** temperatura f del aire [temperätōō'rä del ī're] 185; **~ mattress** colchón m de aire [kōltshōn' de ī're] 185; **~ jet** tobera f de aire fresco [tōbe'rä de ī're fres'kō] 70; **~ conditioning** aire m acondicionado [ī're äkōndēsyōnä'dō] 75; **~ mail** por avión [pōr ävyōn'] 145; correo m aéreo [kōrre'·ō ä·e'reō] 149

aircraft avión m [ävyōn'] 70

airline compañía f aérea [kōmpänyē'ä ä·e'reä] 70

airport aeropuerto m [ä·erōpōō·er'tō] 68; **~ service charge** tasa f del aeropuerto [tä'sä del ä·erōpōō·er'tō] 68

alcohol alcohol m [älkō·ōl] 101

all todo [tō'dō] 80

allergy alergia f [äler'hyä] 169

alley callejón m [kälyehōn'] 120

almond almendra f [älmen'drä] 111

alone solo [sō'lō] 14

already ya [yä] 70

altar altar m [ältär'] 124

alto alto [äl'tō] 176

a.m.: nine ~ las nueve de la mañana [läs nōō·e've de lä mänyä'nä] 30

amber ámbar *m* [äm'bär] 133

ambulance ambulancia *f* [ämbōōlän'-syä] 49

American americano, [ämerēkä'nō] 152; **~ dollars** dólares *m/pl* americanos [dō'läres ämerēkä'nōs] 152; **~ plan** pensión *f* completa [pensyōn' kōmple'tä] 90; **~ studies** estudios *m/pl.* americanos [estōō'dyōs ämerēkä'nōs] 39

amount importe *m* [ēmpōr'te] 151

ampule ampolla *f* [ämpō'lyä] 160

amusement pasatiempo *m* [päsätyem'-pō] 181; **~ park** parque *m* de atracciones [pär'ke de äträksyō'nes] 120

anchor ancla *f* [ang'klä] 75

anchovies anchoas *f/pl* [äntshō'äs] 104

anemia anemia *f* [äne'myä] 169

anesthesia anestesia *f* [äneste'syä] 174

anesthetic anestesia *f* [äneste'syä] 172

ankle tobillo *m* [tōbē'lyō] 166

announcer presentador *m* [presentädōr'] 182

annually todos los años [tōdōs lōs ä'nyōs] 31

another otro [ōt'rō] 83

antidote antídoto *m* [äntē'dōtō] 160

anyone alguien [äl'gyen] 85

anything algo [äl'gō] 80

apartment apartamento *m* [äpärtämen'tō] 81; **~ building** casa *f* de pisos [kä'sä de pē'sōs] 90

apologize pedir perdón [pedēr' perdōn'] 22

appendicitis apendicitis *f* [äpendēsē'-tēs] 169

appendix apéndice *m* [äpen'dēse] 166

appetite apetito *m* [äpetē'tō] 163

applause aplausos *m/pl* [äplou'sōs] 177

apple manzana *f* [mänsä'nä] 111

appointment hora *f*, cita *f* [ō'rä, sē'tä] 173

apprentice aprendiz *m* [äprendēs'] 36

approach *(plane)* vuelo *m* de aproximación [vōō·e'lō de äprōksēmäsyōn'] 70

apricot damasco *m*, albaricoque *m (Sp)*, chabacano *m (Mex)* [dämäs'kō, älbärēkō'ke, tshäbäkä'nō] 111

April abril *m* [äbrēl'] 33

apron delantal *m* [deläntäl'] 134

arch arco *m* [är'kō] 124

archaeology arqueología *f* [ärke·ōlō-hē'ä] 39

architecture arquitectura *f* [ärkētek-tōō'rä] 39

area región *f* [rehyōn'] 120; **~ code** prefijo *m, (Mex)* clave *f* [prefē'hōō, klä've] 149

aria aria *f* [ä'ryä] 177

arm brazo *m* [brä'sō] 166

armchair butaca *f*, sillón *m* [bōōtä'kä, sē'lyōn] 90

armpit sobaco *m*, axila *f* [sōbä'kō, äksē'lä] 166

arrest detener [detener'] 154

arrival llegada *f* [lyegä'dä] 67

art arte *m* [är'te] 39; **~ gallery** galería *f* de arte [gälerē'ä de är'te] 128; **~ history** historia *f* de arte [ēstōr'ya de är'te] 39

artery arteria *f* [ärter'ya] 166

arthritis artritis *f* [ärtrē'tēs] 169

artichoke alcachofa *f* [älkätschō'fä] 109

articles objetos *m/pl* [ōbhe'tōs] 80

artist artista *m + f* [ärtē'stä] 36

ash tray cenicero *m* [senēse'rō] 87

ashore: to go ~ desembarcar [desembärkär'] 72

asparagus espárragos *m/pl* [espä'rrägōs] 110

aspirin aspirina *f* [äspērē'nä] 160

asthma asma *m* [äz'mä] 169

athlete atleta *m* + *f* [ätle'tä] 187

athletic club club *m* deportivo [klōōb depōrtē'vō] 189

atmospheric pressure presión *f* atmosférica [presyōn' ätmōsfe'rēkä] 26

attack ataque *m* [ätä'ke] 169

attorney abogado *m* [äbōgä'dō] 154

audience espectadores *m/pl* [espektä-dō'res] 179

auditorium sala *f* [sä'lä] 179

August agosto *m* [ägōs'tō] 33

aunt tía *f* [tē'ä] 35

auto racing motorismo [*m* mōtōrēz'-mō] 187

autobiography autobiografía *f* [outō-bē·ōgräfē'ä] 130

automatic transmission dispositivo *m* automático [dēspōsētē'vō ōūtōmä'-tēkō] 51

automobile club automóvil club *m* [outōmō'vēl klōōb] 42

avenue avenida *f*, paseo *m* [ävenē'dä, päse'ō] 120

avocado aguacate *m* [ägōō·äkä'te] 109

axle eje *m* [e'he] 51

B

back *(noun)* espalda *f* [espäl'dä] 166; **~ seat** asiento *m* trasero [äsyen'tō träse'rō] 55; **~ wheel** rueda *f* trasera [rōō·e'dä träse'rä] 47

backache dolores *m/pl* de la espalda [dōlō'res de lä espäl'dä] 169

backfire petardeo *m* [petärde'ō] 51

backwards de espaldas [de espäl'däs] 66

bacon tocino *m* [tōse'nō] 100

badminton badminton *m*, volante *m* *(Sp)* [bädmēntōn', vōlän'te] 180

bag bolsa *f* [bōl'sä] 126; **beach ~** bolsa *f* para la playa [bōl'sä pä'rä lä plä'yä] 143; **plastic ~** bolsa *f* de plástico [bōl'sä de pläs'tēkō] 144; **traveling ~**

bolso *m*, bolsa *f* de viaje [bōl'sō, bōl'-sä de vyä'he] 63

baggage equipaje *m* [ekēpä'he] 63; **~ check** resguardo *m*, (Sp) talón *m* [rezgōō·är'dō, tälōn'] 84; **~ check area** consigna *f*, (Mex) "guarda equipaje" [kōnsēg'nä, gōō·är'dä ekēpä'-he] 63; **~ claim area** entrega *f* de equipaje, (Mex) andenes *m/pl* de equipaje [entre'gä de ekēpä'he, än-de'nes de ekēpä'he] 63

baked asado, horneado [äsä'dō, ōr-ne·ä'dō] 102

baker panadero *m* [pänäde'rō] 36

bakery panadería *f* [pänäderē'ä] 128

balance beam barra *f* de equilibrio [bä'rra de ekēlē'brē·ō] 188

balcony balcón *m* [bälkōn] 82; **~** *(theater)* paraíso, (Mex) chilla [pärä·ē'sō, tshē'lyä] 177

ball pelota *f* [pelō'tä] 143; **~ bearings** cojinete *m* de bolas, (Mex) baleros *m/pl* [kōhēne'te de bō'läs, bäle'rōs] 51; **~ point pen** bolígrafo *m*, (Mex) pluma *f* [bōlē'gräfō, plōō'mä] 138

ballet ballet *m* [bäle'] 177

banana plátano *m* [plä'tänō] 112

band conjunto *m*, banda *f* [kōnhōōn'-tō, bän'dä] 177

bandage vendaje *m*, (Mex) venda *f* [vendä'he, ven'dä] 160

bank *(money)* banco *m* [bäng'kō] 151; **savings ~** caja *f* de ahorros [kä'hä de ä·ō'rrōs] 152; **~ account** cuenta *f* bancaria [kōō·en'tä bängkär'yä] 151; **~ charges** derechos *m/pl* del banco [dere'tshōs del bäng'ko] 151; **~ note** billete *m* de banco [bēlye'te de bäng'kō] 151; **~ transfer** giro *m* bancario [hē'ro bängkär'yō] 151

bank *(river)* orilla *f* [ōrē'lyä] 75

banker banquero *m* [bänke'rō] 181

baptism bautismo *m* [boutēz'mō] 124

bar bar *m* [bär] 74

barber shop peluquería f [pelo͞okerē'ä] 74

barge barcaza f, (Mex) chalana f [bär-kä'sä, tshälä'nä] 75

baritone barítono m [bärē'tōnō] 177

barometer barómetro m [bärō'metrō] 25

Baroque barroco m [bärrō'kō] 124

barrier barrera f [bärre'rä] 67

basement sótano m [sō'tänō] 90

bass bajo m [bä'hō] 177

bath baño m [bä'nyō] 82; ~ **attendant** bañero m [bänye'rō] 175; ~ **salts** sales f/pl de baño [sä'les de bä'nyō] 140; **mineral** ~ baño m de aguas minerales [bä'nyō de ä'go͞o·äs menerä-'les] 175; **steam** ~ baño m de vapor, baño m turco [bä'nyō de väpōr, bä'nyō to͞or'kō] 175; **take a** ~ bañarse [bänyär'se] 97

bathing cap gorro m de baño [gō'rro de bä'nyō] 186

bathing suit traje m de baño [trä'he de bä'nyō] 186

bathing trunks bañador m (Sp) [bänyä-dōr'] 186

bathrobe bata f (Sp) albornoz m [bä'tä, älbōrnōs'] 134

bathroom cuarto m de baño [ko͞o·är'tō de bä'nyō] 90

battery (car) batería f, acumulador m (Mex) [bäterē'ä, äko͞omo͞olädōr'] 51

bay bahía f [bä·ē'ä] 75

beach playa f [plä'yä] 81; **private** ~ playa f privada [plä'yä prēvä'dä] 93; **sandy** ~ playa f de arena [plä'yä de äre'nä] 186

beans frijoles m/pl, judías f/pl (Sp) [frē-hō'les, ho͞odē'äs] 110; **green** ~ ejotes m/pl. (Mex), judías verdes f/pl (Sp) [ehō'tes, ho͞odē'äs ver'des] 110

beard barba f [bär'bä] 157

beauty contest concurso m de belleza [kōnko͞or'sō de belye'sä] 181

beauty parlor salón m de belleza [sälōn' de belye'sä] 158

bed cama f [kä'mä] 90; ~ **and two meals** media pensión f [me'dyä pensyōn'] 90; ~ **linen** ropa f de cama [rō'pä de kä'mä] 90; ~ **rug** alfombrilla f, pie m de cama [älfōmbrē'lyä, pye de kä'mä] 90; ~ **side table** mesita f de noche [mesē'tä de nō'tshe] 90; ~ **spread** colcha f, cubrecama m, sobrecama m [kōl'tshä, ko͞obrekä'mä, sōbrekä'mä] 90; **day** ~ sofá-cama m [sōfä'-kä'mä] 91

bedroom dormitorio m, alcoba f, recámara f (Mex) [dōrmētōr'yō, älkō'bä, rekä'märä] 93

beer cerveza f [serve'sä] 113; **bottled** ~ cerveza f de botella [serve'sä de bōte'lyä] 113; **dark** ~ cerveza f negra [serve'sä ne'grä] 113; **draft** ~ cerveza f de barril [serve'sä de bärrēl'] 113; **light** ~ cerveza f clara, rubia (Sp) [serve'sä klä'rä, ro͞o'byä] 113

beeswax cera f de abejas [se'rä de äbe'häs] 143

beets remolachas f/pl [remōlä'tshäs] 110

beige beige [be·ē'he] 194

bell campana f [kämpä'nä] 124

belt cinturón m [sēnto͞orōn'] 134

bet apostar [äpōstär'] 181

bicycle bicicleta f [bēsēkle'tä] 41; ~ **race** carrera f ciclista [kärre'rä sēklēs'-tä] 187; ~ **rider** ciclista m [sēklēs'tä] 187; **ride a** ~ ir en bicicleta [ēr en bēsēkle'tä] 187

bicycling ciclismo m [sēklēz'mō] 187

big grande [grän'de] 127

bike lane pista f de bicicletas [pēs'tä de bēsēkle'täs] 42

bikini bikini m [bēkē'nē] 134

bile bilis f [bē'lēs] 166

bill (money) billete m [bēlye'te] 151

bill cuenta f [ko͞o·en'tä] 89

billfold cartera f [kärte'rä] 153

binoculars prismáticos m/pl [présmä'-tēkōs] 138

biography biografía f [bē·ōgräfē'ä] 130

biology biología f [bē·ōlōhē'ä] 39

birthday cumpleaños m [koōmple-·ä'nyōs] 22; **Happy ~** ¡Feliz cumpleaños! [felēs' koōmple·ä'nyōs] 23

bishop (chess) alfil m [älfēl'] 181

black negro [ne'grō] 194

blackmail attempt extorsión f, chantaje m [ekstōrsyōn', tshäntä'he] 153

bladder vejiga f [vehē'gä] 166

blanket cobija f, frazada f, manta f (Sp) [kōbē'hä, fräsä'dä, män'tä] 87

bleeding hemorragia f [emōrrä'hyä] 169

blinker intermitente m [ēntermēten'te] 51

blizzard ventisca f [ventēs'kä] 26

blonde rubio [roō'byō] 194

blood sangre f [säng'gre] 166; **~ count** hemograma m [emōgrä'mä] 172; **~ poisoning** intoxicación f de la sangre [ēntōksēkäsyōn' de lä säng'gre] 169; **~ pressure** presión f de la sangre, tensión f [presyōn' de lä säng'gre, tensyōn'] 169; **~ test** muestra f de sangre [moō·es'trä de säng'gre] 172; **~ transfusion** transfusión f de sangre [tränsfoōsyōn' de säng'gre] 172

blouse blusa f [bloō'sä] 134

blown (fuse) fundido [foōndē'dō] 55

blow-out pinchazo m, reventón m [pēntshä'sō, reventōn'] 47

blue azul [äsoōl']194; **dark ~** azul marino [äsoōl' märē'nō] 194; **light ~** azul claro [äsoōl' klä'rō] 194; **~ jeans** pantalón m vaquero, tejanos m/pl, jeans m/pl [päntälōn' väke'rō, tehä'nōs, hēns] 134

boar (wild) jabalí m [häbälē'] 108

board (to) ir a bordo [ēr ä bōr'dō] 75;

on **~** a bordo [ä bōr'dō] 75

boarding house casa f de huéspedes [kä'sa de oō·es'pedes] 81

boarding school internado m [ēnternä'dō] 38

boat barco m, lancha f [bär'kō, län'-tshä] 75; **pedal ~** patín m [pätēn'] 186; **~ trip** excursión f en lancha [ekskoōrsyōn' en län'tshä] 120

body cuerpo m [koō·er'pō] 166

body (car) carrocería f [kärrōserē'ä] 51; **~ and fender damage** daños m/pl en la carrocería [dä'nyōs en lä kärrōserē'ä] 49

boiled cocido [kōsē'dō] 102

bolt tornillo m [tōrnē'lyō] 51; **~ nut** tuerca f [toō·er'kä] 51

bone hueso m [oō·e'sō] 166

book libro m [lē'brō] 130; **~ shop** librería f [lēbrerē'ä] 128; **children's ~** libro m para niños [lē'brō pä'rä nē'nyōs] 130; **guide ~** guía f [gē'ä] 130; **phrase ~** libro m de frases [lē'brō de frä'ses] 130; **reference ~** libro m de consulta [lē'brō de kōnsoōl'tä] 130; **story ~** libro m de cuentos [lē'brō de koō·en'tōs] 130; **text ~** manual m [mänoō·äl'] 130

bookkeeper tenedor m de libros [tenedōr' de lē'brōs] 36

bookseller librero m [lēbre'rō] 36

booth cabina f [käbē'nä] 148

boots botas f/pl [bō'täs] 139

border frontera f [frōnte'rä] 78; **~ crossing** paso m de la frontera [pä'so de lä frōnte'rä] 80

botanical gardens jardín m botánico [härdēn' bōtä'nēkō] 120

bottle botella f, frasco m (Mex) [bōte'-lya, fräs'kō] 199

bouquet ramo m de flores [rä'mō de flō'res] 130

bow (ship) proa f [prō'ä] 75

bowel movement deposición f [depōsēsyōn'] 166

bowl tazón *m* [täsōn'] 99

bowling bolos *m/pl* [bō'lōs] 187; **~ alley** bolera *f* [bōle'rä] 187

box *(verb)* boxear [bōkse·är'] 187

box *(noun)* caja *f* [kä'hä] 126; **~ lunch** bolsa *f* de merienda [bōl'sä de meryen'dä] 86; **~ office** taquilla *f* [täkē'lyä] 177

boxer boxeador *m* [bōkse·ädōr'] 187

boxing boxeo *m* [bōkse·ō] 187

boy niño *m*, muchacho *m* [nē'nyō, mōōtshä'tshō] 35

bra sostén *m*, sujetador *m* [sōsten', sōōhetädōr'] 134

bracelet pulsera *f* [pōōlse'rä] 133

braces aparato *m* dental, frenillo *m* [äpärä'tō dentäl', frenē'lyō] 174

brain cerebro *m* [sere'brō] 166

brake drum tambor *m* de freno [tämbōr' de fre'nō] 51

brake fluid líquido *m* de frenos [lē'kēdō de fre'nōs] 51

brake lights luces *f/pl* de freno [lōō'ses de fre'nō] 51

brake pedal pedal *m* de freno [pedäl' de fre'no] 51

brakes frenos *m/pl* [fre'nōs] 51

branch manager gerente *m* or director *m* de la sucursal [heren'te, dērektōr' de lä sōōkōōrsäl] 151

brandy coñac *m* [kōnyäk'] 113

bread pan *m* [pän] 111; **whole wheat ~** pan *m* de trigo integral [pän de trē'gō ēntegräl'] 100; **~ basket** cestilla *f*, canasta *f* del pan [sestē'lyä, känäs'tä del pän] 99

breakdown falla mecánica *f*, avería *f* [fä'lyä mekä'nēkä, äverē'ä] 48

breakfast desayuno *m* [desäyōō'nō] 90; **to have ~** desayunar [desäyōō-när'] 90; **~ room** sala *f* de desayuno [sä'lä de desäyōō'nō] 90

breast pecho *m*, seno *m* [pe'tshō,

se'nō] 166

breathing respiración *f* [respēräsyōn'] 166; **~ problems** dificultades *f/pl* respiratorias [dēfēkōōltä'des respērätō'ryäs] 169

breeze brisa *f* [brē'sä] 75

bricklayer albañil *m* [älbänyēl'] 36

bridge puente *m* [pōō·en'te] 42

bridge *(on ship)* puente *m* de mando [pōō·en'te de män'do] 75

briefcase maletín *m*, cartera *f (Sp)* [mäletēn', kärte'rä] 143

brilliantine brillantina *f* [brēlyäntē'nä] 158

broccoli brécol *m*, brócoli *m* [bre'kōl, brō'kōlē] 110

brochure folleto *m* [fōlye'tō] 130

broken roto [rō'tō] 23

bronchitis bronquitis *f* [brōngkē'tēs] 169

brooch broche *m*, prendedor *m* [brō'-tshe, prendedōr'] 133

broth caldo *m* [käl'dō] 105; **chicken ~** caldo *m* de gallina [käl'dō de gälyē'nä] 105

brother hermano *m* [ermä'nō] 35; **~ -inlaw** cuñado *m* [kōōnyä'dō] 35

brown marrón, café *(Mex)* [märrōn', käfe'] 194; **chestnut ~** castaño [kästä'nyō] 194

bruise contusión *f* [kōntōōsyōn'] 169

brush cepillo *m* [sepē'lyō] 141; **clothes ~** cepillo *m* de ropa [sepē'lyō de rō'pä] 141

Brussel sprouts coles *f/pl* de Bruselas [kō'les de brōōse'läs] 110

bucket cubo *m*, balde *m* [kōō'bō, bäl'-de] 90

buckle hebilla *f* [ebē'lyä] 136

building edificio *m* [edēfē'syō] 119

bulb bombilla *f* [bōmbē'lyä] 51; **light ~** bombillo *m*, bombilla *f (Sp)*, foco *m (Mex)* [bōmbē'lyō, bōmbē'lyä, fō'kō] 92

bumper parachoques *m*, defensa *f* [pärätshō'kes, defen'sä] 51

bungalows bungalows *m/pl*, bungalos *m/pl*, cabañas *f/pl*. *(Mex)* [bōōngä'lōs, bōōngä'lōs, käbä'nyäs] 81

buoy boya *m* [bō'yä] 75

burn *(noun)* quemadura *f* [kemädōō'rä] 169

burned out *(bulb)* fundida(-o) [fōōndē'dä(-ō)] 88

bus autobús *m*, camión *m (Mex)* [outōbōs', kämyōn'] 59; **~ terminal** estación *f* de autobuses [estäsyōn' de outōbōō'ses] 59

bus stop parada *f* de autobuses, de camiones *(Mex)* [pärä'dä de outōbōō'ses, de kämyō'nes] 116

business administration economía *f* de empresas [ekōnōmē'ä de empre'säs] 39

business school escuela *f* de comercio [eskōō·e'lä de kōmer'syō] 39

busy ocupado [ōkōōpä'dō] 148

butcher carnicero *m* [kärnēse'rō] 36

butter mantequilla *f* [mäntekē'lyä] 102

buttocks nalgas *f/pl* [näl'gäs] 166

button botón *m* [bōtōn'] 136

buy comprar [kōmprär'] 126

C

cabaña caseta *f* [käse'tä] 185

cabbage repollo *m* [repō'lyō] 110

cabin *(on ship)* camarote *m*, cabina *f (Mex)* [kämärō'te, käbē'nä] 75; **double ~** camarote *m*, cabina *f (Mex)* doble [kämärō'te, käbē'nä dō'ble] 73; **inside ~** camarote *m*, cabina *f (Mex)* interior [kämärō'te, käbē'nä ēnteryōr'] 73; **outside ~** camarote *m*, cabina *f (Mex)* exterior [kämärō'te, käbē'nä eksteryōr'] 73; **single ~** camarote *m*, cabina *f (Mex)* individual [kämärō'te, käbē'nä ēndēvē-

dōō·äl'] 73

cabinetmaker ebanista *m* [ebänēs'tä] 36

cable cable *m* [kä'ble] 52

cake tarta *f*, torta *f* [tär'tä, tōr'tä] 113

calf *(of leg)* pantorilla *f* [päntōrē'lyä] 166

call *(noun)* llamada *f* [lyämä'dä] 148; **make a phone ~** telefonear [telefōne·är'] 147; **collect ~** cobro *m* revertido, por cobrar *(Mex)* [kō'brō revertē'dō, pōr kōbrär'] 149; **long distance ~** conferencia *f*, llamada *f* de larga distancia *(Mex)* [kōmferen'syä, lyämä'dä de lär'gä dēstän'syä] 149

call *(at port)* hacer escala [äser' eskä'lä] 75

camera máquina *f* fotográfica [mä'kēnä fōtōgrä'fēkä] 132; **movie ~** tomavistas *m*, cámara *f*, filmadora *f* [tōmävēs'täs, kä'märä, fēlmädō'rä] 132

camomile tea manzanilla *f* [mänsänē'lyä] 160

camp (out) acampar [äkämpär'] 95; **~ bed** cama *f* de campaña [kä'mä de kämpä'nyä] 96; **~ site** camping *m* campamento *m (Mex)* [kämpēn', kämpämen'tō] 96; **~ stove** brasero *m* [bräse'ro] 143

camper vehicle cámper *m* [käm'per] 40

camping camping *m*, campismo *m (Mex)* [kämpēn', kämpēz'mō] 96; **~ ID** tarjeta *f* de camping [tärhe'tä de kämpēn'] 96; **~ trailer** caravana *f*, trayler *m (Mex)* [kärävä'nä, trīler] 40

camshaft árbol *m* de levas [är'bōl de le'väs] 51

can opener abrelatas *m* [äbrelä'täs] 143

canal canal *m* [känäl'] 75

cancel anular [änōōlär'] 69

cancer cáncer *m* [kän'ser] 169

candle vela *f* [ve'lä] 143

candlestick candelero *m* [kändele'rō] 143

candy caramelos *m/pl* [kärämeˈlōs] 143

canned goods conservas *f/pl*, enlatados *m/pl* [kōnserˈväs, enlätäˈdōs] 143

cap gorra *f*, gorro *m* [gōˈrrä, gōˈrrō] 134

capers alcaparras *f/pl* [älkäpäˈrräs] 102

capital capital *f* [käpētälˈ] 120

capon capón *m* [käpōnˈ] 107

captain capitán *m* [käpētänˈ] 75; ~'s **table** mesa *f* del capitán [meˈsä del käpētänˈ] 75

car automóvil *m* [outōmōˈvēl] 40; ~ *(railroad)* coche *m*, vagón *m* [kōˈtshe, vägōnˈ] 67; ~ **door** puerta *f* del carro, del coche *(Sp)* [pō̄ōˈerˈtä del käˈrrō, del kōˈtshe] 52; ~ **ferry** transbordador *m* [tränsbōrdädōrˈ] 72; ~ **keys** llaves *f/pl* del carro, del coche [lyäˈves del käˈrrō, del kōˈtshe] 52; ~ **repair service** taller *m* mecánico [tälyerˈ mekäˈnēkō] 45; **to go by** ~ ir en carro, coche *(Sp)* [ēr en käˈrrō, kōˈtshe] 42

carafe garrafa *f* [gärräˈfä] 99

caraway semillas *f/pl* de Alcaravea [semēˈlyäs de älkäräveˈä] 103

carburetor carburador *m* [kärbōōrädōrˈ] 52; ~ **jet** esprea *f* [espreˈä] 52

card *(post)* tarjeta *f* postal [tärheˈtä pōstälˈ] 145; ~ **game** juego *m* de cartas [hōō·eˈgō de kärˈtäs] 181; **greeting** ~ **telegram** telegrama *m* de felicitación [telegräˈmä de felēsētäsyōnˈ] 147

cardiac infarction infarto *m* del miocardio [ēnfärˈtō del mē·ōkärˈdyō] 169

careful! ¡atención! [ätensyōnˈ] 49

carp carpa *f* [kärˈpä] 106

carpenter carpintero *m* [kärpēnteˈrō] 36

carpet moqueta *f*, tapete *m (Mex)* [mōkeˈtä, täpeˈte] 90

carrots zanahorias *f/pl* [sänä·ōˈryäs] 110

cartoon dibujos *m/pl* animados, monitos *m/pl* [dēbōōˈhōs änēmäˈdōs, mōnēˈtōs] 179

cash *(verb)* cobrar [kōbrärˈ] 151

cassette cassette *m or f* [käseˈte] 143

castle castillo *m* [kästēˈlyō] 119

castor oil aceite *m* de ricino [äseˈēte de rēsēˈnō] 160

catalogue catálogo *m* [kätäˈlōgō] 130

category categoría *f* [kätegōrēˈä] 90

cathedral catedral *f* [kätedrälˈ] 119

cauliflower coliflor *f* [kōlēflōrˈ] 110

cave cueva *f* [kōō·eˈvä] 120

cavities caries *f/pl* [kärˈyes] 174

ceiling techo *m* [teˈtshō] 90

celery apio *m* [äˈpyō] 109

cellar sótano *m* [sōˈtänō] 90

cemetery cementerio *m* [sementeˈryō] 120

centimeter centímetro *m* [sentēˈmetrō] 193

ceramics cerámica *f* [seräˈmēkä] 143

cereal cereales *m/pl* [cere·äˈles] 100

certainly desde luego [dezˈde lōō·eˈgō] 21

chains cadenas *f/pl* [käˈdēnäs] 52

chair silla *f* [sēˈlyä] 91; **deck** ~ silla *f* de cubierta, hamaca *f*, tumbona *f* [sēˈlyä de kōōbyerˈtä, ämäˈkä, tōōmbōˈnä] 91

chamber music música *f* de cámara [mōōˈsēkä de käˈmarä] 177

championship competición *f*, concurso *m* [kōmpetēsyōnˈ, kōnkōōrˈsō] 188

change *(noun)* cambio *m* [kämˈbyō] 152

change *(verb)* cambiar [kämbyärˈ] 85

chapel capilla *f* [käpēˈlyä] 124

charcoal pills pastillas *f/pl* de carbón [pästēˈlyäs de kärbōnˈ] 160

charter plane avión *m* charter [ävyōnˈ tshärˈter] 70

chassis chasís *m*, *chasis m (Sp)* [tshäsēs', tshä'sēs] 52

chauffeur chófer *m* [tshō'fer] 41

check *(noun)* cuenta *f* [kōō·en'tä] 115; **~ room** guardarropa *m* [gōō·ärdä-rrō'pä] 177;

check *(verb)* revisar [revēsär'] 50; **~ in** inscribirse [ēnskrēbēr'se] 91

checked a cuadros [ä kōō·ä'drōs] 137

checkers damas *f/pl* [dä'mäs] 181

check-in inscripción *f* [ēnskrēpsyōn'] 91

cheek mejilla *f* [mehē'lyä] 166

cheers! ¡salud! [sälōōd'] 101

cheese queso *m* [ke'sō] 110; **goat ~** queso *m* de cabra [ke'sō de kä'brä] 110; **grated ~** queso *m* rallado [ke'sō rälyä'dō] 111; **smoked ~** queso *m* ahumado [ke'sō ä·ōōmä'dō] 110; **Swiss ~** queso *m* suizo [ke'sō sōō·ē'sō] 111; **white ~** queso *m* blanco [ke'sō bläng'kō] 110

chef jefe *m* de cocina [*he*'fe de kōsē'-nä] 36

chemistry química *f* [kē'mēkä] 39

cherry cereza *f* [sere'sä] 111

chess ajedrez *m* [ähedres'] 180

chessman pieza *f* [pye'sä] 181

chest pecho *m* [pe'tshō] 166

chicken pollo *m* [pō'lyō] 107; **~ pox** varicela *f* [värēse'lä] 169

children niños *m/pl* [nē'nyōs] 185

chills escalofríos *m/pl* [eskälōfrē'ōs] 169

chimney chimenea *f* [tshēmene'ä] 91

china porcelana *f* [pōrselä'nä] 143

chip ficha *f* [fē'tshä] 181

chisel cincel *m* [sēnsel'] 57

chives cebollino *m* [sebōlyē'nō] 103

chocolate chocolate *m* [tshōkōlä'te] 100

choir coro *m* [kō'rō] 124

cholera cólera *f* [kō'lerä] 169

chop *(noun)* chuleta *f* [tshōōle'tä] 108

chorus coro *m* [kō'rō] 177

christening bautizo *m* [boutē'sō] 124

church iglesia *f* [ēgle'syä] 124; **Catholic ~** iglesia *f* católica [ēgle'syä kätō'lēkä] 123; **Protestant ~** iglesia *f* protestante [ēgle'syä prōtestän'te] 116; **~ concert** concierto *m* de música sacra [kōnsyer'tō de mōō'sēkä sä'krä] 124

churchyard campo *m* santo [käm'pō sän'tō] 124

cider sidra *f* [sē'drä] 114

cigar puro *m* [pōō'rō] 140

cigarette cigarrillo *m*, cigarro *m (Mex)* [sēgärrē'lyo, sēgä'rrō] 140; **filtered ~** con filtro [kōn fēl'trō] 140; **unfiltered ~** sin filtro [sēn fēl'trō] 140

cigarillo purito *m* [pōōrē'tō] 140

cinema cine *m* [sē'ne] 179

cinnamon canela *f* [käne'lä] 103

circulation circulación *f* [sērkōōläsyōn'] 166

circulatory problems trastornos *m/pl* circulatorios [trästōr'nōs sērkōōlätō'ryōs] 169

circus circo *m* [sēr'kō] 181

city ciudad *f*, [syōōdäd'] 120; **~ hall** alcaldía *f*, ayuntamiento *m (Sp)* [älkäldē'ä, ayōōntämyen'tō] 120

civil servant funcionario *m* [fōōnsyōnä'ryō] 36

claim *(luggage)* recoger [rekō*h*er] 63; **~ check** talón *m*, recibo *m*, resguardo *m* [tälōn', resē'bō, rezgōō·är'dō] 63

clam almeja *f* [älme'*h*ä] 106

class clase *f* [klä'se] 73; **first ~** primera clase [prēme'rä klä'se] 73; **tourist ~** clase *f* turista [klä'se tōōrēs'tä] 73

clay pigeon shooting tiro *m* al plato [tē'rō äl plä'tō] 189

clear *(sky)* despejado [despe*h*ä'dō] 26

clergyman clérigo *m* [kle'rēgō] 36

climate clima m [klē'mä] 26

clock reloj m [relōh'] 142; **alarm ~** despertador m [despertädōr'] 143

close cerrar [serär'] 65

closet armario m [ärmär'yō] 91

cloth paño m [pä'nyō] 57

clothes hanger percha f, gancho m [per'tshä, gän'tshō] 87

cloud nube f [nōō'be] 26; **~ cover** nuboso, nublado [nōōbō'sō, nōōblä'-dō] 26

cloudburst chaparrón m [tshäpärrōn'] 26

cloves clavos m/pl de especia [klä'vōs de espe'syä] 103

club club m [klōōb] 181

clubs (cards) tréboles m/pl [tre'bōles] 181

clutch cloche m, embrague m (Sp) [klō'tshe, embrä'ge] 52; **~ pedal** pedal m del embrague [pedäl' del embrä'ge] 52

coast costa f [kōs'tä] 75

coastal road camino m de la costa [kämē'nō de lä kōs'tä] 43

coat sobretodo m, abrigo m [sōbretō'-dō, äbrē'gō] 134; **~ check** ficha f del guardarropa [fē'tshä del gōō·ärdä-rrō'pä] 177

coconut coco m [kō'kō] 111

cod bacalao m [bäkälä'·ō] 106

c.o.d. envío m contra reembolso [envē'ō kōn'trä re·embōl'sō] 149

coffee café m [käfe'] 100; **black ~** (espresso) café m solo, expreso m (Mex) [käfe' sō'lō, espre'sō] 100; **de-caffeinated ~** descafeinado [deskäfe·ēnä'dō] 100; **~ and milk** café m con leche [käfe' kōn le'tshe] 100

cognac coñac m [kōnyäk'] 113

coins monedas f/pl, cambio m [mōne'-däs, käm'byō] 148

cold (noun) resfriado m [resfrē·ä'dō] 169

cold (adj.) frío [frē'ō] 25; **~ cuts** fiambres m/pl, carnes f/pl frías (Mex) [fyäm'bres, kär'nes frē'äs] 100

colic cólico m [kō'lēkō] 169

collarbone clavícula f [klävē'kōōlä] 166

collect call cobro m revertido, por cobrar (Mex) [kō'brō revertē'dō, pōr kōbrär'] 149

collision choque m [tshō'ke] 49

cologne agua m de colonia [ä'gōō·ä de kōlō'nyä] 141

color color m [kōlōr'] 127

colored de colores [de kōlō'res] 194

colorful de muchos colores [de mōō'-tshōs kōlō'res] 194

comb (noun) peine m [pe'ēne] 141

comb (verb) peinar [pe·ēnär'] 158

come venir [venēr'] 15; **~ in!** ¡adelante! ¡pase! [ädelän'te, pä'se] 16

comedy comedia f [kōme'dyä] 177

communion comunión f [kōmōōnyōn'] 124

compact polvera f [pōlve'rä] 141

compartment departamento m, compartim(i)ento m [depärtämen'tō, kōmpärtēm(y)en'tō] 67

compass brújula f [brōō'hōōlä] 138

competition competición f, concurso m [kōmpetēsyōn', kōnkōōr'sō] 188

complaint reclamación f, reclamo m [reklämäsyōn', reklä'mō] 91; **register a ~** hacer una reclamación, un reclamo [äser' ōō'nä reklämäsyōn', ōōn reklä'mō] 23

composer compositor m [kōmpōsē-tōr'] 177

compression compresión f [kōmpre-syōn'] 52

concert concierto m [kōnsyer'tō] 177; **~ hall** sala f de conciertos [sä'lä de kōnsyer'tōs] 177

concierge conserje m [kōnser'he] 91

concussion conmoción f cerebral [kōnmōsyōn' serebräl'] 169

condenser condensador m [kŏndensä-dōr'] 52

condolences pésame m [pe'säme] 23

conductor conductor m [kŏndōōktōr'] 67; ~ *(orchestra)* director m de orquesta [dĕrektōr' de ōrkes'tä] 177

confectioner pastelero m [pästele'rō] 36

confess confesarse [kŏnfesär'se] 124

confession confesión f [kŏnfesyōn'] 124

confiscate confiscar [kŏnfeskär'] 154

congratulations! ¡felicitaciones! [felĕ-sētäsyō'nes] 22

conjunctivitis conjunctivitis f [kŏnhōōn-tĕvē'tĕs] 169

connecting rod biela f [bye'lä] 52; ~ **bearing** conjinete m de biela, metales m/pl de bielas [kōhēne'te de bye'-lä, metä'les de bye'läs] 52

connection conección f, correspondencia f [kŏnegsyōn', kŏrrespōn-den'syä] 67

constipation estreñimiento m [estre-nyēmyen'tō] 169

consulate consulado m [kŏnsōōlä'dō] 120

contact contacto m [kŏntäk'tō] 52; ~ **lenses** lentes f/pl de contacto, lentillas f/pl [len'tes de kŏntäk'tō, lentē'-lyäs] 138

contraceptive pills píldoras f/pl anticonceptivas [pēl'dōräs äntēkōnsep-tē'väs] 160

convalescent home casa f de reposo [kä'sä de repō'sō] 175

convent convento m [kŏnven'tō] 124

cook *(verb)* cocinar [kōsēnär'] 96

cook *(noun)* cocinero m [kōsēne'rō] 36

cookies galletas f/pl, pastas f/pl (Sp) [gälye'täs, päs'täs] 112

cooking utensils batería f de cocina [bäterē'ä de kōsē'nä] 96

coolant agua f para el radiador [a'-

gōō·ä pä'rä el rädyädōr'] 45

cordial cordial [kōrdyäl'] 12

cordially yours con un saludo cordial [kōn ōōn sälōō'dō kōrdyäl'] 13

corduroy pana f [pä'nä] 136

corkscrew sacacorchos m, descorchador m [säkäkōr'tshōs, deskōrtshä-dōr'] 143

corn maíz m [mīs] 110; ~ **plaster** parche m para callos [pär'tshe pä'rä kä'lyōs] 160

corner esquina f [eskē'nä] 120; ~ *(sports)* saque m de esquina [sä'ke de eskē'nä] 189

corridor pasillo m, corredor m [päsē'-lyō, kōrrēdōr'] 91

corset corpiño m [kōrpē'nyō] 134

cosmetic salon instituto m de belleza [ēnstētōō'tō de belye'sä] 128

costumes trajes m/pl [trä'hes] 177; ~ **designer** figurinista m [fēgōōrēnēs'-tä] 177

cotton algodón m [älgōdōn'] 136

couchette car coche m literas, camas f/pl (Mex) [kō'tshe lēte'räs, kä'mäs] 64

cough tos f [tōs] 169; ~ **medicine** calmante m de la tos [kälmän'te de lä tōs] 160; ~ **syrup** jarabe m para tos [härä'be pä'rä tōs] 160

counter ventanilla f [ventänē'lyä] 149

country fair fiesta f popular [fyes'tä pōpōōlär'] 181

country road camino m vecinal [kä-mē'nō vesēnäl'] 43

countryside campo m [käm'pō] 120

course rumbo m [rōōm'bō] 75; **of ~** por supuesto [pōr sōōpōō·es'tō] 21

court tribunal m [trēbōōnäl'] 154

courthouse tribunal m, juzgado m [trēbōōnäl', hōōzgä'dō] 120

cousin *(female)* prima f [prē'mä] 35

cousin *(male)* primo m [prē'mō] 35

covered market mercado m cubierto [merkä'dō kōōbyer'tō] 120

coxswain timonel *m* [tēmŏnel¹] 189

crab cangrejo *m* [kängre¹hō] 107

cramps calambres *m/pl* [käläm¹bres] 169

crankshaft cigüeñal *m* [sēgōō·enyäl¹] 52

crayons lápices *m/pl* de color [lä¹pēses de kōlōr¹] 138

cream crema *f* [kre¹mä] 141; **whipped ~** crema *f* batida; nata *f (Sp)* [kre¹mä bätē¹dä, nä¹tä] 112, 113

credit crédito *m* [kre¹dētō] 152; **~ card** tarjeta *f* de crédito [tärhe¹tä de kre¹dētō] 152

creed credo *m* [kre¹dō] 124

crew tripulación *f* [trēpōōläsyōn¹] 75

crib cuna *f* [kōō¹nä] 83

crime delito *m* [delē¹tō] 154

criminal delincuente *m* [delēnkōō·en¹te] 154

croissant croissant *m* [krō·äsänt¹] 100

cross cruz *f* [krōōs] 124; **~ road** travesía *f* [trävesē¹ä] 43

crossing travesía *f* [trävesē¹ä] 75

crown corona *f* [kōrō¹nä] 174

crucifix crucifijo *m* [krōōsēfē¹hō] 124

cruise crucero *m* [krōōse¹rō] 75

crystal vidrio *m*, cristal *m (Sp)* [vē¹drē·ō, krēstäl¹] 143

cubic cúbico [kōō¹bēkō] 193

cufflinks gemelos *m/pl*, mancuernas *f/pl (Mex)* [heme¹lōs, mänkōō·er¹näs] 133

cup taza *f* [tä¹sä] 99

cure cura *f*, tratamiento *m* [kōō¹rä, trätämyen¹tō] 175; **~ tax** impuesto *m* de turismo [ēmpōō·es¹tō de tōōrēz¹mō] 175; **rest ~** cura *f* de reposo [kōō¹rä de repō¹sō] 175

curler rulero *m*, rulo *m (Sp)* [rōōle¹rō, rōō¹lō] 141

curls rizos *m/pl* [rē¹sōs] 158

currency moneda *f* [mōne¹dä] 152; **foreign ~** divisas *f/pl* [dēvē¹säs] 152

current corriente *f* [kōrryen¹te] 90; **alternating ~** corriente *f* alterna [kōrryen¹te älter¹nä] 90

curtain cortina *f* [kōrtē¹nä] 91

curtain *(theater)* telón *m* [telōn¹] 177; **~ time** comienzo *m* [kōmyen¹sō]177; **final ~** fin *m* [fēn] 177

curve curva *f* [kōōr¹vä] 42

custody detención *f* [detensyōn¹] 154; **protective ~** custodia *f* preventiva [kōōstō¹dyä preventē¹vä] 154

customs aduana *f* [ädōō·ä¹nä] 80; **~ control** control *m* aduanero [kōntrōl¹ adōō·ä¹ne¹rō] 80; **~ declaration** declaración *f* de aduana [dekläräsyōn¹ de ädōō·ä¹nä] 80; **~ office** edificio *m* de aduanas [edēfē¹syō de ädōō·ä-näs] 80; **~ officer** aduanero *m* [ädōō·äne¹rō] 80

cut *(noun)* herida *f*, corte *m* [erē¹dä, kōr¹te] 169

cut *(verb)* cortar [kōrtär¹] 181

cutlery cubiertos *m/pl* [kōōbyer¹tōs] 99

cylinder cilindro *m* [sēlēn¹drō] 52; **~ head** culata *f*, cabeza *f (Mex)* del cilindro [kōōlä¹tä, käbe¹sä del sēlēn¹drō] 52; **~ head gasket** junta *f* de la culeta, empaque *m* de cabeza *(Mex)* [hōōn¹tä de lä kōō!ä¹tä, empä¹ke de käbe¹sä] 52

Canadian dollars dólares *m/pl* canadienses [dō¹läres känädyen¹ses] 152

Catholic católico *m* [kätō¹lēkō] 124

Christ cristo *m* [krēs¹tō] 124

Christian cristiano *m* [krēstyä¹nō] 124

Christianity cristianismo *m* [krēstyänēz¹mō] 124

Christmas Navidad *f* [nävēdäd¹] 33; **Merry ~** ¡Feliz Navidad! [felēs¹ nävēdäd¹] 23

D

daily todos los días [tōdōs lōs dē'äs] 31

dairy lechería f [letsherē'ä] 128

damage *(noun)* daños m/pl [dä'nyōs] 49

dance *(verb)* bailar [bīlär'] 184

dance *(noun)* baile m [bī'le] 183; ~ **hall** sala f de baile [sä'lä de bī'le] 183

dancer bailarín m [bīlärēn'] 177

dandruff caspa f [käs'pä] 158

danger! ¡peligro! [pelē'grō] 191

dangerous peligroso [pelēgrō'sō] 185

dark oscuro [ōskōō'rō] 127

darn zurcir [sōōrsēr'] 137

darning thread hilo m para zurcir [ē'lō pä'rä sōōrsēr'] 136

date of birth fecha f de nacimiento [fe'tshä de näsēmyen'tō] 79

daughter hija f [ē'hä] 35

dawn madrugada f [mädrōōgä'dä] 26

day día m [dē'ä] 31; **New Year's** ~ Año Nuevo [ä'nyō nōō·e'vō] 33; ~ **room** sala f de estar [sä'lä de estär'] 96

dead end street callejón m sin salida [kälyehōn' sēn sälē'dä] 120

deal *(cards)* dar [där] 181

dealership garage taller m concesionario [tälyer' kōnsesyōnä'ryō] 49

December diciembre m [dēsyem'bre] 33

decimeter decímetro m [desē'metrō] 193

deck *(ship)* cubierta f [kōōbyer'tä] 76; **boat** ~ cubierta f de botes [kōōbyer'tä de bō'tes] 76; **fore** ~ cubierta f de proa [kōōbyer'tä de prō'ä] 76; **main** ~ cubierta f principal [kōōbyer'tä prēnsēpäl'] 76; **poop** ~ cubierta f de popa [kōōbyer'tä de pō'pä] 76; **promenade** ~ cubierta f de paseo [kōōbyer'tä de päse'ō] 76; **steerage** ~ entrepuente m [entrepōō·en'te] 76;

sun ~ cubierta f del sol [kōōbyer'tä del sōl] 76; **upper** ~ cubierta f superior [kōōbyer'tä sōōperyōr'] 76; ~ **chair** silla f de cubierta, tumbona f, hamaca f [sē'lyä de kōōbyer'tä, tōōmbō'nä, ämä'ka] 76

declare declarar [deklärär'] 80

defeat derrota f [derrō'tä] 188

delicious! ¡muy rico! [mōō·ē rē'kō] 101

delivery truck furgoneta f, camioneta f [fōōrgōne'tä, kämyōne'tä] 40

denomination *(religious)* confesión f religiosa [kōnfesyōn' relēhyō'sä] 125

dental clinic clínica f dental [klē'nēkä dentäl'] 174

dentist dentista m [dentēs'tä] 174

dentistry odontología f [ōdōntōlōhē'ä] 39

dentures dentadura f/pl postiza [dentädōō'rä pōstē'sä] 174

deodorant desodorante m [desōdōrän'te] 141

depart salir [sälēr'] 67

departure salida f [sälē'dä] 67

deposit *(noun)* pago m a cuenta [pä'gō ä kōō·en'ta] 91

deposit *(verb)* ingresar, consignar [ēngresär', kōnsēgnär'] 152

dermatologist dermatólogo m [dermätō'lōgō] 162

destination destino m [destē'nō] 149

detergent detergente m [deterhen'te] 144

detour desviación f, desvío m [desvē·äsyōn', desvē'ō] 42

develop desarrollar, revelar [desärrōlyär', revelär'] 132

dew rocío m [rōsē'ō] 26

diabetes diabetes f [dyäbe'tes] 170

diabetic diabético [dyäbe'tēkō] 164

diagnosis diagnóstico m [dyägnōs'tēkō] 172

dial *(noun)* disco m [dēs'kō] 149

dial *(verb)* marcar [märkär'] 149

diamond diamante *m* [dyämän'te] 153

diamonds diamantes *m/pl* [dyämän'tes] 181

diaphragm diafragma *m* [dyäfräg'mä] 132

diarrhea diarrea *f* [dyärre'ä] 170

dice dados *m/pl* [dä'dōs] 181; **shoot ~** jugar a los dados [hōōgär' ä lōs dä'dōs] 181

dictionary diccionario *m* [dēksyōnä'ryō] 130

diesel gasóleo *m*, diesel *m (Mex)* [gäsō'le-ō, dyesel'] 45; **~ motor** motor *m* diesel [mōtōr' dyesel'] 54; **~ nozzle** tobera *f* [tōbe'rä] 52

diet dieta *f* [dye'tä] 165

differential diferencial *m* [dēferensyäl'] 52

digestion digestión *f* [dēhestyōn'] 166

digestive tablets pastillas *f/pl* para el estómago [pästē'lyäs pä'rä el estō'mägō] 160

digestive tonic gotas *f/pl* para el estómago [gō'täs pä'rä el estō'mägō] 160

dill eneldo *m* [enel'dō] 103

dinghy bote *m* [bō'te] 186

dining car coche-restaurante *m* [kō'tshe-restourän'te] 61

dining room comedor *m* [kōmedōr'] 74

dip stick varilla *f* del nivel de aceite [värē'lyä del nēvel' de äse'ēte] 52

diphtheria difteria *f* [dēfte'ryä] 170

dipped headlights luz *f* de cruce [lōōs de krōō'se] 53

direct directo [dērek'tō] 68; **~ dial** llamar directamente [lyämär' dērektämen'te] 147

direction dirección *f* [dēreksyōn'] 59; **~ sign** indicador *m* de camino [ēndēkädōr de kämē'nō] 42

director director *m* [dērektōr'] 177

disc disco *m* intervertebral [dēs'kō ēntervertebräl'] 166; **~ brake** freno *m* de disco [fre'nō de dēs'kō] 51

discharge dar de alta [där de äl'tä] 172

discothèque discoteca *f* [dēskōte'kä] 180

discount reducción *f* del precio [redōōksyōn' del pre'syō] 176

disease enfermedad *f* [enfermedäd'] 170; **contagious ~** enfermedad *f* contagiosa [enfermedäd' kōntähyō'sä] 170

disembark desembarcar [desembärkär'] 76

dish plato *m* [plä'tō] 101

dishes vajilla *f* [vähē'lyä] 96

disinfectant desinfectante *m* [desēnfektän'te] 160

dislocation dislocación *f* [dēslōkäsyōn'] 170

distilled water agua *f* destilada [a'gōō-ä destēlä'dä] 45

distributor distribuidor *m* [dēstrēbōō-ēdōr'] 52

district of town barrio *m* [bä'rryō] 120

ditch zanja *f* [sän'hä] 120

diuretic diurético *m* [dyōōre'tēkō] 160

dive bucear [bōōse-är'] 186

diving board trampolín *m* [trämpōlēn'] 186

divorced divorciado (-a) [dēvōrsyä'dō (-ä)] 79

dizziness mareo *m*, vértigo *m* [märe'ō, ver'tēgō] 170

dock *(noun)* muelle *m*, embarcadero *m* [mōō-e'lye, embärkäde'rō] 76

dock *(verb)* atracar [äträkär'] 76

doctor médico *m* + *f* [me'dēkō] 36;**~'s office** consultorio *m* [kōnsōōltō'ryō] 163

documentary documental *m* [dōkōōmentäl'] 179

dog perro *m* [pe'rrō] 191; **beware of the ~** ¡cuidado! ¡perro! [kōō-ēdä'dō, pe'rrō] 191

doll muñeca *f* [mōōnye'kä] 144

dome cúpula *f*, bóveda *f* [kōō'pōōlä,

bō¹vedä] 125

door puerta f [pōō·er¹tä] 91; ~ **handle** picaporte m [pĕkäpōr¹te] 91; ~ **lock** cerradura f, chapa f [serrädōō¹rä, tshä¹pä] 52

dormitory dormitorio m [dōrmētōr¹yō] 96

doubles dobles m/pl [dō¹bles] 189

downtown centro m ciudad, centro m urbano [sen¹trō syōōdäd¹, sen¹trō ōōrbä¹nō] 120

dozen docena f [dōse¹nä] 193

draft corriente f [kōrryen¹te] 26

drain desagüe m [desä¹gōō·e] 88

drama drama m [drä¹mä] 177

draw (cards) mover, jugar [mōver¹, hōōgär] 181

draw (noun) empate m [empä¹te] 188

drawer cajón m, gaveta f [kähōn¹, gäve¹tä] 91

dress vestido m [vestē¹dō] 134

dressing gown bata f [bä¹tä] 134

dressmaker costurera f [kōstōōre¹rä] 36

drier secador m [sekädōr¹] 156

drill taladro m [tälä¹drō¹] 57

drink (noun) refresco m [refres¹kō] 114; ~**ing water** agua f potable [ä¹-gōō·ä pōtä¹ble] 96

drip-dry "no se plancha" [nō se plän¹-tshä] 135

drive shaft árbol m del cardán [är¹bōl del kärdän¹] 52

drive-in movie cine m al aire libre [sē¹-ne äl ī¹re lē¹bre] 179

driver conductor m, chófer m [kōn-dōōktōr¹, tshō¹fer] 36

driver's license carnet m de conducir, licencia f de manejar (Mex) [kärnet¹ de kōndōōsēr¹, lēsen¹syä de mäne-här¹] 42

driver's seat asiento m del conductor [äsyen¹tō del kōndōōktōr¹] 55

driveway calzada f [kälsä¹dä] 42

driving instructor profesor m de a escuela [prōfesōr¹ de outō kōō·e¹lä] 36

drops gotas f/pl [gō¹täs] 160; **ear ~** tas f/pl para los oídos [gō¹täs p lōs ō·ē¹dōs] 160; **eye ~** gotas f/p ra los ojos [gō¹täs pä¹rä lōs ō¹ 160

drugs drogas f/pl [drō¹gäs] 154

dry secar [se¹kär] 92; ~ **cleaner's** ti rería f [tēntōrerē¹ä] 128; ~ **go store** mercería f [merserē¹ä] 136

dubbed doblado [dōblä¹dō] 179

dubbing doblaje m [dōblä¹he] 179

duck pato m [pä¹tō] 107

duet dúo m [dōō¹·ō] 177

dune duna f [dōō¹nä] 186

during the morning durante la mañ [dōōrän¹te lä mänyä¹nä] 31

dusk crepúsculo m [krepōōs¹kōōlō 52

duty derechos m/pl de aduana [de tshōs de ädōō·ä¹nä] 80; **pay ~** p derechos de aduana [pägär¹ de tshōs de ädōō·ä¹nä] 80; **export ~** rechos m/pl de salida [dere¹tshō sälē¹dä] 80; **import ~** derechos de entrada [dere¹tshōs de enträ 80

dye tinte m [tēn¹te] 141

dynamo dínamo m + f (Sp f) [dē¹nä 52

dysentery disentería f [dēsente 170

E

ear oreja f [ōre¹hä] 166; ~ **clips** z llos m/pl, aretes m/pl [särsē äre¹tes] 133

eardrum tímpano m [tēm¹pänō] 16

earlier antes [än¹tes] 32

early temprano [temprä¹nō] 31

earrings pendientes m/pl [pendy tes] 133

Easter Pascua f [päs¹kōō·ä] 33

economics ciencias *f/pl* económicas [syen'syäs ekōnō'mēkäs] 39

economy class clase *f* turista [klä'se tōōrēs'tä] 69

education *(subject)* pedagogía *f* [pedägōhē'ä] 39

eel anguila *f* [ängē'lä] 106

egg huevo *m*, blanquillo *m (Mex)* [ōō·e'vō, blängkē'lyō] 100; **soft-boiled ~** huevo *m* pasado por agua, tibio *(Mex)* [ōō·e'vō päsä'dō pôr ä'gōō·ä, tē'byō] 100; **bacon and eggs** huevos *m/pl* con tocino [ōō·e'vōs kōn tōse'nō] 100; **fried eggs** huevos *m/pl* fritos, estrellados *(Mex)* [ōō·e'vōs frē'tōs, estrelyä'dōs] 100; **ham and eggs** huevos *m/pl* con jamón [ōō·e'vōs kōn hämōn'] 100; **scrambled eggs** huevos *m/pl* revueltos [ōō·e'vōs revōō·el'tōs] 100

egg cup huevera *f* [ōō·eve'rä] 99

eight ocho [ō'tshō] 28

eighty ochenta [ōtshen'tä] 28

elastic cinta *f* de goma, caucho *m* [sēn'tä de gō'mä, kou'tshō] 136; **~ bandage** venda *f* elástica [ven'dä eläs'tēkä] 160; **~ stocking** media *f* elástica [me'dyä eläs'tēkä] 160

elbow codo *m* [kō'dō] 166

electric shaver máquina *f* de afeitar eléctrica [mä'kēnä de äfe·ētär' elek'trēkä] 141

electrical connections enchufes *m/pl*, soquetes *m/pl*, dados *m/pl (Mex)* [entshōō'fes, sōke'tes, dä'dōs] 95

electrician electricista *m* [elektrēsēs'tä] 36

elevator ascensor *m*, elevador *m (Mex)* [äsensōr', elevädōr'] 91

embassy embajada *f* [embähä'dä] 120

emerald esmeralda *f* [ezmeräl'dä] 133

emergency brake *(train)* alarma *f* 66

emergency chute rampa *f* de emergencia [räm'pä de emer*h*en'syä] 70

emergency exit salida *f* de emergencia [säle'dä de emer*h*en'syä] 70

emergency landing aterrizaje *m* forzoso [äterrēsä'*h*e fôrsō'sō] 70

emergency ward sala *f* de emergencias [sä'lä de emer*h*en'syäs] 49

emetic emético *m* [eme'tēkō] 160

endive escarola *f* [eskärō'lä] 110

enema enema *f* [ene'mä] 160

engine motor *m* [mōtōr'] 70

engineer *(scientific)* ingeniero *m* [ēnhenye'rō] 36; **~** *(railroad)* maquinista *m* [mäkēnēs'tä] 36

English inglés [ēngles'] 24

enjoy oneself divertirse [dēvertēr'se] 184

enlargement ampliación *f* [ämplē·äsyōn'] 131

enough suficiente [sōōfēsyen'te] 46; **not ~** muy poco [mōō'·ē pō'kō] 127

entrance entrada *f* [enträ'dä] 67

entry entrada *f* [enträ'dä] 79; **~ visa** visa *f*, visado *m (Sp)* de entrada [vē'sä, vēsä'dō de enträ'dä] 79

envelope sobre *m* [sō'bre] 138

eraser goma *f*, borrador *m* [gō'mä, bōrrädōr'] 138

essentials: the ~ lo más necesario [lō mäs nesesä'ryō] 50

eve: New Year's Eve Año Viejo [ä'nyō vye'hō] 33

evening noche *f* [nō'tshe] 183; **Good ~!** ¡Buenas noches! [bōō·e'näs nō'tshes] 12; **in the ~** por la tarde *or* noche [pōr lä tär'de, nō'tshe] 31; **this ~** esta tarde [es'tä tär'de] 31

every cada, todos los [kä'dä, tōdōs lōs] 31; **~ day** todos los días [tōdōs lōs dē'äs] 31

everything todo [tō'dō] 83

exact exacto [eksäk'tō (-ä)] 30

examination *(lab)* análisis *m* [änä'lēsēs] 172; **~** *(of person)* reconocimiento *m* [rekōnōsēmyen'tō] 172

examine examinar, reconocer [eksä-mēnär', rekōnōser'] 172

excavations excavaciones *f/pl* [ekskä-väsyō'nes] 12

excess baggage exceso *m* de equipaje [ekse'sō de ekēpä'*he*] 68

exchange *(verb)* cambiar [kämbyär'] 127; **money ~** *(noun)* cambio *m* de moneda [käm'byō de mōne'dä] 152; **rate of ~** cambio *m* [käm'byō] 151

excursion excursión *f* [ekskōōrsyōn'] 76; **~ program** programa *m* de la excursión *f* [prōgrä'mä de lä ekskōōr-syōn] 76; **land ~s** excursiones a tierra [ekskōōrsyō'nes ä tye'rrä] 72

excuse me! *(apology)* ¡discúlpeme!, ¡discúlpame! *(fam)* [dēskōōl'peme, dēskōōl'päme] 22

excuse me? *(when passing)* ¿permiso? [permē'sō] 20

exhaust escape *m* [eskä'pe] 52

exhibition exposición *f* [ekspōsēsyōn'] 121

exit salida *f* [sälē'dä] 42; **~ visa** visa *f*, visado *m (Sp)* de salida [vē'sä, vēsä'-dō de sälē'dä] 79

expensive caro [kä'rō] 127

exposure exposición *f* [ekspōsēsyōn'] 132; **~ meter** fotómetro *m*, exposímetro *m* [fōtō'metrō, ekspōsē'metrō] 132

express train expreso *m* [ekspre'sō] 60

extend prorogar [prōrōgär'] 79

extension cord cordón *m*, cable *m* de empalme, cable *m* de extensión *(Mex)* [kōrdōn', kä'ble de empäl'me, kä'ble de ekstensyōn'] 91

external externo [ekster'nō] 159

extra week semana *f* suplementaria [semä'nä sōōplementär'yä] 91

extract sacar, extraer [säkär', eksträ·er'] 174

eye ojo *m* [ō'hō] 166; **~ doctor** optometrista *m + f* [ōptōmetrēs'tä] 162;

~ liner trazado *m* de párpado [träsä'dō de pär'pädō] 141; **~ shadow** sombra *f* de ojos [sōm'brä de ō'hōs] 141

eyeball globo *m* del ojo [glō'bō del ō'hō] 166

eyebrow ceja *f* [se'hä] 156; **~ pencil** lápiz *m* de cejas [lä'pēs de se'häs] 141

eyelid párpado *m* [pär'pädō] 166

F

fabric tela *f* [te'lä] 137

face cara *f*, rostro *m* [kä'rä, rōs'trō] 166; **~** *(of clock)* esfera *f* [esfe'rä] 143; **~ mask** mascarilla *f* [mäskärē'-lyä] 156; **~ massage** masaje *m* facial [mäsä'*he* fäsyäl] 156

factory fábrica *f* [fä'brēkä] 121

falling rocks desprendimiento *m* de piedras, zona *f* de derrumbes *(Mex)* [desprendēmyen'tō de pye'dräs, sō'nä de derrōōm'bes] 42

false tooth diente *m* de espiga [dyen'te de espē'gä] 174

family familia *f* [fämē'lyä] 35

fan ventilador *m* [ventēlädōr'] 53; **~ belt** correa *f* de ventilador, banda *f* de ventilador [kōrre'ä de ventēlädōr', bän'dä de ventēlädōr'] 53

far lejos [le'hōs] 59; **as ~ as** hasta [äs'-tä] 40; **how far?** ¿ a qué distancia? [ä ke dēstän'syä] 45

fare precio *m* del boleto, billete *(Sp)* [pre'syō del bōle'tō, bēlye'te] 62; **pay the excess ~** pagar la diferencia [pägär' lä dēferen'syä] 66; **~ discount** tarifa *f* reducida [tärē'fä re-dōōsē'dä] 67

farewell dinner comida *f* de despedida [kōmē'dä de despedē'dä] 76

farmer agricultor *m* [ägrēkōōltōr'] 36

farmhouse granja *f*, cortijo *m (Mex)*

[grän'hä, körtë'hö] 121

far-sighted présbita [pres'bëtä] 138

fashion boutique boutique f [bō-ōōtē'-ke] 128

fashion show desfile m de modas [desfë'le de mõ'däs] 180

fast rápido [rä'pëdō] 42; ~ *(clock)* adelantado [ädeläntä'dō] 31; ~ **train** tren m rápido [tren rä'pëdō] 60

fat *(noun)* grasa f [grä'sä] 102

father padre m, papá m *(Mex)* [pä'dre, päpä'] 35; ~ **-in-law** suegro m [sōō·e'grō] 35

fatty grasiento [gräsyen'tō] 115

faucet grifo m [grē'fō] 88

February febrero m [febre'rō] 33

fee tarifa f [tärë'fä] 97; **rental** ~ tarifa f de alquiler [tärë'fä de älkēler'] 97

fencing esgrima f [esgrē'mä] 188

fender guardabarros m [gōō·ärdäbä'rrōs] 53

ferry transbordador m, ferry m [tränsbōrdädōr', fe'rrē] 72; **train** ~ transbordador m de trenes [tränsbōrdädōr' de tre'nes] 76

fever fiebre f, calentura f *(Mex)* [fye'bre, kälentōō'rä] 170; ~ **cure** antipirético m, antitérmico m [äntēpēre'tēkō, äntēter'mēkō] 161

fiancé prometido m, novio m [prōmetē'dō, nō'vyō] 14

fiancée prometida f, novia f [prōmetē'dä, nō'vyä] 14

fibre fibra f [fē'brä] 137; **synthetic** ~ fibra f sintética [fē'brä sēnte'tēkä] 137

fight *(noun)* pelea f [pele'ä] 187

fig higo m [ē'gō] 111

figure skating patinaje m artístico [pätēnä'he ärtēstē'kō] 188

figurine figura f [fēgōō'rä] 144

file *(noun)* lima f [lē'mä] 57

fill *(tooth)* calzar, empastar *(Sp)* [kälsär', empästär'] 174; ~ **in** (re)llenar

[(re)lyenär'] 78; ~ **it up** lleno [lye'nō] 45

fillet filete m [fēle'te] 108

filling calza f, empaste m *(Sp)* [käl'sä, empäs'te] 174; **temporary** ~ empaste m provisional [empäs'te prōvēsyō-näl'] 174

film *(noun)* rollo m, carrete m *(Sp)* [rō'lyō, kärre'te] 132; ~ *(movie)* película f [pelē'kōōlä] 132; ~ *(verb)* filmar [fēlmär'] 132; ~ **actor** actor m de cine [äktōr' de sē'ne] 179; ~ **festival** festival m cinematográfico [festēväl sēnemätōgräf'ēkō] 179; ~ **screening** sesión f de cine [sesyōn' de sē'ne] 179; **cartridge** ~ rollo m, carrete m *(Sp)* [rō'lyō, kärre'te] 131; **color** ~ película f en color [pelē'kōōlä en kōlōr'] 132; **daylight color** ~ película f en color para luz diurna [pelē'kōōlä en kōlōr' pä'rä lōōs dyōōr'nä] 132; **educational** ~ documental m [dōkōōmentäl'] 179; **feature** ~ largometraje m [lärgōmeträ'he] 179; **reversal** ~ película f reversible [pelē'kōōlä reversē'ble] 132; **roll** ~ carrete m, rollo m [kärre'te, rō'lyō] 132; **sixteen millimeter color** ~ película f de dieciséis milímetros, en color [pelē'kōōlä de dyesē'sē·ēs mēlē'metrōs, en kōlōr'] 131; **thirty-five millimeter** ~ película f de treinta y cinco milímetros [pelē'kōōlä de tre'ēntä ē sēng'kō mēlē'metrōs] 131; **thirty-six exposure** ~ rollo m, carrete m *(Sp)* de treinta y seis fotografías [rō'lyō, kärre'te de tre'ēntä ē se'ēs fōtōgräfē'äs] 131; **twenty exposure** ~ rollo m, carrete m *(Sp)* de veinte fotografías [rō'lyō, kärre'te de ve'ēnte fōtōgräfē'äs] 131

filter filtro m [fēl'trō] 132

fine muy bien [mōō'ē byen] 12

finger dedo m [de'dō] 167; **index** ~ dedo m índice [de'dō ēn'dēse] 167;

middle ~ dedo *m* del corazón [de'dō del kōräsōn'] 167; **ring** ~ dedo *m* anular [de'dō änōōlär'] 167

fire department bomberos *m/pl* [bōm-be'rōs] 49

fire extinguisher extintor *m*, extinguidor *m* [ekstēngtōr', ekstēngōō-ēdōr'] 53

fireplace chimenea *f* [tshēmene'ä] 91

first (1st) primero [prēme'rō] 29

first class primera clase [prēme'rä klä'-se] 62

first-aid puesto *m* de socorros, "primeros auxilios" *(Mex)* [pōō-es'tō de sōkō'rrōs, prēme'rōs ouksē'lyōs] 121; ~ **kit** botiquín *m* [bōtēkēn'] 161; ~ **station** puesto *m* de socorro, "primeros auxilios" *(Mex)* [pōō-es'tō de sōkō'rrō, prēme'rōs ouksē'lyōs] 49

fish *(noun)* pescado *m* [peskä'dō] 107

fish *(verb)* pescar [peskär'] 185

fish market pescadería *f* [peskäderē'ä] 128

fisherman pescador *m* [peskädōr'] 36

fishing pesca *f* [pes'kä] 188; ~ **license** licencia *f* de pescar [lēsen'syä de peskär'] 188; ~ **rod** caña *f* [kä'nyä] 188; ~ **trawler** barco *m* pesquero [bär'kō peske'rō] 75

fit ataque *m* [ätä'ke] 170

five cinco [sēng'kō] 28

fix arreglar [arreglär'] 50

flannel franela *f* [fräne'lä] 137

flash bulb bombilla *f*, foco *m* de flash [bōmbē'lyä, fō'kō de fläsh] 132

flash cube cubo *m* de flash [kōō'bō de fläsh] 132

flashing signal avisador *m* luminoso [ävēsadōr' lōōmēnō'sō] 53

flashlight linterna *f*, foco *m (Mex)*, luz *f* [lēnter'nä, fō'kō, lōōs] 144

flat *(shoes)* bajo [bä'hō] 139

flatulence flatulencia *f* [flätōōlen'syä] 170

flight vuelo *m* [vōō·e'lō] 68; ~ **attendant** azafata *f*, aeromoza *f*, cabinera *f* [äsäfä'tä, ä·erōmō'sä, käbēne'rä] 71

flint piedra *f* [pye'drä] 140

flirt flirteo *m* [flērte'ō] 184

float *(car)* flotador *m* [flōtädōr'] 53

floor piso *m* [pē'sō] 91; **second** ~ segundo piso [segōōn'dō pē'sō] 82

flower pot tiesto *m*, maceta *f* [tyes'tō, mäse'tä] 130

flowers flores *f/pl* [flō'res] 130

flu gripe *f* [grē'pe] 170

fly *(verb)* volar [vōlär'] 71

flying time duración *f* de vuelo [dōōräsyōn' de vōō·e'lō] 71

FM frequencia *f* modulada [frekōō·en'syä mōdōōlä'dä] 182

fog niebla *f* [nye'blä] 27

fond of aficionado a [äfēsyōnä'dō ä] 187

font pila *f* bautismal [pē'lä boutēzmäl'] 125

food comida *f* [kōme'dä] 163; **diet** ~ platos *m/pl* de régimen [plä'tōs de re'hēmen] 98; **vegetarian** ~ platos *m/pl* vegetarianos [plä'tōs vehetäryä'nōs] 98; ~ **poisoning** intoxicación *f* alimenticia [ēntōksēkäsyōn' älēmentē'syä] 170

foot pie *m* [pye] 167; **on** ~ andando [ändän'dō] 116; ~ **brake** freno *m* de pedal [fre'nō de pedäl'] 51

footpath senda *f* [sen'dä] 42

for sale se vende [se ven'de] 191

forehead frente *f* [fren'te] 167

forest ranger guarda *m* forestal [gōō·är'dä fōrestäl'] 36

fork tenedor *m* [tenedōr'] 99

form *(noun)* formulario *m* [fōrmōōlä'-ryō] 78

fortress fortaleza *f* [fōrtäle'sä] 119

forward *(sports)* delantero *m* [delänte'-rō] 189

fountain fuente *f* [fōō·en'te] 121

four cuatro [kōō·äˈtrō] 28

fracture fractura f, quebradura f (Mex) [fräktōōˈrä, kebrädōōˈrä] 170

frame (eyeglass) montura f [mōntōōˈrä] 138

free libre [lēˈbre] 44; ~ **kick** golpe m franco [gōlˈpe frängˈkō] 189; ~ **style** carrera f libre [kärreˈrä lēˈbre] 188; ~ **wheel** (hub) rueda f libre [rōō·eˈdä lēˈbre] 53

freighter carguero m [kärgeˈrō] 77

French francés [fränsesˈ] 24

fresco fresco m [fresˈkō] 125

fresh fresco [fresˈkō] 102

Friday viernes m [vyerˈnes] 33; **Good ~** viernes m santo [vyerˈnes sänˈtō] 33

fried frito [frēˈtō] 102

friend (male) amigo m [ämēˈgō] 14

friend (female) amiga f [ämēˈgä] 14

front (of train) puertas f/pl delanteras [pōō·erˈtäs delänteˈräs] 66; **up ~** en la cabeza [en lä käbeˈsä] 65; ~ **desk** recepción f [resepsyōnˈ] 91; ~ **door** puerta f de entrada [pōō·erˈtä de enträˈdä] 91; ~ **seat** asiento m delantero [äsyenˈtō delänteˈrō] 55; ~ **passenger seat** asiento m delantero del pasajero [äsyenˈtō delänteˈrō del päsäheˈrō] 55; ~ **wheel** rueda f delantera [rōō·eˈdä delänteˈrä] 47

frontal sinus seno m frontal [seˈnō frōntälˈ] 167

frost helada f [eläˈdä] 27

frostbite congelación f [kōnheläsyōnˈ] 170

fruit fruta f [frōōˈtä] 112; ~ **cocktail** coctel m de frutas, macedonia f de frutas (Sp) [kōktelˈ de frōōˈtäs, mäsedōˈnyä de frōōˈtäs] 112; ~ **market** frutería f [frōōterēˈä] 128

fuel gasolina f [gäsōlēˈnä] 53; ~ **injector** bomba f de inyección [bōmˈbä de ēnyeksyōnˈ] 53; ~ **lines** conducto m de gasolina [kōndōōkˈtō de gäsōlēˈnä] 53; ~ **pump** bomba f de gasolina [bōmˈbä de gäsōleˈnä] 53

full beam luz f de carretera [lōōs de kärreteˈrä] 53

full coverage insurance seguro m [segōōˈrō] 41

full-fare precio m normal [preˈsyō nōrmälˈ] 59

fullback defensa m [defenˈsä] 189

funnel embudo m [embōōˈdō] 57

fur coat abrigo m de piel [äbrēˈgō de pyel] 134

fur jacket chaquetón m de piel [tshäketōnˈ de pyel] 134

furrier peletero m [peleteˈrō] 128

fuse fusible m [fōōsēˈble] 53

G

gall bladder vesícula f [vesēˈkōōlä] 167

gall stones cálculos m/pl biliares [kälˈkōōlōs bēlyärˈyes] 170

gallery galería f [gälerēˈä] 119

gallon galón m [gälōnˈ] 193

gambling casino casino m [käseˈnō] 181

game juego m [hōō·eˈgō] 181

gangway plancha f [plänˈtshä] 76

garage garaje m [gäräˈhe] 44; ~ (workshop) taller m mecánico [tälyerˈ mekäˈnēkō] 50

garden jardín m [härdēnˈ] 121

gardener jardinero m [härdēneˈrō] 36

gargle gárgaras f/pl [gärˈgäräs] 161

garlic ajo m [äˈhō] 103

garter belt portaligas m, liguero m [pōrtälēˈgäs, lēgeˈrō] 134

garters ligas f/pl [lēˈgäs] 136

gas gasolina f [gäsōlēˈnä] 53; ~ **bottles** botellas f/pl, cilindros m/pl de gas [bōteˈlyäs, sēlēnˈdrōs de gäs] 95; ~ **station** gasolinera f, estación f de servicio [gäsōlēneˈrä, estäsyōnˈ de servēˈsyō] 45

gasket junta f, empaque m [hōōn'tä, empä'ke] 53

gasoline gasolina f [gäsōlē'nä] 45; ~ **can** bidón m de gasolina [bēdōn' de gäsōlē'nä] 45

gate puerta f [pōō·er'tä] 121

gauze bandage gasa f [gä'sä] 161

gear (car) marcha f, engrane m (Mex) [mär'tshä, engrä'ne] 53; ~ **lever** palanca f de cambios [pälän'kä de käm'byōs] 53; ~ **oil** aceite m lubricante [äse'ēte lōōbrēkän'te] 46; **put in** ~ meter la marcha [meter' lä mär'tshä] 53

gear box caja f de cambios [kä'hä de käm'byōs] 53

general delivery lista f de correos [lēs'-tä de kōrre'ōs] 149

general practitioner médico m general [me'dēkō heneräl'] 162

genital organs órganos m/pl genitales [ōr'gänōs henētä'les] 167

gentlemen señores m/pl, caballeros m/pl [senyō'res, käbälye'rōs] 13

geology geología f [he·ōlōhē'ä] 39

German alemán [älemän'] 24

German measles rubéola f [rōōbe'ōlä] 170

get conseguir [kōnsegēr'] 20; **get in** (vehicle) subir (a) [sōōbēr' (ä)] 67; **get off, out of** (véhicle) bajar (de) [bähär' (de)] 67, 117

gin ginebra f [hēne'brä] 113

ginger jengibre m [henhē'bre] 103

girdle faja f [fä'hä] 134

girl niña f, muchacha f [nē'nyä, mōō-tshä'tshä] 35

gladioli gladiolos m/pl [glädyō'lōs] 130

gland glándula f [glän'dōōlä] 167

glass vaso m [vä'sō] 99; **water** ~ vaso m para agua [vä'sō pä'rä ä'gōō·ä] 99; **wine** ~ vaso m para vino [vä'sō pä'rä vē'nō] 99

glasses lentes f/pl, anteojos m/pl, ga-

fas f/pl (Sp) [len'tes, änte·ō'hōs, gä'-fäs] 138

glazier vidriero m [vēdrē·e'rō] 37

glossy (adj.) brillante [brēlyän'te] 132

glossy (noun) revista f ilustrada [re-vēs'tä ēlōōsträ'dä] 182

gloves guantes m/pl [gōō·än'tes] 134

glue pegamento m [pegämen'tō] 138

glycerine glicerina f [glēserē'nä] 161

goal gol m [gōl] 187; **kick a** ~ meter un gol [meter' ōōn gōl] 190

goalie portero m [pōrte'rō] 190

God Dios [dyōs] 125

gold oro m [ō'rō] 133; ~ **plated** dorado [dōrä'dō] 133

golf golf m [gōlf] 188

good-bye! ¡adiós! [ädyōs'] 17; **say** ~ despedirse [despedēr'se] 17

goods mercancías f/pl [merkänsē'äs] 70

goose ganso m [gän'sō] 107

gospel evangelio m [evänhe'lyō] 125

gothic gótico m [gō'tēkō] 125

government office oficina f pública [ōfēsē'nä pōō'blēkä] 121

grain (noun) contrapelo m [kōnträpe'-lō] 157

grand piano piano m de cola [pē·ä'nō de kō'lä] 177

grandchild nieto m [nye'tō] 35

granddaughter nieta f [nye'tä] 35

grandfather abuelo m [äbōō·e'lō] 35

grandmother abuela f [äbōō·e'lä] 35

grandparents abuelos m/pl [äbōō·e'-lōs] 35

grandson nieto m [nye'tō] 35

grape uva f [ōō'vä] 112

grapefruit pomelo m [pōme'lō] 112; ~ **juice** jugo m, zumo m (Sp) de pomelo, de toronja (Mex) [hōō'gō, sōō'mō de pōme'lō, de tōrōn'hä] 100

grateful agradecido [ägrädesē'dō] 21

grave (noun) sepultura f [sepōōltōō'rä] 125

gray gris [grēs] 194; **ash ~** gris ceniza [grēs senē'sä] 194; **dark ~** gris oscuro [grēs ōskōō'rō] 194; **pale ~** gris claro [grēs klä'rō] 194

grease grasa f [grä'sä] 53

greasy grasiento [gräsyen'tō] 158

green verde [ver'de] 194; **dark ~** verde oscuro [ver'de ōskōō'rō] 194; **light ~** verde claro [ver'de klä'rō] 194

grill room parrilla f [pärrē'lyä] 91

grilled asado a la parrilla [äsä'dō ä lä pärrē'lyä] 102

grocery store tienda f de comestibles, de abarrotes *(Mex)* [tyen'dä de kōmestē'bles, de äbärrō'tes] 95

group fare ticket boleto m colectivo [bōle'tō kōlektē'vō] 62

guarded vigilado [vēhēlä'dō] 44

guest house casa f de huéspedes [kä'sä de ōō·e·s'pedes] 91

guide guía m [gē'ä] 121

gums encías f/pl [ensē'äs] 174

gym shoes zapatos m/pl de tenis, playeras [säpä'tōs de te'nēs, pläye'räs] 139

gymnast gimnasta m + f [hēmnäs'tä] 188

gymnastics gimnasia f [hēmnä'syä] 188; **~ with apparatus** gimnasia f con aparatos [hēmnä'syä kōn äpärä'tōs] 188

gynecologist ginecólogo m [hēnekō'lōgō] 162

H

hair pelo m [pe'lō] 155; **~ spray** laca f [lä'kä] 156; **~ tonic** loción f [lōsyōn'] 157; **~ drier** secador m [sekädōr'] 158; **~ loss** caída f del pelo [kä·ē'dä del pe'lō] 158; **~ style** peinado m [pe·ēnä'dō] 158

hairbrush cepillo m del pelo [sepē'lyō del pe'lō] 141

haircut corte m [kōr'te] 157

hair-do peinado m [pe·ēnä'dō] 158

hairdresser peluquero m [pelōōke'rō] 158

hairpiece postizo m [pōstē'sō] 158

hairpins horquillas f/pl, clips m/pl [ōrkē'lyäs, klēps] 141

half fare boleto m de media tarifa [bōle'tō de me'dya tärē'fä] 62

half past six las seis y media [läs se'ēs ē me'dyä] 30

half time medio tiempo m [me'dyō tyem'pō] 188

hall hall m, vestíbulo m [äl, vestē'bōōlō] 92

ham jamón m [hämōn'] 108

hammer martillo m [märtē'lyō] 57

hammock hamaca f [ämä'kä] 144

hand mano f [mä'nō] 167; **~s** *(on clock)* agujas f/pl, manecillas f/pl [ägōō'häs, mänesē'lyäs] 143; **~ brake** freno m de mano [fre'nō de mä'nō] 51; **~ luggage** bultos m/pl de mano [bōōl'tōs de mä'nō] 63

handbag bolso m, bolsa f *(Mex)* [bōl'sō, bōl'sä] 153

handball balonmano m [bälōnmä'nō] 189

handicrafts labores m/pl de mano [läbō'res de mä'nō] 144

handkerchief pañuelo m [pänyōō·e'lō] 134

handle manecilla f, manija f [mänesē'lyä, mänē'hä] 53

harbor puerto m [pōō·er'tō] 76; **~ police** policía f del puerto [pōlēsē'ä del pōō·er'tō] 76

hare liebre f [lye'bre] 108

hat sombrero m [sōmbre'rō] 134; **straw ~** sombrero m de paja [sōmbre'rō de pä'hä] 134

hay fever fiebre f del heno [fye'bre del e'nō] 170

hazelnut avellana f [ävelyä'nä] 111

head cabeza f [käbe'sä] 167; ~ **clerk** jefe m de recepción [*he*'fe de resep-syōn'] 91; ~ **nurse** enfermera f jefe [enferme'rä *he*'fe] 172

headlight faro m, focos m/pl (Mex) [fä'rō, fō'kōs] 53

head-on collision choque m de frente [tshō'ke de fren'te] 49

health resort estación f climática [estä-syōn' klēmä'tēkä] 175

heart corazón m [kōräsōn'] 167; ~ **attack** ataque m cardíaco [ätä'ke kär-dē'äkō] 170; ~ **problems** problemas m/pl cardíacas [prōble'mäs kärdē'ä-käs] 170

heartburn ardor m del estómago [är-dōr' del estō'mägō] 170

hearts (cards) corazones m/pl [kōrä-sō'nes] 181

heat calor m [kälōr'] 27

heating system calefacción f [kälefäk-syōn'] 53; **central** ~ calefacción f central [kälefäksyōn' senträl'] 90

heel (shoe) tacón m [täkōn'] 139

heel (foot) talón m [tälōn'] 167

helicopter helicóptero m [elēkōp'terō] 71

helm timón m [tēmōn'] 76

helmsman timonel m [tēmōnel'] 76

help ayuda f [äyōō'dä] 21

hemmorrhage hemorragia f [emōrrä'-hyä] 170

hemorrhoids hemorroides f/pl [emō-rrō·ē'des] 170

herbs hierbas f/pl [yer'bäs] 103

here aquí [äkē'] 14

herring arenque m [ären'ke] 106

high alto [äl'tō] 139; ~ **mass** misa f mayor [mē'sä mäyōr'] 123; ~ **pressure** (system) anticiclón m [äntēsē-klōn'] 27; ~ **school** instituto m de bachillerato [ēnstētōō'tō de bätshē-lyerä'tō] 39; ~ **test** (gas) gasolina f extra [gäsōlē'nä eks'trä] 45

high-rise (building) edificio m, torre f [edēfē'syō, tō'rre] 121

highway autopista f [outōpēs'tä] 42; ~ **patrol** policía f de tráfico [pōlēsē'ä de trä'fēkō] 42

hill colina f, cerro m [kōlē'nä, se'rrō] 121

hip cadera f [käde'rä] 167

history historia f [ēstōr'yä] 39

hitch-hike hacer auto-stop, viajar por aventón (Mex) [äser' ou'tō-stōp', vē·ähär' pōr äventōn'] 43

hoarseness ronquera f [rōnke'rä] 170

hockey hockey m [hō'kē] 189

hold-up atraco m [äträ'kō] 153

home casa f [kä'sä] 15; at ~ en casa [en kä'sä] 15

honey miel f [myel] 100

hood capó m, capota f [käpō', käpō'tä] 53

horizontal bar barra f fija [bä'rrä fē'*h*ä] 188

horn bocina f, claxon m, pito m [bōsē'-nä, klä'ksōn, pē'tō] 53

horse caballo m [käbä'lyō] 189; ~ **cart** carro m, carreta f (Mex) [kä'rrō, kä-rre'tä] 41; ~ **race** carrera f de caba-llos [kärre'rä de käbä'lyōs] 189

horseradish rábano m picante [rä'bä-nō pēkän'te] 103

hospital hospital m [ōspētäl'] 49

hostal father encargado m del al-bergue [enkärgä'dō del älber'ge] 96; **hostal mother** encargada f del al-bergue [enkärgä'dä del älber'ge] 96; **hostel parents** encargados m/pl del albergue [enkärgä'dōs del älber'ge] 96

hot caliente [kälyen'te] 94; ~ (spicy) pi-cante [pēkän'te] 102; ~ **chocolate** chocolate m [tshōkōlä'te] 100; ~ **spring** fuente f termal [fōō·en'te ter-mäl'] 175

hotel hotel m [ōtel'] 92; **beach** ~ hotel

m de playa [ōtel' de plä'yä] 92; ~ **restaurant** restaurante *m* del hotel [restouurän'te del ōtel'] 92

hour hora *f* [ō'rä] 31; **every ~** cada hora [kä'dä ō'rä] 31; **quarter ~** cuarto de hora [kōō·är'tō de ō'rä] 87; **half ~** media hora [me'dyä ō'rä] 87

house casa *f* [kä'sä] 92; ~ **key** llave *f* de la casa [lyä've de lä kä'sä] 92; ~ **number** número *m* (de la casa) [nōō'merō (de lä kä'sä)] 121

how como [kō'mō] 12; ~ **are you?** ¿cómo está usted? [kō'mō estä' ōōste'] 12; ~ **far** a qué distancia [ä ke de'stän'syä] 72

hub cubo *m* [kōō'bō] 53; ~ **cap** tapacubos *m*, copa *f* [täpäkōō'bōs, kō'pä] 53

hundred cien, ciento [syen, syen'tō] 28

hundredweight *(approx.)* un quintal [ōōn kēntäl'] 193

hunting caza *f* [kä'sä] 188; ~ **license** licencia *f* de caza [lēsen'syä de kä'sä] 188

hurt herido [erē'dō] 49

husband esposo *m*, marido *m* [espō'sō, märē'dō] 13

hydrogen peroxide agua *f* oxigenada [ä'gōō·ä ōksēhenä'dä] 161

hypertension hipertensión *f* [ēpertensyōn'] 170

I

ice hielo *m* [ye'lō] 27; ~ **cream** helado *m* [elä'dō] 112; **chocolate ~ cream** helado *m* de chocolate [elä'dō de tshōkōlä'te] 112; **strawberry ~ cream** helado *m* de fresa [elä'dō de fre'sä] 112; **vanilla ~ cream** helado *m* de vainilla [elä'dō de vēnē'lyä] 112; ~ **skating rink** pista *f* de hielo [pēs'tä de ye'lō] 180

icy road carretera *f* helada [kärrete'rä elä'dä] 27

identity card documento *m*, carnet *m* de identidad [dōkōōmen'tō, kärnet' de ēdentēdäd'] 79

ignition encendido *m* [ensendē'dō] 54; ~ **cable** cable *m* del encendido [kä'ble del ensendē'dō] 54; ~ **key** llave *f* de contacto [lyä've de kōntäk'tō] 54; ~ **lock** interruptor *m* (del encendido) [ēnterrōōptōr' (del ensendē'dō)] 54

illness enfermedad *f* [enfermedäd'] 170

inch pulgada *f* [pōōlgä'dä] 193

incisor diente *m* incisivo [dyen'te ēnsēsē'vō] 174

included incluido [ēnklōō·ē'dō] 83

indigestion trastornos *m/pl* digestivos [trästōr'nōs dēhestē'vōs] 170

inflammation inflamación *f* [ēnflämäsyōn'] 170

influenza gripe *f* [grē'pe] 170

information información *f* [ēnfōrmäsyōn'] 67

infusion infusión *f* [ēnfōōsyōn'] 172

inhale inhalar [ēnälär'] 175

injection inyección *f* [ēnyeksyōn'] 174

injured *(noun)* heridos *m/pl* [erē'dōs] 48

injury herida *f* [erē'dä] 49

ink tinta *f* [tēn'tä] 138

inn posada *f*, hostal *m* [pōsä'dä, ōstäl'] 81

inner tube cámara *f*, tubo *(Mex)* de aire [kä'märä, tōō'bō de ī're] 46

innocent inocente [ēnōsen'te] 154

inquiry informe *m* [ēnfōr'me] 92

insect repellent insecticida *m* [ēnsektēsē'dä] 161

inside dentro [den'trō] 47

in-sole plantilla *f* [pläntē'lyä] 139

insomnia insomnio *m* [ēnsōm'nyō] 170

inspection light lámpara *f* piloto or de prueba [läm'pärä pēlō'tō, de prōō·e'bä] 57

insulation aislamiento m [īzlämyen'tō] 54

insurance seguro m [segōo'rō] 49; ~ **certificate** tarjeta f de seguro [tärhe'tä de segōo'rō] 79

insure asegurar [asegōorär'] 63

insured mail correo m asegurado [kō-rre'ō äsegōorä'dō] 149

intensive care unit unidad f de cuidados intensivos [ōonēdäd' de kōo-ē-dä'dōs ēntensē'vōs] 172

intermission descanso m, intermedio m, entreacto m [deskän'sō, ēnter-me'dyō, entre-äk'tō] 177

internal interno [ēnter'nō] 159

internist internista m + f [ēnternēs'tä] 162

interpreter intérprete m + f [ēnter'pre-te] 36

interrupt interrumpir [ēnterrōompēr'] 62

interrupter ruptor m [rōoptōr'] 54

intersection cruce m, crucero m (Mex) [krōo'se, krōose'rō] 42

intestinal catarrh enteritis f [enterē'tēs] 170

intestine intestino m [ēntestē'nō] 167

invitation invitación f [ēmbētäsyōn'] 16

invite invitar [ēmbētär'] 183

iodine yodo m [yō'dō] 161

iron planchar [pläntshär'] 92

Islam Islam m [ēzläm'] 125

island isla f [ēz'lä] 76

J

jack (cards) valet m [välet'] 181

jack (tool) gato m [gä'tō] 57

jacket (lady's) chaqueta f [tshäke'tä] 134

jacket (man's) saco m, americana f (Sp), chaqueta f [sä'kō, ämerēkä'nä, tshäke'tä] 134

jackknife navaja f [nävä'hä] 144

jam mermelada f [mermelä'dä] 100

January enero m [ene'rō] 33

jaundice ictericia f [ēkterē'syä] 170

jaw maxilar m, mandíbula f [mäksēlär', mändē'bōolä] 167; **upper** ~ maxilar m, mandíbula f superior [mäksēlär', mändē'bōolä sōoperyōr'] 167; **lower** ~ maxilar m, mandíbula f inferior [mäksēlär', mändē'bōolä ēnferyōr'] 167

jersey jersey m [her'sē] 137

jet plane jet m, avión m a reacción (Sp) [het, ävyōn'ä re·äksyōn'] 71

jetty malecón m, muelle m [mälekōn', mōo·e'lye] 76

Jew judío m [hōodē'ō] 124

jewelry joyas f/pl [hō'yäs] 133; **costume** ~ bisutería f, fantasía f [bēsōote-rē'ä, fäntäsē'ä] 133

Jewish judío [hōodē'ō] 125

joint articulación f [ärtēkōoläsyōn'] 167

joker (cards) comodín m [kōmōdēn'] 181

journalism periodismo m [peryōdēz'-mō] 39

journalist periodista m + f [peryōdēs'-tä] 37

journey viaje m [vyä'he] 43

Judaism judaísmo m [hōodä·ēz'mō] 125

judge juez m + f [hōo·es'] 37

judo yudo m, judo m (Sp) [yōo'dō, hōo'dō] 188

juice jugo m, zumo m (Sp) [hōo'gō, sōo'mō] 100; **fruit** ~ jugo m, zumo m (Sp) [hōo'gō, sōo'mō] 100; **grapefruit** ~ jugo m, zumo m (Sp) de pomelo, de toronja (Mex) [hōo'gō, sōo'mō de pōme'lō, de tōrōn'hä] 100; **orange** ~ jugo m, zumo m (Sp) de naranja [hōo'gō, sōo'mō de nä-rän'hä] 100

juicy jugoso [hōogō'sō] 102

July julio m [hōōˈlyō] 33
jumping salto m [sälˈtō] 189
June junio m [hōōˈnyō] 33

K

kerchief pañuelo m de cabeza [pä-nyōō·eˈlō de käbeˈsä] 144
ketchup salsa f de tomate [sälˈsä de tō-mäˈte] 103
key llave f [lyäˈve] 85
kidnapping secuestro m [sekōō·esˈtrō] 153
kidney riñón m [rēnyōnˈ] 167; ~ **stones** cálculos m/pl renales [kälˈ-kōōlōs renäˈles] 170
kilometer kilómetro m [kēlōˈmetrō] 193
king rey m [reˈē] 181
kiss (noun) beso m [beˈsō] 184
kiss (verb) besar [besärˈ] 184
kitchen cocina f [kōsēˈnä] 92
kitchenette rincón-cocina m, cocineta f [rēnkōnˈ-kōsēˈnä, kōsēneˈtä] 92
knee rodilla f [rōdēˈlyä] 167; ~ **socks** medias f/pl cortas [meˈdyäs kōrˈtäs] 134
kneecap rótula f [rōˈtōōlä] 167
knife cuchillo m [kōōtshēˈlyō] 99; **pocket** ~ navaja f [näväˈhä] 144
knight (chess) caballo m [käbäˈlyō] 181
knot nudo m [nōōˈdō] 76

L

ladies señoras f/pl, damas f/pl [senyōˈ-räs, däˈmäs] 13; ~ **shoes** zapatos m/pl de señora [säpäˈtōs de senyōˈrä] 139
lake lago m [läˈgō] 76
lamb cordero m [kōrdeˈrō] 108; **baby** ~ cordero m lechal [kōrdeˈrō letshälˈ] 108
lamp lámpara f [lämˈpärä] 92; **reading** ~ lámpara f para leer [lämˈpärä päˈrä le·erˈ] 93

land (noun) tierra f [tyeˈrrä] 76
land (verb) tomar tierra [tōmärˈ tyeˈrrä] 76
land (planes) aterrizar [äterrēsärˈ] 71
landing aterrizaje m [äterrēsäˈhe] 71
landing gear tren m de aterrizaje [tren de äterrēsäˈhe] 71
landing stage embarcadero m [embär-kädeˈrō] 76
landscape paisaje m [pīsäˈhe] 121
lane (highway) carril m [kärrēlˈ] 42
lane camino m, sendero m [kämēˈnō, sendeˈrō] 121; **get in** ~ (merge) to-mar fila [tōmärˈ fēˈlä] 43
lard manteca f (de cerdo) [mänteˈkä (de serˈdō)] 103
larynx laringe f [lärēnˈhe] 167
last último [ōōlˈtēmō] 59; ~ **stop** termi-nal m + f [termēnälˈ] 59; ~ **year** año m pasado [äˈnyō päsäˈdō] 32
late tarde [tärˈde] 17; ~ (trains, planes) retraso m [reträˈsō] 61
later más tarde [mäs tärˈde] 15
launch (noun) lancha f [länˈtshä] 75
laundromat lavandería f automática [lävänderēˈä outōmäˈtēkä] 128
laundry lavandería f [lävänderēˈä] 92
lavender lila [lēˈlä] 194
law (subject) derecho m [dereˈtshō] 39
lawyer abogado m + f [äbōgäˈdō] 37
laxative laxante m [läksänˈte] 161
lean magro, macizo (Mex) [mägˈrō, mä-sēˈsō] 102
leash cuerda f [kōō·erˈdä] 144
leather cuero m [kōō·eˈrō] 139; ~ **coat** abrigo m de cuero [äbrēˈgō de kōō·eˈrō] 134; ~ **jacket** chaquetón m de cuero [tshäketōnˈ de kōō·eˈrō] 134
leave dejar [dehärˈ] 44
left izquierda [ēskyerˈdä] 40
leg pierna f [pyerˈnä] 167
lemon limón m, lima f (Mex) [lēmōnˈ, lēˈmä] 103

lemonade limonada *f* [lēmōnä'dä] 114

lend prestar [prestär'] 48

lengthen alargar [älärgär'] 137

lens *(camera)* objetivo *m* [obhetē'vō] 132

lenses lentes *m/pl* [len'tes] 138

letter carta *f* [kär'tä] 34; **local ~** carta *f* local [kär'tä lōkäl'] 145; **registered ~** carta *f* certificada, registrada [kär'tä sertēfēkä'dä, rehēsträ'dä] 145; **special delivery ~** carta *f* exprés, urgente [kär'tä ekspres', ōōrhen'te 145; **~ abroad** carta *f* para el extranjero [kär'tä pä'rä el ekstränhe'rō] 145

librarian bibliotecario *m* [bēblē·ōtekär'yō] 37

library biblioteca *f* [bēblē·ōte'kä] 121

libretto libreto *m* [lēbre'tō] 177

license plate matrícula *f*, placa *f* [mätrē'kōōlä, plä'kä] 54

life belt salvavidas *m* [sälvävē'däs] 76

life jacket chaleco *m* salvavidas [tshäle'kō sälvävē'däs] 71

lifeboat bote *m* salvavidas [bō'te sälvävē'däs] 75

lifeguard vigilante *m* [vēhēlän'te] 185

light *(adj.)* claro [klä'rō] 127

light luz *f* [lōōs] 88

lighter encendedor *m*, mechero *m* [ensendedōr', metshe'rō] 140; **~ fluid** gasolina *f* para el encendedor [gäsōlē'nä pä'rä el ensendedōr'] 140

lighthouse faro *m* [fä'rō] 76

lighting system alumbrado *m*, luces *f/pl* [älōōmbrä'dō, lōō'ses] 54

lightning relámpago *m* [reläm'pägō] 27

lights luces *f/pl* [lōō'ses] 92

lilacs lilas *f/pl* [lē'läs] 130

limbs miembros *m/pl* [myem'brōs] 167

linen lino *m* [lē'nō] 137

lingerie ropa *f* interior [rō'pä ēnteryōr'] 134

liniment linimento *m* [lēnēmen'tō] 161

lining forro *m* [fō'rrō] 136

lip labio *m* [lä'byō] 167

lipstick lápiz *m* de labios, colorete *m* *(Mex)* [lä'pēs de lä'byōs, kōlōre'te] 141

liter litro *m* [lē'trō] 193

liver hígado *m* [ē'gädō] 108; **~ problems** trastornos *m/pl* del hígado [trästōr'nōs del ē'gädō] 170

living room salón *m*, sala *f* de estar [sälōn', sä'lä de estär'] 93

loafers zapatos *m/pl* sin cordones, mocasín *m* [säpä'tōs sēn kōrdō'nes, mōkäsēn'] 139

loan prestar [prestär'] 57

lobby foyer *m* [fōyer' (fōye')] 177

lobster bogavante *m* [bōgävän'te] 106; **spiny ~** langosta *f* [läng-gōs'tä] 106

local call llamada *f* urbana, interna *(Mex)* [lyämä'dä ōōrbä'nä, ēnter'nä] 149

lock cerrar con llave [serrär' kōn lyä've] 92; **~ up** encerrar [enserrär'] 92

locker room vestuario *m* [vestōō·är'yō] 186

locksmith cerrajero *m* [serrähe'rō] 37

locomotive locomotora *f* [lōkōmōtō'rä] 67

long largo [lär'gō] 133; **how ~** cuánto tiempo [kōō·än'tō tyem'pō] 18; **~ distance express** expreso *m* de largo recorrido [ekspre'sō de lär'gō rekōrrē'dō] 60; **~ wave** onda *f* larga [ōn'dä lär'gä] 182

loss pérdida *f* [per'dēdä] 153

lounge salón *m* [sälōn'] 74

love *(noun)* amor *m* [ämōr'] 184

love *(verb)* amar [ämär'] 184

low pressure *(system)* de baja presión [de bä'hä presyōn'] 27

lubricant lubricante *m* [lōōbrēkän'te] 54

lubrication lubricación *f* [lōōbrēkäsyōn'] 46

luck suerte *f* [sōō·er'te] 23; **good ~**

mucha suerte [mōō'tshä sōō·er'te] 23

luggage equipaje *m* [ekēpä'*h*e] 59; **~ car** furgón *m* [fōōrgōn'] 64; **~ locker** consigna *f* automática [kōnsēg'nä outōmä'tēkä] 63; **~ rack** rejilla *f* [rehē'lyä] 67

lunch almuerzo *m*, comida *f* [älmōō·er'sō, kōmē'dä] 92

lung pulmón *m* [pōōlmōn'] 167

M

mackerel caballa *f* [käbä'lyä] 106

magazine revista *f* [revēs'tä] 182; **fashion** ~ revista *f* de modas [revēs'tä de mō'däs] 182

maid camarera *f*, recamarera *f* [kämäre'rä, rekämäre'rä] 92

maiden name nombre *m* de soltera [nōm'bre de sōlte'rä] 79

mail correo [kōrre'ō] 89; **~ box** buzón *m* [bōōsōn'] 145

mailman cartero *m* [kärte'rō] 149

main road carretera *f* principal [kärrete'rä prēnsēpäl'] 43

main station estación *f* central [estäsyōn' senträl'] 60

main street calle *f* principal [kä'lye prēnsēpäl'] 121

manager director *m*, gerente *m* [dērektōr', heren'te] 23

manicure manicura *f* [mänēkōō'rä] 156

manufacturer's spare parts piezas *f/pl* de repuesto originales [pye'säs de repōō·es'tō ōrē*h*ēnä'les] 50

map mapa *m* [mä'pä] 130; **city ~** plano *m* de la ciudad [plä'nō de lä syōōdäd'] 130; **road ~** mapa *m* de carreteras [mä'pä de kärrete'räs] 130; **street ~** plano *m* de la ciudad [plä'nō de lä syōōdäd'] 130

March marzo *m* [mär'sō] 33

margarine margarina *f* [märgärē'nä] 103

marital status estado *m* civil [estä'dō sēvēl'] 79

marksmanship tiro *m* [tē'rō] 189

marriage boda *f* [bō'dä] 22

married casado [käsä'dō (-ä)] 79

mascara pestañina *f*, rímel *m (Sp)* [pestänyē'nä, rē'mel] 141

mass misa *f* [mē'sä] 125

massage *(noun)* masaje *m* [mäsä'*h*e] 175; **massage** *(verb)* dar masaje [där mäsä'*h*e] 175

masseur masajista *m* [mäsä*h*ēs'tä] 175

masseuse masajista *f* [mäsä*h*ēs'tä] 175

mast mástil *m* [mäs'tēl] 76

match *(sports)* partido *m* [pärtē'dō] 188

matches fósforos *m/pl*, cerillas *f/pl (Sp)*, cerillos *m/pl (Mex)* [fōs'fōrōs, serē'lyäs, serē'lyōs] 140

material tejido *m*, tela *f* [te*h*ē'dō, te'lä] 137

mathematics matemáticas *f/pl* [mätemä'tēkäs] 39

matte mate [mä'te] 132

mattress colchón *m* [kōltshōn'] 90

mauve malva [mäl'vä] 194

maxillary sinus seno *m* maxilar [se'nō mäksēlär'] 167

maximum speed velocidad *f* máxima [velōsēdäd' mä'ksēmä] 42

May mayo *m* [mä'yō] 33

maybe quizá(s) [kēsä(s)'] 21

mayonnaise mayonesa *f* [mäyōne'sä] 103

meals comidas *f/pl* [kōmē'däs] 86

meanwhile mientras tanto [myen'träs tän'tō] 32

measles sarampión *m* [särämpyōn'] 171

meat carne *f* [kär'ne] 108; **ground ~** carne *f* molida, picada *(Sp)* [kär'ne mōlē'dä, pēkä'dä] 108

mechanic mecánico *m* [mekä'nēkō] 48

mechanical engineering construcción f mecánica [kōnstrōoksyōn' mekä'-nēkä] 39

medical director médico-jefe m [me'-dēkō-he'fe] 172

medicinal spring aguas f/pl medicinales [ä'gōo·äs medēsēnä'les] 175

medicine medicamento m [medēkä-men'tō] 159

medicine (discipline) medicina f [me-dēsē'nä] 39

meditation meditación f [medētäsyōn'] 125

medium (done) medio cocido, medio asado (Sp) [me'dyō kō sē'dō, me'dyō äsä'dō] 102

meet encontrarse [enkōnträr'se] 184; **glad to ~ you** encantado [enkän-tä'dō] 14

melon melón m [melōn'] 112; **water ~** sandía f [sändē'ä] 112

membership card tarjeta f, carnet m de miembro (Sp) [tärhe'tä, kärnet' de myem'brō] 96

memorial monumento m [mōnōo·men'tō] 121

men's room caballeros [käbälye'rōs] 92

menstruation menstruación f, período m [menstrōo·äsyōn', perē'ōdō] 167

menu carta f [kär'tä] 98

metabolism metabolismo m [metäbō-lēz'mō] 168

metalworker metalúrgico m [metäl-ōor'hēkō] 37

meter metro m [me'trō] 193

middle centro m [sen'trō] 65; **~ ear inflammation** otitis f media [ōtē'tēs me'dyä] 171

midnight medianoche f [medyänō'-tshe] 31

midwife comadrona f, partera f [kōmä-drō'nä, pärte'rä] 37

mile milla f [mē'lyä] 193; **nautical ~** milla f marítima or náutica [mē'lyä märē'tēma, nou'tēkä] 193

mileage indicator cuentakilometros m [kōo·entäkēlō'metrōs] 54

milk leche f [le'tshe 100; **condensed ~** leche f evaporada [le'tshe eväpōrä'-dä] 100

millimeter milímetro m [mēlē'metrō] 193

mine mío [mē'ō] 80

miner minero m [mēne'rō] 37

minerals minerales m/p. [mēnerä'les] 175

miniature golf minigolf m [mēnēgōlf'] 180; **~ course** minigolf m [mēnē-gōlf'] 180

ministry ministerio m [mēnēster'yō] 121

minute minuto m [mēnōo'tō] 86; **just a ~** un momento [ōon mōmen'tō] 16

mirror espejo m [espe'hō] 92

miss señorita f [senyōrē'tä] 13

mist neblina f [neblē'nä] 27

molar muela f [mōo·e'lä] 174

mole malecón m, muelle m [mälekōn', mōo·e'lye] 76

moment momento m [mōmen'tō] 87; **at the ~** de momento [de mōmen'tō] 32

monastery monasterio m [mōnäste'-ryō] 125

Monday lunes m [lōo'nes] 33

money dinero m [dēne'rō] 151; **~ exchange** oficina f de cambio [ōfē-sē'nä de käm'byō] 60

month mes m [mes] 32

monument monumento m [mōnōo-men'tō] 119

moon luna f [lōo'nä] 27

moped ciclomotor m [sēklōmōtōr'] 41

morning mañana f [mänyä'nä] 31; **good ~** buenos días [bōo·e'nōs dē'äs] 12; **in the ~** por la mañana [pōr lä mänyä'nä] 31; **this ~** esta mañana [es'tä mänyä'nä] 31

mortgage hipoteca f [ēpōte'kä] 152

mosaic mosaico m [mōsī'kō] 125

Moslem musulmán m [mōsōōlmän'] 125

mosque mezquita f [meskē'tä] 125

motel motel m [mōtel'] 81

mother madre f, mamá f (Mex) [mä'dre, mämä'] 35

mother-in-law suegra f [sōō·e'grä] 35

motor motor m [mōtōr'] 54; **~ scooter** escúter m [eskōō'ter] 41; **~ oil** aceite m para el motor [äse'ēte pä'rä el mōtōr'] 46

motorail service autotrén m [outōtren'] 60

motorboat lancha f motora, voladora f, motonauta f (Mex) [län'tshä mōtō'rä, vōlädō'rä, mōtōnou'tä] 75

motorcycle motocicleta f, moto f [mōtōsēkle'tä, mō'tō] 41

mountain montaña f [mōntä'nyä] 122; **~ range** montañas f/pl, sierra f, cordillera f [mōntä'nyäs, sye'rä, kōrdēlye'rä] 122; **~ climber** montañero m, alpinista m + f [mōntänye'rō, älpēnēs'tä] 189; **~ climbing** montañismo m, alpinismo m [mōntänyēz'mō, älpēnēz'mō] 189

moustache bigote m [bēgō'te] 157

mouth boca f [bō'kä] 168

mouthwash agua m dentífrica [ä'gōō·ä dentē'frēkä] 141

move (verb) mover [mōver'] 164

move (e.g. apt.) mudarse [mudär'se] 92; **~ in** instalarse [ēnstälär'se] 92; **~ out** abandonar [äbändōnär'] 92

move (e.g. game) jugada f [hōōgä'dä] 181

movie película f [pelē'kōōlä] 179

movies cine m [sē'ne] 179

Mr. señor [senyōr'] 13

Mrs. señora [senyō'rä] 13

mucous membrane mucosa f [mōōkō'sä] 168

mud lodo m [lō'dō] 175; **~ bath** baño m de lodo [bä'nyō de lō'dō] 175; **~ pack** envoltura f [envōltōō'rä] 175

mumps paperas f/pl [päpe'räs] 171

murder asesinato m [äsesēnä'tō] 153

muscle músculo m [mōōs'kōōlō] 168

museum museo m [mōōse'ō] 116

mushrooms champiñones m/pl [tshämpēnyō'nes] 110

music música f [mōō'sēkä] 177; **piece of ~** composición f [kōmpōsēsyōn'] 178

musical musical m [mōōsēkäl'] 177

musician músico m + f [mōō'sēkō] 37

musicology música f [mōō'sēkä] 39

mussels mejillones m/pl [mehēlyō'nes] 107

mustard mostaza f [mōstä'sä] 103

mutton carnero m [kärne'rō] 108

my mi [mē] 80

N

nail (finger) uña f [ōō'nyä] 168

nail (tool) clavo m [klä'vō] 57; **~ file** lima f de uñas [lēmä de ōō'nyäs] 141; **~ polish** esmalte m [ezmäl'te] 141; **~ polish remover** quitaesmalte m [kētä·ezmäl'te] 141; **~ scissors** tijeras f/pl de uñas [tēhe'räs de ōō'nyäs] 141

name nombre m [nōm'bre] 79; **first ~** nombre m de pila [nōm'bre de pē'lä] 79; **middle ~** nombre m segundo [nōm'bre segōōn'dō] 79; **last ~** apellido m [äpelyē'dō] 79; **what's your ~** como se llama [kō'mō se lyä'mä] 19

napkin servilleta f [servēlye'tä] 99

narcoticas narcóticas f/pl [närkō'tēkäs] 154

narrow estrecho [estre'tshō] 127

national park parque m nacional [pär'ke näsyōnäl'] 122

nationality nacionalidad f [näsyōnälē-

däd'] 79; ~ **plate** placa f de nacionalidad [plä'kä de näsyōnälēdäd'] 79
nausea náuseas f/pl [nou'se·äs] 171
nave nave f [nä've] 125
near cerca [ser'kä] 44; ~ **here** cerca de
aquí [ser'kä de äkē'] 44
nearest cercano [serkä'nō] 50
near-sighted miope [mē·ō'pe] 138
neck cuello m [kōō·e'lyō] 168; **nape of
the** ~ nuca f [nōō'kä] 168
necklace collar m [kōlyär'] 133
needle aguja f [ägōō'hä] 136; **sewing**
~ aguja f de coser [ägōō'hä de kōse-
r'] 136
negative negativo m [negätē'vō] 131
nephew sobrino m [sōbrē'nō] 35
nephritis nefritis f [nefrē'tēs] 171
nerve nervio m [ner'vyō] 174
nerves nervios m/pl [ner'vyōs] 168
neuralgia neuralgia f [ne·ōōräl'hyä]
171
neurologist neurólogo m [ne·ōōrō'lō-
gō] 162
neutral (car) punto m muerto [pōōn'tō
mōō·er'tō] 53
never nunca [nōōng'kä] 21
new nuevo [nōō·e'vō] 50
news noticias f/pl [notē'syäs] 182
newsdealer vendedor m de periódicos
[vendedōr' de perē·ō'dēkōs] 129
newspaper periódico m [peryō'dēkō]
181
next próximo [prō'hēmō] 183
nice agradable [ägrädä'ble] 184
niece sobrina f [sōbrē'nä] 35
night noche f [nō'tshe] 83; **all** ~ toda la
noche [tō'dä lä nō'tshe] 44; **at** ~ por
la noche [pōr lä nō'tshe] 31; **good** ~
buenas noches [bōōe'näs nō'tshes]
17; ~ **club** club m nocturno [klōōb
nōktōōr'nō] 180; ~ **duty** guardia f or
turno m [gōō·är'dyä, tōōr'nō] 159, ~
rate tarifa f nocturna [tärē'fä
nōktōōr'nä] 148; ~ **shirt** camisa f de

dormir [kämē'sä de dōrmēr'] 134
nightgown camisón m [kämēsōn'] 134
night's lodging alojamiento m para
una noche [älōhämyen'tō pä'rä ōō'-
nä nō'tshe] 92
nine nueve [nōō·e've] 28
ninepins bolos m/pl [bō'lōs] 189
no no [nō] 21
nobody nadie [nä'dye] 49
non-swimmer no-nadador [nō-nädä-
dōr'] 186
noodles fideos m/pl [fēde'ōs] 105
noon mediodía m [medyōdē'ä] 31; **at** ~
a mediodía [ä medyōdē'ä] 31; **this** ~
hoy al mediodía [oi äl medyōdē'ä] 32
nose nariz f [närēs'] 168
nosebleed hemorragia f nasal [emō-
rrä'hyä näsäl'] 171
notary notario m [nōtär'yō] 37
note nota f [nō'tä] 177
nothing nada [nä'dä] 21
novel novela f [nōve'lä] 130
November noviembre m [nōvyem'bre]
33
now ahora [ä·ō'rä] 32; ~ **and then** a
veces [ä veses] 32
nude desnudo [desnōō'dō] 185
number número m [nōō'merō] 79
nurse enfermera f [enferme'rä] 172;
male ~ enfermero m [enferme'rō]
37; **night** ~ enfermera f de noche
[enferme'rä de nō'tshe] 172
nursery cuarto m de niños [kōō·är'tō
de nē'nyōs] 93
nutmeg nuez f moscada [nōō·es' mōs-
kä'dä] 103
nut nuez f [nōō·es'] 111
nylon nilón m [nēlōn'] 137

O

oarsman remero m [reme'rō] 189
observatory observatorio m [ōbservä-
tōr'yō] 121

occupation profesión f [prŏfesyŏn'] 79
occupied ocupado [ŏkōōpä'dŏ] 66
ocean océano m [ŏse'änŏ] 77
October octubre m [ŏktōō'bre] 33
offer ofrecer [ŏfreser'] 16
office oficina f [ŏfēsē'nä] 121; **lost and found** ~ oficina f de objetos perdidos [ŏfēsē'nä de ŏbhe'tŏs perdē'dŏs] 121; ~ **hours** horas f/pl de consulta [ŏ'räs de kŏnsōōl'tä] 163
officer oficial m [ŏfēsyäl'] 74; **deck** ~ oficial m de guardia [ŏfēsyäl' de gōō·är'dyä] 74; **first** ~ segundo comandante m [segōōn'dŏ kŏmändän'te] 76
off-side fuera de juego [fōō·e'rä de hōō·e'gŏ] 190
oil aceite m [äse'ēte] 45; **please check the** ~ revise el nivel de aceite [revē'se el nēvel' de äse'ēte] 46; ~ **can** aceitera f [äse·ēte'rä] 46; ~ **change** cambio m de aceite [käm'byŏ de äse'ēte] 46; ~ **filter** filtro m de aceite [fēl'trŏ de äse'ēte] 54; ~ **level** nivel m de aceite [nēvel' de äse'ēte] 46; ~ **pump** bomba f de aceite [bŏm'bä de äse'ēte] 54
ointment pomada f [pŏmä'dä] 161; **boric acid** ~ agua f bórica [ä'gōō·ä bŏ'rēkä] 160; **burn** ~ pomada f para quemaduras [pŏmä'dä pä'rä kemädōō'räs] 160
eye ~ pomada f para los ojos [pŏmä'dä pä'rä lŏs ŏ'hŏs] 160
olives aceitunas f/pl [äse'ētōō'näs] 104
one un, uno [ōōn, ōō'nŏ] 28
one way ticket boleto m de ida [bŏle'tŏ de ē'dä] 62
onion cebolla f [sebŏ'lyä] 103
open abierto [äbyer'tŏ] 44
open (verb) abrir [äbrēr'] 65
open market mercado m [merkä'dŏ] 121
opera ópera f [ŏ'perä] 177; ~ **glasses**

gemelos m/pl (de teatro) [jeme'lŏs (de te·ä'trŏ)] 178
operate operar [ŏperär'] 172
operating room quirófano m [kērŏ'fänŏ] 172
operation operación f [ŏperäsyŏn'] 172
operator telefonista m + f, operador m + f (Mex) [telefŏnēs'tä, ŏperädŏr'] 150
operetta opereta f [ŏpere'tä] 177
optician óptico m [ŏp'tēkŏ] 129
oral surgeon cirujano m oral [sērōō-hä'nŏ ŏräl'] 174
orange naranja f [närän'hä] 112; ~ **juice** jugo m, zumo m (Sp), de naranja [hōō'gŏ, sōō'mŏ de närän'hä] 100
orange (color) naranja [närän'hä] 194
orangeade naranjada f [näränhä'dä] 114
orchestra orquesta f [ŏrkes'tä] 178; ~ **seats** patio m (de butacas), platea f, luneta f [pä'tyŏ (de bōōtä'käs), pläte'ä, lōōne'tä] 178
orchids orquídeas f/pl [ŏrkē'de·äs] 130
organ órgano m [ŏr'gänŏ] 125
orthodontist ortodontista m + f [ŏrtŏdŏntēs'tä] 174
orthopedist ortopedista m + f [ŏrtŏpedēs'tä] 162
ounce onza f [ŏn'sä] 193
overture obertura f [ŏbertōō'rä] 178
oysters ostras f/pl, ostiones f/pl (Mex) [ŏs'träs, ŏstyŏ'nes] 104

P

pack (packet) paquete m [päke'te] 126
pad bloc m [blŏk] 138; **scratch** ~ bloc m de notas [blŏk de nŏ'täs] 138; **sketch** ~ bloc m de dibujos [blŏk de dēbōō'hŏs] 138
pail balde m, cubo m (Sp), cubeta f (Mex) [bäl'de, kōō'bŏ, kōōbe'tä] 92
pain dolor m [dŏlŏr'] 171; ~ **killer** algo

contra el dolor [ăl'gō kōn'trä el dō-lôr'] 173; ~ **pills** analgésicos m/pl [änälhe'sēkōs] 161

paint *(noun)* pintura f, barniz m *(Sp)* [pēntōō'rä, bärnēs'] 54

painter pintor m [pēntōr'] 37

pair par m [pär] 126

pajamas pijama f [pēhä'mä] 134

palace palacio m [pälä'syō] 119

palate paladar m [pälädär'] 168

pancreas páncreas m [pän'kre·äs] 168

panties bragas f/pl, pantaletas f/pl *(Mex)* [brä'gäs', päntäle'täs] 134

pants pantalón m [päntälōn']135; ~ **suit** traje m de pantalón [trä'he de päntälōn'] 135

paper papel m [päpel'] 132

paperback libro m de bolsillo [lē'brō de bōlsē'lyō] 130

paper napkins servilletas f/pl de papel [servēlye'täs de päpel'] 144

papers documentación f [dōkōōmen-täsyōn'] 78

paprika pimentón m [pēmentōn'] 103

parallel bars paralelas f/pl [päräle'läs] 188

paralysis parálisis f [pärä'lēsēs] 171

parcel paquete m [päke'te] 145

pardon perdón [perdōn'] 22

parents padres m/pl [pä'dres] 35

park *(verb)* estacionar, aparcar *(Sp)* [estäsyōnär, äpärkär'] 43

park *(noun)* parque m [pär'ke] 121

parka anorac m [änōräk] 135

parking estacionamiento m [estäsyō-nämyen'tō] 42; **no** ~ estacionamiento m prohibido [estäsyōnämyen'tō prō·ēbē'dō] 42; ~ **disc** disco m de estacionamiento [dēs'kō de estäsyō-nämyen'tō] 42; ~ **lights** luz f de población [lōōs de pōbläsyōn'] 53; ~ **lot** aparcamiento m, estacionamiento m [äpärkämyen'tō, estäsyōnä-myen'tō] 42; ~ **meter** parquímetro m

[pärkē'metrō] 42

parsley perejil m [perehēl'] 103

part *(in hair)* raya f, carrera f, línea f [rä'yä, kärre'rä, lē'ne·ä] 157

part *(in theater)* papel m [päpel'] 178

part of town barrio m [bärr'yō] 121

partridge perdiz f [perdēs'] 107

party fiesta f [fyes'tä] 183; ~ **games** juegos m/pl de sociedad [hōō·e' gōs de sōsyedäd'] 182

pass *(on road)* adelantar [ädeläntär'] 42

pass *(mountain)* puerto m (de monta-ña) [pōō·er'tō (de mōntä'nyä)] 42

passenger pasajero m [päsahe'rō] 77

passport pasaporte m [päsäpōr'te] 79; ~ **control** control m de pasaportes [kōntrōl' de päsäpōr'tes] 79

pastime pasatiempo m [päsätyem'pō] 182

pastor pastor m [pästōr'] 125

pastry chef pastelero m [pästele'rō] 37

path camino m [kämē'nō] 42

patient paciente m + f [päsyen'te] 172

patio patio m [pä'tyō] 92

pavillion pabellón m [päbelyōn'] 122

pawn *(chess)* peón m [pe·ōn'] 181

pay pagar [pägär'] 80

payment pago m [pä'gō] 152

peas chícharos m/pl *(Mex)*, guisantes m/pl *(Sp)* [tshē'tshärōs, gēsän'tes] 110

peach durazno m, melocotón m *(Sp)* [dōōräz'nō, melōkōtōn'] 111, 112

peanuts cacahuates m/pl *(Mex)*, caca-huetes m/pl *(Sp)* [käkä·ōō·ä'tes, kä-kä·ōō·e'tes] 110

pear pera f [pe'rä] 112

pearls perlas f/pl [p-er'läs] 133

pedal pedal m [pedäl'] 54

pedestrian peatón m [pe·ätōn'] 122; ~ **crossing** paso m de peatones [pä'sō de pe·ätō'nes] 122

pediatrician pediatra m + f [pedyä'trä] 162

pedicure pedicura f [pedëkoo'rä] 156

pelvis pelvis f [pel'vës] 168

pen *(fountain)* pluma f [ploo'mä] 138

penalty kick penalty m [penäl'tē] 190

pencil lápiz m [lä'pës] 138

penis pene m [pe'ne] 168

pension pensión f [pensyōn'] 81

people personas f/pl [persō'näs] 41

pepper *(spice)* pimienta f (negra) [pēmyen'tä (ne'grä)] 103; ~ **mill** molinillo m de pimienta [mōlēnē'lyō de pēmyen'tä] 99; ~ **shaker** pimentero m [pēmente'rō] 99

peppermint menta f [men'tä] 161

peptic ulcer úlcera f gástrica [ool'serä gäs'trēkä] 171

perch perca f [per'kä] 107

performance *(at the theater)* función f [foonsyōn'] 176

performance *(of a work)* representación f [representäsyōn'] 178

perfume perfume m [perfoo'me] 141

perhaps quizá(s) [kēsä(s)'] 21

permanent wave permanente f [permänen'te] 155

personal personal [persōnäl'] 80

petticoat enaguas f/pl [enä'goo·äs] 135

pharmacist farmacéutico m [färmäse'·ootēkō] 37

pharmacy farmacia f [färmä'syä] 159

pheasant faisán m [fīsän'] 107

phone *(verb)* telefonear [telefōne·är'] 78

phone *(noun)* teléfono m [tele'fōnō] 147; ~ **book** directorio m, guía f (de teléfonos) (Sp) [dērektōr'yō, gē'ä (de tele'fōnōs)] 147; ~ **booth** cabina f [käbē'nä] 148; ~ **call** *(make a)* telefonear [telefōne·är'] 85; **pay ~** teléfono m público [tele'fōnō poo'blēkō] 148

photo fotografía f [fōtōgräfē'ä] 132

photocopies fotocopias f/pl [fōtōkō'pyäs] 138

photograph *(verb)* fotografiar [fōtōgräfē·är'] 132

photographer fotógrafo m [fōtō'gräfō] 74

photographer's studio fotógrafo m [fōtō'gräfō] 129

physics física f [fē'sēkä] 39

pianist pianista m + f [pē·änēs'tä] 178

piano recital recital m (de piano) [resētäl' (de pē·ä'nō)] 178

pick up recoger [rekō*her*'] 41

pickles pepinillos m/pl [pepēnē'lyōs] 103

pickled escabechado [eskäbetshä'dō] 102

picture cuadro m [koo·ä'drō] 144

piece parte f, trozo f [pär'te, trō'sō] 193

pier embarcadero m [embärkäde'rō] 77

pike lucio m [loo'syō] 107

piles almorranas f/pl [älmōrrä'näs] 171

pills pastillas f/pl, píldoras f/pl [pästē'lyäs, pēl'dōräs] 161

pillar columna f [kōloom'nä] 125

pillow almohada f [älmō·ä'dä] 87

pillowcase funda f [foon'dä] 90

pilot piloto m [pēlō'tō] 71

pin alfiler m [älfēler'] 136; **bobby ~** horquillas f/pl, clips m/pl [ōrkē'lyäs, klēps] 140

pincers tenazas f/pl [tenä'säs] 57

pineapple piña f [pē'nyä] 112

ping pong ping pong m [pēnpōn'] 182

pink rosa [rō'sä] 194

pinkie dedo m meñique [de'dō menyē'ke] 167

pint pinta f [pēn'tä] 193

pipe tubo m [too'bō] 54

pipe *(to smoke)* pipa f [pē'pä] 140; ~ **cleaner** escobilla f [eskōbē'lyä] 140

piston émbolo m, pistón m [em'bōlō, pēstōn'] 54; ~ **ring** segmento m de émbolo (de pistón) [segmen'tō de em'bōlō (de pēstōn')] 54

pitcher jarra f [hä'rrä] 99; **cream ~** jarra f para leche [hä'rrä pä'rä le'-tshe] 99

pity lástima f, pena f [läs'tēmä, pe'nä] 22

place of birth lugar m de nacimiento [lōōgär' de näsēmyen'tō] 79

place of residence lugar m de residencia [lōōgär' de resēden'syä] 79

plane avión m [ävyōn'] 68

plate *(dentistry)* plancha f [plän'tshä] 174

plate *(table service)* plato m [plä'tō] 99; **bread ~** platillo m [plätē'lyō] 99; **soup ~** plato m sopero [plä'tō sōpe'-rō] 99

platform andén m [ändēn'] 67

play *(verb)* jugar [hōōgär'] 182

play *(noun)* pieza f de teatro [pye'sä de te·ä'trō] 178

player jugador m [hōōgädōr'] 189

playground parque m infantil [pär'ke ēnfäntēl'] 96

playing cards cartas f/pl, naipes m/pl [kär'täs, nī'pes] 144

please por favor [pōr fävōr'] 20

pleasure gusto m [gōōs'tō] 21

pleurisy pleuresía f [ple·ōōresē'ä] 171

pliers alicates m/pl, pinzas f/pl [älēkä'-tes, pēn'säs] 57

plug clavija f de enchufe [klävē'hä de entshōō'fe] 92

plum ciruela f [sērōō·e'lä] 111

plumber plomero m, fontanero m *(Sp)* [plōme'rō, fōntäne'rō] 37

pneumonia pulmonía f [pōōlmōnē'ä] 171

point punto m [pōōn'tō] 188

poisoning envenenamiento m, intoxicación f [envenenämyen'tō, ēntōksēkäsyōn'] 171

police policía f [pōlēsē'ä] 154; **~ car** carro m, coche m *(Sp)* de la policía [kä'rrō, kō'tshe de lä pōlēsē'ä] 154;

~ station estación f de policía, comisaría f *(Sp)* [estäsyōn' de pōlēsē'ä, kōmēsärē'ä] 154

policeman policía m [pōlēsē'ä] 122

polish pulir [pōōlēr'] 156

political science ciencias f/pl políticas [syen'syäs pōlē'tēkäs] 39

pool hall sala f de billar [sä'lä de bē'-lyär] 180

pork cerdo m, puerco m [ser'dō, pōō·er'kō] 108

port *(land)* puerto m [pōō·er'tō] 77

port *(side)* babor m [bäbōr'] 77; **~ fees** tasa f portuaria [tä'sä pōrtōō·är'yä] 77

portal portal m [pōrtäl'] 125

porter mozo m [mō'sō] 64

portion ración f [räsyōn'] 98

possible posible [pōsē'ble] 22

post office correos m/pl [kōrre'ōs] 122

postage porte m, franqueo m [pōr'te, fränçke'ō] 150

postal clerk empleado m de correos [emple·ä'dō de kōrre'ōs] 150

postal savings book libreta f postal de ahorros [lēbre'tä pōstäl de ä·ō'rrōs] 150

postcard postal f [pōstäl'] 85

postman cartero m [kärte'rō] 150

pot olla f [ō'lyä] 99; **coffee ~** cafetera f [käfete'rä] 99; **tea ~** tetera f [tete'rä] 99

potatoes papas f/pl, patatas f/pl [pä'-päs, pätä'täs] 110

pound libra f [lē'brä] 193

powder polvos m/pl [pōl'vōs] 141; **~ puff** borla f de polvos [bōr'lä de pōl'-vōs] 141

power brake servofreno m [servōfre'-nō] 54

power station central f eléctrica, planta f eléctrica *(Mex)* [senträl' elek'trē-kä, plän'tä elek'trēkä] 122

power steering servodirección f [servōdĕreksyōn'] 54

practice *(train)* entrenarse [entrenär'- se] 188

precipitation precipitaciones *f/pl* [pre- sĕpĕtäsyō'nes] 27

pregnancy embarazo *m* [embärä'sō] 168

prescription receta *f*, fórmula *f* [rese'tä, fōr'mōōlä] 159

present regalo *m* [regä'lō] 80

press *(verb)* planchar [pläntshär'] 137

preview avance *m* [ävän'se] 179

previously antes [än'tes] 32

price precio *m* [pre'syō] 92

priest cura *m* [kōō'rä] 123

print *(film)* copia *f* [kō'pyä] 131

printed estampado [estämpä'dō] 137

printed matter impresos *m/pl* [ēmpre'- sōs] 145

prison cárcel *f* [kär'sel] 154

probably probablemente [prōbäble- men'te] 21

procession procesión *f* [prōsesyōn'] 125

producer productor *m* [prōdōōktōr'] 178

production puesta *f* en escena [pōō·es'tä en ese'nä] 178

program programa *m* [prōgrä'mä] 178; ~ **schedule** programas *m/pl* de la semana [prōgrä'mäs de lä semä'nä] 182

prophylactics preservativos *m/pl* [pre- servätē'vōs] 161

Protestant protestante [prōtestän'te] 125

psychiatrist psiquiatra *m* + *f* [sēkyä'- trä] 163

psychologist psicólogo *m* [sēkō'lōgō] 163

psychology psicología *f* [sēkōlōhē'ä] 39

public garden jardín *m* público [här- dēn' pōō'blēkō] 122

public rest room baños *m/pl*, servicios *m/pl (Sp)* [bä'nyōs, servē'syōs] 122

pulpit púlpito *m* [pōōl'pētō] 125

pumpkin calabaza *f* [käläbä'sä] 110

puncture pinchazo *m* [pēntshä'sō] 47

pupil alumno *m* [älōōm'nō] 37

purple morado [mōrä'dō] 194

purse bolso *m*, bolsa *f (Mex)* [bōl'sō, bōl'sä] 153

purser contador *m* [kōntädōr'] 74

Q

quay muelle *m* [mōō·e'lye] 77

quails codornices *f/pl* [kōdōrnē'ses] 107

quart *(approx.)* litro *m* [lē'trō] 126

quarter cuarto [kōō·är'tō] 30

quarter *(year)* trimestre *m* [trēmes'tre] 32

queen *(chess)* dama *f* [dä'mä] 181

quickly en seguida [en segē'dä] 48

quinine quinina *f* [kēnē'nä] 161

R

rabbi rabino *m* [räbē'nō] 125

rabbit conejo *m* [kōne'hō] 108

race carrera *f* [kärre'rä] 187; ~ **car driver** corredor *m* [kōrredōr'] 187

racing car carro *m*, coche *m (Sp)* de carreras [kä'rrō, kō'tshe de kärre'- räs] 187

radiation therapy radioterapia *f* [rädyō- terä'pyä] 175

radiator radiador *m* [rädyädōr'] 93

radio radio *m*, *(Sp)* *f* [rä'dyō] 182; ~ **play** radioteatro *m* [rä'dyōte·ä'trō] 182; ~ **room** cabina *f* de radio [kä- bē'nä de rä'dyō] 74

rag trapo *m* [trä'pō] 57

railroad ferrocarril *m* [ferrōkärrēl'] 67; ~ **crossing** paso *m* a nivel, cruce *m* de F.C. *(Mex)* [pä'sō ä nēvel', krōō'se de e'fe se] 42; ~ **man** ferroviario *m* [ferrōvyär'yō] 37; ~ **station** estación f [estäsyōn'] 72

rain (noun) lluvia f [lyōō'vyä] 88

rain (verb) llover [lyōver'] 25

raincoat impermeable m [ēmperme·ä'-ble] 135

raisins pasas f/pl [pä'säs] 103

ranch station wagon camioneta f, combi f (Mex) [kämyōne'tä, kōm'bē] 40

rare casi crudo, a la inglesa (Sp) [kä'sē krōō'dō, ä lä ēngle'sä] 102

rash erupción f cutánea, salpullido m (Mex) [erōōpsyōn' kōōtä'ne·ä, säl-pōōlyē'dō] 171

raw crudo [krōō'dō] 102

razor (safety) rasuradora f, maquinilla f de afeitar (Sp) [räsōōrädō'rä, mäke-nē'lyä de äfe·ētär'] 141; ~ **blades** hojas f/pl de afeitar, cuchillas f/pl [ō'häs de äfe·ētär', kōōtshē'lyäs] 141; ~ **cut** corte m a navaja [kōr'te ä nävä'hä] 157; **straight** ~ navaja f [nä-vä'hä] 141

reading room sala f de lectura [sä'lä de lektōō'rä] 74

ready listo [lēs'tō] 50

real estate agency inmobiliaria f [ēn-mōbēlyär'yä] 129

rear trasero [träse'rō] 54; **at the** ~ en la cola [en lä kō'lä] 65; ~ **lights** luz f trasera [lōōs träse'rä] 53; ~ **motor** motor m trasero [mōtōr träse'rō] 54; ~ **view mirror** espejo m retrovisor [espe'hō retrōvēsōr'] 55; ~ **-end collision** accidente m en cadena [äkse-den'te en käde'nä] 49

receipt recibo m, resguardo m (Sp) [re-sē'bō, rezgōō·är'dō] 150

recently recientemente [resyentemen'-te] 32

reception desk recepción f [resep-syōn'] 92

recommend recomendar [rekōmen-

där'] 81

record disco m [dēs'kō] 130; ~ **player** tocadiscos m/pl [tōkädēs'kōs] 182; **phonograph** ~ disco m [dēs'kō] 144

recording tape cinta f magnetofónica [sēn'tä mägnetōfō'nēkä] 144

recreation room salón m de recreo [sa-lón' de rekre'ō] 96

red rojo, colorado [rō'hō, kōlōrä'dō] 194; **bright** ~ rojo vivo [rō'hō vē'vō] 194; **dark** ~ rojo oscuro [rō'hō ōs-kōō'rō] 194; ~ **cabbage** berza f, lombarda f [ber'sä, lōmbär'dä] 110

reduced fare ticket boleto m a precio reducido [bōle'tō a pre'syō redōōsē'-dō] 62

reduced rates rebaja f, descuento m [rebä'hä, deskōō·en'tō] 83

referee árbitro m [är'bētrō] 189

refrain from smoking no fumen [nō fōō'men] 70

refrigerator frigorífico m, refrigerador m (Mex) [frēgōrē'fēkō, refrēherädōr'] 93

register (in hotel) inscribir [ēnskrēbēr'] 84

register (letter) certificar, registrar [sertēfēkär', rehēsträr'] 150

registered letter carta f certificada, registrada [kär'tä sertēfēkä'dä, rehēs-trä'dä] 150

registration (car) papeles m/pl del carro, del coche (Sp) [päpe'les del kä'-rrō, del kō'tshe] 43

registration inscripción f [ēnskrēp-syōn'] 93

regret pesar m [pesär'] 22

regular (gas) normal [nōrmäl'] 45

religion religión f [relēhyōn'] 125

religious religioso [relēhyō'sō] 125

remedy remedio m [reme'dyō] 161

renew renovar [renōvär'] 79

rent (noun) alquiler m, arriendo m [äl-kēler', ärryen'dō] 93

rent *(verb)* alquilar, rentar [älkēlär¹, rentär¹] 93

repair *(verb)* arreglar [ärreglär¹] 46

repair *(noun)* reparación f [repäräsyōn¹] 55; ~ **shop** taller m mecánico [tälyer¹ mekä¹nēkō] 48

replace reponer [repōner¹] 138

reply respuesta f [respōō·es¹tä] 147

report *(to police)* denunciar [denōōnsyär¹] 153

reservation reserva f [reser¹vä] 71

reserve reservar [reservär¹] 62; ~ **fuel can** tarro m de reserva, bidón m de reserva [tä¹rrō de reser¹vä, bēdōn¹ de reser¹vä] 55; ~ **wheel** rueda f de repuesto [rōō·e¹dä de repōō·es¹tō] 47

respiration respiración f [respēräsyōn¹] 168

rest room baños m/pl, servicios m/pl *(Sp)* [bä¹nyōs, servē¹syōs] 93

restaurant restaurante m [restourän¹te] 60

result resultado m [resōōltä¹dō] 188

retailer comerciante m [kōmersyän¹te] 37

retiree pensionista m + f [pensyōnēs¹tä] 37

retread recauchutar [rekoutshōōtär¹] 46

return flight vuelo m de regreso [vōō·e¹lō de regre¹sō] 71

return postage porte m de vuelta [pōr¹te de vōō·el¹tä] 150

reverse *(gear)* marcha f atrás [mär¹tshä äträs¹] 53

rheumatism reumatismo m [re·ōōmätēz¹mō] 171

rib costilla f [kōstē¹lyä] 168

ribbon cinta f [sēn¹tä] 136

rice arroz m [ärōs¹] 105

ride *(on train)* viajar [vyähär¹] 66

ride *(horse)* montar a caballo [mōntär¹ ä käbä¹lyō] 189

rider jinete m [hēne¹te] 189

riding equitación f [ekētäsyōn¹] 189; ~ **stable** cuadra f [kōō·ä¹drä] 180

rifle range campo m de tiro [käm¹pō de tē¹rō] 188

right! ¡eso es! [e¹sō es] 21

right derecha dere¹tshä 40; ~ **of way** preferencia f de paso [preferens¹yä de pä¹sō] 43; ~ **away** en seguida [en segē¹dä] 98

ring sortija f, anillo m [sōrtē¹hä, änē¹lyō] 133; **wedding** ~ anillo m de boda [änē¹lyō de bō¹dä] 133

rinse *(hair)* dar reflejos *(al pelo)* [där refle¹hōs äl pe¹lō] 155

river río m [rē¹ō] 70

road camino m [kämē¹nō] 122; ~ **sign** señal f de circulación [senyäl¹ de sērkōōläsyōn¹] 43; ~ **under construction** obras f, hombres trabajando *(Mex)* [ō¹bräs, ōm¹bres träbähän¹dō] 43

roast beef rosbif m [rōsbēf¹] 108

roasted horneado, asado *(Sp)* [ōrne·ä¹dō, äsä¹dō] 108

rod *(fishing)* caña f [kä¹nyä] 188

role *(theater)* papel m [päpel¹] 178; **leading** ~ papel m principal [päpel¹ prēnsēpäl¹] 178

roll *(bread)* panecillo m, bolillo m *(Mex)* [pänesē¹lyō, bōlē¹lyō] 100

roll rollo m [rō¹lyō] 126

Romance languages filología f románica [fēlōlōhē¹ä rōmä¹nēkä] 39

Romanesque románico [rōmä¹nēkō] 125

roof *(car)* capota f [käpō¹tä] 55

rook peón m [pe·ōn¹] 181

room cuarto m [kōō·är¹tō] 93; ~ **referral** oficina f de alojamiento [ōfēsē¹nä de älōhämyen¹tō] 60; **double** ~ habitación f, cuarto m *(Mex)* doble [äbētäsyōn¹, kōō·är¹tō dō¹ble] 82; **single** ~ habitación f, cuarto m *(Mex)* individual, sencillo *(Mex)* [äbētäsyōn¹, kōo·är'tō ēndēvēdōo·äl', sensē'lyō] 82; **quiet** ~ habitación f, cuarto m (Mex) tranquilo [äbētäsyōn', kōo·är'-tō trängkē'lō (-ä)] 82

root (tooth) raíz f del diente [rä·ēs' del dyen'te] 174; ~ **canal work** tratamiento m de la raíz [trätämyen'tō de lä rä·ēs'] 174

rope cuerda f, cabo m [kōo·er'dä, kä'-bō] 77

rosemary romero m [rōme'rō] 103

roses rosas f/pl [rō'säs] 130

rough seas marejada f [märehä'dä] 77

round redondo [redōn'dō] 156

round-trip ticket boleto m, billete m (Sp) de ida y vuelta [bōle'tō, bēlye'te de ē'dä ē vōo·el'tä] 69

route ruta f [rōo'tä] 43

route (plane) trayecto m [träyek'tō] 71

row fila f [fē'lä] 176

rowing remo m [re'mō] 189

rubber boots botas f/pl de goma [bō'-täs de gō'mä] 139

ruby rubí m [rōobē'] 133

rucksack mochila f [mōtshē'lä] 144

rudder timón m [tēmōn'] 77

ruin ruina f [rōo·ē'nä] 122

S

sacristan sacristán m [säkrēstän'] 125

sacristy sacristía f [säkrēstē'ä] 125

safety pin imperdible m, seguro m (Mex) [ēmperdē'ble, segōo'rō] 136

sail (noun) vela f [ve'lä] 189

sail (verb) navegar a la vela [nävegär' ä lä ve'lä] 189

sailboat barco m de vela [bär'kō de ve'-lä] 189

sailing deporte m de vela [depōr'te de ve'lä] 189; ~ **school** escuela f de vela [eskōo·e'lä de ve'lä] 189

sailor marinero m [märēne'rō] 77

salad ensalada f [ensälä'dä] 104

salesperson dependiente m [depen-dyen'te] 37

saline content salinidad f [sälēnēdäd'] 186

salmon salmón m [sälmōn'] 107

salt sal f [säl] 103; ~ **shaker** salero m [säle'rō] 99

salted salado [sälä'dō] 102

salty salado [sälä'dō] 115

salve pomada f [pōmä'dä] 161

sanatorium sanatorio m [sänätōr'yō] 175

sandals sandalias f/pl [sändä'lyäs] 139; **beach** ~ sandalias f/pl para la playa [sändä'lyäs pä'rä lä plä'yä] 139

sandpaper papel m de lija [päpel' de lē'hä] 57

sanitary napkins compresas f/pl [kōm-pre'säs] 161

sapphire zafiro m [säfē'rō] 133

sardines sardinas f/pl [särdē'näs] 104

Saturday sábado m [sä'bädō] 33

sauce salsa f [säl'sä] 103

saucer platillo m [plätē'lyō] 99

sauna sauna f [sou'nä] 175

sausage salchicha f [sältshē'tshä] 100

savings book caja f de ahorros [kä'hä de ä·ō'rrōs] 152

scarf bufanda f [bōofän'dä] 135

scarlet fever escarlatina f [eskärlätē'-nä] 171

scenery/settings decoración f [dekōrä-syōn'] 178

scheduled flight avión m de línea [ävyōn' de lē'ne·ä] 71

scholar erudito m [erōodē'tō] 37

school escuela f [eskōo·e'lä] 38

sciatica ciática f [syä'tēkä] 171

scientist científico m [syentē'fēkō] 37

scissors tijeras f/pl [tēhe'räs] 136

Scotch tape cinta f adhesiva, cinta f celo (Sp) [sēn'tä ädesē'vä, sēn'tä se'lō] 144

screen pantalla f [päntä'lyä] 179

screenplay guíon m [gë'ōn] 179
screw tornillo m [tōrnē'lyō] 57
screwdriver destornillador m, desarmador m (Mex) [destōrnēlyädōr', desärmädōr'] 57
scuba diving bucear [boose·är'] 186
scuba equipment escafandra f, equipo m de bucear [eskäfän'drä, ekē'pō de boose·är'] 186
scull barca f de remos [bär'kä de re'mōs] 189
sculptor escultor m [eskooltōr'] 37
sea mar m [mär] 77
seasickness mareo m [märe'ō] 171
season temporada f [tempōrä'dä] 93
seasoned condimentado [kōndēmentä'dō] 102
seasoning (spice) especias f/pl [espe'syäs] 103
seat asiento m [äsyen'tō] 62; ~ **belt** cinturón m de seguridad [sēntoorōn' de segoorēdäd'] 55; ~ **reservation** reserva f de asiento [reser'vä de asyen'tō] 62
second segundo m [segoon'dō] 32
second class segunda clase f [segoon'dä klä'se] 62
secretary secretaria f [sekretär'yä] 37
security fianza f [fyän'sä] 152
see ver [ver] 18; ~ **you soon** hasta luego [äs'tä loo·e'gō] 17; ~ **you tomorrow** hasta mañana [äs'tä mänyä'nä] 17
self-service autoservicio m [outōservē'syō] 129
send mandar [mändär'] 147
send (luggage) facturar [fäktoorär'] 63
sender remitente m [remēten'te] 150
separate separado [sepärä'dō] 115
September se(p)tiembre m [se(p)tyem'bre] 33
serious grave [grä've] 164
sermon sermón m, plática f [sermōn', plä'tēkä] 125

service (church) oficio m [ōfē'syō] 123
service servicio m [servē'syō] 83; ~ **station** gasolinera f [gäsōlēne'rä] 48
serving dish fuente f [foo·en'te] 99
set (hair) enrular, marcar (Sp) [enroolär', märkär'] 158
set designer escenógrafo m [esenō'gräfō] 178
setting lotion fijador m [fēhädōr'] 156
seven siete [sye'te] 28
sew coser [kōser'] 137
shampoo champú m [tshämpoo'] 141
shape forma f [fōr'mä] 127
share of stock acción f [äksyōn'] 152
sharp (pain) agudo [ägoo'dō] 163; **eleven** ~ las once en punto [läs ōn'se em poon'tō] 30
shave afeitar [äfe·ētär'] 158
shaving brush brocha f de afeitar [brō'tshä de äfe·ētär'] 141
shaving cream crema f de afeitar [kre'mä de äfe·ētär'] 142
shaving foam espuma f de afeitar [espoo'mä de äfe·ētär'] 142
shaving soap jabón m de afeitar [häbōn' de äfe·ētär'] 142
sheets sábanas f/pl [sä'bänäs] 90
shellfish mariscos m/pl [märēs'kōs] 107
shells conchas f/pl [kōn'tshäs] 186
sherry jerez m [heres'] 113
shin espinilla f [espēnē'lyä] 168
ship barco m, buque m [bär'kō, boo'-ke] 77; **passenger** ~ barco m de pasajeros [bär'kō de päsähe'rōs] 77
shipboard party fiesta f de a bordo [fyes'tä de ä bōr'dō] 77
shipping agency agencia f marítima [ähen'syä märē'tēmä] 77
shipping company compañía f naviera [kōmpänyē'ä nävye'rä] 77
ship's doctor médico m de a bordo [me'dēkō de ä bōr'dō] 77
shirt camisa f [kämē'sä] 135

shock shock *m* nervioso [shōk nervyō'-sō] 171; **~ absorber** amortiguador *m* [ämōrtēgōō·ädōr'] 55

shoe zapato *m* [säpä'tō] 139; **~ horn** calzador *m* [kälsädō'r] 139; **~ laces** cordones *m/pl* [kōrdō'nes] 139

shoemaker zapatero *m* [säpäte'rō] 37

shoot tirar [tērär'] 189

shop tienda *f* [tyen'dä] 122; **antique ~** tienda *f* de antigüedades [tyen'dä de äntēgōō·edä'des] 128; **barber ~** peluquería *f* [pelōōkerē'ä] 128; **butcher ~** carnicería *f* [kärnēserē'ä] 128; **china ~** artículos *m/pl* de porcelana [ärtē'kōōlōs de pōrselä'nä] 128; **dressmaker's ~** modista *f* [mōdēs'tä] 128; **electrical appliance ~** (tienda *f* de) electrodomésticos [(tyen'dä de) elektrōdōmes'tēkōs] 128; **flower ~** florería *f*, floristería *f*, (Sp) [flōrerē'ä, flōrēsterē'ä] 128; **hat ~** sombrería *f* [sōmbrerē'ä] 128; **lingerie ~** lencería *f*, corsetería *f* [lenserē'ä, kōrseterē'ä] 129; **photo ~** tienda *f* de artículos fotográficos [tyen'dä de ärtē'kōōlōs fōtōgrä'fēkō's 129; **shoe ~** zapatería *f* [säpäterē'ä] 129; **souvenir ~** recuerdos *m/pl* [rekōō·er'dōs] 129; **tailor ~** sastre *m* [säs'tre] 129; **textile ~** tienda *f* de tejidos [tyen'dä de tehē'-dōs] 129; **watchmaker's ~** relojería *f* [relōherē'ä] 129; **wine ~** bodega *f* [bōde'gä] 129

shopping (go) ir de compras [ēr de kōm'präs] 118; **~ mall** centro *m* comercial [sen'trō kōmersyäl'] 122

shore (on) en tierra [en tye'rrä] 77

short corto [kōr'tō] 133; **~ circuit** cortocircuito *m* [kōrtōsērkōō·ē'tō] 55; **-sleeved** de manga corta [de män'gä kōr'tä] 135; **~ subject** cortometraje *m* [kōrtōmeträ'he] 179; **~ wave** onda *f* corta [ōn'dä kōr'tä] 175

shorten acortar [äkōrtär'] 137

shorts pantalón *m* corto [päntälōn' kōr'tō] 135

shoulder hombro *m* [ōm'brō] 168

shower ducha *f*, regadera *f* (Mex) [dōō'tshä, regäde'rä] 82

shower (weather) chubasco *m*, aguacero *m* [tshōōbäs'kō, ägōō·äse'rō] 27

shrimp gambas *f/pl*, camarones *m/pl* (Mex) [gäm'bäs, kämärō'nes] 104

shuffle barajar [bärähär'] 181

shutter obturador *m* [ōbtōōrädōr'] 132; **~ release** disparador *m* [dēspär-ädōr'] 132; **automatic ~** disparador *m* automático [dēspärädōr' outō-mä'tēkō] 132

sick enfermo [enfer'mō] 162; **I feel ~** me siento mal [me syen'tō mäl] 70; **~ bay** hospital *m* [ōspētäl'] 74

side (on the) lateral(es) [läteräl'(es)] 176; **~ road** calle *f* lateral [kä'lye läteräl'] 122; **~ wind** viento *m* de costado [vyen'tō de kōstä'dō] 43

sideburns patillas *f/pl* [pätē'lyäs] 158

sidewalk acera *f*, banqueta *f* (Mex) [äse'rä, bängke'tä] 122

sightseeing turismo *m* [tōōrēz'mō] 122

sign up inscribir [ēnskrēbēr'] 85

signature firma *f* [fēr'mä] 84

silk seda *f* [se'dä] 137; **artificial ~** seda *f* artificial [se'dä ärtēfēsyäl'] 137; **~ thread** hilo *m* de seda [ē'lō de se'dä] 136

silver (adj.) plateado [pläte·ä'dō] 194

silver (noun) plata *f* [plä'tä] 133; **~ plated** plateado [pläte·ä'dō] 133

silverware vajilla *f* de plata [vähē'lyä de plä'tä] 99

since desde [des'de] 32

sinew tendón *m* [tendōn'] 168

singer cantante *m* [käntän'te] 178

singing canto *m* [kän'tō] 178

single soltero [sōlte'rō (-ä)] 79

singles (tennis) individual [ēndēvēdōō·äl'] 190

sink lavabo m, lavatorio m [lävä'bō, lävätōr'yō] 93

sir señor m [senyōr'] 13

sister hermana f [ermä'nä] 35; **~ -in-law** cuñada f [kōōnyä'dä] 35

six seis [se'ēs] 28

size talla f [tä'lyä] 133

skate patinar [pätēnär'] 188

skater patinador m [pätēnädōr'] 188

skates patines m/pl [pätēn'es] 188

ski (verb) esquiar [eskē·är'] 189

ski (noun) esquí m [eskē'] 189; **~ binding** fijación f [fēhäsyōn'] 189; **~ jump** trampolín m de saltos [trämpōlēn' de säl'tōs] 189; **~ lift** telesquí m [teleskē'] 189

skiing esquí m [eskē'] 189

skin piel f, cutis m [pyel, kōō'tēs] 168; **~ disease** enfermedad f de la piel [enfermedäd' de lä pyel] 171; **~ lesion** lesión f de la piel [lesyōn' de lä pyel] 171

skirt falda f [fäl'dä] 135

skull cráneo m [krä'ne·ō] 168

sky cielo m [sye'lō] 26

slack flojo [flō'hō] 51

slacks pantalones m/pl [päntälō'nes] 135

Slavic languages eslavística f [eslävēs'tēkä] 39

sled trineo m [trēne'ō] 144

sleep dormir [dōrmēr'] 164

sleeper/sleeping car coche-cama m, camarín m, alcoba f (Mex) [kō'tshekä'mä, kämärēn', älkō'bä] 60; **~ reservation** boleto m, billete m (Sp) de coche-cama, de alcoba, de camarín (Mex) [bōle'tō, bēlye'te de kō'tshekä'mä, de älkō'bä, de kämärēn'] 62

sleeping bag saco m, bolsa f (Mex) de dormir [sä'kō, bōl'sä de dōrmēr'] 96

sleeping pills somníferos m/pl [sōmnē'ferōs] 161

slide transparencia f, diapositiva f (Sp) [tränspären'syä, dyäpōsētē'vä] 132; **~ frame** marquito m [märkē'tō] 132

sliding sun roof techo m corredizo [te'tshō korredē'sō] 55

slippers zapatillas f/pl, pantuflas f/pl [säpätē'lyäs, päntōōf'läs] 139

slippery resbaladizo, resbaloso [resbäládē'sō, resbälō'sō] 25; **~ road** piso m resbaloso, resbaladizo [pē'sō resbälō'sō, resbälädē'sō] 43

slow despacio [despä'syō] 42

slow (clock) retrasado [reträsä'dō] 31

small pequeño [peke'nyō] 127

smallpox viruela f [vērōō·e'lä] 171

smoked ahumado [ä·ōōmä'dō] 102

smoking (sign) fumadores [fōōmädō'res] 66; **no ~** (sign) no fumadores [nō fōōmädō'res] 66

smuggling contrabando m [kōnträbän'dō] 154

snails cangrejos m/pl [kängre'hōs] 104

snow (verb) nevar [nevär'] 25

snow (noun) nieve f [nye've] 27; **~ chains** cadenas f/pl antideslizantes [käde'näs äntēdezlēsän'tes] 52; **~ flurries** copos m/pl de nieve [kō'pōs de nye've] 27

soap jabón m [häbōn'] 87; **cake of ~** pastilla f de jabón [pästē'lya de häbōn'] 87

soccer fútbol m [fōōt'bōl] 189; **~ game** partido m de fútbol [pärtē'dō de fōōt'bōl] 187; **play ~** jugar al fútbol [hōōgär' äl fōōt'bōl] 189

sociology sociología f [sōsyōlōhē'ä] 39

socket enchufe m, soquet m (Mex) [entshōō'fe, sōket'] 90; **~ wrench** llave f de dado [lyä've de dä'dō] 57

socks medias f/pl, calcetines m/pl (Sp) [me'dyäs, kälsetē'nes] 135

soda (bicarbonate of) bicarbonato m sódico [bēkärbōnä'tō sō'dēkō] 160

soft blando [blän'dō] 102; **~ drink** refresco *m* [refres'kō] 114

solder soldar [sōldär'] 55

sole *(verb)* poner suela [pōner' sōō·e'lä] 139

sole *(noun)* suela *f* [sōō·e'lä] 139; **leather ~** suela *f* de cuero [sōō·e'lä de kōō·e'rō] 139; **rubber ~** suela *f* de goma [sōō·e'lä de gō'mä] 139

sole *(fish)* lenguado *m* [leng·gōō·ä'dō] 107

solid color de un solo color [de ōōn sō'lō kōlōr'] 137

soloist solista *m + f* [sōlēs'tä] 178

somebody alguien [al'gyen] 41

sometimes a veces [ä ve'ses] 32

son hijo *m* [ē'hō] 35

song canción *f* [känsyōn'] 178; **folk ~** canción *f* popular [känsyōn' pōpōō·lär'] 178; **~ recital** recital *m* (de canto) [resētäl' (de kän'tō)] 178

soon pronto [prōn'tō] 32

soprano soprano *m* [sōprä'nō] 178

sore throat dolor *m* de garganta [dōlōr' de gärgän'tä] 171

sorry (I'm) lo siento [lō syen'tō] 22

soup sopa *f* [sō'pä] 105; **fish ~** sopa *f* de pescado [sō'pä de peskä'dō] 105; **garlic ~** sopa *f* de ajo [sō'pä de ä'hō] 105; **lentil ~** sopa *f* de lentejas [sō'pä de lente'häs] 105; **noodle ~** sopa *f* de fideos [sō'pä de fēde'ōs] 105; **tomato ~** sopa *f* de tomate [sō'pä de tōmä'te] 105; **vegetable ~** sopa *f* de verduras [sō'pä de verdōō'räs] 105

sour agrio [ä'grē·ō] 115

souvenir recuerdo *m* [rekōō·er'dō] 80

spa balneario *m* [bälne·är'yō] 175

space sitio *m* [sē'tyō] 44

spades *(cards)* picos *m/pl* [pē'kōs] 181

spare parts piezas *f/pl* de repuesto [pye'säs de repōō·es'tō] 50

spare wheel rueda *f* de recambio, de repuesto [rōō·e'dä de rekäm'byō, de repōō·es'tō] 50

spark chispa *f* [tshēs'pä] 55; **~ plug** bujía *f* [bōōhē'ä] 55

speak hablar [äblär'] 15

speaking! *(on telephone)* ¡soy yo! [soi yō] 148

special especial [espesyäl'] 46; **~ delivery** exprés, urgente, entrega *f* inmediata [ekspres', ōōrhen'te, entre'gä ēnmedyä'tä] 150; **~ delivery letter** carta *f* exprés, carta *f* de entrega inmediata, urgente *(Sp)* [kär'tä ekspres', kär'tä de entre'gä ēnmedyä'tä, ōōrhen'te] 150; **~ issue stamp** estampilla *f,* sello *m (Sp),* timbre *m (Mex)* conmemorativo [estämpē'lyä, se'lyō, tēm'bre kōnmemōrätē'vō] 150

specialist especialista *m* [espesyälēs'tä] 163; **ear, nose and throat ~** otorrinolaringólogo *m + f* [ōtōrrēnōlärēngō'lōgō] 162

speed velocidad *f* [velōsēdäd'] 43; **~ limit** límite *m* de velocidad [lē'mēte de velōsēdäd'] 43

speedometer taquímetro *m* [täkē'metrō] 54

spell deletrear [deletre·är'] 24

spinach espinacas *f/pl* [espēnä'käs] 110

spinal cord médula *f* espinal [me'dōōlä espēnäl'] 168

spine espina *f* dorsal [espē'nä dōrsäl] 168

spleen bazo *m* [bä'sō] 168

sponge esponja *f* [espōn'hä] 142

spoon cuchara *f* [kōōtshä'ra] 99; **soup ~** cuchara *f* sopera [kōōtshä'ra sōpe'rä] 99; **tea ~** cucharita *f* [kōōtshärē'tä] 99

sport shirt camisa *f* deportiva [kämē'sä depōrtē'vä] 135

sports deportes *m/pl* [depōr'tes] 187; **~ event** pruebas *f/pl* deportivas [prōō·e'bäs depōrtē'väs] 186; **~ fan**

aficionado m [äfêsyōnä'dō] 190

sportswear trajes m/pl de deportes [trä'hes de depōr'tes] 135

spot remover quitamanchas m [kētämän'tshäs] 144

sprain (noun) torcedura f, falseo m [tōrsedōō'rä, fälse'ō] 171

spring ballesta f [bälyes'tä] 55

spring (season) primavera f [prēmäve'rä] 33

square (adj.) cuadrado [kōō·ädrä'dō] 193

square (noun) plaza f [plä'sä] 122

square (chess) casilla f [käsē'lyä] 181

stadium estadio m [estä'dyō] 122

stage escena f, escenario m [ese'nä, esenär'yō] 178; ~ **director** director m de escena [dērektōr' de ese'nä] 178

stain mancha f [män'tshä] 137

staircase escalera f [eskäle'rä] 93

stairwell hueco m de escalera [ōō·e'kō de eskäle'rä] 93

stake puesta f [pōō·es'tä] 182

stamp (verb) franquear [fränke·är'] 150

stamp (noun) estampilla f, sello m (Sp), timbre m (Mex) [estämpē'lyä, se'lyō, tēm'bre] 150; ~ **machine** distribuidor m automático de estampillas, sellos (Sp), timbres (Mex) [dēstrēbōō·ēdōr' outōmä'tēkō de estämpē'lyäs, se'lyōs, tēm'bres] 150

standard (oil) normal f [nōrmäl'] 46

star estrella f [estre'lyä] 27

starboard estribor m [estrēbōr'] 77

start (of race) salida f [sälē'dä] 188

starter arranque m, marcha f (Mex) [ärrän'ke, mär'tshä] 55

station (train) estación f [estäsyōn'] 67

station (TV etc.) emisora f [emēsō'rä] 180; ~ **master** jefe m de estación [he'fe de estäsyōn'] 67; ~ **wagon** camioneta f, combi f (Mex) [kämyōne'tä, kōm'bē] 40

Stations of the Cross estaciones f/pl de la vía Crucis [estäsyō'nes de lä vē'ä krōō'sēs] 125

statue estatua f [estä'tōō·ä] 119

steak bistec m [bēstek'] 108

steamed cocido al vapor [kōse'dō äl väpōr'] 102

steamer vapor m [väpōr'] 77

steep downgrade bajada f (peligrosa) [bähä'dä (pelēgrō'sä)] 43

steep upgrade cuesta f, subida f [kōō·es'tä, sōōbē'dä] 43

steering dirección f [dēreksyōn'] 56; ~ **wheel** volante m [vōlän'te] 56

stern popa f [pō'pä] 77

stew potaje m [pōtä'he] 105

steward camarero m [kämäre'rō] 74; **chief ~** jefe m de camareros [he'fe de kämäre'rōs] 74

stewed estofado, guisado [estōfä'dō, gēsä'dō] 102

still aún [ä·ōōn'] 31

stitch in the side puntadas f/pl en el costado [pōōntä'däs en el kōstä'dō] 171

stock acciones f/pl [äksyō'nes] 152

stockings medias f/pl [me'dyäs] 135

stole estola f [estō'lä] 135

stomach estómago m [estō'mägō] 168; ~ **pain** dolores m/pl de estómago [dōlō'res de estō'mägō] 171

stop parada f [pärä'dä] 59

stop (verb) parar [pärär'] 43

stopover escala f [eskä'lä] 71

stopped up tapado, atascado [täpä'dō, ätäskä'dō] 88

stopping (no) prohibido detenerse [prō·ēbē'dō detener'se] 42

store tienda f [tyen'dä] 128; **candy ~** confitería f [kōnfēterē'ä] 128; **department ~** grandes almacenes m/pl [grän'des älmäse'nes] 128; **drug ~** (sundries) droguería f [drōgerē'ä] 128; **drug ~** (pharmacy) farmacia f [färmä'syä] 128; **furniture ~** tienda f de muebles [tyen'dä de mōō·e'bles] 128; **grocery** ~ tienda f de alimentación, de abarrotes *(Mex)* [tyen'dä de älementäsyōn', de äbärrō'tes] 128; **hardware** ~ ferretería f [ferreterē'ä] 128; **jewelry** ~ joyería f [hōyerē'ä] 128; **leather goods** ~ artículos m/pl de piel, marroquinería f [ärte'kōōlōs de pyel, marrōkēnerē'ä] 129; **liquor** ~ tienda f de bebidas alcohólicas, licorerías *(Mex)* [tyen'dä de bebē'däs älkō·ō'lēkäs, lēkōrerē'äs] 129; **music** ~ tienda f de música [tyen'dä de mōō'sēkä] 129; **record** ~ tienda f de discos, discoteca f *(Mex)* [tyen'dä de dēs'kōs, dēskōte'kä] 129; **shoe** ~ zapatería f [säpäterē'ä] 129; **sporting goods** ~ tienda f de artículos de deporte [tyen'dä de ärte'kōōlōs de depōr'te] 129; **stationery** ~ papelería f [päpelerē'ä] 129; **toy** ~ juguetería f [hōōgeterē'ä] 129

storekeeper tendero m [tende'rō] 37

storm tormenta f [tōrmen'tä] 27

stove estufa f, cocina f *(Sp)* [estōō'fä, kōsē'nä] 93

straight ahead todo derecho [tō'dō dere'tshō] 40

strait estrecho m [estre'tshō] 77

strawberry fresa f [fre'sä] 111

street calle f [kä'lye] 192

strict riguroso [rēgōōrō'sō] 165

string cordel m, cuerda f [kōrdel', kōō·er'dä] 57

stroke apoplejía f [äpōplehē'ä] 171

student estudiante m + f [estōōdyän'te] 37

stuffed relleno [relye'nō] 102; ~ **animal** animal m de trapo [änēmäl' de trä'pō] 144

subject asignatura f [äsēgnätōō'rä] 39

subtitled subtitulado [sōōbtētōōlä'dō] 179

suburbs afueras f/pl [äfōō·e'räs] 122

suburban train tren m de cercanías, tren m local *(Mex)* [tren de serkänē'äs, tren lōkäl'] 60

subway métro m [me'trō] 122

success éxito m [e'ksētō] 23

suède ante m [än'te] 139; ~ **coat** abrigo m de ante [äbrē'gō de än'te] 135; ~ **jacket** chaqueta f de ante [tshäke'tä de än'te] 135

sugar azúcar m [äsōō'kär] 100; ~ **bowl** azucarera f, azucarero m *(Sp)* [äsōōkäre'rä, äsōōkäre'rō] 99

suit *(lady's)* traje m de chaqueta, traje m sastre [trä'he de tshäke'tä, trä'he säs'tre] 135

suit *(man's)* traje m [trä'he] 135

suitcase maleta f [mäle'tä] 63

summer verano m [verä'nō] 33; ~ **dress** vestido m de verano [vestē'dō de verä'nō] 135

sun sol m [sōl] 27; ~ **tan cream** crema f solar, bronceadora f [kre'mä sōlär', brōnse·ädō'rä] 142; ~ **tan lotion** loción f solar, loción f para broncearse [lōsyōn' sōlär', lōsyōn' pä'rä brōnse·är'se] 142; ~ **tan oil** aceite m solar, bronceador m *(Mex)* [äse'ētē sōlär', brōnse·ädōr'] 142

sun roof techo m corredizo [te'tshō kōrredē'sō] 55

sunbath: take a ~ tomar el sol [tōmär' el sōl] 186

sunburn quemadura f del sol [kemädōō'rä del sōl] 171

Sunday domingo m [dōmēn'gō] 33

sunglasses lentes f/pl, anteojos m/pl, gafas f/pl *(Sp)* de sol [len'tes, änte·ō'hōs, gä'fäs de sōl] 138

sunlamp lámpara f solar ultravioleta [lämp'ärä sōlär' ōōlträvyōle'tä] 175

sunrise salida f del sol [sälē'dä del sōl] 27

sunset puesta f del sol [pōō·es'tä del sōl] 27

sunstroke insolación *f* [ēnsōläsyōn'] 171

supermarket supermercado *m* [sōō-permerkä'dō] 129

supplement suplemento *m* [sōōplemen'tō] 66

suppository supositorio *m*, calillo *m (Mex)* [sōōpōsētōr'yō, kälē'lyō] 161

suppuration supuración *f* [sōōpōōräsyōn'] 171

surcharge suplemento *m* [sōōplemen'tō] 83; **seasonal ~** suplemento *m* por temporada [sōōplemen'tō pōr tempōrä'dä] 83

surgeon cirujano *m* [sērōōhä'nō] 163

surroundings alrededores *m/pl* [älrededō'res] 122

suspenders tirantes *m/pl* [tērän'tes] 135

sweater jersey *m*, suéter *m* [her'sē, sōō·e'ter] 135

swelling hinchazón *f* [ēntshäsōn'] 171

swim nadar, bañarse [nädär', bänyär'se] 186

swimmer nadador *m* [nädädōr'] 186

swimming *(go ~)* ir a nadar, ir a bañarse [ēr ä nädär', ēr ä bänyär'se] 96

swimming *(noun)* natación *f* [nätäsyōn'] 190; **no ~** ¡prohibido bañarse! [prō·ebē'dō bänyär'se] 185; **~ pool** piscina *f* [pēsē'nä] 74

swimsuit traje *m* de baño [trä'he de bä'nyō] 135

switch interruptor *m* [ēnterrōōptōr'] 56

swollen hinchado [ēntshä'dō] 164

symphony concert concierto *m* sinfónico [kōnsyer'tō sēnfō'nēkō] 178

synagogue sinagoga *f* [sēnägō'gä] 122

synthetic thread hilo *m* sintético [ē'lō sēnte'tēkō] 136

system time table *(trains)* guía *f* de ferrocarriles [gē'ä de ferrōkärrē'les] 67

system time table *(planes)* horario *m* de vuelos [ōrär'yō de vōō·e'lōs] 71

T

table mesa *f* [me'sä] 93; **~ tennis** ping pong *m* [pēn pōn'] 182

tablecloth mantel *m* [mäntel'] 93

tablet comprimido *m* [kōmprēmē'dō] 161

tailor sastre *m* [säs'tre] 37

take off despegue *m*, descolaje *m* [despe'ge, deskōlä'he] 71

talcum powder talco *m* [täl'kō] 161

tampon tampón *m* [tämpōn'] 142

tangerine mandarina *f* [mändärē'nä] 111

tape cinta *f* [sēn'tä] 136; **~ measure** cinta *f* métrica [sēn'tä me'trēkä] 136; **~ recorder** magnetófono *m* [mägnetō'fōnō] 182

target blanco *m* [bläng'kō] 189

tartar sarro *m* dental, tártaro *m* [sä'rrō dentäl', tär'tärō] 174

taxi taxi *m* [tä'ksē] 89; **~ stand** parada *f*, sitio *m (Mex)* de taxis [pärä'dä, sē'tyō de tä'ksēs] 116

tea té *m* [te] 100; **camomile ~** té *m* de manzanilla [te de mänsänē'lyä] 100; **mint ~** té *m* de menta, de hierba buena *(Mex)* [te de men'tä, de yer'bä bōō·e'nä] 100

teacher profesor *m*, maestro *m* [prōfesōr', mä·es'trō] 37

tease *(hair)* enredar, cardar *(Sp)* [enredär', kärdär'] 156

technical técnico [tek'nēkō] 39; **~ college** escuela *f* superior técnica [eskōō·e'lä sōōperyōr tek'nēkä] 39

technician técnico *m* [tek'nēkō] 38

telegram telegrama *m* [telegrä'mä] 147; **~ form** impreso *m* de telegrama [ēmpre'sō de telegrä'mä] 147

telegraphic telegráfico [telegrä'fēkō] 152

telephone teléfono *m* [tele'fōnō] 150

television televisión *f* [televēsyōn']

182; ~ **play** telefilm m [telefēlm] 182

tell decir [desēr'] 20

teller's window caja f [kä'hä] 152

temperature temperatura f [temperätōō'rä] 27; **what's the** ~? ¿a cuántos estamos? [ä kōō·än'tōs estä'mōs] 25; ~ **chart** curva f de temperatura [kōōr'vä de temperätōō'rä] 173

temple (of head) sien f [syen] 168

temple templo m [tem'plō] 122

temporarily por el momento [pōr el mōmen'tō] 32

temporary provisionalmente [prōvēsyōnälmen'te] 173

ten diez [dyes] 28

tender tierno [tyer'nō] 102

tendon tendón m [tendōn'] 168; **pulled** ~ distorsión f de un tendón [dēstōrsyōn' de ōōn tendōn'] 171

tennis tenis m [te'nēs] 190; **play** ~ jugar al tenis [hōōgär' äl te'nēs] 190; ~ **ball** pelota f de tenis [pelō'tä de te'nēs] 190; ~ **court** pista f, cancha f de tenis [pēs'tä, kän'tshä de te'nēs] 190

tenor tenor m [tenōr'] 178

tent carpa f, tienda f (Sp), casita f (Mex) de campaña [kär'pä, tyen'dä, käsē'tä de kämpä'nyä] 97

terrace terraza f [terrä'sä] 93

terrific ¡estupendo! [estōōpen'dō] 21

tetanus tétano m [te'tänō] 172

thank you gracias [grä'syäs] 21

thanks a lot ¡muchas gracias! [mōō'tshäs grä'syäs] 21

thaw deshielo m [desye'lō] 27

theatre teatro m [te·ä'trō] 178; ~ **schedule** programa m [prōgrä'mä] 178

theft robo m [rō'bō] 153

there allá [älyä'] 40

thermometer termómetro m [termō'metrō] 144

thermos bottle termo m [ter'mō] 144

thermostat termostato m, toma f de

agua (Mex) [termōstä'tō, tō'mä de ä'gōō·ä] 56

thief ladrón m [lädrōn'] 154

thigh muslo m [mōōs'lō] 167

thimble dedal m [dedäl'] 136

third tercero [terse'rō] 29

thorax tórax m [tō'räks] 168

thread hilo m ē'lō 136; **screw** ~ rosca f [rōs'kä] 56

three tres [tres] 28

thriller novela f de suspense, de misterio [nōve'lä de sōōspen'se, de mēster'yō] 130

throat garganta f [gärgän'tä] 168

through car coche m directo [kō'tshe dērek'tō] 64

throw-in saque m de línea [sä'ke de lē'ne·ä] 190

thumb pulgar m [pōōlgär'] 167

thunder trueno m [trōō·e'nō] 27

thunderstorm tempestad f [tempestäd'] 27

Thursday jueves m [hōō·e'ves] 33

ticket boleto m, billete m (Sp) [bōle'tō, bēlye'te] 59

ticket (plane) billete m, pasaje m [bēlye'te, päsä'he] 71; **one-way** ~ boleto m, billete m, pasaje m de ida solo [bōle'tō, bēlye'te, päsä'he de ē'dä sō'lō] 117; ~ **sales** despacho m de localidades [despä'tshō de lōkälēdä'des] 178; **transfer** ~ boleto m, billete m, pasaje m de correspondencia [bōle'tō, bēlye'te, päsä'he de korrespōnden'syä] 117; ~ **window** despacho m de billetes, taquilla f [despä'tshō de bēlye'tes, täkē'lyä] 60

tie corbata f [kōrbä'tä] 133

tight (brakes) tenso [ten'sō] 51

tight (shoes) estrecho [estre'tshō] 139

tighten apretar [äpretär'] 55

time hora f [ō'rä] 30; **at what** ~? a qué hora [ä ke ō'rä] 15; **what** ~ **is it?** ¿qué hora es? [ke ō'rä es] 30; **have a**

good ~ diviértase, diviertete *(fam)* [dĕvyer'täse, dĕvyer'tete] 20; **from ~ to** ~ de vez en cuando [de ves en kōō·än'dō] 32; **any** ~ de un momento a otro [de ōōn mōmen'tō ä ō'trō] 32; **in** ~ a la hora, a tiempo [ä lä ō'rä, ä tyem'pō] 32; ~ **table** horario *m* [ōrär'yō] 60

tincture of iodine tintura *f* de yodo [tĕntōō'rä de yō'dō] 161

tint dar color, dar reflejos [där kōlōr', där refle'hōs] 158

tire neumático *m*, llanta *(Mex)* [ne·ōōmä'tēkō, lyän'tä] 47; ~ **change** cambio *m* de neumático, de llanta *(Mex)* [käm'byō de ne·ōōmä'tēkō, de lyän'tä] 47; ~ **pressure** presión *f* de los neumáticos, de las llantas *(Mex)* [presyōn' de lōs ne·ōōmä'tēkōs, de läs lyän'täs] 47

tires neumáticos *m/pl*, llantas *f/pl* *(Mex)* [ne·ōōmä'tēkōs, lyän'täs] 47

tissues pañuelos *m/pl* de papel [pänyōō·e'lōs de päpel'] 142

toast pan *m* tostado [pän tōstä'dō] 100

tobacco tabaco *m* [täbä'kō] 140

tobaggan trineo *m* [trēne'ō] 190

tobagganing ir en trineo [ēr en trēne'ō] 190

today hoy [oi] 68

toe dedo *m* del pie [de'dō del pye] 168

together junto [hōōn'tō] 115

toilet wáter *m*, lavabo *m*, excusado *m* *(Mex)* [ōō·ä'ter, lävä'bō, ekskōōsä'dō] 82; ~ **articles** artículos *m/pl* de tocador [ärtē'kōōlōs de tōkädōr'] 142; ~ **kit** neceser *m* [neseser'] 142; ~ **paper** papel *m* higiénico, papel *m* sanitario [päpel' ēhē·e'nēkō, päpel' sänētär'yō] 142

tomato tomate *m* (Sp) jitomate *m* (Mex) [tōmä'te, hētōmä'te] 110

tomb sepulcro *m* [sepōōl'krō] 123

tomorrow mañana [mänyä'nä] 31; **the**

day after ~ pasado mañana [päsä'dō mänyä'nä] 31

ton tonelada *f* [tōnelä'dä] 193

tongue lengua *f* [len'gōō·ä] 168

tonic tónico *m* [tō'nēkō] 161; ~ **water** tónica *f* [tō'nēkä] 114

tonight esta noche [es'tä nō'tshe] 31

tonsilitis anginas *f/pl* [änhē'näs] 172

tonsils amígdalas *f/pl* [ämēg'däläs] 168

too también [tämbyen'] 47

too *(degree)* demasiado [demäsyä'dō] 31

tool box *(kit)* caja *f* de herramientas *f/pl* [kä'hä de errämyen'täs] 57

tools herramientas *f/pl* [errämyen'täs] 57

tooth diente *m* [dyen'te] 168; ~ **brush** cepillo *m* de dientes [sepē'lyō de dyen'tes] 142; ~ **paste** pasta *f* de dientes [päs'tä de dyen'tes] 142; **wisdom** ~ muela *f* del juicio [mōō·e'lä del hōō·ē'syō] 174

toothache dolor *m* de muelas [dōlōr' de mōō·e'läs] 174

toothpick palillo *m* [pälē'lyō] 99

top *(car)* capota *f* [käpō'tä] 56

tough duro [dōō'rō] 102

toupé postizo *m* [pōstē'sō] 158

tour visita *f* [vēsē'tä] 119; **guided** ~ visita *f* guiada [vēsē'tä gē·ä'dä] 119; ~ **guide** guía *m* [gē'ä] 94

tour guide's office dirección *f* del crucero [dēreksyōn' del krōōse'rō] 74

tow remolcar [remōlkär'] 49; ~ **line** cable *m* de remolque [kä'ble de remōl'ke] 49; ~ **truck** grúa *f*, coche *m* grúa *(Sp)* [grōō'ä, kō'tshe grōō'ä] 49

towel toalla *f* [tō·ä'lyä] 142; **bath** ~ toalla *f* de baño [tō·ä'lyä de bä'nyō] 142

tower torre *f* [tō'rre] 123

towing service servicio *m* de remolque [servē'syō de remōl'ke] 49

town ciudad *f* [syōōdäd'] 123

toy juguete *m* [hōōge'te] 144

track vía f [vē'ä] 67; ~ **and field** atletismo m en pista [ätletēz'mō en pēs'tä] 190; ~ **suit** chándal m, sudadera f [tshän'däl, sōōdäde'rä] 135

traffic tráfico m, circulación f [trä'fēkō, sērkōōläsyōn'] 123; ~ **light** semáforo m, disco m [semä'fōrō, dēs'kō] 123; ~ **regulations** reglamentos m/pl de la circulación [reglämen'tōs de lä sērkōōläsyōn'] 43

tragedy tragedia f [trähe'dyä] 178

trailer remolque m [remōl'ke] 41; **camping** ~ caravana f, trayler m (Mex) [kärävä'nä, trīler] 40

train tren m [tren] 60; **suburban** ~ tren m de cercanías, tren local (Mex) [tren de serkänē'äs, tren lōkäl'] 60

trainee aprendiz m [äprendēs'] 38

tranquilizer calmante m, sedante m [kälmän'te, sedän'te] 161

transfer (bus) correspondencia f [kōrrespōnden'syä] 59

transfer (money) giro m [hē'rō] 152

translate traducir [trädōōsēr'] 24

translation traducción f [trädōōksyōn'] 130

translator traductor m [trädōōktōr'] 38

transmission transmisión f [tränsmēsyōn'] 56

travel agency agencia f de viajes [ähen'syä de vyä'hes] 82

traveler's cheque cheque m de viaje [tshe'ke de vyä'he] 127

tray charola f, bandeja f (Sp) [tshärō'lä, bände'hä] 99

trick (cards) baza f [bä'sä] 181

trip viaje m [vyä'he] 61; **have a good** ~ buen viaje [bōō·em' byä'he] 17

tripe callos m/pl [kä'lyōs] 108

tripod trípode m [trē'pōde] 132

trout trucha f [trōō'tshä] 107

truck camión m [kämyōn'] 40; ~ **driver** chófer m, camionero m [tshō'fer, kämyōne'rō] 38

trump triunfo m [trē·ōōn'fō] 181

trunk portamaletas m, maletero m, cajuela f (Mex) [pōrtämäle'täs, mälete'rō, kähōō·e'lä] 56

tube tubo m [tōō'bō] 126

tubeless (tire) neumático m, llanta f (Mex) sin cámara [ne·ōōmä'tēkō, lyän'tä sēn kä'märä] 47

Tuesday martes m [mär'tes] 33

tug remolcador m [remōlkädōr'] 77

tulips tulipanes m/pl [tōōlēpä'nes] 130

tumor tumor m [tōōmōr'] 172

tuna atún m [ätōōn'] 107

turbot rodaballo m [rōdäbä'lyō] 107

turkey guajolote m (Mex), pavo m (Sp) [gōō·áhōlō'te, pä'vō] 107

turn (the car) dar la vuelta, virar [där lä vōō·el'tä, vērär'] 43

turn (into a road) entrar en [enträr' en] 43

turn off (a road) doblar, torcer (Sp) [dōblär', tōrser'] 43

turn off apagar [äpägär'] 182

turn on poner [pōner'] 182

turnip nabo m [nä'bō] 110

tweezers pinzas f/pl [pēn'säs] 142

two dos [dōs] 28

two-piece de dos piezas [de dōs pye'säs] 135

two-stroke motor motor m de dos tiempos [mōtōr' de dōs tyem'pōs] 54

typewriter máquina f de escribir [mä'kēnä de eskrēbēr'] 138; ~ **paper** papel m para la máquina de escribir [päpel' pä'rä lä mä'kēnä de eskrēbēr'] 138

typhoid fever tifoidea f [tēfō·ēde'ä] 172

U

ulcer úlcera f [ōōl'serä] 172

ultrasonics ultrasonido m [ōōlträsō-nē'dō] 175

umbrella paraguas m [pärä'gōō·äs]

144; **garden** ~ sombrilla f, parasol m [sōmbrē'lyä, päräsōl'] 91

umpire árbitro m [är'bētrō] 190

uncle tío m [tē'ō] 35

underpants *(men's)* calzoncillos m/pl [kälsōnsē'lyōs] 135

undershirt camiseta f [kämēse'tä] 135

undertow corrientes f/pl [kōrryen'tes] 185

underwear ropa f interior [rō'pä ēnteryōr'] 135

university universidad f [ōōnēversēdäd'] 39

unlock abrir con llave [äbrēr' kōn lyä've] 92

unstamped sin franquear [sēn frängke·är'] 150

until hasta [äs'tä] 32

urgent urgente [ōōrhen'te] 147

urine orina f [ōrē'nä] 168

urinalysis análisis m de orina [änä'lēsēs de ōrē'nä] 165

urologist urólogo m [ōōrō'lōgō] 163

use uso m [ōō'sō] 80

usher acomodador m [äkōmōdädōr'] 179

uterus útero m [ōō'terō] 168

V

vacant libre [lē'bre] 65

vacation vacaciones f/pl [väkäsyō'nes] 78

vaccinate vacunar [väkōōnar'] 164

vaccination vacunación f [väkōōnäsyōn'] 78; ~ **certificate** certificado m de vacunación [sertēfēkä'dō de väkōōnäsyōn'] 78

vagina vagina f [vähē'nä] 169

valerian drops gotas f/pl de valeriana [gō'täs de väleryä'nä] 161

valid válido [vä'lēdō] 62

valley valle m [vä'lye] 123

valuables objetos m/pl de valor [ōbhe'-tōs de välōr'] 84

value declaration declaración f de valor [dekläräsyōn' de välōr'] 150

valve válvula f [väl'vōōlä] 56

vanilla vainilla f [vīnē'lyä] 103

vase florero m [flōre'rō] 130

vaseline vaselina f [väselē'nä] 161

veal ternera f, ternero m *(Mex)* [terne'-rä, terne'rō] 108

vegetable market verdulería f [verdōō-lerē'ä] 129

vehicle vehículo m [ve·ē'kōōlō] 41

vein vena f [ve'nä] 168

velvet terciopelo m [tersyōpe'lō] 137

venereal disease enfermedad f venérea [enfermedäd' vene're·ä] 172

ventilation ventilación f [ventēläsyōn'] 94

verdict sentencia f [senten'syä] 154

very muy [mōō'ē] 21

vest chaleco m [tshäle'kō] 135

veterinarian veterinario m [veterēnär'-yō] 38

veterinary medicine veterinaria f [veterēnär'yä] 39

victory victoria f [vēktōr'yä] 188

video cassette cassette m + f de vídeo [käse'te de vē'de'ō] 144

view finder visor m [vēsōr'] 132

village pueblo m, aldea f [pōō·e'blō, älde'ä] 123

vinegar vinagre m [vēnä'gre] 103

vintage wine vino m añejo [vē'nō änye'-hō] 113

violet *(adj.)* violeta [vyōle'tä] 194

violets violetas f/pl [vyōle'täs] 130

violin recital recital m de violín [resētäl' de vē·ōlēn'] 178

visa visa f, visado m *(Sp)* [vē'sä, vēsä'-dō] 78

visit visitar [vēsētär'] 183

visiting hours horas f/pl de visita [ō'räs de vēsē'tä] 173

vitamin pills pastillas f/pl de vitaminas

[pästē'lyäs de vĕtämē'näs] 161

vocational school escuela *f* de formación profesional [eskōō-e'lä de fōr-mäsyōn' prŏfesyŏnäl] 39

vodka vodka *f* [vŏd'kä] 114

volleyball vol(e)ibol *m*, balónvolea *m (Sp)* [vōlēbōl', bälŏnvōle'ä] 190

voltage voltaje *m* [vŏltä'he] 86

volume *(of series)* tomo *m*, volumen *m* [tō'mō, vōlōō'men] 130

vomiting náuseas *f/pl* [nou'se-äs] 172

voyage *(sea)* viaje *m* (por mar) [vyä'he (pōr mär)] 77

W

wait esperar [esperär'] 87

waiter camarero *m*, mesero *m (Mex)* [kämäre'rō, mese'rō] 98

waiting room sala *f* de espera [sä'lä de espe'rä] 60

waitress camarera *f*, mesera *f (Mex)* [kämäre'rä, mese'rä] 38

walk *(take a ~)* pasear, dar una vuelta [päse-är', där ōō'nä vōō-el'tä] 184

walking shoes botas *f/pl* para caminar [bō'täs pä'rä kämēnär'] 139

wall *(city)* muralla *f* [mōōrä'lyä] 123

wall pared *f*, tabique *m* [päred', täbē'-ke] 94

wallet monedero *m* [mōnede'rō] 144

ward unidad *f*, sección *f* [ōōnēdäd', seksyōn'] 173

warning triangle triángulo *m* de peligro [trē-än'gōōlō de pelē'grō] 56

warship buque *m* de guerra [bōō'ke de ge'rrä] 77

wash lavar [lävär'] 155; **~ and set** lavar y enrular [lävär' ē enrōōlär'] 155; **~ cloth** manopla *f* de baño [mänō'plä de bä'nyō] 142; **~ rooms** lavabos *m/ pl* [lävä'bōs] 95

washer arandela *f* [ärände'lä] 56

washing line cuerda *f*, soga, lazo *m*

[kōō-er'dä, sō'gä, lä'sō] 144

watch *(noun)* reloj *m* [relō(*h*)'] 153; **pocket ~** reloj *m* de bolsillo [relō(*h*)' de bōlsē'lyō] 143; **stop ~** cronómetro *m* [krŏnō'metrō] 143; **wrist ~** reloj *m* de pulsera, de pulso [relō(*h*)' de pōōlse'rä, de pōōl'sō] 153; **~ band** pulsera *f* de reloj [pōōlse'rä de relō(*h*)'] 143

watchmaker relojero *m* [relōhe'rō] 38

water agua *f* [ä'gōō-ä] 45; **bottled ~** agua *f* purificada [ä'gōō-ä pōōrēfē-kä'dä] 114; **distilled ~** agua *f* destilada [ä'gōō-ä destēlä'dä] 45; **drinking ~** agua *f* potable [ä'gōō-ä pōtä'ble] 144; **fresh ~** agua *f* dulce [ä'gōō-ä dōōl'se] 114; **running ~** agua *f* corriente ä'gōō-ä kōrryen'te 82; **~ skiing** esquí *m* acuático [eskē' akōō-ä'-tēkō] 185; **~ temperature** temperatura *f* del agua [temperätōō'rä del ä'gōō-ä] 186

waterfall cascada *f*, salto *m* de agua, caída *f* de agua [käskä'dä, säl'tō de ä'gōō-ä, kä-ē'dä de ä'gōō-ä] 123

wave ola *f* [ō'lä] 186

weather tiempo *m* [tyem'pō] 25, **~ prediction** pronóstico *m* [prŏnōs'tēkō] 27; **~ report** parte *m* meteorológico [pär'te mete-ōrōlō'hēkō] 25

wedding boda *f* [bō'dä] 123

Wednesday miércoles *m* [myer'kōles] 33

week semana *f* [semä'nä] 32; **this coming ~** la semana *f* que viene [lä semä'nä ke vye'ne] 32; **a ~ from now** de hoy en ocho días [de oi en ō'tshō dē'äs] 31; **two ~s from now** de hoy en quince días [de oi en kēn'se dē'äs] 31

weekly cada semana [kä'dä semä'nä] 32

welcome *(greeting)* ¡bienvenido! [byenbenē'dō] 12

welcome *(noun)* acogida f [äkōhē'dä] 12; **you're ~** de nada [de nä'dä] 21

well bien [byen] 12; **get ~ soon** que se mejore, te mejores *(fam)* [ke se mehō're, te mehō'res] 20; **~ done** bien hecho, bien asado, bien cocido [byen e'tshō, byen äsä'dō, byen kōsē'dō] 102

wet mojado [mōhä'dō] 155

what? ¡qué? [ke] 18; **~ for?** ¿para qué? [pä'rä ke] 18

wheel rueda f [rōo·e'dä] 56

when? ¿cuándo? [kōō·än'dō] 18

where? ¿dónde? [dōn'de] 18; **~ from?** ¿de dónde? [de dōn'de] 18; **~ to?** ¿adónde? [ädōn'de] 18; **~ is...?** ¿dónde está...? [dōn'de estä'] 19

which? ¿cuál? [kōō·äl'] 18

whisk(e)y whisk(e)y m [ōō·es'kē] 114

white blanco [bläng'kō] 194

who? ¿quién? [kyen] 18

wholesaler mayorista m + f [mäyōrēs'tä] 38

whom *(to ~)* ¿a quién? [ä kyen] 18

whom *(with ~)* ¿con quién? [kōn kyen] 18

whose? ¿de quién? [de kyen] 18

why? ¿por qué? [pōr ke] 18

wide ancho [än'tshō] 127

widowed viudo [vyōō'dō (-ä)] 79

wife esposa f, mujer f [espō'sä, mōōher'] 35

wig peluca f [pelōō'kä] 158

win ganar [gänär'] 188

wind viento m [vyen'tō] 27; **north (east) ~** viento m del norte (este) [vyen'tō del nōr'te, (es'te)] 27; **south (west) ~** viento m del sur (oeste) [vyen'tō del sōōr, (ō·es'te)] 27

windbreaker cazadora f [käsädō'rä] 135

winding road camino m sinuoso [kämē'nō sēnōō·ō'sō] 43

window ventana f [ventä'nä] 94; **~**

pane vidrio m, cristal m *(Sp)* [vē'-drē·ō, krēstäl'] 94; **~ seat** asiento m de ventanilla [äsyen'tō de ventänē'-lyä] 67

windshield parabrisas m [päräbrē'säs] 56; **~ washer** lavaparabrisas m [läväpäräbrē'säs] 56; **~ wiper** limpiaparabrisas m [lēmpyäpäräbrē'säs] 56

wine vino m [vē'nō] 113; **dry ~** vino m seco [vē'nō se'kō] 113; **house ~** vino m de la casa [vē'nō de lä kä'sä] 113; **new ~** vino m nuevo [vē'nō nōō·e'vō] 113; **red ~** vino m tinto [vē'nō tēn'tō] 113; **rosé ~** vino m rosado [vē'nō rōsä'dō] 113; **sweet ~** vino m dulce [vē'nō dōōl'se] 113; **vintage ~** vino m añejo [vē'nō äñe'hō] 113; **white ~** vino m blanco [vē'nō bläng'-kō] 113

wing ala f [ä'lä] 71

winter invierno m [ēmbyer'nō] 33

wire *(tool)* alambre m [äläm'bre] 57

wire telegrama m [telegrä'mä] 147

withdraw retirar [retērär'] 152

within dentro [den'trō] 32

witness testigo m [testē'gō] 49

wood carvings tallas m /pl de madera [tä'lyäs de mäde'rä] 144

wool lana f [lä'nä] 137; **pure ~** lana f pura [lä'nä pōō'rä] 137; **pure virgin ~** pura lana f virgen [pōō'rä lä'nä vēr'hen] 137

words palabras f /pl [pälä'bräs] 147

work *(noun)* obra f [ō'brä] 178

worker obrero m [ōbre'rō] 38

worsted estambre m [estäm'bre] 137

wound herida f [erē'dä] 172; **~ salve** ungüento m [ōōngōō·en'tō] 161

wrapping paper papel m de envolver, de embalar *(Sp)* [päpel' de envōlver', de embälär'] 138

wrench llave f inglesa [lyä've ēngle'sä] 57

wrestle luchar [lo͞otshär'] 190
wrestler luchador m [lo͞otshädōr'] 190
wrestling lucha f [lo͞ot'shä] 190
wrist muñeca f [mo͞onye'kä] 168
write escribir [eskrēbēr'] 24
writer escritor m [eskrētōr'] 38
writing paper papel m de carta [päpel' de kär'tä] 138

X

x-ray *(noun)* radiografía f, rayos m/pl equis [rädyōgräfē'ä, rä'yōs e'kēs] 173
x-ray *(verb)* hacer una radiografía [äser' o͞o'nä rädyōgräfē'ä] 173

Y

yacht yate m [yä'te] 77
yard *(approx.)* metro m [me'trō] 126
year año m [ä'nyō] 32; **happy new ~** próspero año nuevo [prōs'perō

ä'nyō no͞o·e'vō] 23
yellow amarillo [ämärē'lyō] 194
yes sí [sē] 21
yesterday ayer [äyer'] 31; **day before ~** anteayer [änte·äyer'] 31
you usted [o͞oste'] 12
young joven [hō'ven] 35
younger más joven [mäs hō'ven] 35
your su [so͞o] 13
youth group grupo m juvenil [gro͞o'pō ho͞ovenēl'] 97

Z

zebra crossing paso m de peatones, paso m cebra [pä'sō de pe·ätō'nes, pä'sō se'brä] 43
zero cero [se'rō] 28
zipper cierre m, cremallera f [sye're, kremälyer'ä] 136
zoo jardín m zoológico [hardēn sō·ō-lō'hēkō] 123
zoology zoología f [sō'ōlōhē'ä] 39